THE ART OF DOSTOEVSKY

The Art
of Dostoevsky

DELIRIUMS AND
NOCTURNES

Robert Louis Jackson

Princeton University Press
Princeton, New Jersey

For My Mother and Father

CONTENTS

PREFACE

The Art of Dostoevsky is a continuation of a study of Dostoevsky that began intensively at the Russian Institute, Columbia University, thirty-five years ago, when I wrote a master's thesis on "The Sociological Method of V. F. Pereverzev."[1] A good part of that work was devoted to Pereverzev's attempt at a sociological analysis of Dostoevsky's "enchanted circle of images." I carried away a deep respect for the integrity of Pereverzev's pioneering sociological study of Dostoevsky but nonetheless found his approach, even when fruitful, to be one-sided and limiting.

I encountered Dostoevsky a second time when writing my book, *Dostoevsky's Underground Man in Russian Literature* (1958). A work with a predominantly literary-historical orientation, this second study focused on the inner content of *Notes from the Underground* and the complex problem of its ideological reception in Russian literature of the prerevolutionary and early postrevolutionary periods. It provided me with new insights into *Notes from the Underground* and a deeper awareness of the dramatic relations that have always existed between Dostoevsky and his author-readers. In *Dostoevsky's Underground Man*, I stressed the ambivalence of Dostoevsky's attitude toward his protagonist, an ambivalence that was later to characterize the point of view of many Russian and European writers who found in *Notes from the Underground* a clue to contemporary complexities.

I left behind *Dostoevsky's Underground Man* with a sense of restlessness and a renewed interest in Dostoevsky. Wanting to understand his work more comprehensively, I turned to a study of his aesthetics. *Dostoevsky's Quest for Form—A Study of his Philosophy of Art* (1966) was the result of my efforts. This study, it seemed to me, came close to the basic concerns of Dostoevsky and the creative tensions or dialectic that characterize his work. It did not include analyses of concrete works but focused primarily on Dostoevsky's aesthetic ideas and explored their interconnections in his poetics. As I wrote in the preface to that study, however, "it is necessary to turn to his belles lettres . . . for the whole Dostoevsky."[2] *The Art of Dostoevsky* is an attempt to turn to the whole of Dostoevsky. It grew out of my continuing effort to grasp and present Dostoevsky not only abstractly, or in the form of his general artistic thought, but as his thought or vision was directly embodied in the text. In short, I wished to come to terms with the work of art as such.

In *The Art of Dostoevsky*, as in my previous work on Dostoevsky, the question of *Notes from the Underground* and its interpretation continued to haunt me. It was in my close reading of *Notes from the House of the Dead* (hereafter referred to as *House of the Dead*[3]) that I came to realize the monumental importance of that work for an understanding of *Notes from the Underground* and Dostoevsky's other works from the first half of the 1860s. Indeed, it is no exaggeration to say that almost every work of Dostoevsky in the last two decades of his life can and must be read in the context of *House of the Dead*.

My understanding of *House of the Dead* owes much to my study of Dostoevsky's aesthetics. In an early essay on the narrator of *House of the Dead*, I dwelled on the disjunction between Dostoevsky's resentful attitude toward the prison convicts (as may be ascertained from his letters and the reminiscences of people who knew him in prison) and the particularly calm and objective, all-forgiving and all-reconciling point of view of the narrator toward these convicts.[4] I emphasized, also, the importance of Dostoevsky's bitter prison experience for his formulation of the complex problem content of the theme of loving one's neighbor in his later novels. Finally, I pointed to the importance of the mythopoetic or religious framework of Dostoevsky's prison work for an understanding of its inner content. But it was only after studying Dostoevsky's aesthetic thought that I fully understood its central role in the writing and dynamics of *House of the Dead*. Only through an appreciation of his poetics was I able to resolve, to my own satisfaction, the contradiction (or apparent contradiction) between *Dichtung* and *Wahrheit*, "poetry" and "truth," in Dostoevsky's artistic shaping of his prison experiences. Indeed, *House of the*

Dead now presented itself to me as a kind of programmatic statement of a Christian poetics of insight and transfiguration that Dostoevsky had not only lived through in prison but had thought through there as well. "I thought it all out to the last word back in Omsk," Dostoevsky wrote to his friend A. E. Vrangel in 1856 about an article, "Letters about Art," he was then preparing—a work "essentially on the significance of Christianity in art."[5] Dostoevsky never published this work, and the manuscript is not extant, but there is little doubt that *House of the Dead* constitutes the artistic embodiment of his aesthetic and spiritual thought.

House of the Dead, which has received relatively little attention in scholarship, thus seemed to me to deserve careful analysis. And in fact, what at superficial glance might appear simple autobiography turned out to be the pivotal literary and spiritual work in Dostoevsky's writing career. Furthermore, apart from its intrinsic interest as a great human document, *House of the Dead* struck me as, perhaps, the most profound meditation on Russia and the Russian people in the nineteenth century from the social and psychohistorical point of view.

The various chapters in *The Art of Dostoevsky* are united not only by themes that pervade Dostoevsky's work—the problem of human nature, its possibilities and limitations, questions of fate, freedom and responsibility, gambling, the ideal, evil, conscience and suffering, and so forth—but by the "shape" that these apparently disparate themes are given in Dostoevsky's work. These themes are dealt with by an artist with a coherent vision, and not merely by an orchestrator of many "voices." There is, to be sure, polyphony in the Dostoevsky novel. But as in any great musical composition or literary epic (such as Tolstoy's *War and Peace*), the voices are integral to a grand conception. Dostoevsky has a point of view—that is, he looks upon the world from a point of view—and the more we study him, the more we become aware of this unifying view, a vision that permeates all of his work, all of his deliriums and nocturnes.

My study of Dostoevsky and of Russian literature in general, though grounded in my own special interests and disposition, is not marked by any particular established approach or methodology.

I have learned much from Marx, Nietzsche, and Dostoevsky, from the old "New Critics" and the modern existential philosophers. Like every student of Dostoevsky, I have profited from the conscientious, meticulous, biographical and historical work of such outstanding Soviet Russian Dostoevsky scholars as Leonid Grossman and Arkady Dolinin. Yet if I feel a kinship with any group of Dostoevsky interpreters, it is with the metaphysically and ontologically oriented group of Russian critics—with Vladimir Solovyov, Vasily Rozanov, Vyacheslav Ivanov, Nicholas Berdyaev, Leo Shestov, Paul Evdokimoff, and others. What has always drawn me to these thinkers, even when I have disagreed with them, is not only their attempt to come to grips with the whole Dostoevsky but their ability to feel his thought, to be moved by what moves him, and to address themselves to the "ultimate questions" that concerned him and must concern anybody who wishes deeply to comprehend Russian literature.

"In every serious philosophical question uncertainty extends to the very roots of the problem," Ludwig Wittgenstein has remarked. "We must always be prepared to learn something *totally new*."[6] This is certainly true where Dostoevsky is concerned. His world, like that of Tolstoy, is a continually expanding universe. The important moments in scholarship when problems are "resolved" appear, in retrospect, merely to be clear anticipations or formulations of new enigmas. What is substantial and lasting—and what one hopes, in the end, to convey—is the sense of excitement and complexity of the quest.

I am very grateful to Robert Lamont Belknap, William Mills Todd III, and Gary Saul Morson for their careful and perceptive reading of the manuscript. I also wish to thank Lou Anthony for typing the manuscript and catching my errors and Tam Curry for her meticulous and always thoughtful editing of the final manuscript. Finally, I thank my wife, Leslie, who has always shared my thoughts, my journey, and my wonderment over Dostoevsky.

ACKNOWLEDGMENTS

Segments of this text have appeared in earlier versions and translations: "The Narrator in Dostoevsky's *Notes from the House of the Dead*," in *Studies in Russian and Polish Literature. In Honor of Wacław Lednicki*, ed. Zbigniew Folejewski (The Hague: Mouton, 1962), pp. 192-216; "Dmitrij Karamazov and the 'Legend'," in *Slavic and East European Journal* (the official scholarly journal of the *American Association of Teachers of Slavic*), 9, no. 3 (1965), 257-267; "Quelques Considérations sur 'Le Rêve d'un homme ridicule' et 'Bobok' du point de vue esthétique," in *Russian Literature*, no. 1 (1971), pp. 15-27; "On the Uses of the Motif of the Duel in Dostoevskii's 'A Gentle Creature'," in *Canadian-American Slavic Studies* 6, no. 2 (1972), 256-264; "Philosophical Pro and Contra in Part One of *Crime and Punishment*," in *Twentieth Century Interpretations of Crime and Punishment*, ed. Robert Louis Jackson (Englewood Cliffs, N.J.: Prentice-Hall, Inc., 1974), pp. 26-40; "Vynesenie prigovora Fedoru Pavlovichu Karamazovu" [The Sentencing of Fyodor Pavlovich Karamazov], in *Dostoevskii. Materialy i issledovaniia*, ed. G. M. Fridlender (Leningrad: Nauka Publishing House, 1978), pp. 173-183; "The Triple Vision: Dostoevsky's 'The Peasant Marey'," in *The Yale Review* 67, no. 2 (copyright Yale University), 225-235. I am grateful to Princeton University Press for permission to quote from Charles S. Singleton's translation of Dante's *Inferno* and *Purgatory*, Bollingen Series LXXX, Vol. 1 (Princeton, N.J.: Princeton University Press, 1970).

THE ART OF DOSTOEVSKY

*"Who are you that, against the blind stream,
have fled the eternal prison?"* said he, *moving those
venerable plumes. "Who has guided you,
or what was a lamp to you issuing forth from the deep night
that ever makes the infernal valley black?
Are the laws of the abyss thus broken? Or is
some new counsel changed in Heaven that though damned
you come to my rocks?"*

DANTE, Purgatory

Introduction

THE WORKS EXAMINED in this book belong to the major period of Dostoevsky's writing, the last twenty years of his life (1861-1881). Three areas of concentration may be singled out. The first embraces the works of the first half of the 1860s, which may be said to be dominated for the most part by problems, ideas, and themes raised in *House of the Dead* (1860-1862). These works include *Winter Notes on Summer Impressions* (1863), *Notes from the Underground* (1864), and *Crime and Punishment* and *The Gambler* (1866). The second group consists of short stories or sketches that appear in *Diary of a Writer* (1873, 1876-1877) and that reflect the aesthetic ideas and radical experiments with genre in that work. Among them are "Bobok," "A Boy at Christ's Christmas Party," "The Peasant Marey," "A Gentle Creature," and "The Dream of a Ridiculous Man." *The Brothers Karamazov* constitutes the third. *The Art of Dostoevsky* opens with a discussion of the poetics of insight and transfiguration in Dostoevsky's sketch on his prison experience, "The Peasant Marey," and then turns to a substantial analysis of his *House of the Dead*, the seminal work of his post-Siberian period.

Writers and critics have long ago acknowledged the singular quality and importance of *House of the Dead*. Nietzsche described it as "one of the most human books ever written"; he most certainly had it in mind when he spoke of Dostoevsky's work as "the most valuable psychological material known to me."[1] Tolstoy talked of *House of the Dead* as an "amazing piece"; frequently praising it, he once called it the "best" that Dostoevsky had written "because it is integral in an artistic sense."[2] In a preface to *War and Peace* Tolstoy cited *House of the Dead* in connection with his assertion that not a single artistic prose work of significance in Russian literature from the time of Pushkin would "completely fit the form of novel, narrative poem or novella"; all represent "deviations from European form."[3] Indeed, in recent times *House of the Dead* has been variously defined as a work that "borders on an artistic sketch, on the one hand, and memoirs, on the other,"[4] as a "novel of a special genre . . . encompassing the life of a large body of people," as a "documentary novel,"[5] as a transitional form arising out of the "sketch, notes for a social-philosophical novel."[6] Dostoevsky himself once grouped *House of the Dead* among his "novels."[7]

Yet however we define *House of the Dead* as a genre, or boundary genre, what is certain is that it is an artistic work. In it, concerns of the documentary (the description of prison life and milieu) merge with those of hagiography (the story of a people's historical martyrdom) and spiritual autobiography (the discovered meaning of personal history) to form a series of gigantic frescoes of human experience and destiny. The epoch of Nicholas I, wrote Alexander Herzen in the early 1860s, has left us

> one terrifying book, a sort of *carmen horrendum* that will forever denote the passage from the dark reign of Nicholas, like Dante's inscription at the entrance to hell: this is Dostoevsky's *Notes from the House of the Dead*, a fearful narrative in which the author himself probably did not suspect that by drawing the images of his fellow convicts with his fettered hand, he had created out of a description of the customs of a Siberian prison, frescoes in the spirit of Buonarroti.[8]

The liberating ethos of *House of the Dead* indeed reflects the momentary—but for the time momentous—"thaw" of the late 1850s, a thaw involving the signal social and economic event of the century: the emancipation of the serfs in 1861. Herzen's comparison of Dostoevsky's work with the religious frescoes of Michelangelo also points to the vital allegorical dimension of *House of the Dead*: the drama of birth, death, fall, and redemption that constitutes the symbolic structure of the work. Not without reason is the narrative in *House of the Dead,* as in "The Peasant Marey," framed, as it were, by the events in the life of Christ.

A consideration of the problem of the narrator in *House of the Dead* opens the way to an outlook on the work as a whole. We speak of the historical Dante, or poet, who wrote *The Divine Comedy,* and of Dante the pilgrim or traveler who makes the journey through hell, purgatory, and paradise.[9] Even if at times the two figures seem to merge, the distinction between them is real. But what of Dostoevsky and his fictional narrator, Alexander Petrovich Goryanchikov? Did not the historical Dostoevsky, the poet himself, literally make the journey that his narrator takes through the prison hell? To be sure, Dostoevsky and Goryanchikov share certain actual experiences. The prison world they encounter is recognizably the same despite differences in detail and emphasis. Yet the two journeys are different. The first, historical journey of Dostoevsky was an involuntary one, an excruciating experience that left deep psychological wounds and bitter feelings. The second, literary journey in *House of the Dead,* like the journey of Dante the traveler, was an expedition to see and learn. The Dostoevsky who made the second journey in the figure of Goryanchikov was a person who had come to see himself and his subject in a new light. In this way *House of the Dead* becomes vision and not autobiography, and the writing of that work becomes a process of self-overcoming.

Nowhere is this more plain than in "The Peasant Marey" where vision as an aesthetic and religious category structures Dostoevsky's understanding of his prison experience. Though it appears many years after *House of the Dead,* "The Peasant Marey" in fact may be regarded as a kind of prologue, or vital key, to Dostoevsky's prison work and to the dialectic of poetry and truth that constitutes its dynamic.

"Every exceptional life," Herzen observed, "once we examine it closely may provide us more answers and more questions than the hero of any novel."[10] The Soviet scholar V. Kirpotin cites this observation with some approval and notes that Dostoevsky generalized about man on the basis of his experience with many "exceptional lives." Kirpotin nonetheless reproaches Dostoevsky "for not making allowances for the exceptional character of the milieu into which he fell, for the artificiality of the assortment of people, the peculiar way in which morality and psychology is refracted in the convict 'people'." He continues: "In 'anthropological,' philosophical, and political respects he equated the criminal inhabitants of the prison with people living in freedom, with the masses of people." Dostoevsky's moral humanism, Kirpotin emphasizes, is revealed here, but "he erred in putting an equals sign between the protest expressed in crime and social and political protest." The absence of a "necessary corrective" on Dostoevsky's part, according to Kirpotin, in general threw off Dostoevsky's thinking in historical-philosophical and political realms.[11]

We may recall here Tolstoy's reply to the Russian critic N. N. Strakhov whose constant complaint was that Dostoevsky wrote about himself in his works while imagining that he was writing about people at large. "And so?" Tolstoy exclaims, "The result is that not only people close to him like us, but foreigners as well, recognize themselves, their spirit in these exceptional characters."[12] Dostoevsky, to be sure, especially calls attention in the opening pages of *House of the Dead* to the "different sorts of people" there were in prison; every section of Russia "had its representative." But what is central is that he recognized in the exceptional convicts, in the exaggerated and even abnormal content of their personalities and histories, precisely the problems that had been afflicting the Russian people and nation for centuries. He found reflected in the convicts, and in their exceptional prison situation, issues and problems that in one form or another have dogged historical man at every stage of his development. It may be noted here that Dostoevsky's concept of the "exceptional" and "fantastic" as often constituting the very essence of reality—a concept that lies at the center of his poetics in the 1860s and 1870s—owes much to his prison experience.

House of the Dead, then, is extraordinarily rich and important precisely on the psychohistorical plane of investigation. Dostoevsky apprehended deeply and fully the social and psychological tragedy of a people that had been subjected to serfdom and autocracy for hundreds of years, an "unfortunate" people that comprehended its tragedy as "fate." Just here, of course, "protest expressed in crime"—that is, anarchic despair and revolt—gives eloquent expression to the tragic historical experience of the Russian people. This experience is in the foreground of Dostoevsky's consciousness in *House of the Dead*; it is in the substratum of his philosophically and ethically profound *Notes from the Underground*, a work that perhaps would have been inconceivable in any other European nation in the nineteenth century. My analysis of *House of the Dead*, though not primarily sociological or historical in orientation, nonetheless inevitably focuses the aesthetic, psychological, and philosophical issues of that work against the background of Dostoevsky's own deep concern with Russian man and history.

In its themes and preoccupations *House of the Dead* anticipates the problem content of Dostoevsky's novels in the 1860s and 1870s. The frightening "story" told by Akulka's husband, the convict Shishkov, is at the center of the discussion of Dostoevsky's approach to the problem of evil in Russian life and in human existence in general. The significance of Shishkov's story in the context of Dostoevsky's broader statement in *House of the Dead* has been a subject of controversy.[13] Does Dostoevsky affirm the existence of absolute evil or does he view evil as dependent upon environment? It would appear that he affirms neither extreme but insists that man is his own environment. The instinct for power, acquisition, and sexual aggression—for Dostoevsky the locus of evil—is a force that is encouraged or discouraged by environment, but it is not a *product* of environment in the most fundamental sense. The potential for good and evil lies within man. Though he does not possess absolute freedom from evil in the face of human nature, he can nonetheless, through the awakening of his own moral and spiritual forces, improve himself and in turn improve society.

Dostoevsky, then, appeals in *House of the Dead* to the moral and civic consciousness of Russia. He affirms man's essential inner freedom and therefore his responsibility for himself and his environment. At the same time, he depicts the Russian peasant-convict as a victim of centuries of disordered history. In this connection, nothing is more striking to the reader familiar with Dostoevsky's later works (for example, *Crime and Punishment*) than the insistence of the narrator that the ordinary convict felt no pangs of conscience for his crimes. Dostoevsky advances no single reason for this phenomenon that so engages his attention. But he points to the Russian people's sense of total alienation from the social and cultural structures of Russia's ruling class and to a morally disabling feeling of helplessness before an implacable historical fate.

In contrast to the typical peasant-convict, the narrator, a man from the nobility, judged himself and his past severely. An upper-class background, of course, does not in any way signify the presence of an active conscience in a man, as Dostoevsky makes clear in several graphic examples. But in *House of the Dead*, moral conscience as it is conventionally understood seems to be the attribute of an educated, spiritually developed consciousness.

Later in his life Dostoevsky appears to have felt uncomfortable with the interpretation he gave of the popular conscience in *House of the Dead*. He insists in *Diary of a Writer* in 1873 that the convicts were *not* indifferent to the crimes they committed. At the same time, he adopts a moralistic and militant point of view toward the malefactor among the Russian masses. Dostoevsky's partial revision of his thinking in this area, however, suggests that the full ambience of his attitude toward the peasant-convict was not expressed in *House of the Dead*. This is a work in which all elements of purely moral criticism of the people, to say nothing of personal resentment for years of insult and humiliation, are muted in favor of a compassionate study of the character of the Russian people and of their historical tragedy.

In his later writings Dostoevsky tends to idealize suffering and to view it as having a salutary influence in the life of the individual and of the Russian people at large. Although such a point of view finds real expression in the personal drama of the narrator of *House of the Dead*, it finds little development in the drama of the common peasant-convict. For the most part, Dostoevsky explores the suffering of the Russian people from a social and psychological point of view. He finds in the common conflict's passive submission to suffering, for example, a kind of perverse and stubborn resistance to a cruel fate. As later in *Notes from the Underground*, he links suffering in general closely with man's primordial craving for freedom, with his need to express his deepest creative instincts and energies. The evolution of Dostoevsky's views on conscience and suffering in the 1860s and 1870s is among the most important problems of Dostoevsky scholarship, and it is one of the most psychologically and ideologically complex. What is certain is that this problem cannot even be posed without the most searching examination of *House of the Dead* and of Dostoevsky's whole orientation to his prison experience.

Notes from the Underground has been called the prologue or "philosophical preface" to the great novels of Dostoevsky.[14] Little attention, however, has been given the dependence of this work on *House of the Dead* for its main psychological and philosophical insights.[15] The complex themes of *Notes from the Underground*— problems of fate, freedom, suffering, underground revolt—are all embodied first in *House of the Dead*. Indeed, Goryanchikov's "Scenes from the House of the Dead" and the Underground Man's "confession" from a certain point of view can be regarded as complementary responses to the devastating experience of the "dead house." Dostoevsky, to be sure, conceives the Russian convict and Underground Man as entirely different social types. They stand in relation to each other—on the ideological plane of Dostoevsky's discourse—as hero and antihero. Yet we recognize in the convict's instinctual striving for freedom, in his thirst for life and movement, and in the various ways he resists the paralyzing force of his prison environment, a prototype of tragic underground revolt and despair.

Dostoevsky's own experience in prison (he later spoke of it as a "compulsory communism") and his reflections there on the question of freedom deeply influenced his complex—indeed, in some respects, ambivalent—treatment of this theme in *Notes from the Underground*. "The revolt of the Underground Man," I wrote in *Dostoevsky's Underground Man in Russian Literature*, "is a tragicomic rebellion of the ego, crazed by its impotence, against an overpowering and humiliating reality. The Underground Man's entire life is one continuous attempt to make contact with the world and with himself; isolated, unable to act, he is a social zero. He is the negation of the negation."[16]

In its critique of anarchic individualism and in its underlying social ethic, *Notes from the Underground* marks one of the lofty achievements of the Russian cultural renaissance of the nineteenth century. It marks the recognition, to use the words of Dostoevsky, that the "law of the 'I' must merge with the law of humanism," that the opposition of "I" and "everybody" must disappear in a union that will recreate the basis for the genuine development of personality.[17] Yet at the same time, in its depiction of the total catastrophe of the individual and of personality, *Notes from the Underground* constitutes a tragic acknowledgment of the fundamentally premature, indeed utopian, character of that ideal in Russian social reality. "The concept of personality among us is only just taking shape," the Russian critic V. G. Belinsky wrote in 1847, "and therefore the Gogolian types *for the time being* are the most authentic Russian types."[18]

Russian literature of the nineteenth century, deeply spiritual and national, in its own way disputed with Belinsky on this point; it took up the cause of the Russian people, of the "little man," of Russian "personality," and created out of Russian life images of original beauty. *Notes from the Underground* was part of this quest for form, but its humanity is expressed almost totally in pain. It gives expression to Dostoevsky's militant defense not of anarchic individualism, but of the violated individual, of his aborted personal freedom, dignity, and happiness. The disfigured and anarchic character of the Underground Man's protest points to the overwhelming force arrayed against the individual, a force foredooming him to impotence and despair. Dostoevsky here raises once again the agonizing question posed by Pushkin in his narrative poem, *The Bronze Horseman* (the contradiction between the harsh ideals and impersonality of the imperial state, indeed of history itself, and the humble, human strivings and needs of the individual), but raises it now almost exclusively in the desperate human terms of ruined personality.[19] The grandeur of the Petrine state is now reduced to a terrifying abstraction, its historical reality to the primordial swamp upon which Petersburg was founded. Man is swallowed up by nature and environment. It is a "misfortune" to inhabit Petersburg, observes the Underground Man, "the most abstract and intentional city in the whole world."

The philosophical complexities of *Notes from the Underground*—its multiperspectival approach to the question of human freedom, its rejection both of reactionary utopia and of anarchic liberty, yet its recognition that human freedom must begin and end with the notion of the sanctity of human personality—take on special meaning when examined in the light of conditions specific to Russian life and history. The Russian "renaissance" had arrived in all its splendor in the late eighteenth and early nineteenth centuries, but it found the dead house everywhere in place.[20] The passionate appeal of Dostoevsky in his postexile work for a Christian change in consciousness, for a change based upon the Christian ethic of love and self-sacrifice—an appeal coupled with a rejection of the path of action of the socialist and revolutionary forces of his day—derives much of its strength and pathos from a deep and in many respects well-justified social-historical pessimism.

All roads in Dostoevsky lead to and from the dead house. Here Dostoevsky explored the questions of freedom, alienation, and rebellion from the psychological and ethical points of view.[21] The revolt of alienated man is not only a reaction; it is rooted in man's natural need to affirm himself. In Dostoevsky's recognition that this natural egoism was both necessary to man and a part of his historical evolution, and at the same time in conflict with man's highest spiritual ideal of love and self-sacrifice, we find the philosophical and ethical conundrum that lies at the heart of *Notes from the Underground* and that has resisted all one-sided solutions.

The experience of the Russian convict in prison became for Dostoevsky a metaphor expressing the moral and spiritual tragedy of man in a fate-ruled universe. The Underground Man is a victim not so much of a hostile world, but of his own skeptical and fatalistic outlook on the world. Central in Raskolnikov's movement toward catastrophe is his fundamentally pessimistic judgment of man and the world and a rationalistic and fatalistic outlook that denies freedom of choice or moral responsibility. In "The Gentle Creature" Dostoevsky again exposes the tragic link between a world view that denies any coherence in the universe—one that posits fate as the determinant in man's life—and personal and social catastrophe. But without doubt the most thorough examination of the moral, spiritual, and social implications of a belief in chance is to be found in *The Gambler*, a work in which Dostoevsky draws not only upon his own experience in gambling in the early 1860s but also upon his whole psychological experience in prison.[22]

Few subjects provide such a remarkable point of conjunction for so many areas of thought and human experience as does the phenomenon of gambling. Here, to borrow a phrase from Dmitry Karamazov, "all shores meet": social, psychosexual, economic, philosophical, religious. As *The Gambler* and *House of the Dead* attest, Dostoevsky perceived the relevance and ramifications of the gambling impulse in all these areas.

In *House of the Dead* the theme of gambling is embodied not so much in games of chance—for example, constant card playing— as in the convicts' craving for "risk" and in the way they confront their environment. It would, perhaps, not be incorrect to say that on the psychological plane Dostoevsky perceived the convicts as gamblers. The worlds of the dead house, the underground, and the gambler are the same in a psychological sense. It is the players who are different. Different, too, is Dostoevsky's attitude toward the real Russian convicts as compared with his attitude toward the metaphysical convicts, the Underground Man, and the hero in *The Gambler*. Yet in all cases the gamblers are men who live in an enclosed, seemingly finite universe; in all cases the gambling impulse expresses a deep insecurity and a sense of danger in the face of a threat to personality—the threat of spiritual inertia, death to the spirit. "If the whole future were laid bare to us beyond today," George Eliot has written, "we should rush fiercely to the Exchange for our last possibility of speculation, of success, of disappointment."[23] The convicts find themselves in precisely this situation, and their efforts to overcome the inertia of their world—mostly benign, but occasionally malignant—represent a form of desperate "speculation." In one sense, they seek in uncertainty a kind of freedom; in another sense, they seek to determine their ontological situation before the unknown.

INTRODUCTION

We need not argue, as does one student of gambling, that "gambling is a 'universal neurosis'—like religion itself"[24] to recognize that in Dostoevsky's universe gambling is an alternative to religion, that the gambling neurosis as such is linked with a failure to resolve the religious question. The convicts, of course, were not involved with posing or solving religious questions. Religion, moreover, did not play a deep role in the way they related to reality. But Dostoevsky's case was different. The dead house for him later became the metaphor for an enclosed, godless universe, a place where hope or salvation was absolutely denied. Man confined in such a universe could only conceive of the world as being directed by blind fate; that is, he could only relate to it as a gambler. The ordinary Russian convict, whatever his religious convictions, related to prison in this way. Dostoevsky—in *House of the Dead* at least—seems to see the Russian peasant-serf in general as relating to his condition, (on the psychohistorical plane) in the same way—that is, as determined by fate.

The step from *House of the Dead* to *The Gambler* is not as great as might be assumed at first glance. *The Gambler* is indubitably among the most psychologically profound and artistically successful of Dostoevsky's works. What has stood in the way of a full appreciation of this work and its meaning has been the tendency to see in it a simple mirroring of Dostoevsky's own gambling experiences and adventures with Apollinaria Suslova.[25] As D. S. Savage has observed in his fine essay on *The Gambler*, Dostoevsky's novel about gambling "is no mere scandalous revelation of a personal history but, as is usual with Dostoevsky's work, a dominating and shaping imaginative *idea* to which everything in the action is related."[26] That idea, as Savage rightly understands it, involves the exploration of the "interior dialectic of unbelief," a tragic dialectic that Dostoevsky explores in many of his great characters.

Diary of a Writer is certainly one of Dostoevsky's most complex artistic experiments.[27] Deeply involved with the artistic process, it afforded Dostoevsky, first of all, a unique means for exploring and experimenting with his concepts of art and reality. "The Peasant Marey," "Bobok," "A Boy at Christ's Christmas Party," "The

Dream of a Ridiculous Man," and "A Gentle Creature" each constitute unique statements on a whole range of aesthetic questions. Indeed, it is impossible to grasp these works in all their complex problem content apart from their conscious effort to project and embody aesthetic problems. What Dostoevsky says in "The Dream of a Ridiculous Man," for example, is inseparable from the artistic ideas the story exemplifies. "Fantastic realism" here is a philosophy. "The Peasant Marey" has often been taken as a simple piece of autobiography. Yet this seemingly casual recollection of a recollection of a childhood incident is not so much autobiography as it is an example of the creation of biography, that is, of artistic self-creation on the part of Dostoevsky as both convict and memoirist. Only in recognizing this artistic element—which Dostoevsky hardly conceals in his sketch—can we assess the great importance of this sketch as spiritual autobiography. We are not dealing in "The Peasant Marey" with self-parody, but with serious irony. My discussion of "The Peasant Marey," a prologue to the discussion of *House of the Dead*, also serves as an examination of the artist in process.

"A Boy at Christ's Christmas Party" is a "Christmas story" in which Dostoevsky mixes sentimentality with brutal realism. He interweaves the theme of the suffering child—at the center of this story, as it is at the center of Ivan Karamazov's "rebellion"—and the theme of heavenly happiness with the theme of "incredible" reality. What is real or fantastic is relative to the perspective of the viewer. What is not relative, what is absolute, is the dignity and worth of the human being.

"A Boy at Christ's Christmas Party" embodies the kind of fantastic realism we find in "The Dream of a Ridiculous Man." In the latter story and in "Bobok" Dostoevsky provides the reader—through his play with two different kinds of fantasy—with the most complete idea of his view of the nature of realism and reality. In "Dream" we find an almost programmatic example of Dostoevsky's notion of fantastic realism; his concept of time and space gives expression to his entire moral-philosophical outlook. "Bobok," on the other hand, is fantasy of another kind: a didactic pseudogrotesque in which Dostoevsky explores the secular imagination of naturalism.

The view that "The Dream of a Ridiculous Man" is an antiutopia has been argued a number of times.[28] My own view is that Dostoevsky is not criticizing the utopian mentality in this story but giving embodiment and expression to his own "law of striving for the ideal." What is ridiculous about the hero of "Dream" in the worldly sphere, but heroic and necessary in Dostoevsky's view, is his affirmation of the ideal in the face of his sober awareness that the ideal is unrealizable. The notion that man strives—and must strive—for a lofty ideal that is unattainable on earth is one that Dostoevsky elaborates in his notebook in the early 1860s. These ideas find full expression in "The Dream of a Ridiculous Man."

The ridiculous man plainly articulates another of Dostoevsky's cardinal thoughts, one expressed both in his notebooks and novels—namely, the idea that life is higher than the consciousness of life. The ridiculous man is not Dostoevsky, of course, yet this type of "holy fool" or *iurodivyi* (as the ridiculous man is called by the fallen people of his dream paradise) was deeply congenial to him. In the final analysis, what Dostoevsky once wrote in a letter about his characterization of Zosima in *The Brothers Karamazov* might equally well have been written about the ridiculous man: "Although indeed I fully share the thoughts he expresses, yet if I were to express them personally as coming *from myself*, then I would have expressed them in another form, in another language. But he *could not* express them in another language *or another spirit* than that which I have given to him. Otherwise an artistic figure would not have been created."[29] This Russian Don Quixote, who ultimately went beyond his Spanish prototype, was dear to Dostoevsky.

"A Gentle Creature" is one of the great stories in world literature. Innovative in form, it remains one of the most extraordinary explorations of the labyrinth of guilty solitude, of the dialectic of conscience and reason, of the processes of rationalization in human consciousness. Aron Steinberg has written that to overcome his absolute isolation the " 'proud man' of the new age might even contemplate the creation by sheer willpower of another human being whose relationship to the self-appointed creator would be similar to that of man to God."[30] Such creation, of course, falls into the realm of the demonic. The account of such an experiment in creation is recorded in "A Gentle Creature," a work that in important ways draws upon the Faust legend.

It is impossible, of course, to disclose in a few words the incredibly rich content of the sketches in *Diary of a Writer*. "Bobok," M. Bakhtin rightly insists, is "almost a microcosm" of Dostoevsky's art. In it we encounter the central ideas, themes, and images of his entire oeuvre.[31] The same may be said of all of the short masterpieces that form an integral part of *Diary of a Writer*. The whole work of Dostoevsky is reflected in these brilliant and profound microcosms, like the sun in a drop of water.

The concepts of *obraz* (image or form, but also icon) and *bezobrazie* (shapelessness, the monstrous, or deformed) are structuring moral and aesthetic categories in Dostoevsky's art and find their source in traditional Christian theology and symbolism. God created man in His own image. But this image becomes obscured, even disfigured. It is never completely lost, however; it remains to be rediscovered, "restored"—in theological terms, redeemed—in all its original purity. The fundamental concerns of Dostoevsky in his art are always related to this task of restoration. The "basic idea" in all art in the nineteenth century, a "Christian" idea, he insisted in 1861, is the "restoration of the fallen man." This idea was first embodied in Dostoevsky's work in *Poor Folk* and other stories in the 1840s. The same idea wholly defined Dostoevsky's efforts in *House of the Dead*, a work in which the theme of the restoration of fallen man is interwoven with the theme of Christian redemption on the deepest level of the work's meaning.

The concepts of *obraz* and *bezobrazie* enter deeply into the artistic fabric and design of *The Brothers Karamazov*. Fyodor Karamazov emerges before the reader in the chapter entitled "Over the Brandy" as the very incarnation of *bezobrazie*—not only as one whose image is literally and figuratively deformed but as one who desecrates all that is sacred in Russian life, including the icon itself.[32] Both Zosima and Alyosha perceive the inner image of

Fyodor, but they are unable to prevent his fatal plunge to disaster.
The Christian law of brotherly love is overwhelmed in *The Brothers
Karamazov* by what Vyacheslav Ivanov has termed the tragic "law
of the progressively gathering momentum of events."[33]

"I think if the devil doesn't exist, but man has created him,"
Ivan remarks to Alyosha, "he has created him in his own image
and likeness." This observation, of course, mocks the concept of
man as created in God's image. And indeed, Ivan finds it difficult
to find even traces of God's image in man. He is doubtful about
the possibility of any kind of genuine Christian love in man. Yet
he himself constitutes a refutation of his own pessimistic outlook.[34]
The Russian people, Dostoevsky believed, preserved in their hearts,
throughout the misery and disfiguration of centuries, the image
of beauty, the image of Christ and the saints. It is precisely because
Ivan has preserved in his heart the "precious" image of Christ that
he finds it difficult to reconcile Christian truth with evil, *obraz*
with *bezobrazie*. Beneath his desire to suffer with his indignation
lies a desire to imitate Christ.

Dmitry Karamazov's drama is central to the novel. In the context
of Ivan's legend of the Grand Inquisitor, Dmitry represents the
generality of mankind, those millions of tormented people who
in the eyes of the Grand Inquisitor are unable to endure their inner
conflicts or bear the burden of their moral freedom. Yet the fate
of Dmitry suggests that man, while compromising with his ideals
in life, nonetheless will continue to struggle for them. The positive
resolution of Dmitry's immediate crisis in the novel is signaled by
his discovery of a "new man" in himself. This new man, like the
obscured image of God in man's countenance, is not yet visible.
But Dmitry's awareness of him marks a new stage in his development. On the symbolic plane of the novel's meaning, it marks
a new stage in the development of humanity.

The Triple Vision:
"The Peasant Marey"

Aus meinem Leben. Dichtung und Wahrheit.
GOETHE

IN "THE PEASANT MAREY" (1876) Dostoevsky recalls how as a convict in Siberia early in Easter week 1850 he recoiled in horror before the depravity and violence of his fellow convicts. The words of a Polish political prisoner addressed to him on this occasion, *"Je hais ces brigands,"* seem to express his own sense of disgust, hatred, and despair. But Dostoevsky writes that he lay down on his bunk in the barracks a few moments later and recalled in a daydream a childhood encounter with the kindly peasant Marey.[1] As a result of that recollection, he recalls, something unusual happened to Dostoevsky the convict. Just what happened he describes at the end of "The Peasant Marey":

> And so when I got off the bunk and looked round, I remember, I suddenly felt that I could look at these unhappy creatures with quite a different glance, and that suddenly, as though by some miracle, all hatred and anger vanished from my heart. I went about looking into the faces of people I encountered. This rascal of a peasant with shaven head and branded face, intoxicated, bawling out his drunken hoarse song,—why, he too may be the very same Marey: after all I really can't look into his heart.

The daydream-recollection of Dostoevsky the convict certainly brought about an important change, or transfiguration, in his heart, and this change is intimately connected with his daydream image of Marey. At that moment, he felt that he could look at the convicts with new eyes, that is, look beyond their raw, frightening exterior. Yet when Dostoevsky, looking into the faces of the convicts, speculates that this or that peasant "may be the very same Marey," he adds, oddly: "after all, I really can't look into his heart."

We can count five words in the passage quoted above that have to do with vision. Dostoevsky must have been fully aware of the curious non sequitur presented by that last phrase. So we come to the question: how is it possible to have a new view of the convicts, that is, a view of their basic humanity, without the capacity to look into their hearts? How can there be belief without insight? We will leave aside the testimony of Jesus, his gentle admonition to the once doubting Thomas: "blessed are they that have not seen, and yet have believed" (John 20:29). The answer to this question involves not only an understanding of the precise nature—and limits—of the action of the daydream-recollection in a psychological and aesthetic sense but a recognition that the vision of Dostoevsky the convict is only an intermediate level in a three-stage vision and transfiguration of reality. This triple vision involves the encounter of the nine-year-old Dostoevsky with Marey, the convict Dostoevsky's daydream-recollection of the encounter, and the recollection of the recollection in "The Peasant Marey"—all that constitutes section three, chapter one of the February 1876 issue of *Diary of a Writer*.

In analyzing this sketch or testimony, we must continually bear in mind some important remarks Dostoevsky makes midway in the story. The daydream, he indicates, was for him both an escape and a creative occupation in prison. All through those four years he would "incessantly" recall his past, "relive [his] whole past life." These recollections, he notes, would arise spontaneously:

I rarely evoked them of my own will. It used to begin with some spark, traits, sometimes almost imperceptible, and then little by little grew into a whole picture, into some kind of strong and integral impression. I would analyze these impressions, add new features to things that had happened long ago, and, mainly, I would correct, continually correct the picture, and herein lay my whole pleasure.

There is no doubt at all that Dostoevsky the convict did indeed dream and think in this manner, that he would correct—that is, shape, or give form and moral meaning to—the impressions and experiences of his past. But these remarks also provide us with the aesthetic key to "The Peasant Marey" as a whole, and to the serious play of Dostoevsky the artist here, sacred play involving his fundamental aesthetic, spiritual, and populist outlook.

Perhaps more than any other work of Dostoevsky, "The Peasant Marey" constitutes a *profession de foi*, that is, a declaration of faith and convictions. Everything else, including the recollection of the peasant Marey, is subordinated to this objective. The opening lines of "The Peasant Marey," commenting on the short discussion of the Russian people in the section of *Diary of a Writer* just preceding the sketch, read as follows:

> But these *professions de foi*, I think, are very boring to the reader, and therefore I will relate an anecdote, or rather something that is not even an anecdote: just one little distant recollection which for some reason I very much want to relate precisely at this point, at the conclusion of our little treatise on the people.[2]

Dostoevsky's *professions de foi*, of course, point forward to his anecdote as well as backward to his treatise on the people. They are extremely relevant to "The Peasant Marey."

The short piece that precedes "The Peasant Marey" is entitled "About Love for the People. A Necessary Contract with the People." In the so-called anecdote or distant recollection that follows, Dostoevsky presents the reader with precisely the moment when he made his contract with the people, that is, when he attained to the most important vision of his life. In this vision, aesthetic, religion, and populism form a grand trinity. We say "moment," yet an analysis of "The Peasant Marey" suggests that the moment existed at a number of points in historical time, and therefore exists out of time, or only in the ideality of time created by the artist himself.

We cannot overestimate the critical, indeed agonizing, importance that the people—the problem of understanding them and being reconciled with them—played in Dostoevsky's life, outlook,

and art. It was "agonizing" because Dostoevsky came to understand through direct experience that any authentic understanding
or reconciliation would have to endure a terrifying journey before
it reached the interior, the immense spiritual yearnings, of this
wounded and unhappy people. In the so-called treatise on the
people that precedes "The Peasant Marey" Dostoevsky formulates the problem of love for the people in characteristically aesthetic terms:

> Where the Russian common man of the people is concerned,
> one must be able to abstract his beauty from the alluvial
> barbarism. Owing to the circumstances of almost our entire
> history our people have been subjected to depravity and have
> been debauched, tempted, and constantly tortured to such an
> extent that it is still amazing how it managed to survive and
> still preserve a human image, to say nothing of preserving
> its beauty. But it preserved the beauty of its image as well.
> A true friend of humanity . . . will excuse all the impassable
> alluvial filth in which our people are sunk and be able to seek
> out diamonds in this filth.[3]

Dostoevsky, then, distinguishes between repulsive, yet alluvial,
filth in Russian life—that is, a surface *bezobrazie*, or disfiguration—and an inner, organic form—*obraz*, or image.[4] Diamonds
in filth. In this extended metaphor the diamond, or image, represents the luminous, refulgent ideals preserved in the heart of
the people—"all those sacred things it longs for," everything that
we find in its "saints," saints who "themselves glow and illumi-
nate the path for us all." The ideals of the people, Dostoevsky
insists, are "strong and sacred"; these ideals "saved" the people
in centuries of suffering: "they became one with its spirit. . . .
And if despite all this there is so much filth, then the Russian
suffers from it himself more than anybody else, and believes that
all this is only alluvial and temporal, a diabolical suggestion, that
the darkness will disappear and eternal light without fail will
beam out some day."[5]

What conceals or disfigures the image, or icon, of the Russian
people, then, is not merely ugly but evil—a "diabolical sugges-

tion," something alien, accidental, slanderous—as the Russian word for "alluvial," *nanosnyi,* implies. In turn, the revelation of the beauty of the image, the removal, as it were, of layers of filth from the icon, will also be a triumph over evil. It will be a revelation of light in the broad aesthetic and religious sense. The aesthetic act, the revelation of light and beauty, is in this sense apocalyptic: it presages rebirth and transfiguration. In the deepest sense, though, Dostoevsky would say of the artist and his aesthetic act what the Gospel says of John the Baptist: "he was not that Light, but was sent to bear witness of that Light" (John 1:8).

Who, according to Dostoevsky, bears witness to the luminous image of the Russian people? Who gives birth to images? Or, as he puts it, who "seeks out diamonds in filth"? Russian literature, the Russian artist, of course. The poem, Dostoevsky wrote in 1869, "is like a natural precious stone, a diamond in the soul of the people." But "if it is not [the artist] himself who is the creator," Dostoevsky adds, "then at least his soul is that very mine which gives birth to the diamonds."[6] It is only in contact with common interests, only "in sympathy with the mass of society and its direct, immediate demands," Dostoevsky wrote again in 1847, "not in drowsiness, not in indifference—from which the mass disintegrates—not in solitude, that man's treasure, his capital, his good heart can be refined into a precious, inimitable, brilliant diamond."[7]

It is no surprise, then, that Dostoevsky insists in 1876 in his treatise on the people that it is precisely the Russian artist who has been mining and refining diamonds in filth. "All that is truly beautiful in Russian literature has been taken from the people." The great writers "borrowed from the people its simple-heartedness, purity, gentleness, breadth of mind, and kindliness, in contrast to all that is twisted, false, alluvial, and slavishly borrowed." Russian literature—Turgenev, Goncharov, and others—has the merit of having "recognized the people's ideals as genuinely beautiful." "In all this," Dostoevsky remarks, "it has been guided by artistic sense rather than good will."[8] Aesthetic rather than abstract moral criteria, significantly, stand in the foreground for Dostoevsky: where good will is easily frustrated, artistic sense, acting independently, discerns beauty and the deepest layers of reality in man.

Aesthetic vision, revelation, the simultaneous discovery of light and truth in the midst of darkness, penetrating the alluvial filth, in a word, artistic sense is what "The Peasant Marey" is about. But when did the miracle take place? In the summer of 1830, when the nine-year-old Dostoevsky met Marey in the woods? In prison during Easter week 1850, when at the age of twenty-nine Dostoevsky the convict recollected Marey? Or in February 1876, in St. Petersburg, when Dostoevsky the fifty-five-year-old writer recollected the recollection of Marey and embodied it in "The Peasant Marey"?

Easter Monday, though a traditional moment of joyous expectation for the believer, was a terrifying time for the convict Dostoevsky, in Omsk, Siberia, in 1850. Dostoevsky accents the terrible degradation, violence, and brutality of the convicts around him:

> Monstrous, vile songs, groups of convicts playing cards under the bunks; several of the convicts, who had been sentenced by their own comrades for running amok, to be beaten till they were half dead, were lying on the bunk, covered with sheepskins till they should recover and come to themselves again; knives had already been drawn several times—for these two days of holiday all this had been torturing me to the point of illness. And indeed I was never able to endure without repulsion the drunken orgies of the people, and here, in this place in particular.

Dostoevsky had just rushed out of the barracks "half mad" when six convicts beat the drunken, monstrous Tatar Gazin nearly to death (Dostoevsky describes Gazin in *House of the Dead* as "having the appearance of a huge spider the size of a man"). But he returned to the barracks fifteen minutes later with the words of the Polish political prisoner ringing in his ears: "*Je hais ces brigands.*"

In the midst of this nightmare of violence and debauch, Dostoevsky relates, he lay down on his bunk on his back and closed his eyes. "I liked to lie that way: people don't bother a person who is sleeping, and meanwhile one can dream and think." Little by little he forgot his surroundings and "imperceptibly sank into memories." What follows is the recollection of Dostoevsky the convict, in the rendition of Dostoevsky the writer, of his experience as a child on a walk through a wooded area called Losk (that is, "shine" or "lustre") one late summer's day. We shall not dwell on the extraordinary description Dostoevsky gives of himself in the woods hunting beetles, lizards, and mushrooms—fearing only snakes. "These impressions remain with you for your whole life," Dostoevsky says. Suffice it to say that there is something distinctly idyllic about this scene; it is a kind of garden of Eden, the kind of garden that is rarely to be found in Dostoevsky's works. But suddenly in this garden the child hears a cry, "A wolf is coming!" "I shrieked and, beside myself with fright, and screaming at the top of my lungs, I rushed out to the clearing and straight to the ploughing peasant," to the kindly and benevolent Marey. It turns out that the boy was the victim of an hallucination. The peasant Marey gently calmed him, Dostoevsky the convict recalls; he "extended his hand and suddenly stroked" the child's cheek and made the sign of the cross. With a "broad motherly smile," "he quietly stretched out his thick earth-bespattered finger with its blackened nail and gently touched my trembling lips."[9] The episode is almost iconographic in its detail. And as though to emphasize its importance, Dostoevsky repeats his description of it a few moments later. This passage deserves the utmost attention. Dostoevsky recalls again how he

remembered this entire meeting with such clarity, to the finest detail . . . this tender, motherly smile of that poor serf, his sign of the cross, the nodding of his head . . . and especially that thick finger bespattered with earth with which quietly and with such shy tenderness he touched my trembling lips. Of course, anybody would have comforted a child, but here in this lonely encounter it seems that something quite different happened, and if I had been his own son, he could not have looked at me and beamed a more luminous glance of love; yet who compelled him to do it? . . . The meeting was a solitary one, in an empty field, and only God, perhaps, saw from above with what profound and enlightened human feeling, and with what delicate, almost feminine tenderness, the heart of a coarse, savagely ignorant Russian serf was filled, a serf who at the time neither expected nor dreamt of his emancipation. [10]

The miracle of Dostoevsky the convict's change of heart is, of course, the miracle of the memory-purified image of Marey, an image expressed in his "gentle motherly smile" (mentioned three times), his "shy, . . . feminine tenderness," his "luminous glance of love." At the moment of contact with the boy Dostoevsky Marey is the very embodiment of love and motherly compassion.

Dostoevsky, it is clear, has selected this name, "Marey," for the peasant of his childhood memory, [11] for he remarks, significantly, on his first mention of the peasant, "I do not know if there is such a name." The name, if indeed it exists, is certainly a rare one. It is in any case not accidental that the name or word "Marey" could very easily have been associated in the popular mind with the dialect pronunciation of "Maria" (Mary), which is "Mareia." The peasant Marey in all his essential characteristics—his tenderness and motherly compassion—is an imitation of the Holy Mary. In this sense, the nine-year-old Dostoevsky, like the child Alyosha Karamazov whose mother held him up before the icon-image of Mary, may be said to have come under the protection of the Madonna.

The symbolic meaning of his encounter with Marey, of course, dawned upon Dostoevsky only as a convict in prison. This encounter, as Dostoevsky the writer conceives it, suggests what a depth of feeling and concept underlay his assertion in the last section of *Diary of a Writer* in 1873 that at the basis of his "change of convictions" lay "direct contact with the people, brotherly unity with it in the common misfortune." [12] Contact with the people for Dostoevsky, as for Alyosha Karamazov in the chapter "Cana of Galilee," was not only a contact with the rejuvenating powers of the earth but a hidden revelation. Thus the special words of Dostoevsky, "something quite different happened," point to a mystical experience, a religious moment of consecration—a solitary one, as Dostoevsky puts it, in an empty field with only God looking on.

Let us briefly review the experience remembered in "The Peasant Marey." In prison, surrounded by coarse and frightening peasant-convicts, Dostoevsky closes his eyes and recalls a moment in his childhood when, alone in the woods, he had a terrible fright about a wolf (in Russian, the word for "wolf" is *volk*). We have an obvious parallel in experience here. On the one hand, we have the moment of panic in the woods in which the boy fears a terrible wolf; this all turns out to have been an hallucination. On the other hand, we have a moment of panic in the barracks in which Dostoevsky the convict is terrorized by monster-convicts; this also turns out to have been something of an hallucination, a nightmare, a diabolical suggestion, for it involved a deep misunderstanding of the true nature of the convicts, or Russian people. (The German word for "the people," *das Volk*, comes to mind here.) Dostoevsky had been deceived in his judgment by alluvial filth, the diabolical mask of ugliness. In the first instance, the terrified child is touched on the lips and cured of his hallucination by the compassionate Marey with his "gentle motherly smile." In the second instance, Dostoevsky the convict is cured of his hatred and anger, his moral blindness, by what he calls the "gentle smile of memory":

> All this I recalled at once, I do not know why, but with amazing accuracy of detail. I suddenly came to and sat up in my bunk and, I remember, I could still feel the gentle smile of memory on my face. For another minute I went on recalling that incident of my childhood.

The gentle smile of memory, of course, spreads across the hardened, embittered face of Dostoevsky the convict, comforts him in his suffering, and above all—momentarily, to be sure—banishes from his heart all hatred and anger. The psychological-aesthetic impact of the daydream-recollection with its glowing image of

Marey is such as to make him feel—precisely feel—that he could
look at the convicts with quite different eyes.

And yet for Dostoevsky the convict, in the very first months
of his imprisonment, there was as yet no real seeing into the
inner human core of the convicts. Under the impact of his daydream-recollection he only sensed or supposed the existence of
other peasant Mareys under the harsh exterior of the convicts.
"But after all I cannot really look into his heart," he says. If we
read correctly the concluding passage from "The Peasant Marey,"
we realize that the daydream-recollection constituted a form of
intuition by analogy; the purified dream-image of Marey momentarily came between Dostoevsky and the convicts. What the
daydream-recollection did for Dostoevsky the convict was to open
up for Dostoevsky the artist the possibility of a new "quite different glance"; it opened the way for those months and years of
purifying recollection of his years in prison, years of slow spiritual recovery, years of preparation of *House of the Dead*, the pivotal work in Dostoevsky's postexile artistic development. In the
latter work, in which aesthetic idealism merges with a Christian
faith and mythology, Dostoevsky simultaneously defines his aesthetic of transfiguration and signals his own personal and artistic
triumph over the raw, naturalistic, lethal reality of Russian life.

The daydream-recollection, then, is analogous to the artistic
process. As Dostoevsky himself notes in "The Peasant Marey,"
it is an active creative process working toward a final, integral,
complete "picture." Further, the daydream-recollection, as a com-
pleted memory image, in all its artistic detail, acts upon the dreamer like a work of art: it momentarily transforms him, inwardly
and outwardly. Yet the convict Dostoevsky's daydream-recollection was not art in itself. It became art in the final recollection of
the recollection, that is, when the anecdote or distant recollection,
after much analysis and correction, after prolonged search for
form and meaning, was finally embodied in artistic imagery.

In sum, we can distinguish three intersecting levels of vision or
aesthetic-spiritual experience. The first vision pertains to the appearance of Marey before the nine-year-old Dostoevsky. Something happened to the child in the field: he was not merely com-

forted; his lips were touched, consecrated by earth; he was blessed by the archetypal man of the people, the peasant Marey. The poet discovers in this the inner, mystical moment of his spiritual formation and calling. This whole "adventure," as Dostoevsky calls it, along with the memory of Marey, was of course quickly forgotten by the child. But nothing is ever lost. It only waits to be recovered. The second vision was experienced by the convict Dostoevsky in prison on the second day of Easter week. Just as the Russian peasant was saved in centuries of suffering by the luminous, embodied ideals of the people, so the image of Marey, as Dostoevsky puts it, "came back when it was needed," came back in the purifying form of a daydream-revelation. The third and final vision involved the crucial artistic embodiment of all that the child experienced, the convict unearthed, and artistic memory refined. The miracle of the encounter that became the miracle of the daydream now becomes the miracle of the resurrection. Here memory and imagination, always prompting one another, merge into the image. The poet is no longer witness, but creator. "The time is fulfilled" (Mark 1:15). Here the lips of the poet open, the dream becomes prophecy, and prophecy, the word.

At the beginning of "The Peasant Marey" Dostoevsky recalls the words of the Polish convict, "*Je hais ces brigands.*" He concludes his story with a final reference to these words. On the very evening of his daydream, Dostoevsky writes, he met the Polish convict again. "Unfortunate one!" he exclaims, "Now he could not have had any recollections about any Mareys or any other view of these people except, '*Je hais ces brigands!*' No, these Poles endured more than we did at that time!" In this final line Dostoevsky brings the reader back to the reality of the prison, the reality of suffering, the reality of reality as he himself had experienced it during his four years in Omsk. The words of hatred he attributes to the suffering Polish convict he clearly uttered countless times himself. The recollection of the recollection of Marey, after all, was not Dostoevsky's only recollection. "Even now at nights," he writes in "The Peasant Marey," "I sometimes dream of that time, and I have no dreams more agonizing than these." "Those four years," Dostoevsky wrote his brother Andrey on his release from prison in 1854, "I consider a time in which I was buried alive and closed up in a coffin. I haven't the strength to tell you, my friend, what a frightful time this was. It was inexpressible, endless suffering, because every hour, every minute weighed on my soul like a stone."[13]

"Man does not live his whole life, but *composes himself*," Dostoevsky once wrote in his notebook.[14] Anecdote and distant recollection merge in "The Peasant Marey." Without doubt there is material of biographical interest here, though it is clear that this material has been reshaped and that the image of Marey is an idealized one.[15] Yet the real importance of the sketch as a work of art lies not in its measure of literal truthfulness to incidents in Dostoevsky's life, but in the way it signals the manner in which he approached his prison experiences in the critical period of his Siberian exile. His emphasis upon the role of "artistic sense" as opposed to "good will" in the Russian writer's perception of the Russian people may also be taken as something of an artist's confession. Dostoevsky the convict certainly felt no good will toward the convicts with whom he lived those four terrible years. But with his artistic sense he discerned an inner truth, the truth of their essential humanity. This is the real message of "The Peasant Marey." It does not seem likely that Dostoevsky experienced any sudden revelation about the Russian peasant, though we cannot exclude the possibility of a mystical experience in prison. The author of *Poor Folk* surely had many revelations of the humanity that lay beneath the coarse exterior of the Russian peasant-convict. What Dostoevsky does in "The Peasant Marey," however, is to dramatize the miracle of artistic revelation, the miracle of the artistic process itself, involving aesthetic distancing, the interplay of memory and imagination, and the perception of the inner "idea" of reality.

"The Peasant Marey," then, points directly to Dostoevsky's artistic and spiritual resolution of his crisis in prison, a crisis involving not only his personal sufferings and feelings of hatred and resentment but also his recognition of the tragedy of the Russian people and its history. Dostoevsky did not merely dis-

CHAPTER I

cover a people buried, like himself, in prison, but a people buried
in the alluvial barbarism of Russian life and history. The aesthetic
and spiritual processes whereby Dostoevsky overcame his disil-
lusionments, as well as his own misery with its accumulation of
bitterness and hatred, the processes whereby he reassembled broken dreams and ideals on the basis of a renewed Christian faith—
this is the real subject of "The Peasant Marey." Though written
almost a decade and a half after *House of the Dead*, "The Peasant
Marey" in fact forms a fitting prologue to that work, to its poetics
and the problems involved in its creation.

"Perhaps is will be noted that until this day I have hardly ever
spoken in print about my life in prison," remarks Dostoevsky in
"The Peasant Marey." "Now I wrote *Notes from the House of
the Dead* fifteen years ago in the person of a fictitious character,
a criminal who was supposed to have killed his wife. I may add,
incidentally, as a minor detail that from that time many people
have believed and even now maintain that I was exiled for the
murder of my wife." An analysis of the problem of the fictitious
narrator of *House of the Dead* leads to the heart of some of the
central aesthetic and ideological problems of that work.

The Narrator in
House of the Dead

Take ye away the stone!
JOHN 11:39

IN THE INTRODUCTION TO *House of the Dead* the editor—a fictitious person whom Dostoevsky interposes between himself and the narrator Alexander Petrovich Goryanchikov—relates how he met the exconvict Goryanchikov in a small Siberian town. A former Russian landowner and nobleman, we are told, Goryanchikov had been sentenced to prison for murdering his wife. He had murdered her out of jealousy and then turned himself in to the police. After Goryanchikov's death a short while later at the early age of thirty-five,[1] the editor came into possession of one

> rather bulky notebook filled with writing but unfinished, thrown aside, perhaps, and forgotten by the author himself. It contained a description, although a disconnected one, of ten years of life in penal servitude undergone by Alexander Petrovich. In places this description was interrupted by some other narrative, some other kind of strange, terrible recollections jotted down in an uneven, convulsive sort of way as though under some sort of compulsion. I read through these fragments several times and almost convinced myself that they had been written in madness. But the prison memoirs— "Scenes from the House of the Dead"—as he himself calls them somewhere in his manuscript, seemed to me to be not without interest. I was carried away by a completely new, hitherto unknown world, by the strangeness of some of the facts, by certain particular remarks about a lost people, and I read something of it with curiosity. Of course, I may be mistaken. As a test I am picking out two or three chapters to begin with; let the public judge....*

* Dostoevsky frequently uses trailing ellipses in his text for dramatic effect. I have used tightly spaced points to distinguish them from regular punctuation.

The editor has nothing further to say about the strange and terrible reminiscences that constitute the secondary narrative in Goryanchikov's notebook. But whatever their specific content—perhaps an account of his domestic tragedy—their disturbed character suggests that the main narrative, the controlled and objective "Scenes from the House of the Dead," is incomplete as an expression of Goryanchikov's whole personality. Indeed, the ex-convict, described as a very polite, morally irreproachable man making his living by tutoring in French, emerges in the introduction as a strange and troubled man: "mistrustful to an insane degree," "terribly unsociable," "enigmatic." Goryanchikov could greet an unexpected visitor with "hatred" on his face. The very suggestion of meeting with people seemed to alarm him, and conversation left him with a look of "suffering and weariness."[2] He refused to communicate with his family and, in general, made it his business to "hide himself as securely as possible from the whole world." In the months before his untimely death he hardly did anything; he did not open a book (though he had been a great reader) but would merely walk about his room thinking and sometimes talking to himself. His only human contact was his landlady's ten-year-old granddaughter Katya whom he treated affectionately. He was religious: "every time St. Catherine's day came around he had a requiem said for somebody."

It is this tormented, misanthropic, yet gentle man, shattered by his experiences, who writes "Scenes from the House of the Dead"; and in this work his fellow convicts in prison, men who had contributed mightily toward his misery and misanthropy, are depicted in the warm light of reconciliation. "Such people," the philosopher Leo Shestov remarked of Goryanchikov, "do not write their reminiscences, but if they do write them down they do so most certainly not in the tone of *Notes from the House of the Dead*. Where would they get the eyes to see the convicts' amusements and distractions? Where would they find the vitality to be moved by all sorts of 'good' sought out by Dostoevsky in prison?"[3]

Whether or not we agree with Shestov here, his remarks do raise some important questions. How is the reader to respond to the Goryanchikov of the introduction? What place does the introduction, with its description of Goryanchikov's somber character and tragic fate, play in *House of the Dead* at large? We may note, for example, that the Goryanchikov of the introduction who is sentenced to prison for the murder of his wife emerges quite plainly in his prison memoirs as a political prisoner. Indeed, the Russian reading public in the 1860s had no difficulty identifying the narrator of *House of the Dead* with its author. Dostoevsky's use of a fictitious narrator may have been motivated, in part, by his concern for the censor. Yet his designation of Goryanchikov later on as a political prisoner would indicate that his concern for the censorship, at least with respect to Goryanchikov's true situation, had proven groundless.

Dostoevsky nonetheless retained the introduction when he republished *House of the Dead* in book form; he did not even bother to change the criminal status of Goryanchikov from that of a murderer to that of a political offender. We might conclude, not unreasonably, that he did not wish to tamper with a fictional formula with which the public was already familiar. Yet other factors clearly entered into his decision to retain the introduction in its original design. The introduction is certainly flawed if we view it from the standpoint of its representation of Goryanchikov as a murderer. On this point, it embodies an approach to the narrator that Dostoevsky obviously abandoned. It is also true that the image of the narrator, in the memoirs proper, as a person full of the will to survive his ordeal seemingly stands in contradiction to the tragic fate of Goryanchikov as conveyed in the introduction. Yet an examination of *House of the Dead* as a whole and of the author's approach to the narrator suggests that Dostoevsky regarded the introduction as central to his artistic and spiritual design. In this design the introduction is not to be viewed as a flaw, but as vital counterpoint in a drama of suffering, death, and resurrection that, in its conception at least, rivals Dante's *Divine Comedy*.

1

In the final line of *House of the Dead* Goryanchikov, who has just had his fetters struck off in anticipation of his release from prison after ten years' incarceration, echoes his fellow convicts' words of farewell, "God be with you!" with the words: "Yes, God was with us! Freedom, a new life, resurrection from the dead.... What a glorious moment!"[4] The paradox of these lines for the reader who has read the fictitious editor's introduction to Goryanchikov's "Scenes"—in which we learn what happened to the narrator after leaving prison—is that Goryanchikov gains freedom only to die a short while later a lonely and broken man. This tragic denouement is of course the direct consequence of the power of the dead house. Victor Shklovsky has maintained that the "hopelessness of the denouement" is underscored by the ending of the memoirs. The final paragraphs, which tell of how Goryanchikov's fetters were removed, recall in the reader's mind, he suggests, an earlier chapter in which the narrator describes the death of the convict Mikhailov. There he describes the terrible impression created by the naked corpse wearing only fetters and relates how the corpse was removed and the fetters struck off. "Thus," Shklovsky writes, "the novel both in the beginning and at the end tells of a crushed human being." Shklovsky regards the final lines about new life and resurrection merely as "words of good cheer," inserted, presumably, to counteract the impression of the preceding lines with their allusion to the convict Mikhailov's death.[5]

The scene in which Goryanchikov's fetters are struck off does arouse a tragic association in the reader's mind, and in this sense, the euphoric mood of the scene is in some degree undercut. But the notion that the line, "Freedom, a new life, resurrection from the dead...," is artificially inserted here surely is incorrect (the importance Dostoevsky gave to this line is indicated by his use of ellipses). The movement from freedom to death that marks Goryanchikov's personal fate on leaving prison is reversed on the spiritual and broadly ideological plane of action of *House of the Dead*. This action, which finds its summation in the last lines of Goryanchikov's "Scenes," involves the restoration of the image of a "lost people,"[6] the justification of a pariah-people, the symbolic redemption of the Russian people.

Some comments Dostoevsky made about Victor Hugo, which

appeared in 1862 shortly after Dostoevsky published *House of the Dead*, have direct bearing on the central idea and theme of this epic work. The idea of Hugo's art, according to Dostoevsky, is the "basic idea" of all nineteenth-century art, a "Christian and supremely moral idea." The formula of this idea, he wrote, is

> the restoration of the fallen man, crushed unjustly by the yoke of circumstances, by the stagnation of centuries, and by social prejudices. This idea is the justification of the pariahs of society, humiliated and rejected by all. Of course, allegory is unthinkable in such an artistic work as, for example, *Notre-Dame de Paris*. But to whom does it not occur that Quasimodo is the embodiment of the oppressed and despised French people of medieval times, dumb and disfigured, gifted only with fearful physical strength, but in whom there sleeps, finally, love and a thirst for justice and, at the same time, along with it, a consciousness of its truth and its still untested, boundless strength.[7]

This idea, Dostoevsky notes, in what is surely an indirect allusion to *House of the Dead*, will perhaps be embodied in a great work of art that will "express the strivings and characteristics of its time quite as fully and eternally as, for example, *The Divine Comedy* expressed its epoch of medieval Catholic faith and ideal."[8] There can be no question that Dostoevsky conceived of *House of the Dead*, a work in which the Russian people find themselves still enthralled in a quasi-medieval world, in terms of the Christian and supremely moral idea he found in Hugo and nineteenth-century art. There can be no question, too, that Dostoevsky deeply pondered Dante's *Divine Comedy* at the time he wrote his prison epic.[9] The tragic drama of the Russian convict gives expression, in the first instance, to the historical drama of the Russian people. In words that signal Dostoevsky's deepest intentions Goryanchikov observes toward the end of his "Scenes":

> And how much youth has been buried wrongfully within those walls, what great forces have perished here in vain! Really the whole truth must be told: these really were ex-

ceptional people. They are really perhaps the most highly gifted and strongest of all our people. But powerful forces perished in vain, perished unnaturally, wrongfully, irrevocably. And who is to blame? That is just it: who is to blame? (II, 10)

Here, as in *Notre-Dame*, are the representatives of an oppressed and despised people. The disfigured and, at least outwardly, coarse Russian convict is the Quasimodo of the Russian people. In *House of the Dead*, as later on in "The Peasant Marey," Dostoevsky stresses the initially frightening aspect of the Russian convict. But just as Quasimodo embodies for Dostoevsky the French people's "consciousness of its truth and its still untested boundless strength," just as the very word *quasimodo* ("low Sunday," first Sunday after Easter) points to the idea of resurrection, so the Russian convict in Dostoevsky's conception expresses the vast untested creative potential of the Russian people.

Dostoevsky embodies his idea of resurrection in a crucial image or metaphor, one that recalls the verse from the Gospel of John (12:24) that serves as epigraph to *The Brothers Karamazov*: "Verily, verily, I say unto you, except a corn of wheat fall into the ground and die, it abideth alone; but if it die, it bringeth forth much fruit." In the chapter in *House of the Dead* entitled "Theatricals," where the theme of moral transfiguration is linked with the action of drama, art, and illusion upon man, the narrator observes: "One need only remove the outer, superficial husk and look at the kernel itself more attentively, closely, and without prejudice, to see things in the people which he had never suspected." The pure and vital kernel here is the intrinsic humanity of Russian man:

> Every man, whoever he may be, and however abased he may be, nonetheless requires, if only instinctively, if only unconsciously, that his dignity as a human being be respected. . . . No brands, no fetters can compel him to forget that he is a human being. And since he really is a human being it follows that he must be treated in a humane way. My God!

THE NARRATOR IN *House of the Dead*

why really *humane* treatment could humanize even a person in whom the image of God has been long obscured. (I, 8)

The action of *House of the Dead*, as Dostoevsky conceived this work, is the aesthetic concomitant of humane treatment of the Russian convict. It reveals the long obscured image of God in man, that "human image," as Dostoevsky put it in "The Peasant Marey," which the Russian people had preserved through centuries of alluvial barbarism. What is involved in this for Dostoevsky is not a falsification of man's human condition, but a restoration of man's true image.

The central social, or Christian, theme of *House of the Dead*, then—the restoration of fallen man—points to its aesthetic premises, or its poetic. It points to the view that reality, or the "whole truth" of man, is only accessible to an art that is capable of penetrating the naturalistic, time-bound reality of the historical moment and disclosing man in the aspect of his timeless humanity. The exultant words at the end of *House of the Dead*, "resurrection from the dead," serve as a metaphor for the whole accomplishment of the book: the raising of the Russian people.

At the conclusion of his memoirs the narrator Goryanchikov observes that if he were to put down "successively and in order" everything that happened and that he saw and experienced during his ten years in prison it would all become "too monotonous." The reader, he hopes, has formed a good notion of prison life: "I wanted to present our prison and all I lived through during these years in one graphic and clear picture." In these lines Dostoevsky speaks almost directly of his approach to *House of the Dead*, of his striving to subordinate the particular and the arbitrary, the welter of surface detail and naturalistic truth, to overall design and comprehension, that is, to an inner, poetic truth.

Central to Dostoevsky's striving for poetic truth was the choice of a frame for his picture: one year, the first year, in the prison life of Goryanchikov. The choice of this frame facilitated the presentation of prison life in the perspective of Goryanchikov's "later years," but without sacrificing the shock of the first encounter. This frame, in the last analysis, gives *House of the Dead* its iconographic and apocalyptic dimension as a drama of death and resurrection.

At the basis of *House of the Dead*, and defining its action on the deepest level of its symbolic meaning, is a rudimentary drama of suffering, sacrifice, death, and rebirth that finds expression in the seasonal cycle of the year. Goryanchikov enters his prison in winter. His descent into this hell of human suffering—symbolized so dramatically by the Dantesque scene of the prison bathhouse with its crowded tiers of monstrously disfigured bodies in chains, its filth and stench, its shrieks and cries, its groans and curses—is relieved momentarily by Christmas, the hope of the "birth," and by the theatricals in which the convicts through art discover an inner freedom and sense of communion, and in which their "moral nature was changed, even if only for a few minutes."

The long and harrowing hospital scenes that open part two of *House of the Dead* lead down to the deepest level of Dostoevsky's hell, to "Akulka's Husband. A Story," a tale of disfiguration that concludes with a symbolic shedding of blood. "But now it was already the beginning of April, and Holy Week was already drawing near." With these words, Dostoevsky opens the chapter that follows the story told by Akulka's husband. The feverish and oppressive atmosphere of the hospital scenes is now broken. Lent, Communion, the symbolic resurrection, all coincide with new yearnings for freedom evoked by spring, with the awakening of the earth, with the naive hopes aroused by the coming of a prison inspector who would presumably right the prison wrongs. An atmosphere of subdued hope—the "second realm" of which Dante speaks—seems to pervade the last five chapters of *House of the Dead*. Summer brings thoughts of freedom, the release of the crippled eagle, the abortive protest of the convicts, the failed escape; and all lead directly to the liberation of Goryanchikov. Goryanchikov leaves the prison in winter, exactly ten years from the time he entered; he leaves to die in solitude, like the crippled eagle. But the symbolic significance of his liberation—and with it is linked the affirmative character of *House of the Dead*—is inseparable from the whole movement of the seasons, from winter to spring, from Christmas to Easter, from death to resurrection: "Freedom, a new life, resurrection from the dead.... What a glorious moment!"

The last line of Goryanchikov's "Scenes" carries the reader back to the introduction with its report on the death of Goryanchikov and the discovery of his "Scenes from the House of the Dead." A man dies, the one-time representative of a ruling class separated from the people by the "profoundest of gulfs." But by means of his "Scenes" he crosses that gulf and a whole people is reborn. This continual cycle of death and resurrection (the structure of the story provides an impression of a continuous cycle or of circular movement) expresses the tragic optimism of *House of the Dead*, its triumph over the finite. The death of Goryanchikov and the historic raising of the Russian people express, finally, the profoundly Christian and populist resolution of Dostoevsky's own personal crisis in his years of prison and exile—all that he later called the "regeneration of my convictions."

2

Dostoevsky believed that he had presented the whole truth about the Russian convict and the Russian hell. But had he presented the whole truth of the convict Dostoevsky's agony, bitterness, and despair in that experience? Had he given sufficient emphasis to the hostility he had felt toward the Russian convicts at the time he was in prison with them? In some notes prepared for his prison work Dostoevsky, seeking to rebut the censor's incredible view that *House of the Dead* depicted prison life as too easy for the convict, stressed the terrible meaning of deprivation of freedom for a man: "One is a man—and yet one is not: one's legs are fettered, a sharp picket fence surrounds you, and behind you is a soldier with a bayonet; it's up in the morning at the beat of a drum, and to work under threat of being beaten, and if you want to have a good time—well, take your choice of two hundred and fifty comrades...." At this point Dostoevsky formulates the response of the gentleman-convict to his comrades: "But I don't want them! I don't like these people—these murderers. I want to pray while they sing filthy songs. Now how can one live with people whom one does not like, does not respect?"[10] Dostoevsky never integrated these remarks into the published text of *House of the Dead*. The horror of life in prison, after all, was amply clear to his general reader, even if it was not to the censor. Yet it is also apparent that these remarks about the convicts disclose too vividly the hatred that the narrator felt for the convicts during the period of his incarceration.

P. K. Martyanov, who knew Dostoevsky in prison, remembers Dostoevsky as a tragically embittered, stonyfaced man who withdrew in proud silence from the convicts around him. Dostoevsky wore his hat down over his brows, Martyanov recalls; his "face was gloomy, concentrated, unpleasant, his head bowed and his eyes directed down toward the earth. The convicts did not like him, but they recognized his moral authority."[11] The Pole Szymon Tokarzewski, a political prisoner with Dostoevsky in Omsk, describes Dostoevsky not only as nervous, sick, irascible, and violently anti-Polish but as a person who repeatedly called attention to his noble origins:

> "Nobility," "nobleman," "nobility," "I am a nobleman," "we, the nobility," he would constantly repeat. And when he would turn to us, Poles, saying: "We, the nobility," I would always interrupt him: "Excuse me, sir, I think that in this prison there are no gentry, there are only men deprived of rights, only convicts." Then he would foam with anger: "And you, sir, are evidently pleased that you are a convict," he shouted with anger and irony. "That I am just such a convict as I am, I am happy," I would answer quietly.[12]

Tokarzewski's recollections of Dostoevsky, in contrast to Dostoevsky's generally sympathetic portrayal of the Polish political prisoners in *House of the Dead*, are harsh and bitter. Part of the reason is undoubtedly Tokarzewski's resentment of the way Dostoevsky accents Goryanchikov's humanitarian views of the ordinary Russian convict against the background of the Poles' alleged "exclusiveness." Clearly, Tokarzewski viewed Goryanchikov not as a person who had the moral autonomy of a literary character,

but as transparent fiction, as an insincere effort on the part of
Dostoevsky to conceal the inner content of his attitude toward the
ordinary Russian convict in prison.

However biased the recollections of Tokarzewski or Martyanov,
they are certainly a warning. The biographer of Dostoevsky must
approach *House of the Dead* with extreme caution. O. F. Miller,
Dostoevsky's early biographer, recognized here "splendid material" for a biography. But he wisely added that the title of
Goethe's own creative autobiography, *Aus meinem Leben. Dichtung und Wahrheit*, might well be applied to Dostoevsky's *House
of the Dead*.[13] Miller, however, does not indicate where in that
work *Dichtung* begins and *Wahrheit* ends, or what purpose was
served by their peculiar blend. In any case, the artist's concern
with *Dichtung* and *Wahrheit* in the creative process is not at all
the same as the biographer's interest in these elements: what the
biographer seeks to sunder (if he can), the artist, instinctively or
not, seeks to join.

Whatever relationship *House of the Dead* has to Dostoevsky's
real experience in prison (and the notion of "real" in this instance
is by no means simple or self-explanatory), Dostoevsky clearly
conceived of it as an artistic work in which he strove for maximum truth through poetic generalization. With this aim in mind,
a choice of a fictitious narrator—however transparent the fiction
from one point of view—was inevitable. Examining *House of the
Dead* in this light, the literary critic cannot impugn Dostoevsky's
integrity or morally reproach him for deviating from some abstract norm of truth in his characterization of Goryanchikov. On
the other hand, an examination of this work against the background of Dostoevsky's letters, notes, and the recollections of
people who knew him in prison reveals much about Dostoevsky's
creative process in general and about his artistic intentions in particular.

In the broadest sense, of course, Dostoevsky did not envisage
Wahrheit—that is, "truth," or "reality"—as excluding *Dichtung*—or "poetry." Poetic truth, the truth of man's ideals and
aspirations, is part of man's reality. And reality is "all available
human meaning," as Dostoevsky writes in "Two Suicides," in the

October 1876 issue of *Diary of a Writer*. "We cannot exhaust the whole of a phenomenon, we can never reach its ends and beginnings."[14] Yet in his art, Dostoevsky was driven to explore reality through precisely these ends and beginnings. Poetry in *House of the Dead*, a work dominated by the material of terrible personal experience, seeks first of all to overcome the tyranny of congealed time and space, all that impedes the exploration of a phenomenon in terms of its ends and beginnings, all that hinders presentation of man in the hierarchy of his history and essential humanity. The psychological and aesthetic problem faced by Dostoevsky in approaching his prison experiences was mastering the bias of direct experience, a bias that prevented him, figuratively speaking, from *seeing*.

Nietzsche has outlined the problem of seeing for the artist-psychologist in *Twilight of the Idols* (written after his reading of *Notes from the Underground* and *House of the Dead*). His remarks here could almost be read as direct comments upon the two radically different types of narrators that appear in these works:

> One *must* not eye oneself while having an experience; else the eye becomes an "evil" eye. A born psychologist guards instinctively against seeing in order to see. . . . Learning to *see*—accustoming the eye to calmness, to patience, to letting things come up to it; postponing judgment, learning to go around and grasp each individual case from all sides. That is the *first* preliminary school for spirituality: not to react at once to a stimulus, but to gain control of all the inhibiting, excluding instincts. Learning to *see*, as I understand it, is almost what, unphilosophically speaking, is called a strong will: the essential feature is precisely *not* to "will"—to be *able* to suspend decision. All un-spirituality, all vulgar commonness, depends on the inability to resist a stimulus: one *must* react, one follows every impulse. In many cases, such a compulsion is already pathology, decline, a symptom of exhaustion—almost everything that unphilosophical crudity designates with the word "vice" is this physiological inability *not* to react.[15]

THE NARRATOR IN *House of the Dead*

The Underground Man, of course, is a perfect example of the person who is unable to suspend decision or resist a stimulus. By contrast, Goryanchikov the memoirist (as opposed to Goryanchikov the convict) is precisely the kind of person who has learned how to see. He has overcome all the deeply hostile feelings that blinded him to the truth in his first encounters with the common convicts. Nietzsche's observations, in short, are dramatically relevant to the aesthetic-psychological problems Dostoevsky faced as he reviewed his prison experiences before and after his release from prison and contemplated setting them down.

The magnitude of Dostoevsky's problem of "learning to see"— of learning to suspend judgment, avoiding the temptation to eye himself alone, overcoming the whole pathology of resentment— may be discerned from his long commentary on his life in prison in one of the first letters he wrote to his brother after his release from prison (1854). The story that pours forth here is one of martyrdom of the body and spirit:

> I first got acquainted with the convict people in Tobolsk, and here in Omsk I settled down to live with them for four years. These are coarse, angry, and embittered people. Their hatred for the nobility exceeds all limits, and therefore they greeted us, the nobility, with hostility, maliciously rejoicing over our misfortune. They would have devoured us if they had been allowed to. Judge then how much defense we had when we were obliged to live, drink, eat, and sleep with these people for several years, and when it was even impossible to complain about the countless insults of all kinds. "You are members of the nobility, iron beaks, you have pecked at us. Formerly you were masters and tormented the people, but now you are lowest of the low and have become one of us": here is the theme that was played four years long. One hundred and fifty enemies could not let up in their persecution; this gave them pleasure; it was a distraction, an occupation; and if anything saved us from woe, it was our indifference, our moral superiority which they could not but understand and respect, along with our unwillingness to bend to their will.

CHAPTER II

They always recognized that we were above them. They had no conception of our crime. We ourselves were silent about this and therefore did not understand each other, and so we were obliged to endure all the revenge and persecution which they thrive on and nourish toward the nobility. We had a very bad time of it.

A military prison is much worse than a civilian one. I spent the entire four years locked up in the fortress, behind walls, and would only leave it for work. I did heavy work, of course, not always, and sometimes would reach the breaking point, in foul weather, in damp and slush, or in the unbearable cold of winter. Once I spent four hours on special work when the mercury was frozen and it was perhaps forty degrees below zero. My foot was frostbitten. We lived heaped all together in one barracks. Just imagine an old, rickety wooden building, one which should have been torn down a long time ago and which was no longer of any use. In summer the stifling heat was unbearable, and in winter the cold was unendurable. All the floors were rotten. The filth was an inch thick on the floor, so that one could slip and fall. The small windows were covered with frost so that at any time of day it was almost impossible to read. There was an inch of ice on the panes. There was dripping from the ceilings and draughts everywhere. We were packed like herrings in a barrel. The stove took six logs at a time; still there was no heat (the ice barely melted in the room) and the fumes were unbearable: and this all winter long.

Here in this same barracks the convicts washed their clothes and splashed water all over. There was no space to turn around. From twilight to dawn one could not go outside to relieve oneself since the barracks were locked, and tubs were placed in the passages—hence an unendurable, stifling stench. The convicts all stank like pigs and would say that it was impossible not to act like pigs, for after all "we are living human beings." We slept on bare planks and were allowed one pillow. We covered ourselves with very short sheepskin coats, and our feet were always uncovered all night long.

THE NARRATOR IN *House of the Dead*

You would shiver throughout the night. Fleas, lice, cockroaches by the bushel. In winter we wore these short sheepskin coats, often of the worst kind, which provided almost no warmth; on our feet we had leg coverings with low galoshes—try that out in freezing weather. To eat we had bread and cabbage in which there was supposed to be a quarter of a pound of beef per person, but they chopped up the beef and I never saw any of it. On holidays there was gruel with hardly any fat. On fast days—cabbage and water and practically nothing else. I had unbearable stomach disorders and was ill several times. Judge for yourself whether it would have been possible to live without money; indeed if there had not been money I would certainly have died; nobody, no convict, could have endured such a life. But everybody did some work, sold something and had a few kopecks. I drank tea and occasionally had a piece of beef, and this saved me. It was impossible also not to smoke tobacco, because without it one might have suffocated in that stifling atmosphere. All this was done on the sly.

I was often ill in the hospital. Because of my disordered nerves I had epileptic attacks, but this, however, happened rarely. I still have rheumatism in my legs. Apart from this I feel reasonably well. Add to all these pleasantries the fact that it was almost impossible to get hold of a book, that if you did get one it had to be read on the sly; the eternal enmity and brawling around one; the cursing, shouting, noise, uproar; the fact that one was always under surveillance, never alone; and all this for four years without end: really one might be forgiven for saying that it was bad. Besides this there was the possibility at any moment of being disciplined for something, fetters, and a total oppression of the spirit—and there you have an image of my daily situation.

What happened to my spirit, my beliefs, my mind, and heart in those four years I will not tell you. It would take too long to relate. But eternal concentration within myself where I took refuge from bitter reality bore its fruits. I now have many needs and hopes of a kind that I had not even dreamed. But these are all enigmas and therefore past. One thing only: do not forget me, and help me.[16]

Dostoevsky's commentary here on prison life is a grim account of a struggle for survival. It is a kind of naked, physiological realism. The prison surroundings and convicts concern the writer from only one standpoint: the devastating impact they had on his life, body, and spirit. Dostoevsky penned these lines directly after leaving prison, but he wrote as though still in prison, still in pain, still suffering from the immediacy of the experience. The reader sees no more of the prison world than meets the naked eye: on the one hand, brutal, inescapable reality; on the other hand, Dostoevsky nearly crushed by this reality. Realism here is a cry of pain and anger.

The passage cited above is interesting not only for its expression of Dostoevsky's harsh and unreconciled attitude toward the convicts ("one hundred and fifty enemies") but for the presence of an element to which the Polish convict Tokarzewski called attention: Dostoevsky's identification with the nobility in a feeling of moral superiority before the common convicts, the idea that "we were above them." In *House of the Dead* Dostoevsky ascribes these feelings to the Polish convicts: "The Poles (I speak only of political prisoners) bore themselves toward the other convicts with a kind of refined offensive courtesy, were extremely uncommunicative and quite unable to conceal their loathing for the others, who understood this very well and repaid them in their own coin." Dostoevsky, as we have noted, was in general far more generous in his view of the Polish convicts than Tokarzewski was in his view of Dostoevsky. Goryanchikov asserts that the Poles "looked with deep prejudice at those around them, saw in the convicts nothing but bestiality and could not, even did not, want to see in them a single good feature, anything human." But he adds: "And this too was quite understandable: they had been brought to this unhappy point of view by the force of circumstances, by fate." Nonetheless, Tokarzewski's unflattering view of the convict Dostoevsky finds ample confirmation in Dostoevsky's letter to his brother Mikhail in 1854.

The same letter contains other observations that point to the broadly impersonal and objective focus of *House of the Dead*. These observations indicate that even at the time he was in prison Dostoevsky's attitude toward the common Russian convicts could by no means be summed up by the phrase "one hundred and fifty enemies." Several paragraphs after his long commentary on his life in prison, Dostoevsky remarks with emphasis: "I need to live, brother. These years will not have passed fruitlessly." He needs money and books. His situation, he hopes, may change, "and now I will not write about rubbish." At this moment in his life—he is faced with punitive service in the army—he fears only "people and arbitrariness," the tyranny of a commanding officer who can ruin a man. " 'You'll find only simple people there,' people say encouragingly to me," Dostoevsky writes. "But it's just the simple person I fear more than the complex one."

At this point in his letter Dostoevsky's line of thought draws him back to his prison experiences:

> All the same, people are people everywhere. Even in prison among brigands, I, in the course of four years, discerned at last people. Will you believe it: there are profound, strong, beautiful characters, and how joyful it was to find gold beneath the coarse crust. And not one, not two, but a number. Some one cannot but respect; others are absolutely beautiful. I taught one Circassian (sent to prison for robbery) to read and write Russian. With what gratitude did he repay me. Another convict wept when he parted from me. I gave him money—but was it much? But his gratitude was boundless. Yet at the same time I developed a bad disposition; I was capricious with them. They respected my spiritual condition and bore everything without a murmur.[17]

Dostoevsky in this passage is sober and factual. Returning almost accidentally to the theme of his prison life, he reveals that the convicts were more to him than enemies. "Even . . . among brigands," he allows, he "discerned at last people." These people were entirely missing from his description of prison life in the early part of his letter. He mentions a Circassian (Aley in *House of the Dead*) here and a servant (Sushilov). He refers to his bad disposition and capriciousness. He is aware that his own tormented state of mind, bitterness, and malevolence stood in the way of a more objective evaluation of the convicts as human beings.

This awareness emerges even more strikingly in the moving letter Dostoevsky wrote to N. D. Fonvizina at about the same time he wrote to his brother in 1854. Dostoevsky speaks here frankly of his bad disposition and of the effect this state of mind had on his judgment of, and behavior toward, the convicts around him:

> It will soon be five years since I have been under escort in a crowd of people and have not been alone for a single hour. To be alone is as normal a need as drinking and eating, otherwise you become a misanthrope in this compulsory communism. The society of people becomes a poison and a plague and it is just from this unbearable torture that I have suffered most of all these past four years. I had moments when I hated everyone I encountered, the just and the guilty, and looked upon them as upon thieves who, unpunished, were stealing my life from me. The most unbearable misfortune is when you yourself become unjust, evil, foul; you recognize all this, you even reproach yourself—but you cannot master yourself. I experienced this. I am certain that God spared you this. I think that in you, as a woman, there would be far greater strength to endure and to forgive.[18]

These are the recollections of a human being who, even in the midst of intolerable personal suffering and degradation, did not lose the capacity to evaluate his outlook and behavior in a broad moral and spiritual context. It is worth recalling in this connection some observations of N. N. Strakhov, Dostoevsky's one-time literary intimate and early biographer:

> [Dostoevsky] was a particularly striking example of a special kind of duality: one in which a man may give himself over

in a very lively way to certain thoughts and feelings, while at the same time preserving in his soul an unyielding and unshakeable point from which he observes himself, his thoughts and feelings. Dostoevsky himself sometimes would talk of this duality and call it reflexion. As a result of this psychic makeup, a person always preserves the possibility of judging what fills his soul. Various feelings and moods are able to manifest themselves in the soul, but without fully possessing it. And from this deep spiritual center surges an energy that animates and transforms the whole activity and whole content of mind and creation.[19]

Strakhov's remarks contribute much to an understanding of Dostoevsky's state of mind in prison.

Dostoevsky's final comments on prison life and people in his letter to his brother Mikhail in 1854 indicate how alive the artist was in Dostoevsky during his years of incarceration and what he meant by the words, "and now I will not write about rubbish":

Apropos: how many national types, characters have I not brought out of prison with me! I lived closely with them, and thus, perhaps, know them quite well. How many stories of tramps and brigands and, in general, stories of a dark, wretched everyday existence. There's enough for whole volumes. What a marvelous people! In general, my time was not lost. If I didn't come to know Russia, then I came to know the Russian people well, so well that perhaps very few people know it as I do. But that is my little vanity! I hope it is forgivable.[20]

Dostoevsky's comments to his brother here are remarkable for their artistic detachment. His first comments on prison life had focused entirely on its impact on him. There was a strong emphasis upon the class antagonism between the gentlemen-convicts and the common convicts. "We had a very bad time of it"—that is, the gentlemen did. In the later comments the emphasis shifts from class antagonism—"one hundred and fifty enemies"—to human relationships—"people are people."

His remark about finding "gold beneath the coarse crust" anticipates the central image of the kernel and the husk in *House of the Dead*. Dostoevsky is no longer concerned with himself and his own sufferings, but with what lies beneath the coarse crust, with the essential humanity of the Russian people. "I . . . know them quite well," he writes toward the end of the letter. He recognizes in the convicts the Russian people at large and he sees them not merely as brigands but as "national types, characters," as people who have emerged from "a dark, wretched everyday existence," that is, as people with a tragic history. He has come to know Russia and its people. This, of course, is the author of *House of the Dead*. In his comments on prison life, then, Dostoevsky moves from the egoism of suffering, with its limited perspective, to the altruism of artistic vision; from judgments rooted in years of excruciating pain ("when you yourself become unjust, evil, foul") to objective evaluation of the prison world; from a reactive subjectivity to controlled artistic cognition and intuition.

During his years of exile in Siberia Dostoevsky's concern for the "marvelous" Russian people developed into an ideology. He wrote the poet Apollon Maikov in January 1856 of how close to his heart was "everything Russian": "so much so that even the convicts did not frighten me. These were Russian people, my brothers in misfortune, and I had the happiness indeed more than once to discover magnanimity in the soul of the brigand, precisely because I could understand him; because I myself was Russian."[21] In his letter to Maikov, the ideologist in Dostoevsky moves to the foreground; he omits entirely any reference to the bitterness and hatred that had so clouded his deeper comprehension of the Russian convict. Yet allowing for exaggeration on the personal side, Dostoevsky's thought here points to his broad artistic design in *House of the Dead*, a design that took embryonic shape in prison. He speaks in his letter to Maikov of the unbearable torment of not being able to write in prison, but adds that "at the same time, there was tumultuous inner work. Something good came out of it; I felt that."[22]

In this same letter Dostoevsky remarks of the dramatist Alexander N. Ostrovsky whose works he had begun to read: "Perhaps he knows well a certain class in Russia, but it seems to me he is not an artist. Moreover, he seems to me to be a poet without an ideal."[23] Whether or not Dostoevsky's observations are a fair evaluation of the art of Ostrovsky, they are of particular interest because they are made at a time when he was himself trying to come to grips with the raw material of his own prison experiences. Without question the central demand he made upon himself was to approach his subject not only with ruthless honesty but as a *poet with an ideal*.

The choice of artistic form was obviously a crucial one for Dostoevsky. Would memoirs in his own name enable him to present the dead house in all its human and historical ambience? How much attention could be given to the purely subjective side of his experience—his experience of himself—without undermining his larger artistic intention of restoring the image of this "marvelous" people? Dostoevsky's letters provide only rare indications of how he approached these questions. One comment in his letter to Maikov in 1856 does suggest the direction his thought was taking, however. He writes that in his spare moments he is putting down on paper "some of the more noteworthy things" from his prison recollections. "However," he adds, "there is very little of the purely personal here."[24] Dostoevsky says nothing in his letter about an artistic structuring of his recollections, but it is clear that his focus has shifted from himself—that is, from the narrator—to his surroundings.

Three years later he commented on his matured plan for *House of the Dead*. His primary focus would be on the world of the convicts, he said, but he had decided upon a fictional form. He wrote his brother Mikhail in October 1859 that he had in his head "a full and definitive plan":

> My person will disappear. These are the notes of an unknown individual; but I vouch for the appeal of the book. It will really be of capital interest. You will find in it much that is serious, somber, and humorous, the popular tongue with its special prison camp flavor (I read you several of the expressions I had written down *on the spot*) and a depiction

of personalities *unheard of* in literature; there will be much
that is touching and, finally, most important—my name.[25]

Dostoevsky carried out his design. His "person," of course, does
not disappear in a fundamental sense in *House of the Dead*.
Everything in that work filters through a mind and sensibility
that is recognizably that of Dostoevsky. But the use of an unknown narrator made it possible for him to structure his experiences and impressions on the basis of his deepest insights. He
freed himself from the exacting and distracting demand of adher-
ing to the temporal and spiritual timetable of his own personal
experiences. Removing himself from the center of attention, Dostoevsky was able artistically to shape himself. Above all, he
sought to eliminate as far as possible the contradiction that had
clearly rended his own spirit: the contradiction between subjective
bias and objective insight, personal hatred and loving understanding, all that is summed up in Zosima's remark in *The Brothers
Karamazov*: "Love is a cruel thing." He did this first of all by
directing the main attention of his fictional narrator Goryanchikov away from himself and his recollection of his personal suffering, and secondly, by presenting the narrator's responses to
the convicts in the reconciling light of hindsight.

3

The central focus of *House of the Dead* is upon the broad pano-
rama of prison life and personalities; its central theme is the discovery of the Russian people and the restoration of its image.
Goryanchikov at times is almost forgotten in his fascinating descriptions of the convicts, in his depiction of the prison world, in
his reflections on crime and punishment and the nature of freedom, and so forth. Yet there are glimpses into the inner world of
Goryanchikov the convict. The moments of introspection that
Goryanchikov the narrator recalls point to a devastating solitude,
suffering, and despair. Thus, for example, he describes his
thoughts when he first arrived in prison:

"Here is the end of my wanderings: I am in prison!" I constantly repeated to myself; "here is my berth for many long years, my corner which I enter with such a mistrustful, such a painful feeling.... And who knows? Perhaps when, after many years, the time comes for me to leave it, I shall be sorry to go!" I added not without a touch of that malignant pleasure that sometimes reaches the point of a craving deliberately to reopen one's wounds, as though one wanted to revel in one's pain, as though the consciousness of the magnitude of one's unhappiness was a real pleasure. (I, 5)

Such comments as these suggest how familiar Goryanchikov was with the moral-psychological "underground" that Dostoevsky explored so thoroughly shortly after his prison work in *Notes from the Underground*—that spiritual state in which man at the "last wall" takes malignant pleasure in trampling upon his hopes and expresses his protest by inflicting suffering upon himself. It is no accident that the chapter that opens with this intimate view of Goryanchikov's spiritual state should close with a discussion of convicts who suddenly go on a wild and destructive rampage just in order to affirm their integrity as human beings. Goryanchikov discovers his identity with the common convict precisely on this deepest and most disfigured level of suffering.

Perhaps the most poignant allusion to Goryanchikov's inner condition in the first period of his incarceration is to be found in his portrayal of the crippled eagle that is brought into the prison. Malevolent but exhausted, the eagle hobbles off to a corner of the prison fortress where it crouches—solitary, mistrustful, and spiteful—looking at everybody with the "proud and fierce gaze of a wounded king." After three months the convicts decide to release him. "Let him kick the bucket, only not in prison," said some of them. "That's right, he's a wild, free bird, he'll never get accustomed to prison," others assented. "He's clearly not like us," somebody put in. "Hey now, what sort of nonsense is that?" replied another convict. "He's a bird, while we're people." *House of the Dead* is ambivalent on this point. People are not like birds; they have the capacity to adapt to unfreedom. Yet even in adapting, they never lose their need for freedom.

CHAPTER II

The eagle struggles and bites even as it is carried to the prison wall. "Let him go, Mikitka!" remarks one convict. "He knows what he wants, and there's no covering up. Give him freedom, real freedom." About twelve convicts watch the eagle as it hobbles off into the steppe grass without looking back. The deeply human Goryanchikov, of course, looks back before he dies, and what he sees is the unobscured image of man.

Man, Goryanchikov observes at one point, "losing his purpose and hope often will turn into a monster out of anguish...." But in his "passionate desire for resurrection, renewal, a new life," Goryanchikov writes at the conclusion of his memoirs, he finally did pull himself together: "I would wait, I would mark off every day. . . . I remember that during all this time, in spite of hundreds of companions, I was terribly alone, and in the end I came to love this solitude." In his "spiritual solitude," Goryanchikov notes, he reviewed his whole life and judged himself sternly:

> I thought, I determined, I swore to myself that in my future life there should be none of the mistakes, the backsliding there had been in the past. I sketched out for myself a program for my whole future and firmly resolved to keep to it. A blind faith was born in me that I would and could carry all this out.... I waited, I called for freedom to come as quickly as possible; I wanted to test myself anew in fresh struggle. At times I was seized by a convulsive impatience.... But it is painful for me now to recall the state of my soul at that time. Of course, all this only concerns me alone.... But the reason I have set this down is that it seems to me that everybody will understand it, because the same thing must happen to anybody who lands in prison for a term in the flower of his years and strength. But why dwell on this?.... I had better talk of something else so as not to conclude so abruptly. (II, 9)

Goryanchikov's recollections of his painful spiritual state give poignant expression to Dostoevsky's own profound anguish. But his remark, "of course, all this concerns me alone," testifies to Dostoevsky's cardinal decision in *House of the Dead* to free the narration from the tyranny of a deeply troubled, misanthropic subjectivity, from the baleful glance of a man driven to the limits of hatred through years of a debased, herdlike existence. "The last time I wrote you I was sick in body and soul," Dostoevsky wrote N. D. Fonvizina in February 1854, "I was devoured by anguish, and I think I wrote you an extraordinarily muddled letter. This long, difficult, and bleak life physically and morally crushed me." Apropos of his first letter, Dostoevsky adds characteristically, "writing letters at such moments is always sad for me; moreover I think it pusilanimous to impose one's anguish at such a time upon another person, even a person very well disposed towards one."[26] This attitude clearly prevailed when Dostoevsky wrote *House of the Dead*.

Dostoevsky spent four terrible years in prison and six in Siberian exile, but he condemned Goryanchikov to ten years in prison. He gave him, as it were, six more years to gain some perspective, to get over the first years of bitterness and despair, to come to those conclusions that Dostoevsky grasped as an artist even as he walked in prison, head bent forward, "eyes directed down toward the earth," but that ripened in him only over a ten-year period of prison and exile. "I repeat," Dostoevsky wrote at the end of *Diary of a Writer* in 1873 about his change of convictions that came through direct contact with the people, "this did not take place quickly, but gradually and only after a very, very long period of time."[27]

Goryanchikov's "Scenes from the House of the Dead" is, significantly, not a diary (ideal for directly presenting the workings of a person's mind), but a gathering of recollections pertaining, chiefly, to the first year, the first months, even the first days of his incarceration. "The later years somehow have been effaced in my memory." His recollections are first presented in chronological sequence—arrival in prison, first impressions, the first month, and so forth—and thereafter in the broad framework of the seasons and holidays of the first year—winter (Christmas), spring (Easter). Goryanchikov is released from prison in the winter of his tenth year.

This timetable does not prevent Goryanchikov from moving

freely back and forth across the space of time in his ruminations on people, incident, and detail. Yet the timetable is there and it serves a vital function: it enables the narrator to present and evaluate the experiences and thoughts of his first year in prison against the background of the experiences and insights of later years. The image of Goryanchikov that takes shape in the reader's eye is primarily that of the reflective, all-seeing memoirist who corrects, as it were, the distorted first impressions of Goryanchikov the convict at the very moment he recalls them. Thus, the memoirist Goryanchikov writes in different places in his memoirs:

> The anguish of that whole first year in prison was unbearable and had an irritating, lacerating effect on me. As a result of that anguish, I did not notice much around me that first year. I covered my eyes and did not want to look closely. Among my malicious and hateful fellow convicts I did not notice the good people who were capable of thinking and feeling in spite of all that repulsive crust that covered them on the surface. (II, 5)

> But as I have already mentioned in part, I was unable and even did not know how to penetrate the inner depths of this life at the beginning of my imprisonment, and therefore all its outward manifestations tormented me and were a cause of unutterable anguish at the time. Sometimes I simply began to hate those people who were sufferers like myself. (II, 7)

> Yes, it is often very difficult to make a person out even after long years of acquaintance! That is why at first glance the prison really could not appear to me in that real light in which I saw it later. (I, 5)

It is noteworthy that Goryanchikov's failure to empathize with the common convicts is formulated by Dostoevsky here, as in "The Peasant Marey," as a failure of vision or insight: "I did not notice," "I covered my eyes and did not want to look closely." Reality here is not simply the outward manifestations of life, the

"repulsive crust" that is everywhere evident in prison life, but
the inner world of other people who also suffer, think, and feel.
To look is to penetrate into the inner depths of this world.[28]

Goryanchikov tells the reader that even in the first period of
his stay in prison he had had an intuition about the inner nature
of the convicts. In the early part of his memoirs he recalls his
thinking in the very first days of his imprisonment that the convicts in prison were " 'not really so very much worse than
those—*the others*, who have *remained* there, outside the prison.'
I thought this and nodded my head at my own thought, and yet—
my God! If I had only known at that time to what an extent this
thought was the truth!" The suggestion is that he would have
been spared much mental anguish had he been able to see the
convicts in the context of Russian life and the fate of the people
at large.

The reader begins his journey into the Russian hell with insights that were not fully appreciated by Goryanchikov the convict in his first year or so in prison. Goryanchikov the memoirist
alludes once to his "hatred" of the convicts, but he relates it
mainly to the early period of his stay in prison. With respect to
the general misunderstandings, suspicions, and hatred with which
he was greeted by the convicts, he suggests that things were different later on. Thus, he writes at different points in his memoirs:

> The hatred that I, as a noble, experienced without letup dur-
> ing my first years in prison became intolerable to me and
> poisoned my whole life. In those first years I would often go
> into the hospital, although I was not at all ill, solely in order
> not to be in the prison, solely in order to get away from that
> stubborn, implacable general hatred. (II, 5)

> I could see very well now that they despised me because I
> wanted to work just as they did, because I did not pamper
> myself or put on airs in front of them; and although I knew
> for certain that they would be compelled to change their
> opinion of me later, still the thought that for the present
> they would have the right, as it were, to despise me, thinking

that I was trying to ingratiate myself before them at work—this thought greatly pained me. (I, 6)

I had to live in the prison for almost two years in order to gain the favor of some of the convicts. But the majority of them, in the end, grew fond of me and judged me a "good" fellow. (I, 2)

I have already said that I got accustomed, finally, to my situation in prison. But this "finally" came about with great difficulty and pain, and far too slowly. In fact, it took me almost a year's time to get to this point, and that year was the most difficult one of my life. (II, 7)

It is not always clear what "later," "in the end," or "finally" means to Goryanchikov; but by his tenth year, he writes at the conclusion of his memoirs, he found life easier. "In the first place," he says, "by now I had many friends and well-wishers among the convicts who finally had decided that I was a good man. Many of them were devoted to me and sincerely fond of me." Yet even those convicts who grew fond of Goryanchikov later on never met him "on an equal footing." And when he left prison, he notes, only a few people shook his hand in a comradely way.

A careful reading of the memoirs suggests that Goryanchikov's relationships with the convicts from the people had a limited, utilitarian character. Goryanchikov describes the "plan of action" he formulated for dealing with the convicts: he would carry himself as simply and independently as possible; he would not seek friends but neither would he repulse those who wished to be friends. The convicts, he asserts, expected him to value and respect his noble origins in front of them:

That is, I should have pampered myself, given myself airs, scorned them, turned up my nose at everything, played the fine gentleman. That was their precise understanding of nobility. Of course, they would have abused me for all this, but still they would have respected me for it privately. Such a role was not for me; I had never been a nobleman according to their notions; but on the other hand, I promised myself that I would never debase before them by any compromising action my education or my way of thinking. (I, 6)

Yet later on in his memoirs Goryanchikov confirms what is already evident from his description of his relationships with the common convicts: willy nilly he was compelled in certain matters to act the fine gentleman, that is, to surround himself with people who fulfilled the role of servants. Though he insists that he always wanted to do everything himself, yet it always happened, he acknowledges, that he was never able to shake off the various "servitors and hangers-on" who took possession of him. Thus, it always turned out that "my outward appearance showed that I was, indeed, too lordly to do without servants and playing the fine gentleman. I found this, of course, very vexatious."

How many "servitors and hangers-on" were among Goryanchikov's "friends and well-wishers" in later years? The "meek and humble, really downtrodden" Sushilov, who wept when Goryanchikov left prison, acted like a servant for him, though he was "incapable of carrying on a conversation." Goryanchikov "always got along very well" with Osip the cook, though he too was "somehow incapable of sustaining a conversation," a defect not surprising in "this Hercules with the level of a seven-year-old." The enigmatic, fearful, but usually meek Petrov was also devoted to Goryanchikov and appears to have performed various menial roles for him. But like Sushilov and Osip, Petrov was "not an especially communicative or talkative man." Apart from these convicts, Goryanchikov appears to have been on good terms—among the common Russian convicts—with the quiet and modest Sirokin, a youth with an unusually "beautiful face" who also "spoke little and laughed rarely"; with the universally-liked Baklushkin, who first appears in the role of a menial to Goryanchikov in the bathhouse; and with the Jew, Isay Fomich Bumstein—a person with whom Goryanchikov was "great friends." "He was unique, and even now I cannot recall him without laughter. . . . Our Jew, Isay Fomich, was like as two drops of water to a plucked chicken. . . . He was a man of about fifty, small in stature and puny, cunning and yet distinctly stupid." But Goryanchikov's relationship with Isay Fomich was a special one.

Many are the convicts from among the people with whom Goryanchikov appears to have communicated at one time or another, but it is clear that most of these relationships were superficial ones. A few truly friendly faces, often among the non-Russian convicts, stood out in the prison milieu. One could not but notice, Goryanchikov writes, the "kindly, sympathizing face" of the Lezghian, Nurra, "among all the angry, sullen and mocking faces of the other convicts. In the first half hour of my arrival in prison he patted my shoulder as he passed by and laughed good-naturedly at me."

Among the convicts from the people, it is only with the handsome and gentle Dagestan Tatar, Aley, that Goryanchikov appears to have had a gratifying friendship: "His smile was so trustful, so childishly simple-hearted; his large black eyes were so soft, so caressing, that I always felt a special satisfaction, even a relief in anguish and grief, looking at him"; "he was as chaste as a pure young girl, and any ugly, cynical, filthy or unjust or violent action lit the fires of indignation in his beautiful eyes." Aley stands out as an exception, particularly among the Russian convicts. His moral and physical beauty contrast sharply with the spiritually impoverished and often physically disfigured appearance of the common convict.

Yet Aley, both as a real and symbolic incarnation of perfect moral beauty, occupies a central place in the spiritual design of *House of the Dead*: this Christlike figure is emblematic of that inner, unobscured image of man that Goryanchikov finally glimpses after long peering into the "mocking, mutilated, and terrible" faces around him. Profoundly relevant, also, to *House of the Dead* and its underlying moral-religious ethic is the conversation Goryanchikov has with Aley concerning their joint reading of the Sermon on the Mount.

I noticed that he would pronounce some parts of it with particular feeling. I asked him whether he had liked what he read. He looked up quickly and his face grew flushed. "Oh, yes!" he answered. "Yes, Jesus is a holy prophet. Jesus spoke the words of God. How good!" "What do you like best of all?" "Where He says: 'Forgive, love, do not offend, and love your enemies.' Ah, how well He speaks!" (I, 4)

It is significant that it is the Christlike Aley and not Goryanchikov who utters Christ's words, "Forgive, love, do not offend, and love your enemies." Goryanchikov the convict could only have remained silent when Aley spoke these words—and not because he rejected these Christian commandments (Goryanchikov's deep religious feelings are clear), but because he did not find in himself *at the time* the Christlike capacity to forgive and love his "enemies." In *House of the Dead* Dostoevsky mutes this side of Goryanchikov's experience—which is, of course, his own as well. Yet as we know from his letter to N. D. Fonvizina, he was acutely aware of his own incapacity at the time to forgive his enemies. It was precisely this anguished and profoundly moral awareness of his own all-too-human nature that made it possible for him to forgive and love on the transfigured plane of art.

4

The remarkable Mr. Kurtz in Joseph Conrad's *Heart of Darkness* left behind him a report of his activities in the Congo, written for the "International Society for the Suppression of Savage Customs." Seventeen pages of close writing were filled with "burning noble words" on the ability of "we whites" to "exert a power for good practically unbounded."

> There were no practical hints to interrupt the magic current of phrases, unless a kind of note at the foot of the last page, scrawled evidently much later, in an unsteady hand, may be regarded as the exposition of a method. It was very simple, and at the end of that moving appeal to every altruistic sentiment it blazed at you, luminous and terrifying, like a flash of lightning in a serene sky: "Exterminate all the brutes!"[29]

The strange symbiotic relationship between altruistic and misanthropic sentiments is a problem encountered in any close study of the personality of Dostoevsky and some of his heroes. N. N. Strakhov dwelled almost savagely in a letter to Leo Tolstoy of November 23, 1883 on what he considered the disparity between Dostoevsky the "preacher of humanity" and Dostoevsky's real personality, between the pose of a "fabricated and literary humanity" and the reality of an "evil, envious, debauched" man who "imagined himself happy, a hero, and tenderly loved himself alone." The characters who most resemble Dostoevsky, Strakhov maintained, are the hero of *Notes from the Underground*, Svidrigailov in *Crime and Punishment*, and Stavrogin in *The Devils*. With such a nature, Strakhov wrote, Dostoevsky "was very much inclined toward sweet sentimentality, lofty and humanitarian dreams; these dreams illustrate his bent, his literary muse and his path. In essence, moreover, all his novels represent *self-justification*, prove that all kinds of vileness can co-exist with nobility in man."[30]

Strakhov's extraordinarily self-righteous observations here are heavily burdened by the unusual spite of a friendship gone to seed. He had written about Dostoevsky earlier and with insight.[31] These remarks are nonetheless of interest, not so much for their bearing on Dostoevsky's complex nature as for their relevance to Dostoevsky's fictional characters. The question to which Strakhov calls attention—the disjunction between negative personal attitudes toward people and abstract or "literary" humanism—was certainly one that Dostoevsky pondered deeply in prison, both as an individual and as a representative of an upper-class intelligentsia educated in the liberal traditions of Russian and Western humanism. Contact with the Russian masses—with Russian reality—came as a rude shock to Dostoevsky. "I was blind, believed in theories and utopias," he wrote E. I. Totleben in 1856. "I know I was condemned for dreams, for theories."[32] Through his own experience he became acutely aware of his separation from the masses as a representative of his class. Goryanchikov insists that the Russian nobleman is not and can never be a friend or comrade of the ordinary people. He will be eternally tormented by the consciousness of his "alienation and solitude."

THE NARRATOR IN *House of the Dead*

The broad social, psychological, and ideological problems—national in scope and consequence—that Dostoevsky pondered in the period of his imprisonment and Siberian exile are at the center of his development of many of his later heroes. Ivan Karamazov, a disillusioned idealist and abstract humanist divorced from the people and the national "soil," expresses in theory and practice—that is, in his life drama—a problem that Dostoevsky sharply confronted in prison: "One can love one's neighbors in the abstract, or even at a distance," he observes cynically, "but at close quarters it's almost impossible." Dostoevsky raises this same question at the beginning of *The Brothers Karamazov*. In reply to Mrs. Khokhlakova's complaint about the inadequacy of a "love for humanity" that can be easily dissipated by a feeling of "ingratitude," Zosima remarks:

> That's exactly what a doctor used to tell me a long time ago, to be sure. He was already well on in years and unquestionably an intelligent person. He spoke just as frankly as you, although in jest, but in sorrowful jest. "I love humanity," he would say, "but I really wonder at myself: the more I love humanity in general, the less I love people in particular, that is, as separate, individual people. In my dreams," he would say, "I would often arrive at passionate schemes for the service of humanity and, perhaps, I really would have gone to the cross for people if it had been suddenly necessary; and yet I am incapable of living in the same room with anyone for two days, as I know from experience. No sooner is he near me than his personality weighs upon my vanity and cramps my freedom. In twenty four hours I come to hate even the finest of people: one because he spends too long at dinner, another because he has a cold and is constantly blowing his nose. I become the enemy of people practically at the very moment I come into contact with them. On the other hand, it always happens that the more I hated people in particular, the more passionate would become my love for humanity in general. (II, 4)

The outlook of Zosima's doctor-friend resembles—though in a

benign and banal way—the complex moral-psychological ambivalence of Dostoevsky in prison. Indeed, the doctor's peculiar tendency to love humanity in general the more he hated people in particular might almost be viewed as a cruel parody of Dostoevsky's capacity to convert his own bitterness and resentment into a purified Christian humanism. In his discussion of the painful and ugly beginnings of "bad conscience" in *On the Genealogy of Morals* Nietzsche has remarked:

> This secret self-ravishment, this artists' cruelty, this delight in imposing a form upon oneself as a hard, recalcitrant, suffering material and in burning a will, a critique, a contradiction, a contempt, a No into it, this uncanny, dreadfully joyous labor of a soul voluntarily at odds with itself that makes itself suffer out of joy in making suffer—eventually this entire *active* "bad conscience"—you will have guessed it—as the womb of all ideal and imaginative phenomena, also brought to light an abundance of strange new beauty and affirmation, and perhaps beauty itself. After all, what would be "beautiful" if the contradiction had not first become conscious of itself, if the ugly had not first said to itself "I am ugly"?[33]

Dostoevsky's art in the period after his exile could be defined, from a psychological point of view, as Nietzsche's "contradiction" (the *active* bad conscience) "becomes conscious of itself"—not, however, in the bitter and self-ridiculing way of an Ivan Karamazov, an Underground Man, or a Versilov (*The Raw Youth*), but in the self-overcoming way of a Goryanchikov. We need not embrace Nietzsche's profound mistrust and critique of the Christian ethic of love, self-sacrifice, and self-denial to recognize that he is exploring authentic psychological processes in the artist, processes that Dostoevsky explored first of all in his own painful experience and then later projected in his art. To recognize in art and in the artist the psychological and aesthetic phenomenon of sublimation and transfiguration, of course, in no way devalues the fruit of that transfiguration, or the moral-aesthetic integrity of the process of sublimation in the artist himself.

Contradiction and paradox, nonetheless, lie at the very center of the world view that Dostoevsky elaborates after—and out of—his prison experience. The bitterness and despair that he felt but rejected in himself is formulated in the remarkable letter he wrote to N. D. Fonvizina in 1854. Here contradiction takes on the form of a creative dialectic; we find what might be termed the Christian existentialist core of Dostoevsky's world view in his art. He speaks of himself as a "child of the century, a child of disbelief and doubt." Yet he speaks too of his terrible "thirst to believe, which is all the more powerful in my soul the more the opposite proofs accumulate in me." Nonetheless, God has provided him with moments of absolute tranquility:

> In these moments I love, and I find that I am loved by others, and in such moments I have formed in myself a symbol of faith in which everything is clear and sacred. This symbol is very simple, here it is: to believe that there is nothing more beautiful, profound, attractive, intelligent, manly, and perfect than Christ, and not only is not, but I say with jealous love to myself: cannot be. Even more, if somebody proved to me that Christ was outside the truth, and it *really* were true that the truth was outside Christ, then I would rather remain with Christ than with the truth.[34]

It was this paradoxical faith, this thirst to believe in the face of "opposite proofs," that inspired Dostoevsky in *House of the Dead* and made possible a work of exemplary truth and beauty.

Dostoevsky could not have allowed Goryanchikov to speak bluntly in the bitter and questioning manner of Ivan Karamazov about the impossibility of loving man at close quarters. Such a presentation would have been possible only if Dostoevsky had himself succumbed to the spiritual crisis he suffered in prison. Such a presentation would have been confession in the style of a disillusioned idealist, of an embittered man from the underground, and not affirmation in the style of a man who had survived his spiritual crisis. The author of "Scenes from the House of the Dead" is a man who has already come to grips with the ethical and spiritual problems that such men as Ivan Karamazov, the Underground Man, Zosima's friend the doctor, or Versilov in *The Raw Youth* can only pose. He has gone through an experience that has purged him of empty and abstract humanism. Goryanchikov makes no impossible utopian demands upon life. He is not a dreamer. There is nothing bookish or sentimental about his reminiscences. He looks at people without illusions, yet at the same time looks into their lives with compassion.

The journey of Dostoevsky's fictitious hero led him into a hell of solitude and alienation from which there was no return. His life journey in this sense is finite. But his journey back through that alienation as exconvict and writer in "Scenes from the House of the Dead" is redemptive. Redeemer of a lost people, he is himself redeemed, purged of the guilt, the misanthropy, and the despair that was the legacy of those terrible years in prison. The hero of Dostoevsky's spiritual autobiography in the decade of 1850-1860 is thus perhaps the only true or successful "positive hero" in Dostoevsky's work, the only one, at least, to complete the spiritual journey that Dostoevsky later charted for his "great sinner."

On December 22, 1849 Dostoevsky was led out of the Peter-Paul fortress in St. Petersburg to Semyonov Square. There he was sentenced to be shot with his fellow prisoners for participation in the Petrashevsky Circle. At the last moment, however, through the tsar's "infinite mercy," the death sentence was commuted and Dostoevsky was sentenced to prison and exile in Siberia. With the joy of a man brought back from the dead, Dostoevsky wrote from his cell a few hours later to his brother Mikhail:

> Brother! I have not been grieving and I have not lost spirit. Life everywhere is life, life is in ourselves and not in something external. Alongside of me will be people, and to be a *human being* among people and to remain so forever, not to grieve or falter whatever the misfortunes—this is what life is about, that is its purpose. I realized this. This idea entered

my flesh and blood. Yes! It is the truth! . . . Life is a gift,
life is happiness, every minute could be a century of happiness. *Si jeunesse savait!* Now, changing my life, I am reborn
in a new form. Brother! I swear to you that I shall not lose
hope and shall keep pure my heart and soul. I shall be born
again for the best. That is all my hope, all my comfort.[35]

Ten bitter years in prison and exile put to a severe test Dostoevsky's resolve to be born again into a new form, but Dostoevsky survived his second encounter with death. *House of the Dead*
attests to his triumphant "resurrection from the dead." In "The
Peasant Marey" Dostoevsky located the symbolic moment of his
spiritual crisis and renewal in Easter week 1850. Four years later
he left prison, at the age of thirty-three. It is idle to speculate on
the role of coincidence in the spiritual autobiography of a person,
but in the case of Dostoevsky, a question may be asked that is
relevant to our understanding of some of his characters: could
Dostoevsky have been unaware that Jesus traditionally is pre-
sumed to have been thirty-three years old at the time of the
resurrection?

The Nethermost Pit and the Outer Darkness: "Akulka's Husband. A Story"

> *How frozen and faint I then became, ask it not, reader, for I*
> *do not write it, because all words would fail. I did not die and*
> *I did not remain alive: now think for yourself, if you have*
> *any wit, what I became, deprived alike of death and life!*
> DANTE, Inferno

AT THE CONCLUSION of the third hospital scene in *House of the Dead* Goryanchikov recalls the long evenings he used to spend when ill in the prison hospital ward. There in the dim candle light, in the fetid and stifling air, he would begin to "dream, recall the past, and broad and vivid pictures would appear in [his] imagination"; or he would speculate on the future, how and when he would leave the prison; or perhaps, he would simply begin to count "one, two, three," in the hope of falling asleep:

> Somewhere in a corner others also are not sleeping and are talking together from their cots. One begins to tell something of his past, something far off, long gone by—of tramping about the roads, of children, of his wife, of the old days. You feel from the very sound of that remote whisper that all that he is talking about will never come back to him, that he, the speaker, is totally cut off from it. Another person listens. Only a quiet, even whisper is audible, like water trickling far away.... I remember, once, one long winter's night I heard a story. At first it seemed to me like a feverish dream, as though I had been lying feverish and had fancied all this in a high temperature, in delirium. (II, 3)

These words form the prelude to the last of the hospital scenes, entitled "Akulka's Husband. A Story." It is no mere stylistic touch that the narrator of "Scenes from the House of the Dead" compares the story to a feverish dream. The tale of the convict Ivan Semyonych Shishkov is a nightmare of Russian life.

"Akulka's Husband. A Story" is paradigmatic in Dostoevsky's work: Raskolnikov's dream of the beating of the mare and Ivan's stories of cruelty to children resemble this story in content, symbolic detail, and function within the larger work. All three episodes concentrate on the darkest sides of Russian life. All three are associated with sickness and delirium. Shishkov tells his story to another convict with "feverish intensity," while Goryanchikov listens in as though in delirium. Raskolnikov's dream comes at a time when he himself is psychologically distraught, physically exhausted, on the verge of a breakdown. Ivan's stories about cruelty to children are told at a moment when illness is breaking in upon him ("You talk with a strange look on your face," Alyosha remarks on this occasion, "as though you were in some state of madness"). All three episodes focus on the theme of insensate violence (beatings) and injured innocence; their realism is brutal. The violence constitutes a terrible indictment of human nature. Yet all three are part of larger works in which the author, Dostoevsky, seeks to refute the view that man is irredeemably evil.

1

"Akulka's Husband" is the deepest level of Dostoevsky's hell. It is, in the words of Dante, the "bottom of the whole universe." It follows upon the three hospital scenes that open part two of *House of the Dead* and must be considered in this context in particular. "Soon after the holiday I became ill," remarks Goryanchikov in the opening line of part two. In the poetic subtext of *House of the Dead* the narrator's illness points back to the concluding words of the preceding chapter when, lifting his head in terror one Christmas night, Goryanchikov peered at his sleeping companions, "at their pale faces, their poor beds, at all that hopeless destitution and poverty." At that moment he convinced himself that "all this was not the continuation of a monstrous dream but the real truth." The illness of Goryanchikov, though physical, is also an anguish of the spirit. It is a reaction to the whole calamity of prison and to the abyss of Russian life that opens up beyond it. Dostoevsky's focus is directly upon this abyss in the hospital scenes and in the "story" that completes this cycle.

The hospital scenes are filled with a variety of incident and detail, character sketch and commentary. Yet they concentrate on the outer and inner landscape of violence; there is a steady descent into the misery and degradation of man and human nature. Goryanchikov passes from a general description of the hospital milieu to a detailed discussion of the ways men suffer and make each other suffer; from a description of indirect methods of torturing the sick and dying to a detailed probing of the direct punishments of beatings; from a discussion of the sensations and psychology of the victims of torture to an analysis of the frightening mentality of the torturers themselves.

The motif of pollution in the opening hospital scene is introduced by the discussion of the dressing gown that the convicts all wore ("filthy beyond all measure"): "I was overcome by revulsion . . . and immediately and involuntarily, filled with curiosity and disgust, began to examine the dressing gown I had just put on." It smelled powerfully of medicines, plasters, and pus, "which was not to be wondered at since from time immemorial it had not left the shoulders of sick men." In addition, Goryanchikov notes, the gown was impregnated with the wounds of men who had run the gauntlet, victims of terrible, often fatal beatings. The page-long description of the dressing gown occupies a central place in Dostoevsky's design. Commenting on the huge, fat lice that were often to be found in the gown, Goryanchikov concludes: "Although apart from the intolerable smell everything in the ward viewed from the outside seemed as clean as possible, we could not speak much of an inner, so to speak, cleanliness of the lining." A perfectly naturalistic detail of life in the prison hospital, the dressing gown becomes a symbol of evil incarnate. Impregnated with the wounds of the sick and beaten convicts, it testifies not merely to physical filth but to corruption in the very core of Russian life.

"There is no need to punish the sick," remarks Goryanchikov. "It is terrible and disgusting now for me to picture to what degree our already poisoned air must have been further poisoned at night when the tub [serving as a latrine] was brought into the warm ward where people were suffering illnesses that absolutely required some outlet." The tub remained there all night. Thus, "the sick convict had to bear his punishment even when he was sick." Goryanchikov has no idea who first introduced this procedure: "I only know that there was no real sense in it and that the essential uselessness of all bureaucratic regulations was never more clearly demonstrated, for example, than in this case." Goryanchikov is baffled—at least ostensibly—as he seeks a reason for what he calls a "useless cruelty." One reason, he suggests, might have been to make sure that the convicts could not escape when going to the latrine outside the ward. Yet he goes on to demonstrate the absurdity of such a thought. His question, "what for?" echoes in the reader's mind. At the same time, as though groping for an answer, Goryanchikov comes up with the hypothesis that "this procedure was established for the sole purpose of punishment." He immediately rejects this hypothesis as "senseless calumny."

But in fact there is no senseless calumny here. Dostoevsky obliquely raises the problem of gratuitous cruelty in Russian life, cruelty that is not directly called for but that arises out of a tragic existence in which men have been so inured to cruelty that they cannot do without it. On the psychological side, the problem of useless cruelty is connected with a major problem center in Dostoevsky's writing: cruelty that is perpetrated for the satisfaction of the perpetrator and accepted with satisfaction by the victim. Such cruelty, of course, may take on wholly impersonal forms. It may take the form of bureaucratic rules and regulations whose *raisons d'être* have been lost in time but which have become so much a part of everybody's daily life—indeed, have become so much a way of life—that one can only ask in utter perplexity, "what for?" and be inclined to dismiss the obvious answer as senseless calumny. Cruelty here is a social illness involving all members of society.

Gorky perceived the enormous significance of Dostoevsky's writings for a psychohistorical interpretation of Russian life. Dostoevsky, he insisted in a letter to the literary historian D. N. Ovsyaniko-Kulikovsky, was a writer who "with the greatest power and lucidity depicted the spiritual illnesses grafted upon us from the Mongol, the mutilations inflicted on our soul by our painful Muscovite history."[1] Several years later, in an article entitled "On Karamazovism" (1913), Gorky spelled out these illnesses as the "sadistic savagery of the completely disillusioned nihilist and its opposite, the masochism of the beaten, frightened creature who is capable of enjoying his suffering, not without malicious pleasure, however, parading it before everybody and before himself; he has been mercilessly beaten, and he brags about it."[2]

Discussion of punishment of the sick and dying leads Goryanchikov to another "enigmatic fact": "I am speaking of the fetters from which no illness delivers the convicted criminal. Even consumptives have died in fetters before my eyes." Here again Goryanchikov seemingly finds it "impossible to believe that this is only done for the sake of punishment." But what is impossible to believe has already become a major theme in *House of the Dead*. The first of the hospital scenes concludes with the death of the convict Mikhailov, perhaps the most moving and tragic scene in Goryanchikov's memoirs. Dying with his fetters on, Mikhailov in his last moments tears off his blanket and bedclothes:

> It was terrible to look at that long, long body with its arms and legs wasted to the bone, the sunken belly, the raised breastbone, the ribs as clearly defined as those of a skeleton. All that remained on his body was a wooden cross and a reliquary, and his fetters through which at this point he could have passed his wasted leg. . . . Finally, with a wandering and uncertain hand he groped for the reliquary and tried to tear it off, just as though it were a burden and was troubling and oppressing him. The reliquary was removed. Ten minutes later he died. (II, 1)

The naked and dead man is carried away to have his fetters struck off.

The scene, and chapter, conclude with the narrator's laconic but meaningful comment, one frequently employed by Dostoevsky for special emphasis: "But I have digressed from my subject."

"AKULKA'S HUSBAND"

The terrible description of Mikhailov's death, of course, is not at all a digression. In one sense, it is but another example of gratuitous cruelty, but in another, it offers a tragic counterpoint to the theme of resurrection in *House of the Dead*. The image of the wandering hand groping for the reliquary and the cross and seeking to remove them captures—in the symbolic religious context of Dostoevsky's narrative—a deeply tragic moment. The sense of completely abandoned humanity presented by this scene is only barely offset by the almost reverential response of all the witnesses to the scene. "He, too, must have had a mother!" remarks one convict as the body is carried out. The cross is silently restored to the neck of the dead man, but the somber implications of the scene remain.

The second of the hospital scenes is given over largely to minute descriptions of the beatings and punishments endured, or not endured, by the convicts. These stories, told by the convicts themselves, Goryanchikov remarks, "sometimes made my heart rise into my throat and begin to thump heavily and violently." The depraved, indeed almost insane, prison guards Zherebyatnikov and Smekalov are the center of some of the most vivid descriptions. The narrator writes of Lieutenant Zherebyatnikov:

I saw him in the flesh when he was on guard duty. He was a man of about thirty, tall, fat, bloated, with puffy greasy red cheeks, white teeth, and a booming laugh reminding you of Gogol's Nozdryov. It was apparent from his face that he was the most unreflecting man in the world. As officer in charge of corporal punishments, he was passionately fond of flogging and punishing with the rods. I hasten to add that even at that time I regarded Lt. Zherebyatnikov as a monster among his own kind, and, indeed, even the convicts viewed him as such. There were others like him, to be sure, in the past, it goes without saying in that recent past about which "the memory is fresh and it is hard to believe," who enjoyed performing their task conscientiously and zealously. But for the most part things were done plainly and without especial enthusiasm. The lieutenant, however, was something of a refined connoisseur of corporal punishment. He loved, passionately loved the art of punishing, and loved it purely as art. He took pleasure in it and, like a jaded patrician of the Roman Empire, worn out with pleasures, he could invent for himself various refinements and unnatural variations in order somehow to stimulate and agreeably tickle his soul lapped in its fat. (II, 2)

In the figure of Zherebyatnikov (his name recalls the Russian words for "stallion," "horse-laugh," and "horsemeat") the theme of pleasure in beatings finds its sharpest expression. Zherebyatnikov emerges as a distinctly Sadean type. The pleasures he obtains in beating the convicts have a sensual character. He clearly anticipates a later "patrician" and sensualist who prided himself on his Roman nose, who approved the beating of peasants and found the thrashing of girls quite appropriate—Fyodor Pavlovich Karamazov.

Zherebyatnikov's pleasure in beatings takes on a demonic, carnival-like character. After promising a convict a light punishment, he would order the convict to be flayed mercilessly and then would run after the victim along the line

laughing, laughing, overcome with laughter, holding both his sides, doubled up with laughter and hardly able to stand, so that in the end one would feel sorry for the good-hearted creature. He is happy and finds it all very amusing, and only occasionally is there a pause in his hearty, rollicking, booming laughter, and one hears again: "Flay him, flay him! Make it hot for him, the thief, make it hot for him, the orphan!" (II, 2)

The "fatherly" Lieutenant Smekalov, too, would carry out punishments with a "smile and a joke." While the rods were being brought, he would sit down and light his pipe:

The convict would begin to entreat him.... "Oh, no, brother, lie down; it's no use..." Smekalov would say. The convict would sigh and lie down. "Well, now, my good fellow, do you know such-and-such verses?" "Why, of course I do, your honor; we are Christians and we learnt them from childhood." "Say them, then." (II, 2)

The convict then would begin to recite, "Our Father who art in heaven"; but when he reached the well-known words, "in heaven," the excited lieutenant would shout with an inspired gesture, "Enough!" and then, "let him have it!" And the terrible beatings would begin. Like Zherebyatnikov, Smekalov would roar with laughter: "The soldiers standing around also grinned, the executioner grinned, even the victim almost grinned." Smekalov exulted in particular because he had created a rhyme out of the Russian words *na nebesi* ("in heaven") and *podnesi* ("let him have it"). He would leave the scene of punishment, Goryanchikov notes, terribly pleased with himself. And the man who had been flogged would go away "almost pleased with himself and with Smekalov." Within the hour, he would be telling the prison how the joke, repeated thirty times, had now been repeated for the thirty-first time: "No doubt about it, he's quite a fellow! He's got a real sense of humor!"

In this scene Dostoevsky underscores not only the sadism and inhumanity of Lieutenant Smekalov but the tragic fact that everybody—Smekalov, the man who does the beating, the soldiers standing about, the mass of convicts in the prison barracks, and even the victim himself—participates in this carnival of violence. Like the peasants who watch Mikolka in *Crime and Punishment* beating his mare to death, these people are not only not indignant over the suffering and degradation perpetrated upon one of their own kind, but, on the contrary, they enjoy the spectacle. This is the sadomasochistic syndrome in the Russian people about which Gorky wrote apropos of Dostoevsky's work.

The special tragedy of this scene is deepened by the seeming inability of Christianity—so openly mocked by the recitation of the Lord's Prayer—to exercise any power over the habits of men. The ritual words, learned by everybody from childhood, ring out emptily in this world. Smekalov's "joke," on the other hand, parodies in a particularly brutal way the place of suffering in the doctrine of Christianity. Indeed, in Smekalov's ritual drama the promise of heaven is a joke that is followed by hell.

2

"It is time for us to cease our apathetic complaints about environment—that it has ruined us," Goryanchikov observes at the beginning of the hospital scene in which Zherebyatnikov and Smekalov figure so prominently. "It is true, let us grant, that our environment destroys much that is in us, but not everything." Man, in short, even in dire circumstances, retains a measure of moral freedom. The appeal to environment, moreover, can be used not only to cover up "weakness"—the failure to exercise one's freedom—but to cover up and excuse "out-and-out vileness." The excuse of environment can never be justified, Goryanchikov writes with regard to the few doctors who cover up wrongdoing in the prison hospital, "especially if they have lost love of humanity." As for the prison doctors in general, Goryanchikov praises them for their kindness and compassion. Nobody, after all, would have bothered if they had treated the convicts differently, that is, "more coarsely and inhumanely: consequently they were good out of a real love for man." Thus, to the indubitable power of environment or fate, Dostoevsky opposes the power of the human heart. Man, in the final analysis, is his own environment and cannot evade the responsibility he bears for his actions. Whatever the influence of environment, the potential for real love of man, like the potential for evil, lies within man's heart.

The question of the nature of man—perhaps the central question in all of Dostoevsky's great work—is clearly put by Ivan Karamazov. Regarding man's inability (in Ivan's view) to love his neighbor, he asks: is this because of "bad elements in people's character," or does it come about "simply because that is their nature?" In other words, does man behave in an evil manner because he is merely susceptible to temptation (the implication here is that man is not irredeemably bad), or because he is inherently, by nature, evil? Raskolnikov poses essentially the same question after his first visit to the Marmeladovs.

This problem of man's nature, though it is not directly formulated as a question, is very much on Dostoevsky's mind in *House of the Dead*. Some insight into Dostoevsky's resolution of this question may be gained by turning to Goryanchikov's observations on violence in the third hospital scene. The scene opens with a discussion of corporal punishment, Goryanchikov displaying an intense interest in all its details. But in the midst of his analysis of the pain of flogging and the special qualities of the birch rod, Goryanchikov suddenly shifts to a broadly moral and social plane of discussion:

> I don't know how it is now, but in the not too distant past there were gentlemen to whom the power of flogging a victim afforded a pleasure resembling that of the Marquis de Sade and [Marquise] de Brinvilliers. I think there is something in this sensation, both sweet and painful, that sends a thrill through the hearts of these gentlemen. There are people who like tigers thirst for the taste of blood. Whoever has once experienced this power, this limitless domination over the body, blood, and spirit of a person like himself, created like himself, a brother in the law of Christ; whoever has experienced this power and boundless opportunity to inflict the most extreme humiliation upon another being made in the image of God,—such a person whether he wills it or not has somehow lost control over his sensations. Tyranny is a habit; it has the capacity to develop and does develop into a disease. I affirm that the best of men through habit can be reduced to the crude and unthinking state of an animal. Blood and power intoxicate: coarseness and debauchery follow; the most abnormal phenomena begin to appeal to the mind and feelings, become sweet to them. Man and citizen perish in the tyrant forever, and regeneration, repentance, a return to human dignity now becomes for him almost impossible. What is more, the example, the possibility of such arbitrary use of power has a corrupting effect on all of soci-

ety; such power is a temptation. A society that regards indifferently such a phenomenon is already corrupted at its
very roots. In a word, the right of corporal punishment given
to one man over another is one of the ulcers of society, one
of the most powerful forces destructive of every germ, every
effort in society towards civic feeling, and a full cause for its
inevitable and irretrievable destruction. (II, 3)

The power and pathos of Dostoevsky's appeal here for humaneness in Russian society is almost unexampled in his works.
He directs his call to the civic consciousness of the citizen and
points to the delicate and laborious process of creating a community with a sense of civic responsibility. He indicts any society
that sanctions corporal punishment, but he has in mind, of course,
specifically Russian society, which had been nurtured for hundreds of years on the institutionalized violence of serfdom and
autocracy. Indeed, Dostoevsky is addressing himself to a society
that legally abolished serfdom only in 1861, the year in which he
published *House of the Dead.*

Dostoevsky clearly recognizes the enormous role of society in
the development of good or bad habits in its citizens. Precisely in
this connection he is concerned with violence as a psychological
phenomenon, that is, as an instinct in man for power and possession, an instinct that he directly links with unbridled sensuality
(the Marquis de Sade). The example and possibility of violence is
a temptation to man; it arouses his most antisocial instincts. The
very best of men can through habit become degraded to the level
of a beast, can lose control over their sensations. Man is made in
the image of God; but the potential for evil in him, like the potential for good, Dostoevsky clearly implies, is rooted in his nature.

It is not only executioners and debauchees like Zherebyatnikov
and the Marquis de Sade who are open to the temptation of
power:

Society abhors the professional executioner, but by no means
the gentleman-executioner. It is only recently that an opposing view has been expressed, but so far only in books, in the

abstract. Even among those who express it not all have yet succeeded in stifling in themselves this need for absolute power. Every manufacturer and employer must inevitably experience a sharp pleasure in the fact that his workmen and their families sometimes are wholly and solely dependent upon him. (II, 3)

In employers and manufacturers, as in the slaveholder and executioner, the lust for power finds direct expression; and it finds social sanction as well. But the need for absolute power is expressed even in people who in the abstract oppose violence. It is expressed—as Dostoévsky noted much later in a piece entitled "Environment" (1873)—in the juror as well:

It seems to me that one feeling common to all jurors throughout the world, and to our [peasant] jurors in particular (apart, of course, from other feelings) must be the feeling of power or, to put it more felicitously, absolute power. This can sometimes be a vile feeling, that is, if it should happen to dominate other feelings. . . . I believe that this somehow emerges from the very laws of nature.[3]

Dostoevsky's particular emphasis here upon the Russian peasant is noteworthy. It is not only in the slaveholder but in the slave as well that the instinct for power and possession finds deep expression. The archetypal Russian "executioner," in fact, is the peasant Mikolka in Raskolnikov's nightmare, who repeatedly brings down his iron bar on the back of his mare, the words, "my property!" ever on his lips. He is the peasant husband in the "funny and unaffectedly gay" skit, "The Miller and his Wife," that is staged by the convicts in the Christmas theatricals:

The miller finishes his work, picks up his hat, takes his whip, goes up to his wife and explains to her by signs that he has to go out, but that if she invites in anybody in his absence, then...and he points to his whip. His wife listens and nods her head. That whip probably was very familiar to her. (I, 11)

The fictional miller in the comic skit that delights all the convicts is only a mirror image of the witless but terrifying "husband," Shishkov, who mercilessly and endlessly flogs his wife in the tragic story, "Akulka's Husband." Shishkov's enjoyment of absolute power is the same as that of the slaveholder, manufacturer, juror, debauchee. The pleasures of power he obtains are linked directly with the unwritten but absolute feudal right of possession he enjoys over his wife. And these pleasures include the right to exploit, the right to flog, and the right to sexually dominate. Shishkov, no less than the peasant Mikolka, is a property owner.[4] In one case, the property is a mare—in the other, a wife. It is perfectly natural for Shishkov to take his whip with him to his first marital night.

Dostoevsky deliberately associates the theme of absolute power and violence with the Marquis de Sade and the Marquise de Brinvilliers.[5] The disease of violence, as Dostoevsky conceives it, draws upon the same instincts as does unbridled sensuality. When Goryanchikov writes that "blood and power intoxicate" and that "the most abnormal phenomena begin to appeal to the mind and feelings," he makes no distinction between violence and sensuality. He is repelled most of all by those convicts in whom the flesh gains supremacy over the spirit. He describes the depraved convict and nobleman Aristov as a "moral Quasimodo," "a lump of flesh with teeth and a stomach and with an insatiable thirst for the coarsest, most animal physical pleasures." He is "an example of how far the purely physical side of a man [can] go, unrestrained by any inner norm, any sense of law." Goryanchikov concludes: "No, better fire, better plague and hunger, than such a being in society." So, too, Goryanchikov recoils before the notorious brigand Korenev, a man in whom the "flesh had gained the upper hand over all his spiritual characteristics to such an extent that you saw at once from a single glance at his face that nothing was left in him but a wild thirst for physical pleasures, sensuality, the carnal."

Unbridled sensuality, the craving for absolute power, and possessiveness (the acquisitive instinct) form the syndrome of evil in Dostoevsky's universe. This syndrome, in whatever realm it manifests itself—economic, social, political, or sexual—constitutes for him the main threat to civilization.

"The attributes of the executioner are found in embryo in almost every contemporary man," Goryanchikov observes. Yet Dostoevsky does not approach human nature in a fatalistic way. Goryanchikov goes on to point out that the "animal attributes do not develop equally in all men. . . . If they overpower in their development all other attributes, then that individual, of course, will become terrible and monstrous." Yet the reverse is also possible: people can bring their animal attributes under control; they can become masters of their instincts; even more, they can, like many of the doctors in the prison hospital, find in themselves "a real love for humanity."

Goryanchikov recalls a poor widow in the town where his prison was situated who in a spirit of love and sacrifice did everything possible to alleviate the miseries of the prison convicts. "Some people say (I have heard and read) that the most lofty love for one's neighbor is at the same time the greatest egoism. But what egoism there was here is beyond my understanding." Dostoevsky here affirms the principle of moral freedom. People are not irredeemably bad. They are capable of acting humanely and cultivating the humane attributes of the citizen, as opposed to those of the despot. They are capable of altering their environment. "Indeed," Dostoevsky wrote later in 1873, "by becoming better ourselves we will reform the environment and make it better."[6] Here, as always, Dostoevsky finds the root of the problem and at least its partial amelioration in man himself.

Tyranny is a habit, however; little by little a person can be reduced to the unthinking state of an animal, become terrible and monstrous. The tragedy of violence in prison is not just a question of senseless penal regulations but of a people and society habituated to violence. The process of humanization, the rediscovery of human dignity and image, the stimulation of a civic sense in man, Goryanchikov makes clear, is a long and difficult process:

A generation does not so quickly tear itself away from what

it has inherited; a man does not so soon renounce what has entered into his blood, what he has taken in, so to speak, with his mother's milk. Speedy revolutions of this sort do not occur. The recognition of guilt and ancestral sin amounts to little, far too little; one must wean oneself completely from it. And this is not done so quickly. (II, 3)

Goryanchikov does not elaborate here upon the nature of "ancestral sin." The emphasis, however, is surely not upon metaphysical or religious sin, but upon a concrete history of depravity and temptation under despotism—in short, upon everything that stimulates in man his inclination toward violence of all kinds. Thus it is not enough for the peasant, manufacturer, or repentant nobleman to recognize his guilt and ancestral sin; he must unlearn the habits of violence and humiliation that have entered into all aspects of his daily life, into his social and personal existence.

Dostoevsky's observations on violence and power—the fruit of ten years of experience in prison and exile—constitute a somber judgment of Russian history. *House of the Dead* testifies to Dostoevsky's ultimate faith in the nature of the Russian people, but it is a nature buried in an agonizing history of disfiguration. It is the frightening truth of this history that emerges with ever increasing force in the hospital scenes.

Goryanchikov's general reflections on violence in Russian society momentarily interrupt his detailed discussion of prison punishments. In the third hospital scene he resumes the thread of his narration with an examination of the professional executioner as a type. This executioner, Goryanchikov writes, evokes among the people horror and loathing, "a kind of inexplicable, almost mystical terror." A person of vanity, "he exerts himself for the sake of his art." Like an actor, he is concerned with the response of his public. "Of course, a living man is not a machine," Goryanchikov says, "the executioner flogs because he must, but he also may get worked up sometimes; but although he flogs not without pleasure, he feels, on the other hand, almost no personal hatred for his victim." He may take offense and redouble the punishment if the victim does not beg for mercy, however. And before the punishment commences, he feels in "an excited state of mind, senses his strength and is conscious of his mastery. . . . It is not without pleasure that he cries out to his victim before the first stroke the familiar and fatal words: 'Ready now, I'm going to flay you!' It is difficult to conceive to what an extent human nature can be distorted."

With these words, the narrator concludes a discussion of the executioner that had opened with the words, "the attributes of the executioner are found in embryo in almost every contemporary man." Significantly, Dostoevsky has Goryanchikov directly follow his remarks on the distortion of human nature with a confession: "In that first period in the hospital I listened spellbound to all these stories of the convicts." Goryanchikov himself is carried away by the terrible stories he has heard. On three occasions in the third hospital scene he speaks of the impact upon him of these stories of violence: "I was agitated, disturbed, and frightened." Yet he impatiently begins to probe into all the details of punishment, to question the convicts closely as to the exact nature of the pain of beatings—beatings that sometimes excited the nerves beyond endurance. "I really do not know why I was after all this," Goryanchikov writes. "I only remember one thing, that it was not from idle curiosity. I repeat that I was agitated and shaken."

These remarks suggest in a cryptic way what Goryanchikov himself states in general terms a few lines later in his disquisition on violence: that "blood and power intoxicate" and that the example of violence is a temptation. Goryanchikov, it is clear, did not remain immune to this temptation. He yielded to it as eager voyeur. The obsessive intensity of his concern for the details of floggings betrays in him a vicarious enjoyment of power and dependency. Here, indeed, there is more than curiosity; here is precisely that instinct of the executioner that may be found "in embryo in every contemporary man." The confession that not only torturer and victim succumb to the disease of violence but the observer as well—indeed, even the avowedly moral observer—

CHAPTER III

remains one of the most important and grave messages that we carry away from *House of the Dead.*

Violence, reaching deeply into man's being, engenders mental confusion, madness, even demonism. As the hospital scenes progress, the motif of madness not only serves as a point of topical interest but as a metaphor for total moral chaos. Goryanchikov himself is feverishly excited by the violence he witnesses. The perpetrators of violence, too, men like Zherebyatnikov and Smekalov, are like men possessed. Their wild excitement and roars of laughter not only single them out as demons of this veritable hell but contribute to a sense of rampant evil, the dissolution of all controls and norms, the collapse of all reason.

But madness, real or simulated, is also manifest in the victims of torture. There were "real madmen" among the convicts who were brought into the hospital for observation. "It was terribly difficult and painful for me to see these unfortunate people," observes Goryanchikov. "I could never look coldbloodedly at madmen." But he is also pained by other types of madmen. Goryanchikov dwells at length on the case of a "strange madman"— a convict awaiting execution of his sentence—who in the disordered fantasy of his mind believed that he would of a certainty escape punishment. He imagined that the colonel's daughter was in love with him and would intercede for him. "It was strange what the fear of punishment had done in this timid soul," remarks Goryanchikov: "Perhaps he really had seen somebody from the window, and the madness begotten of terror intensifying with every hour had suddenly at one stroke found its outlet and form. But the authorities were not convinced of his madness; he was put down as *'sanat'* and his sentence was carried out."

Who is healthy and who is sick here: the convict who goes mad in order to escape unreason and terror, or the men who adjudge him *sanat*? What is clear is that madness, in the deepest moral and spiritual sense, defines the atmosphere of the dead house. The sense of vertigo, of an upside-down world, a world without foundations, is vividly conveyed in the final episode of the third hospital scene—the convict Shapkin's story of how he landed in prison. Shapkin, a convict with long ears who has a reputation for telling tall tales, relates a truly fantastic, indeed, mad story. This story, or "chatter," blurring all lines between the real and the fantastic, forms a fitting introduction to the last and most fantastic story in the hospital scenes—"Akulka's Husband. A Story."

3

Goryanchikov describes the thirty-year-old narrator of "Akulka's Husband," Ivan Semyonych Shishkov, as an empty, moody, cowardly type: "one could very easily make him to do anything." In a state of feverish excitement, Shishkov tells his story to another convict, Cherevin, "a man of about fifty, a sullen, coldly moralizing pedant and a conceited fool." Shishkov's story in its barest outlines discloses a life in the Russian village that is frightening, primitive, and brutal.

The story begins with Shishkov and his friend Philka Morozov working for the rich peasant Ankudim Trofimych. Morozov at one point quarrels with Ankudim, whose daughter Akulka he appears to have been courting, and decides to leave the job and drink up his money. Taking his leave, he slanders Akulka by saying that he has slept with her, does not want to marry her anyway, and will see to it that nobody else marries her "because now she's dishonored." Morozov goes on a three-month spree, joined later by Shishkov. They gratuitously jeer at Akulka in the street, call her a slut, and smear her gate with tar so as to shame her publicly:

And so we smeared up her gates. And then they thrashed her, really thrashed her for that at home.... Marya Stepanovna shouted: "I'll wipe her off the earth!" And the old man says: "In the olden days," he says, "when the good patriarchs lived, I would have chopped her up at the stake, but nowadays," he says, "the world's all darkness and decay." At times the neighbors on the whole street would hear Akulka howling—they beat her from morning to night. (II, 4)

CHAPTER III

Shishkov's mother finally suggests that he, Shishkov, marry Akulka: "They'll be glad to marry her even to you now, and give you three hundred roubles on top of it all. . . . The marriage wreath covers it all; so much the better for you if she ends up guilty before you her whole life." Shishkov decides to marry Akulka, but he takes a whip to the marriage bed "to have a bit of fun with Akulka" and to show that he had not gotten married with his eyes closed. "Quite right!" exclaims Shishkov's interlocutor at this point in the story. "That's so she would feel it always after that...."

Akulka, Shishkov discovers that night, turns out to have been innocent of wrongdoing. Drunk, he goes out looking for Morozov to punish him. But Morozov strikes back by telling him that he, Shishkov, was not sober on the marriage night and thus could not know what was what. Home again, Shishkov shouts to his mother: " 'You,' I say, 'married me when I was drunk! . . . Let me at Akulka!' Well, and then I began to knock her about; I knocked her about, brother, really knocked her about, knocked her about for almost two hours, till I nearly collapsed myself; she didn't get out of bed for three weeks." Well, of course," Cherevin observes phlegmatically, "if you don't beat them they'll...."

At the instigation of Morozov, people make a laughingstock of Shishkov. Morozov then threatens to beat up Akulka in his presence. Fearing that Morozov would come and "dishonor" him, the cowardly Shishkov begins to beat Akulka regularly. "But why go on beating?" Cherevin asks. "To beat them too much is also not good. Punish them, give them a lesson, and then be affectionate. That's what a wife is for." But Shishkov felt offended by Morozov: "Then I got into the habit again: some days I'd beat her from morning till night; she would do everything wrong. When I didn't beat her, I was bored. At times she would sit silently, looking out the window and weeping.... Sometimes she'd be crying all the time, and I'd feel sorry for her, but I'd go on beating her." No pleas from her family (who were now convinced of her innocence) would avail: "I don't even want to listen to you now! Whatever I want to do to all of you now, that's what I'm going to do, because I'm no longer in control of myself; and Philka

Morozov . . . is my companion and best friend." Morozov, for his part, hires himself out to be a soldier and plays the despot with the family whose son he will substitute for in the army. Just before he leaves for the army, however, he suddenly bows down to Akulka and proclaims his love for her. Akulka declares that she loves Morozov as well. Shishkov, angered, takes her out and cuts her throat. Such, in brief, is the story told by Shishkov and overheard by Goryanchikov.

The slander of Akulka, the tarring of her gates, her public humiliation, the terrible beatings she endures at the hands of her parents and her husband, and, finally, her murder all define the central theme of "Akulka's Husband": the desecration and disfiguration of the human image. The object of this disfiguration is the iconic Akulka. Defenseless, she stands alone, mute sacrifice to the demonic forces raging about her.

The fate of Akulka is that of the absolutely dependent person: the Russian woman in social and sexual bondage. She is property, owned by her parents who exercise absolute rights over her, including the right to violence. When they marry her off to Shishkov—in effect, sell her—they lose their rights to possession and violence, as they would in the case of any commodity, material or animal. Akulka—like Mikolka's mare in Raskolnikov's nightmare or the tortured children in Ivan Karamazov's stories—is totally defenseless. And "it is precisely the defenselessness of these creatures," Ivan notes, "that tempts the tormentors, the angelic trustfulness of the child who has nowhere to go and no one to talk to, that inflames the vile blood of the torturer." Ivan speaks about the tormentors of children in particular, but his understanding of the psychology of these people applies to man in general. "In every man," he observes, "there lurks an animal, an animal capable of being roused to anger, an animal capable of being inflamed to a peak of sensuality by the cries of the tortured victim, an unrestrained animal let off the chain, an animal nursed in the debauch of diseases, gout, kidney ailments, and so on."

Ivan expands on a theme that lies at the center of *House of the Dead*, but one that Dostoevsky develops there with less rhetoric. Noteworthy in Ivan's remarks, however, is the explicit connection he establishes between the pleasures of violence and sensuality. Shishkov does not dwell on the pleasures he obtains in beating Akulka, yet the reader who has followed Goryanchikov's discussions of violence has no difficulty in recognizing the specific character of his pleasure.

Dostoevsky presents Shishkov's dully contemptuous and cruel attitude toward women as normative in Russian peasant life. The occasional comments of Cherevin make it clear that Shishkov was not an exceptional husband. Cherevin not only approves of Shishkov's cruelty but recalls his own cruelty to his wife. Cherevin responds to Shishkov's story with chilling blandness:

> "Hm.... Well, of course, if you don't beat them, no good will come of it!" coldly and pedantically observed Cherevin, once again taking out his sniff horn. He began taking long sniffs at intervals. "Now there again, my lad," he continued, "you yourself turned out to be very stupid [for murdering Akulka]. I too once came upon my wife with a lover that way. So I invited her to the shed; I doubled up the halter. 'To whom,' I say, 'did you swear an oath? To whom did you swear an oath?' And then I went ahead and thrashed her, thrashed her with that halter, just thrashed and thrashed, for a whole hour and a half I thrashed her,—and then this from her: 'I'll wash your feet,' she screams, 'and I'll drink the water.' Avdotya was her name." (II, 4)

With these lines, Dostoevsky concludes "Akulka's Husband." Cherevin's casual observation here that "if you don't beat them, no good will come of it" points to the whole tragedy of good in the peasant world of Shishkov and Cherevin. "Good," as Cherevin uses the word, is not ethical, but utilitarian good. Beating one's wife makes her more efficient and obedient. In killing his wife instead of beating her, Cherevin suggests, Shishkov lost some useful labor. Akulka was no longer good for anything.

Dostoevsky's concern with the despotism of the Russian peasant husband and the aesthetics of wife-beating does not cease with *House of the Dead*. In his sketch "Environment"—an article, significantly, in which he recalls again his prison experiences—Dos-

toevsky mentions the case of a peasant woman who hanged herself as a result of a terrible beating at the hands of her husband.
The husband was tried, Dostoevsky writes with irony, "and was
found deserving of clemency." "But for a long time I kept dreaming about the whole situation, and I am still dreaming now." He
conjures up an image of a bloated, brutal, cruel peasant who
would catch a chicken and hang it head-downwards by its legs
"for pleasure: this was a form of recreation; a most splendid and
typical feature!" The peasant would beat his wife over a period
of several years with whatever happened to be around—rope,
sticks, whatever. Dostoevsky proceeds to analyze this imaginary
case.

> I believe that he himself did not know why he was beating
> her; probably it was for the same motives that he hung the
> chicken. . . . Peasant life is devoid of aesthetic pleasures—
> music, theaters, journals; naturally, something must take its
> place. After binding his wife and thrusting her legs into the
> opening of a floorboard our good little peasant would prob-
> ably begin—methodically, phlegmatically, even sleepily—
> with measured blows, not listening to the screams and en-
> treaties; that is, precisely listening to them, listening with
> pleasure; or else what would be the satisfaction in beating?[7]

The scene depicted here is no different from similar scenes in
"Akulka's Husband." But in the earlier story the narrator Goryanchikov stood at removes from the action; he let the story
speak for itself. In "Environment" Dostoevsky with savage irony
discloses the sensations of the peasant and—one feels this—in his
obsessive concern for brutal detail, betrays the psychological confusion of a guilty witness of violence.

What gives the wife-beating episode in "Environment" a special interest to the reader of *House of the Dead* is not only Dostoevsky's close-up portrait of a Russian peasant but his conception
of the peasant's wife. At one point, Dostoevsky breaks off his
terrifying account of the beating with a startling question addressed to his readers: "Do you know, gentlemen, that people are
born in different surroundings? Is it possible you do not realize

that this woman in other circumstances might have been a Juliet or Beatrice from Shakespeare, a Gretchen from *Faust?*" She might have been a person with "a loving, even lofty heart, a character full of the most original beauty?" After posing this question, Dostoevsky resumes his description of the beating, but this time naming, as it were, the peasant woman: "And just this very Beatrice or Gretchen is being whipped, whipped like a cat"; " 'I'll wash your feet and drink the water,' screams Beatrice, finally, in an inhuman voice."[8] By naming the peasant wife, by identifying her with the heroines of Shakespeare and Goethe, Dostoevsky dramatically heightens the reader's response to the episode. It is not simply an anonymous peasant woman who is being beaten, but a figure of spiritual beauty.

Shishkov, needless to say, does not identify Akulka with any literary heroine. Yet Dostoevsky endows her with the lofty attributes of a heroine. A simple Russian peasant girl, Akulka, in Dostoevsky's spare but symbolic portrait, is a person of original beauty, purity, love, and charity. The motif of defenselessness in Akulka merges with the motifs of mute innocence and spirituality. Central in Dostoevsky's characterization of Akulka—and in this he follows the tradition of Russian iconographic portrayal of the saints—is the exclusive use of eyes to express a concentration of spiritual life and beauty. In response to Shishkov's abuse of her on the street, the frail Akulka just "looked" at him; "her eyes were so big." On her wedding night Akulka "sat there all white, not a drop of blood in her face. She was scared, of course. . . . She had big eyes. And she would always be silent, you wouldn't hear her, it was like having a dumb woman living in the house. She was a strange one altogether." In answer to Shishkov's announcement that he was going to kill her, she simply looked at him, frightened and silent.

With the exception of the reference to her long flaxen hair, there are no other references to Akulka's physical features. The image of Akulka, of course, is presented by the dull Shishkov. Yet his limited vision serves Dostoevsky's inner idea in the portrayal of Akulka. "The less the body moves," writes Eugene N. Trubetskoi in his study of the Russian icon, "the better do we perceive the movement of the spirit, for the corporeal world becomes its transparent shell. By expressing spiritual life with *nothing but the eyes* of a perfectly motionless figure, the artist symbolically conveys the immense power of the spirit over the flesh."[9] Dostoevsky's portrayal of Akulka—even as she takes shape in Shishkov's murky mind—accomplishes just this effect. Like a Madonna in an icon, Akulka "lives" in her eyes and emerges as a perfect embodiment of spiritual beauty and innocence, a triumph of spirit over flesh.

Shishkov, as we have noted, took a whip with him to the marriage bed. But Akulka turned out to be "as innocent as could be," absolutely untouched. Akulka's innocence, of course, extends beyond her virginity. She stands innocent in a disfigured, evil world; and her death, or sacrifice, has profound symbolic meaning in the poetic subtext of *House of the Dead.* In both her personality and behavior Akulka is exemplary. "You've got a wife," Morozov remarks sarcastically to Shishkov, "only for display" (*U tebia zhena dlia modeli, chtoby liudi gliadeli,* literally, "You have a wife who is a model for other people to look at").

Morozov here unconsciously formulates the truth about Akulka: she is a model, somebody to be "looked at" and imitated in her embodiment of virtue, simplicity, and suffering innocence. The loftiness of her nature is expressed not only in her readiness to bear misfortune but in her capacity to love and forgive Morozov. Shishkov describes Akulka's reconciliation with Philka Morozov at the time he leaves for the army and recalls his own vile response to this reconciliation:

> When Philka saw her just at our gate, "Stop!" he cries, and leaps out of the cart and straightway bows down to the earth before her. "My heart," he says, "my precious one, I have loved you for two years, and now they are taking me off to be a soldier with music. Forgive me," he says, "honorable daughter of an honorable father, because I've been a scoundrel to you—it's all my fault!" And once again he bows down to the earth before her. Akulka stood there, at first she seemed scared, and then gave him a low bow, and says: "You

forgive me too, good youth, I bear you no malice." I follow her into the house. "Now you lousy bitch, what did you say to him?" And believe it or not she looks at me and says: "I love him now more than all the world." (II, 4)

Akulka's almost superhuman capacity for forgiveness, and, it would seem, for love, is unencumbered by her own terrible experiences with Morozov.

But this mute Russian Beatrice or Gretchen—her only words in the story are the words of love and forgiveness addressed to Philka Morozov—pays for her candid innocence. The morning after Morozov's departure, Shishkov drives Akulka a short distance into the woods, orders her out of the wagon, and announces his intention to kill her: "Your end has come."

She looked at me, frightened, and stood before me silently. "I'm sick of you," I say, "say your prayers!" Then I seized her by the hair: she had long thick braids, and I wound them around my hand, and I gripped her from behind on both sides with my knees, drew out my knife, bent her head back, and slashed her throat with the knife.... She screams, the blood spurts forth, and I threw down the knife, threw my arms around her from the front, lay on the ground, embraced her and screamed over her, I yelled and roared; and she screamed and I screamed; she was writhing, struggling to get out of my hands, while blood was simply pouring over me, blood was streaming, just streaming on my face and on my hands. I shook her off, I was overcome with terror, left the horse, and just set off running, running myself, homewards; I ran along the back ways and right into the bathhouse. We have an old bathhouse standing unused; I crouched in under the benches and there I sat. I sat there till nightfall. (II, 4)

Hell is a state of being, a moment of suspended time, a "place" unmediated by any vision of space or grace. Svidrigailov in *Crime and Punishment* conceives of eternity as "just a little room . . . something like a village bathhouse, grimy and with spiders in every corner, and that's all eternity is." Both the prison bath-house, described so vividly by Goryanchikov, and the bathhouse in which Shishkov hides are variants of Svidrigailov's narrow, temporal eternity. Yet the paradox of the prison bathhouse, and indeed of Dostoevsky's whole encircled prison world, is that its seething humanity (all that Dostoevsky later called the "kara-mazov earthly force") forms a vital counterpoise to the crushing limitations of time and place. As an organic life force, it eternally contradicts and denies the Euclidian, twice-two-is-four world that everywhere and every minute encloses it, stifles it, sentences it to death. It is noteworthy, therefore, that the image of the bath-house, which appears earlier in *House of the Dead* as a veritable hell of disfigured, fragmented, compacted humanity, reappears in "Akulka's Husband" old, empty, and deserted of its humanity— a symbol of the absolute triumph of evil, of empty and narrow form, of suspended time and circumscribed space. On the ethical plane, the deepest level of hell for Dostoevsky, as for Dante, is not the throng of alienated, unhappy, and loveless humanity thrashing about in its coffinlike existence, but the emptiness and mad isolation of the individual—man alone in his Euclidian uni-verse, man vanishing into the blindness and darkness of his ice-bound self.

Few scenes in Dostoevsky's work arouse a greater sense of horror, nausea, and despair than does the final murder scene in "Akulka's Husband." The slaughter of the innocent Akulka, in a real and in a symbolic sense, is a crime of the most fearful mag-nitude for Dostoevsky; the theme of disfiguration of the human image—the dark theme of *House of the Dead*—here reaches its apogee in the desecration of sacred beauty. The tragicomic Stepan Trofimovich Verkhovensky in *The Devils* speaks out in outrage against "the stinking and debauched lackey who first will mount the ladder with a pair of scissors in his hands and slash the divine countenance of the great ideal [Raphael's Sistine Madonna]." In the heart of Russia the stinking lackey Shishkov enacts that crime in his murder of a simple peasant woman—a creature whom Dos-toevsky has invested with all the tragic beauty of a Russian Ma-donna.

The death of Akulka is unatoned for in the historical time and space of the story. In the journey of Goryanchikov, the murder of Akulka—a triumph of Russian *bezobrazie*, disfiguration—is a moment of total eclipse. The words of Akulka's despotic patriarchal father, "the world's all darkness and decay," are indeed applicable here. Yet it is a moment atoned for—and this is implicit in the central position Dostoevsky gives "Akulka's Husband" in the overall work—by the terrible suffering of the Russian people. On the symbolic or mythopoetic plane, Akulka's death may be viewed as a sacrifice generating hope for the rescue of mankind.

Thus, the opening line of "Summer Time," the chapter that follows the terrible scene of bloodletting, is heavily laden with meaning: "But now it was the beginning of April and Holy Week was already drawing near." A sense of catharsis pervades the opening pages of this chapter. Lenten services with their solemn prayers and deep reverence stir up in Goryanchikov distant memories of childhood: "I recalled how at times, as a child, standing in church, I would look at the common people crowded near the entrance. . . . There at the entrance, so it seemed to me at the time, they were praying not as we did, but humbly, fervently, bowing to the ground, and with a full consciousness of their lowly state." Goryanchikov, observing that the common convicts were zealous in their devotions and always brought to church a kopeck for a candle, reflects:

> Perhaps as he gave it he thought or felt, "I too, after all, am a man, and all men are equal before God...." We took communion at the early mass. When the priest, with the chalice in his hands, read the words: "Accept me, O Lord, even as the thief," almost everybody, apparently applying these words literally to themselves, fell to the earth, their fetters clanking. (II, 5)

In "The Peasant Marey" Easter week is the occasion for a radical shift in the narrator's attitude toward the common convict. There is no direct indication in *House of the Dead* that Goryanchikov experienced a dramatic change of heart toward the convicts in this period of his first year in prison. Yet his deeply sympathetic impressions of the convicts' zealous devotions are juxtaposed with childhood recollections of humble and devout peasants at the church door. In *House of the Dead* as in "The Peasant Marey," moreover, memory and imagination at this point merge to create a new and softened image of the suffering convict.[10] In any case, Lent is a dramatic turning point in Goryanchikov's memoirs: the nightmare of sickness, terror, madness, and demonism is broken. Goryanchikov passes from the most painful phase of his recollections to less oppressive recollections of prison life and people. His narrative moves swiftly toward the moment of his liberation.

4

The theme of repentance that dominates Goryanchikov's discussion of the Lenten services is woven into the drama of Shishkov's peasant comrade, Philka Morozov. It is Morozov who is perhaps the most dramatic embodiment of self-will in "Akulka's Husband," but it is Morozov who in the end bows down to Akulka and in effect acknowledges her as the model or pattern. Though barely developed as a character, Morozov occupies a central place in "Akulka's Husband." Through him Dostoevsky establishes a link between the psychology of desperation of the Russian convict and the psychology of anarchic revolt of the Russian peasant.

Philka Morozov anticipates such Dostoevsky types as Rogozhin in *The Idiot* and Dmitry Karamazov. His is the "broad" Russian nature. He embodies the principle of violent centrifugal movement. He attains to a quasi-stability only after he has tested his limits. Whereas Shishkov is essentially covert, weak, and cowardly, Morozov is open, direct, and scornful of his environment. He vaunts his independence—or what he imagines to be his independence—and sees no virtue in the accumulation of money or property, in family, or in security of any kind. When he suddenly decides to leave Ankudim's farm, he accuses the latter of being a skinflint. He is sick of all this scrounging: "One saves and skimps and skimps and saves, and all one gets is the devil." "I've a will of my own," he remarks, launching himself on what turns out to be a three-month drinking spree: "As soon as I've run through my money . . . I'll sell the house, I'll sell everything, and then I'll hire myself out as a soldier in someone else's place, or else I'll become a tramp." Morozov would be drunk from morning till night and would drive about with a pair of horses with bells on. In his final act of abandon, he hires himself out as a soldier in somebody else's place. The anarchism of Morozov's personality—indeed, of the Morozov type—is fully revealed in his final debauch. Shishkov observes:

> Now in our parts, if a man's hiring himself out as a soldier in somebody else's place, up to the very day he's taken away everything in the house has got to give way to him and he's absolute master over everything. He gets all his money when he joins up, but until then he lives in the house of the person he's substituting for, sometimes he lives there for half a year, and what doesn't he do to the people of the house— better take the icons out of the house! "I'm substituting for your son in the army," they say, "which means I'm your benefactor, so you'd better respect me or else I'll refuse to go." Just that way Philka was raising hell at the tradesman's house, sleeping with the daughter, pulling the father's beard after dinner every day,—doing everything that he pleases. It would be every day a bath, with him insisting on making steam with vodka and requiring the women to carry him in their arms into the bath. Coming back to the house after partying about, he would stand on the street: "I don't want to go in through the gate, pull down the fence!"—so they had to pull down the fence in another place beside the gate and he would go through. (II, 4)

Violence here, though different in form and degree of cruelty from prison brutality, has the same psychological components: self-will, sadism, and caprice. Intoxicated with his freedom-of-the-moment, the freedom to do anything he wishes, the Russian peasant runs amok. "Whatever I want to do to all of you now, that's what I'm going to do," Shishkov exclaims, "because I'm no longer in control of myself." The "amiable" convict Baklushin ends up in prison for his senseless murder of an old man who sought to block his marriage to a girl. Holding a gun to the head of his enemy, he shouts in wild excitement: "Do you know that at this moment I can do anything I want with you?" He is not so far from the executioner whose first stroke is meant "to show off before his victim, strike terror into him, at the very beginning to stun him so that he may understand with whom he is dealing, in a word, to display himself."

The convict Luchka remarks of a certain "major" whom he murdered that the latter once declared to him: "I am tsar, and I am also God!" Such phrases, and others like it, Goryanchikov notes at this point, were in frequent use "long ago" among many prison commandants. Here Goryanchikov writes with tongue in cheek, for the hated prison major Krivtsov also acted like God in his uniform. "Do you know what it is to be a major?" Krivtsov is reported to have remarked. "A man like the major always needs somebody to oppress, something to take away, somebody to deprive of his rights, in short, an opportunity to play the martinet."

Those who play God and refer to themselves as God and tsar, Goryanchikov notes, are usually people who have risen from the ranks. After they have "groaned under the yoke for a long time and worked through all grades of subordination, they suddenly behold themselves officers" and have an "exaggerated notion of their own power and importance; but only, of course, in relation to the ranks subordinate to them." Such men as Major Krivtsov have much in common with the Morozovs, though the status of one is infinitely greater than that of the other. Morozov, reveling in his moment of absolute power and glory in the family of the boy whose place he is taking as a recruit, does not differ psychologically from the major who almost by instinct plays the despot. And from Morozov to the major, and from the major to the tsar, there stretches a chain of despots whose singular interest and pleasure lies in tormenting and lording it over their subordinates.

The theme of men obsessed with the freedom to transgress deeply concerns Dostoevsky in _House of the Dead_. As the cases of Shishkov, Morozov, and others indicate, the problem of transgression for Dostoevsky is only partially defined in terms of criminal psychology. The roots of the problem run deep into the social and historical life of the Russian people.

The general psychology of Shishkov is more transparent than that of Morozov. His cowardliness and fear of ridicule motivate his behavior toward Akulka. There is no apparent motivation, however, for Morozov's slander of Akulka and his public calumnies. If we are to believe Morozov when he leaves the village, his love for Akulka had been longstanding. What, then, motivated him to shame and disgrace her? The answer to this question is inseparable from the broader questions: what motivated him to give up everything—job, money, home, security, marriage, wife, family—and to plunge into drink and debauchery? What motivated him to hurl himself into the abyss of army service? In short, what lies at the basis of this all-consuming drive toward disfiguration and self-destruction? And finally, how do we explain his sudden repentance at the end of his anarchic revolt?

Morozov is an early example in Dostoevsky's fiction of a "Russian national type" in whose psychology Dostoevsky later (in his article, "Vlas," in *Diary of a Writer*, in 1873) discerned an "urge for the extreme . . . for negation . . . of the most sacred thing in one's heart, of one's loftiest ideal which only a moment before one had worshiped." "The kindest man," Dostoevsky insists, "suddenly may be turned into a most vile debauchee and criminal." This same type, however, with "equal force and impetuosity," thirsts for self-preservation and repentance, and usually saves himself from the abyss when he has reached the "utmost limit." "But it is most significant," Dostoevsky goes on to say, "that the reverse drive, the drive for restoration and salvation of self is invariably more serious than the former impulse of negation and self-destruction."[11]

Dostoevsky's generalizations unquestionably have great relevance to his conception of Morozov's character. But in *Diary of a Writer* Dostoevsky does not explain the appearance of the Russian national type in social terms. In *House of the Dead* the psychology of Morozov is instructively juxtaposed with that of the Russian convict. In his discussion of the behavior of malefactors both inside and outside the prison Dostoevsky links the instinct to destruction that often accompanies the crime or rebellious outburst with the individual's despairing will to assert his own repressed self, to experience "freedom, or, at least, some dream of freedom" in his enclosed and stifling world. The plunge toward destruction, the impulse toward self-negation is to be viewed in the last analysis as part of the tragic dialectic of freedom in a world where authentic freedom and self-mastery are not attainable.

Morozov's frenzied and irrational behavior belongs to the same category of despairing revolt that Dostoevsky singles out among the peasants or convicts. In drink and debauchery, then, Morozov expresses his scorn for the mundane world and his desire for an independence and freedom that is unobtainable. His sudden and abrupt decision to give up everything reflects an instinctive desire to break out of the stupefying world of routine and emptiness, to test his power, to act according to his own free will. But revolt in the conditions of Russian life, a world structured for centuries by serfdom and the exercise of arbitrary power, can only take the form of wild and fruitless manifestations of self-will. Such rebellion is fatally shaped—as is every rebellion—by the nature of the power it is rebelling against.

Tolstoy defined the Morozov type of anarchistic revolt with great insight in one of the scenes in *War and Peace*. Pierre, alone in Moscow and mentally shaken by his experiences, is excited by the danger that would be involved in an attempt on the life of Napoleon. Two feelings inspire him: the first is the feeling that the common misfortune required of him "sacrifice and suffering"; the other is the "vague, exclusively Russian feeling of contempt for everything conventional, artificial and human, everything that the majority of people consider the world's highest good." He is overcome by the "strange and fascinating feeling" that "wealth, power and life—all that men strive to attain and preserve"—are meaningful only in relation to the "pleasure with which one could renounce it all."

But Tolstoy, like Dostoevsky, explores a deep human—and, as

far as Russians are concerned, psychohistorical—dimension of this wild joy of renunciation:

> This was the same feeling that impels the volunteer recruit to drink up his last kopeck, a drunken man to smash mirrors and glass for no apparent reason, knowing all the time that it will cost him his last kopeck; this is the feeling that causes a man who is committing actions judged insane (in the banal sense) to test, as it were, his personal authority and power, thereby affirming the presence of some higher judgment of life beyond all human conditions. (Vol. III, pt. 3, sect. 27)

It is just this testing of personal power and authority (illusory, of course), this affirmation of some higher judgment of life, that underlies and unites the sometimes irrational outbursts of the convicts and the rampages of the volunteer recruit Morozov in Dostoevsky's *House of the Dead*. Both Tolstoy and Dostoevsky concur in their psychological understanding of the national-historical Morozov type of anarchy. At the same time, both recognize the destructive and self-destructive character of this kind of insanity. Pierre himself is a victim of this kind of insanity in deserted Moscow. So, too, is the half-deranged Makar Alekseevich who in the scene under discussion, "evidently imagining some heroic scene," waves a pistol about and has to be forcibly subdued.[12]

Morozov's abrupt rejection of Akulka, then, may be interpreted, in the context of Dostoevsky's understanding of the psychology of the Russian national type, as an unconscious act of despair, a trampling upon of everything he longs for but believes inaccessible. In turn, we may recognize in Morozov's declaration of love for Akulka the "reverse drive, the drive for restoration and salvation of self" that Dostoevsky later marked out as a particular characteristic of the Russian nature. For Morozov, that reverse drive involves a rediscovery of a feeling for the sacred and ideal.

Yet, as Dostoevsky makes amply clear in *House of the Dead*, man is his own environment. Objectively, Morozov belongs to the dark world that the better part of his nature consciously or unconsciously rejects. His experiment with freedom is tragic because it is an experiment with self-will, caprice, and power, because it is based upon negation of the dignity and rights of others and upon self-negation. Even his efforts to amend his past are caught up in a fateful, irreversible movement toward disaster. Blind in his avowal of love, as he was earlier in his malice, he declares his love in the presence of the unrepentant Shishkov and thus brings about the desecration and destruction of that image of beauty that he worships and before which he bows. Morozov, this Russian national type, remains an ambiguous figure. Relevant here is the keen and troubled observation of Arkady Dolgoruky in *The Raw Youth*:

A thousand times I have been amazed at this faculty of man (and, it seems, chiefly Russian man) for cherishing in his soul the most lofty ideal side by side with the most extreme vileness, and all this absolutely sincerely. Whether this is a special breadth in Russian man which will take him far, or simply vileness—that is the question. (pt. III, ch. 3, sect. 1)

There seems little doubt that this question deeply preoccupied Dostoevsky in *House of the Dead*.

5

The overwhelming impression of Shishkov's world in "Akulka's Husband" is not merely its brutality but its mindless, shapeless, uncontrolled gyrations. There is no moral pivot. The theme of drunkenness is paradigmatic here: stupefied by poverty, hard labor, and ignorance, people are beside themselves and drink; or, put another way, they drink and are beside themselves. They beat and befoul people, places, things; the sons beat their mothers, the mothers beat their daughters, the husbands beat their wives, and everybody beats the mute and helpless. Nothing seems sacred in this environment. Yet the rituals of the church are observed, and the icon—the model, the "image of God"—is before everybody's eyes. Akulka's father is well-read in the scriptures; he "was always reading something religious." Furthermore, amidst all the foulness, people seem preoccupied with virtue, shame, and honor. Morozov is certain that nobody will marry Akulka because she has been "dishonored." Shishkov prides himself on the fact that his family has no dishonor attached to it. He threatens to shame Morozov but fears that Morozov will shame him in everybody's eyes by beating up his wife; and for this reason, he starts to beat her himself. Akulka, he discovers, is virtuous—"honorable and from an honorable home"—while her parents, who had once thrashed her mercilessly day and night, now vainly beg Shishkov to forgive their virtuous daughter. "Better take the icons out of the house!" Shishkov remarks to Cherevin apropos of the typically disgraceful behavior of the substitute recruit. But he himself does not have icons on his mind when he remorselessly beats Akulka. After he learns that she has been virtuous (he calls himself a "fool" and a "scoundrel" and asks her to forgive him), he can only wonder why she had had to endure such "torments." But the fear of shame quickly turns him into an animal again.

The much proclaimed concern for the virtue of women goes hand in hand in Shishkov's world with a profound contempt for them. Woman emerges here as a double prisoner of Russian life: slave of the system and slave of her husband. Akulka's drama is thus the focal point for Dostoevsky's exploration of the most terrible kind of slavery. Here the husband embodies the attributes of property owner, executioner, and debauchee. Here the problem of slavery and its consequences—the subterranean theme of *House of the Dead*—finds its most tragic embodiment.

The notions, then, of virtue, shame, decency, disgrace, honor, dishonor, forgiveness, God, and the sacred saints are on everybody's lips, but not in their hearts. Love seems to have no power in Shishkov's world, as it has none in prison. There *are* models, but nobody is imitating them. The old man Ankudim's nostalgia for the "olden days when the good patriarchs lived" and when people were chopped up and burnt at the stake only discloses the profound contradiction of Russian village life: this is a patriarchal world that has adopted the symbols, forms, and rituals of Christian religion but has not realized its central idea of the dignity of man and respect for human personality. There is belief in some kind of deity, but the message of Jesus has not been heard.

Was the message heard by the Russian peasant-convicts? What role did Christianity play in their lives? Dostoevsky addresses these questions cautiously and, for the most part, descriptively in *House of the Dead*. The religious holidays, Christmas and Easter, as we have noted, are stages in the journey of Goryanchikov and in the symbolic design of *House of the Dead*. They are also concrete occasions for directing attention to the religious habits of the convicts. These days (there were three of them) were anticipated and enjoyed as brief moments of change or respite in the dreary routine of prison life; there was no work; it was a "real holiday." "And, finally," remarks Goryanchikov, "who knows how many memories must have stirred in the hearts of those outcasts with the arrival of such a day! The major religious holidays are sharply etched in the memory of the common people from their earliest childhood. These are days of rest from their heavy labors, days of family gatherings. But in prison they must be recalled with pain and anguish."

Goryanchikov speaks of the almost "punctilious" regard of the convicts for the "solemn day" of Christmas. He describes the piety of their devotions at Christmas as well as Easter services. He notes, however, that for the most part it was the elderly who prayed; "the young men did not pray much; they hardly crossed themselves even on a religious holiday." Indeed, there is no evidence that the majority of the Russian peasant-convicts in any way shared the deep and daily piety and moral rectitude of the Old Believer to whom they entrusted their money.

What role, then, did the Christian religion and its holidays play in their lives? On this point, Goryanchikov's testimony is the same for Christmas as for Easter:

> Along with his innate reverence for the great day, the convict unconsciously felt that through his observance of the holiday he in some way came into contact with the whole world, that as a result he was not entirely an outcast, a lost soul, cut off

from everything, and that even in prison things were the same as among other people. (I, 10)

Thus, the religious experience for the Russian convict, as Goryanchikov intuits it ("the convict unconsciously felt," "who knows"), is a moment of purification—a recollection, in a real and in a symbolic sense, of his image, of the lost shape of his existence. Dostoevsky later insisted that the Russian peasant had preserved his human image this way throughout centuries of alluvial barbarism. The peasant-convict, we might say, found his image in the beauty and symbolism of the orthodox holiday ritual. On the deepest and unconscious level of his being, Dostoevsky seems to suggest, the Russian peasant-convict apprehends, or feels, the Christian message of the dignity of man and of his humanity; but he does not carry it into his daily life, either in prison or in the village.

"It has always seemed to me that with us only forms constitute civilization," Dostoevsky wrote in his notebook in 1875, "and that if we didn't have forms everybody at balls would exchange blows, because we do not have any inner need to respect another person, as is still the case and continues to be in Europe, and that this has been taught us only in a mechanical way, while there always remains: *grattez le russe*."[13] Dostoevsky's remarks were directed at the educated upper classes, but they are just as applicable to the people at large. In his notebook, as in *Diary of a Writer* at this time, Dostoevsky stresses the importance of religion as a saving force in the life of the masses of people: "All morality comes from religion, because religion is only a formulation of morality."[14] "The people are debauched," he acknowledges, "but it has religion, there one finds ideals, a guide."[15] Yet clearly Dostoevsky recognized that religion had not yet entered into the life of the Russian people as an effective structuring moral force. *House of the Dead* provides at least indirect evidence of this fact.

The holidays in prison were the occasion for much drinking and roistering about. The narrator's anguished and angry cry in

the unused draft pages of *House of the Dead*—"I want to pray
they sing filthy songs"—says much about the moral-religious feelings of the common convicts. In the end, of course, it is Goryanchikov, and not the peasant convict, who is most deeply and
consciously religious and who recollects the lost shape of his existence. It is he, and not the "lost people," who goes forth from
the prison morally cleansed and spiritually redeemed to disclose
the people's inner image and to prophesy their ultimate redemption.

Is this not the hidden, even fantastic symbolism of the last part
of the bathhouse scene where the convict Petrov, with strange and
measured ceremony, thoroughly washes Goryanchikov ("so that
you'll be nice and clean") and, finally, to the latter's embarrass-
ment, washes his *"little feet"*? "The common people," remarks
Goryanchikov as he squeezes into the hell of unwashed humanity
in the bathhouse, "wash very little with hot water and soap." He
buys the place of a convict who forthwith vanishes under the bench,
"where it was dark, filthy and where the sticky moisture had
accumulated everywhere to the depth of almost half a finger."
Petrov proceeds to wash Goryanchikov. Did not Dostoevsky, rec-
ollecting his own past prison experience and seeking out its acquired
meaning for himself (redemption through "direct contact with the
people"), paint here a scene of his own mysterious annointment
at the hands of the people—an annointment after the manner in
which Jesus washed the feet of the protesting Peter and declared:
"If I wash thee not, thou hast no part with me" (John 13:4-10)?
Here, of course, is an incident (one that is simultaneously a literary
construct) that is analogous in meaning to Dostoevsky's daydream
of the peasant Marey and the moment the latter gently touched
the lips of the child Dostoevsky and blessed him. Dostoevsky does
not refer to such an incident in *House of the Dead*. But his discussion of the impact of the Easter festival upon Goryanchikov as
well as his structuring of the last episode in the bathhouse scene
suggests that the dream of the peasant Marey and the incident
itself in the woods belong to Dostoevsky's real spiritual, if not
actual, autobiography.

6

In his essay on *House of the Dead* Victor Shklovsky has written:

> Along with Aley [the embodiment of absolute good] there is
> absolute evil. The story "Akulka's Husband" enters the
> novel in the form of a separate story, "Akulka's Husband."
> This is a story about a guilty man who is guilty not because
> others offended him, but because he is a bad man who loves
> evil and revenges himself for his insignificance.[16]

There is no question that Shishkov's account of Russian village
life conveys an impression of triumphant evil. But there is a question as to whether Shishkov—vile and disgusting as he is—is
viewed by Dostoevsky as the embodiment of absolute evil. The
question is not an academic one; it touches on Dostoevsky's
whole approach to evil. Aley indubitably emerges as a symbolic
embodiment of absolute good. Yet if Dostoevsky finds an incarnation of absolute evil in anybody in *House of the Dead*, it is not
in Shishkov, but—in a moral and social sense—in the consciously
cynical and vile nobleman Aristov, whom Goryanchikov calls a
"moral Quasimodo," and, perhaps—in a qualified and purely
symbolic sense—in the Jew, Isay Fomich.

Dostoevsky's attitude toward the prison moneylender, Isay Fomich, is deeply ambivalent. It is clear that he was attracted to this
bizarre figure for whom religion and money were passions. Goryanchikov and Isay Fomich were "great friends." Dostoevsky's
fleeting description of Isay Fomich entering prison for the first
time—"he cowered to such an extent that he did not even dare
to raise his eyes to the mocking, mutilated, and terrible faces
crowding closely around him"—recalls medieval paintings of
Christ surrounded by the grotesque and fearful faces of his flag-
ellators. But for the most part, Isay Fomich emerges as the ster-
eotypical Jew—comical and greedy. Dostoevsky makes little effort
to lift the comic curtain that conceals this tragic figure.[17]

It is highly significant that Dostoevsky introduces Isay Fomich
directly following the account about Aley. The back-to-back juxtaposition of these two figures sharpens the contrast: on the one

hand, the symbolic Christ; on the other hand, the Jew who in the convicts' taunt "sold Christ." In his attitude toward money, Isay Fomich stands apart from the rest of the convicts. For them money is "minted freedom"; money does not long remain in their pockets and their use of it expresses their yearning for freedom. For Isay Fomich, money is not a means, but an end in itself. His goal is quite bourgeois: he wants "to get married." It is noteworthy, finally, that in the prison bathhouse—which evokes in Goryanchikov's mind the image of hell—Isay Fomich is to be found "on the very highest shelf . . . roaring with laughter" and "screaming out a tune in a shrill, insane voice."

Without question, Aley and Isay Fomich Bumstein, as symbolic types, stand in sharp contrast to one another. The distinction between Shishkov and Aristov is touched upon by Dostoevsky later on in _Diary of a Writer_ (1873). In a review of a drama, or better, melodrama, Dostoevsky distinguishes between two types of lost souls—the "innocent" and the "guilty"—that may be found among socially and economically deprived people. To the first category belongs the poor girl Matryosha who "behaves in a vile way almost without knowing herself that she is vile." "A tragic fate," concludes Dostoevsky. "A human being is turned into a rotten worm and is completely satisfied with herself and her miserable outlook. Here there is environment, here there is _fatum_, the unfortunate one is not guilty and you understand this." But opposed to this worm is a factory lad—"depraved, drunken, despicable." The circumstances and the environment are the same, Dostoevsky notes—drunkenness, the disintegrating family, the factory—but there are noteworthy differences in the two types. The factory lad

is not simple-minded like Matryosha, he has come to believe in depravity. He is not simple-mindedly vile, as she is, but loves it; he has introduced himself into his vileness. He understands that depravity is depravity, and knows what it means not to be depraved, but he has come to love depravity consciously, and despises honor. He now consciously negates the old order of the family and its customs; he is stupid and dull, that is true, but in him there is a kind of enthusiastic voluptuousness and the vilest and most cynical materialism. He is no longer a mere worm like Matryosha, in whom everything is petty and dried up. He stands at a meeting of the village community and you feel that he no longer understands or is capable of understanding anything about it, that he is no longer "of this world" and has definitely broken with it.[18]

We may question, of course, whether Matryosha and the factory lad are really such radically different "worms" from an objective point of view. But Dostoevsky's distinction between the two types is nonetheless an important one. The most dangerous and intolerable evil for him is one that has become conscious of itself and even reaches the point of enthusiasm.

There is no reason, to be sure, to insist that Shishkov fit wholly into one or the other of Dostoevsky's two categories of depraved people. He is carried away by evil, and evil takes recognizable forms in him. In a deep, psychological sense, moreover, this wife-beating husband enjoys his depravity. Yet in the final analysis, his is not the kind of conscious evil that repels Dostoevsky in the convict-nobleman Aristov, or in Prince Valkovsky (*The Insulted and Injured*), Svidrigailov (*Crime and Punishment*), or Stavrogin (*The Devils*). Shishkov is more or less the unconscious embodiment of a stupefied and brutalized world. The absolute evil we find in "Akulka's Husband" is the evil of a total human situation, or environment, that brings out the potential for evil in man. What this episode says about man, of course, is devastating, especially if we take it in isolation from the mitigating context of the rest of *House of the Dead*.

Yet to say that environment brings out the worst in people is not to say that environment creates the evil in us, that is, the proclivity toward evil. "The attributes of the executioner are found in embryo in almost every contemporary man," Goryanchikov observes. The Soviet scholar V. Kirpotin, seeking to deflect the thrust of this observation, argues that Dostoevsky "found the embryo of the executioner not in human nature in general, but in *contemporary* man." By contemporary man, according to Kirpotin, Dostoevsky meant a people disfigured by centuries of serfdom and exploitation. Kirpotin goes on to argue that the executioners Shishkov, Morozov, and others were "nurtured by environment, and if one had succeeded in reforming the environment, then the causes giving birth to torturers and executioners would gradually have been overcome."[19]

Dostoevsky was deeply, indeed, agonizingly aware of the corrupting character of the Russian historical environment; moreover, he placed great hopes upon a social environment based on a Christian ethic and education that would bring out the best in men. The long and detailed theatrical scenes in *House of the Dead* give expression to Dostoevsky's belief—formulated earlier by Friedrich Schiller in his letters *On the Aesthetic Education of Man*—in the possibility of the aesthetic humanization of man. But his approach to the problem of evil was not a naive one. His deep concern in *House of the Dead* and elsewhere with violence—with the instinct for power, acquisition, and sexual aggression—suggest a notion of evil as something involving more than a corrupt social environment. The "riddle of life" that preoccupies Dostoevsky in his work and of which the "editor" speaks in the introduction to *House of the Dead* is not only that of the Russian people and their history but that of all mankind. He did not believe that people were irredeemably bad, but he did believe that the attributes of both evil and good were to be found in them and that they constituted a given. This given could be influenced by environment, but social engineering could not eradicate the fundamental contradiction between the egoistic and spiritual strivings; it could not overcome the essential ambivalence of human nature. In short, there could be no total triumph over evil on earth.

7

There are many "stories" told in *House of the Dead*, and the majority are related by Goryanchikov. But a few are told directly by the convicts. Dostoevsky refers to one such story in his chapter entitled "Isay Fomich. The Bath. Baklushin's Story." The term used here for "story," *rasskaz*, appears again as part of the chapter title "Akulka's Husband." But in the latter the word *rasskaz* appears beneath the main title, thus creating the curious impression that what follows differs generically from the rest of the narrative. Shishkov's story, of course, is not fiction. It is not an imaginative story of Russian life inserted by Goryanchikov to dramatize his ideas or feelings about Russian life (although it is not at all impossible that elements of Dostoevsky's creative imagination entered into this particular story). Yet Dostoevsky's special designation of "Akulka's Husband" as "a story" does point to its almost incredible content. Revelatory of Dostoevsky's intent here is the comment of the ridiculous man, in "The Dream of a Ridiculous Man," on the incredulous response of people to his dream of beauty: " 'He had a dream,' they say, 'an hallucination, a delirium.' Oh! Is that really so clever? And they are so proud! A dream? What is a dream? And is not our whole life a dream?" "Akulka's Husband" is just such a dream—that is, a nightmare of Russian life. This nightmare may seem incredible, Dostoevsky seems to suggest, but it is a fact. Later in *Diary of a Writer* (in 1876) Dostoevsky will playfully dramatize the purely conventional character of the notion of fiction by interweaving accounts of children from everyday life with imaginative but eminently real stories about children.

"Akulka's Husband" clearly occupies a special place among the stories of *House of the Dead*. For an extended period of time Dostoevsky leaves the reader in a dark chaos without a guide, Goryanchikov, without a faithful Virgil, and with seemingly no way out. Goryanchikov, indeed, never comments directly on the story or its implications (the earlier hospital scenes, to be sure, amply provide the reader with the narrator's point of view). The story is told by a narrator, Shishkov, who is locked in his own narration. He can see nothing beyond the "repulsive crust" of Russian life. Indeed, he is that crust. It is this fact that gives his story its unusually terrifying impact: the frightening reality of violence and disfiguration is conveyed without feeling, without any mitigating pity or compassion, without any insight into life or people. In this sense, "Akulka's Husband" differs radically from Raskolnikov's nightmare and Ivan's stories about the suffering of children. There the sense of the horror and disgrace of human deeds is offset by the paralyzing pain, pity, and rage experienced by the dreamer or narrator.

Shishkov's story, then, from one point of view, is a one-sided representation of Russian life. Moreover, it is typical of the naturalism that Dostoevsky detested and that, in fact, he transcends in *House of the Dead* as a whole. But as a representation of the naturalism of Russian life, of its repulsive crust, it embodies truth—a truth that finds its most tragic expression in the despiritualized reality of the dead house. Yet the incompleteness of Shishkov's truth is demonstrated by Goryanchikov's deep and many-sided exploration of the personality and life of the Russian peasant convict—an exploration that takes into account not only the given, biological man, but the tragic historical, social, and economic factors that went into the shaping of Russian man. The Russian peasant emerges in Goryanchikov's portrayal as a rich personality with enormous strength and creative potential. *House of the Dead* as a whole, then, while it confirms the indictment of Russian life that is contained in "Akulka's Husband," rejects a wholesale indictment of Russian man. In the same way, *The Brothers Karamazov* as a whole constitutes a refutation—albeit a hard fought one—of the total cynicism and pessimism of the Grand Inquisitor.

Dostoevsky set for himself a double task in *House of the Dead*: to view the Russian peasant-convict in the aspect of his concrete life and history, a history of accumulated violence that finds its most fearful embodiment in the dead house; and to view him in the timeless aspect of the human spirit. If we view the journey of the narrator Goryanchikov as ultimately a journey into the spirit of a lost people, into the realm of suffering and disfiguration, trampled dignity and lost hopes, then what appears to be, and is, historically, at the center of Russian life—violence and disfiguration—turns out to be the repulsive crust; and what appears to be alluvial, transitory, and of only tangential meaning—

the living humanity of the Russian convict—turns out to be the true center or vital kernel of Russian life and man.

In this perspective, the reader perceives in Akulka what Shishkov cannot see and Morozov only fleetingly glimpses—a pure embodiment of Russian spirituality, which, like the Russian icon, is both concrete and emblematic. Akulka, whose name is connected etymologically with the word "eagle," symbolizes Russia's soaring spirituality. She embodies in her life the principle of love and self-sacrifice that Dostoevsky placed above all other values. Her death—indubitably the most tragic occurrence in *House of the Dead*—in the framework of Shishkov's story is in vain. In the broader context of Dostoevsky's whole narrative, however, her death is redemptive. Paul Evdokimoff's general observation is wholly applicable to Dostoevsky's understanding of Akulka: "Dostoevsky traces a saint's face and hangs it on the wall in the background like an icon; and it is by its revelatory or therapeutic light that one deciphers the meaning of the events that take place on the stage of the world."[20]

The Problem of Conscience and Suffering in *House of the Dead*

> *Infirmity and misery do not, of necessity, imply guilt. They
> approach or recede from the shades of that dark alliance in
> proportion to the probable motives and prospects of the
> offender and the palliations, known or secret, of the offense,
> in proportion as the temptations to it were potent from
> the first and the resistance to it, in act or in effort,
> was earnest to the last.*
> THOMAS DE QUINCEY, Confessions of an English Opium Eater

IN HIS ARTICLE or sketch entitled "Environment" in *Diary of a
Writer* (1873) Dostoevsky, recalling his life among "dyed-in-the-
wool" criminals, asserts that "not a single one of them ceased to
regard himself as a criminal." Silent and contemplative, the criminals did not speak about their crimes, nor was it considered
proper to do so. "But I say truthfully," Dostoevsky declares,
"that perhaps not a single one of them evaded long, spiritual
suffering within himself, the kind that is most purifying and
strengthening. . . . O, believe me, not one of them considered
himself innocent in his soul!"[1]

Dostoevsky, we feel, presses his point more anxiously than
usual. "But I say truthfully," he insists; "O, believe me." Why
this unusual concern? Had he not definitively presented the Russian convict's attitude toward his crime and punishment well over
a decade earlier in *House of the Dead*? Had he not probed there
the problem of the convict's conscience? He had indeed. Yet a
close reading of that work suggests that the typical convict did
not view himself as a criminal in any deep moral or spiritual
sense; he did not experience any pangs of conscience over his
crime. He does not emerge as a man who has endured "spiritual
suffering of the kind that is most purifying and strengthening."
Dostoevsky, writing in 1873, clearly is reinterpreting some aspects of his prison experience in the light of his subsequent emphasis on the beneficent role of suffering in the destiny of the

CHAPTER IV

Russian people. What were some of his impressions in *House of the Dead* on the question of conscience and suffering among the convicts?

1

The narrator Goryanchikov does not reproach the convict for his crimes. But the question of conscience is very much on his mind. He is acutely interested in how the convicts respond to their crimes as well as to their punishment. He introduces the question casually at the very beginning of his memoirs, recalling the silent farewell of a convict leaving prison after twenty years: this convict had "entered the prison for the first time, young, carefree, thinking neither about his crime nor his punishment. He left a grey-haired old man, with a sad and sullen face." What were the convict's thoughts on his crime and punishment? The narrator does not assay an answer. A moment later he remarks that there were "murderers so cheerful, so totally unreflecting, that one could have sworn that their conscience never reproached them with anything. But there were also morose people who were almost always silent." What were these silent ones thinking about their crimes? Or were they thinking about them at all?

Apropos of his first encounters with particularly moody and unsociable convicts, Goryanchikov notes that he liked to "look into their sullen, branded faces and guess at what they were thinking." But of what were they thinking? The convicts, he asserts, spoke little of their past; "they did not like to talk about it, and, clearly, tried not to think of it." One convict's story about how he had deceived a five-year-old boy with a toy and then murdered him was shouted down by the whole barracks; but this was not out of "indignation," Goryanchikov notes; it was simply that "there was *no need* to talk *about that* . . . it was not the thing to talk *about that*." Certainly there were no feelings of guilt or squeamishness on the part of the convicts: further on in his memoirs Goryanchikov observes that only in prison had he heard "stories about the most fearful and unnatural actions, the most monstrous murders related with the most unrestrained,

childishly merry laughter." The presence of childlike laughter, of
course, gives another dimension to the question of conscience.
Goryanchikov frequently compares the convicts to children.

How did these grown-up children view their crimes? Goryanchikov approaches the question first in connection with a discussion of the convict's response to his immediate surroundings.
Prison, penal servitude, hard labor, Goryanchikov insists, develop
in the convict

> hatred, a thirst for forbidden pleasures, and terrible flip-
> pancy. . . . It sucks the living juices out of a man, saps his
> spirit, weakens and cows him, and then presents the morally
> dried up, half imbecilic mummy as a model of reform and
> repentance. Of course, the criminal, rebelling against society,
> hates it and almost always thinks himself innocent and it
> guilty. What is more, he already has been punished by it
> and for this reason almost considers himself cleansed—all
> accounts settled. From this point of view, finally, one might
> conclude that one was almost obliged to justify the criminal
> himself. (I, i)

The criminal's attitude toward his crime is thus placed directly in
a social context. Hatred of society precedes the criminal act, and
punishment—particularly the inhuman kind described by Goryanchikov—only supports the criminal in his rationalization of
his crime and feeling of innocence.

But the problem of conscience is not exhausted. Other factors
enter into crime besides social ones. "In spite of the many possible points of view," Goryanchikov continues, "everyone will
agree that there are certain crimes which always and everywhere,
from the beginning of the world, no matter what the legal code,
have been considered indisputable crimes and will be so considered as long as men are men." Here he cites the monstrous parricide in prison who appeared to have felt no remorse for his
terrible crime. The "animal insensibility" of this convict strikes
Goryanchikov as almost "impossible." It betrays "some consti-
tutional defect, some physical and moral abnormality still unknown to science, and not simply crime." The alleged parricide

CHAPTER IV

later turns out to have been innocent, in fact, as the "publisher" of Goryanchikov's memoirs informs the reader in an aside in chapter seven, part two of *House of the Dead*.[2] Yet there are other convicts who have committed "indisputable crimes" and who remain untroubled by their acts.

Orlov, "an evil-doer such as is rarely to be found, a man who coldbloodedly murdered old men and children" and who had confessed to many murders, attracts the particular attention of Goryanchikov. Goryanchikov tries to make him talk of the things he has done. Though Orlov always answers frankly, he always frowns at these "interrogations." "But when he grasped that I was trying to get at his conscience and trying to discover some element of repentance in him, he would look at me with the utmost scorn and contempt, as though I had suddenly become in his eyes a sort of foolish little boy with whom it was impossible to discuss things as you would with a grown-up." Orlov would look at Goryanchikov with pity in his face, then laugh at him with the most "good-hearted amusement, without a trace of irony." The generally mild and enigmatic, but fearless and volatile convict Petrov—"he would cut your throat if he took it into his head, just cut your throat without any qualms or remorse"—also views Goryanchikov as an innocent "child, almost like a baby, incapable of understanding even the simplest things in the world." You are "a man with too good a heart," he remarks to Goryanchikov on one occasion, and "so very innocent, so innocent that one just feels pity for you." To approach crime from a moral point of view is, for these convicts, to exhibit the naiveté and innocence of a child. Yet these same convicts, as Goryanchikov stresses more than once, look upon crime and much of life in general with the attitudes of children.

The efforts of the "innocent" Goryanchikov to discover anything resembling conscience or remorse in the convicts are without success. The convicts affect an outward tone of "peculiar personal dignity," as though the status of the convict were a kind of "honorable rank," Goryanchikov notes early in his memoirs. "Not a sign of repentance!"

CONSCIENCE AND SUFFERING

I have already said that in the course of several years I never once saw among these men the slightest sign of repentance, not even a faintly troubled thought about their crime, and that the majority of them inwardly believed themselves to be completely innocent. This is a fact. Of course, vanity, bad example, youth, bravado, false shame were the cause of much of this. On the other hand, who could say that he had sounded the depths of these lost souls and read in them what was hidden from all the world? Yet it really should have been possible after so many years to observe, catch a glimpse, detect in these souls at least a speck of something that might attest to some inner anguish or suffering. But there was nothing, positively nothing. Yes, it would seem that crime cannot be interpreted from any fixed, conventional point of view, and that its philosophy is rather more difficult than has been supposed. (I, i)

Something in Goryanchikov's repeated asseverations on the absence of conscience or remorse in the convict and in his obvious wish to linger in doubt on the matter suggests that his discovery—Dostoevsky's discovery—carried with it, initially at least, a sense of shock and disbelief. It was no doubt this deeply unsettling discovery that led Dostoevsky to examine more deeply the tragic social and historical conditions that led to the formation of the Russian popular consciousness.

2

Among the special songs that were to be heard in prison Goryanchikov recalls a particularly mournful one, "probably the work of some exile, and the words were sentimental and rather illiterate." He cites a few verses:

> My eyes will never see that land
>   In which I was born;
> I have been forever condemned
>   To suffer torments without guilt.
> On the roof a screech owl cries out,

Echoes through the forest.
My heart aches, pines away,
I'll never be there.

This song, Goryanchikov notes, was never sung in chorus, but always as a solo. The song is noteworthy not only for the way in which its persona alludes to the eternal torments of his hell and his own sense of innocence but for the way this feeling merges with a sense of hopelessness and fatality. In rebelling against society, Goryanchikov had noted, the criminal "hates it and almost always thinks himself innocent and it guilty." Yet the feeling of hatred, strangely, is not expressed by any overt resentment or anger on the part of the convict at his incarceration or punishment. In place of these sentiments is found a general sense of resignation and misfortune in life. " 'We are a lost people,' they would say, 'we did not know how to live in freedom, so now it's "run the gauntlet" and "form ranks."'—"You wouldn't obey your father and mother, so now step to the drum."—"You wouldn't do fine needlework, now break stones." ' All this was said often," Goryanchikov notes, "both in the form of moral precepts and as ordinary proverbs and sayings, but never in earnest. These were only words. It is unlikely that a single one of them inwardly acknowledged his lawlessness."

The absence of any sense of guilt or repentance in the convict clearly is linked with his sense of resignation, his feeling of being caught up in a destiny beyond his control. The sense of fatality finds eloquent expression in the common people's designation of the convicts as "unfortunates":[3]

[The common people] never reproach a convict with his crime, however terrible it may be, and forgive him everything because of the punishment he has undergone and, in general, because of his misfortune. Not without reason do the people all over Russia call crime misfortune and convicts unfortunates. It is a profoundly significant designation; it is all the more meaningful because it is applied unconsciously, instinctively. (I, 4)

The common people's readiness to exculpate the convict is but the obverse side of their own sense of misfortune. The notion that crime is a misfortune, or more literally, a stroke of bad luck, and not a matter of personal responsibility, speaks to the heart of the problem of conscience in the convict. Where fate is supreme there can be no freedom; and where there is no freedom there can be no sense of responsibility or recognition of inner lawlessness. The moral precepts and sayings of the convict, then, are but words, empty formulas that grace the convict's real sense of guiltlessness and impotence before the common misfortune or fate.

The attitudes that define the convict's view of his crime are reflected in his response to his punishment. Here misfortune takes a more specific form, and the sense of guiltlessness before the powers-that-be is more pronounced:

It cannot be, I sometimes used to think, that they consider themselves wholly guilty and deserving of punishment, especially when they have committed an offense not against one of their own kind, but against the authorities. The majority of them did not blame themselves at all. I have already said that I did not notice any pangs of conscience even in those cases when the crime was directed against somebody of their own social group. As for crimes against the authorities, they did not count for anything. It sometimes seemed to me that in this latter case they had their own special, so to speak, practical—or, rather, realistic—view of the matter. They took into account fate, incontrovertible fact, and they did so not with any special deliberation, but rather, unconsciously, like some kind of faith. The convict, for example, although always inclined to feel himself innocent of crimes against the authorities, so that even the very question is unthinkable, nonetheless in practice recognizes that the authorities take quite a different view of his crime, and, therefore, that he must be punished, and that's that. It is a mutual struggle. Furthermore, the criminal knows, without any doubt, that he will be acquitted by the court of his own milieu, the common people, who will never—this, too, he knows—definitively condemn him, but for the most part, in-deed, will exonerate him completely, provided that his sin be not against his peers, his brothers, against the common peo-ple to whom he belongs. His conscience is at peace, and he is strong in the power of his conscience and is not morally troubled, and that is the main thing. He feels, as it were, that he has something to lean upon, and therefore does not hate but accepts what happens to him as an ineluctable fact which he did not initiate and will not end and which will continue for a long, long time as part of a long-established, passive but stubborn struggle. What soldier personally hates the Turk when he wars with him; and yet this very Turk cuts him down, runs him through and puts a bullet into him. (II, 2)

The problems raised in this extraordinary passage, though they pertain most immediately to the psychology of the peasant-con-vict, have far-reaching implications. The real context of Dostoev-sky's discussion is Russia and the Russian peasant-serf and the profound abyss separating the popular consciousness from Rus-sian "civilization"—civilization here meaning not only the op-pressive political, social, and economic apparatus of the state (en-vironment, fate) but the whole heritage of enlightenment, ethical culture, and religion that inspired the best representatives of the educated classes.

What is crucial in the formation of the convict's response to his crime and punishment is the history of his entire relation-ship—as serf or soldier—to the authorities—here, the state. The Russian serf was a permanent victim of the state. When he ran afoul of its juridical arm, his psychology of resistance did not change; his encounter with the state as criminal was but a more concentrated embodiment of his everyday condition. Because he viewed his punishment as part of his fate, and therefore, as ine-luctable, his outward stance was one of curious resignation. But not all was peaceful beneath the surface.

These unfortunates, who do not feel guilty yet who accept their punishment with outward resignation, are perceived by Dostoevsky as engaged in a "long-established, passive but stubborn struggle" with an enemy who is as much a part of his landscape as the hated Turk was of the Russian soldier's (the comparison here is a significant one). The hatred of the convict for his enemy—an enemy who is everywhere and is supreme—takes on a peculiarly passive, sublimated, and therefore disagreeable form: the deliberate acceptance of suffering or punishment. The psychologically underground character of the convict's struggle with his enemy ✕ is fully apparent. The Underground Man too speaks of man in the extremity of misfortune as prepared to prove his humanity "if only on his back," that is, through voluntary acceptance of punishment and humiliation.

The hero of *The Raw Youth* sets forth in detail the psychology of underground resistance. As an orphan in school he was mistreated and humiliated by his teacher. He would retaliate by redoubling his zeal as the teacher's lackey:

> Was there spite in me? I don't know, perhaps there was. Strange to say, I always had, perhaps from my earliest childhood, one characteristic: if I were ill-treated, absolutely wronged, insulted to the last degree, I always showed at once an inexhaustible desire passively to submit to insult and even increase my humiliations beyond the desires of the person offending me. "All right, you have humiliated me. Well, I will humiliate myself even more; look and enjoy it!" . . . If they want me to be a lackey, well then, I'll be a lackey; if I'm to be a menial—well then, let me be a menial! I could keep up a passive hatred and underground spite in this way for years. (pt. II, ch. 10, sect. 1)

The usually "submissive and obedient" convict in *House of the Dead* from time to time has "strange outbursts of impatience and rebellion" (by his very nature the convict is "cantankerous and mutinous"). But for the most part, his rebellion takes on a typically underground form that only results in his own redoubled punishment and misery.

The convict, then, emerges in Dostoevsky's portrait as a kind of underground man—an inarticulate one, to be sure—who outwardly accepts his punishment as part of a struggle with an Euclidian universe that is not of his own creation and from which he cannot escape. His stance may be compared to that of the Underground Man, who bows down before the "stone wall" of "twice two is four," but who, grinding his teeth, at the same time refuses to accept it. He chooses suffering instead and rationalizes his situation with the paradoxical thought that he is "guilty but without guilt before the laws of nature."

This last phrase admirably encapsulates the convict's own paradoxical relationship to his "wall," that is, his prison world with its inescapable suffering, humiliation, and punishment: on the one hand, he insists that he is innocent (he will not recognize the moral authority of the law that condemns him); on the other hand, he recognizes that he is faced by the unmovable law of authority (his "realistic" way of looking at things, his acknowledgment of "fate, incontrovertible fact") and that he must capitulate before it. His capitulation, as we have noted, takes on a typically underground character: the revolt of suffering. Revolt here bears witness to his permanent enslavement to the enemy—the authorities, the dead house, the law, fate, the implacable and omnipresent "Turk."

In the final analysis, this tragic psychodrama of the Russian convict and Russian serf constitutes the broad historical context for what Dostoevsky later termed the "tragedy of the underground." Many years later Dostoevsky confided in his notebook:

I take pride in the fact that I was the first to bring forth the real man of the *Russian majority* and was the first to expose his disfigured and tragic side. The tragedy consists in the consciousness of disfiguration. . . . I alone brought into the open the tragedy of the underground, consisting in suffering, self-punishment, the consciousness of something better and the impossibility of achieving that something, and chiefly consisting in the clear conviction of these unfortunate people that all are alike, and hence it is not even worth trying to improve! What is there to support those who wish to reform themselves? Consolation, faith? There is consolation from no

one, faith in no one! But another step from here and one
finds depravity, crime (murder). Mystery.[4]

The full dimensions of this tragedy of the underground that af-
fects the Russian majority became apparent to Dostoevsky in the
dead house.

In *Winter Notes on Summer Impressions* (1863) Dostoevsky
dramatically illustrates his idea of the tragedy of the underground
in a description of the poverty-stricken masses of London:

> We are surprised at this nonsense of succumbing to palsy
> and becoming vagabonds; we do not realize that all this rep-
> resents a separation from our social formula, a stubborn, un-
> conscious separation; an instinctive separation made at any
> cost for the sake of salvation, a separation from us full of
> disgust, and horror. These millions of people, abandoned, ex-
> pelled from the human feast, shoving and crushing each
> other in subterranean darkness into which their elder broth-
> ers have pushed them, grope for any gate at all to knock at,
> and seek an exit in order not to smother in the dark under-
> ground. Here is a final, despairing effort to form their own
> group, their own mass, and to break with everything, even
> with the human image, just so as to be able to act as one
> wishes, just so as not to be together with us. (ch. 5)

What Dostoevsky has to say about the "outcasts of society" in
London applies as well to the "insulted and injured" that he encountered in prison, to say nothing of the people he encountered
earlier in the lower depths of St. Petersburg.

Goryanchikov's discussion of the convict's response to his
crime and punishment is important for its profound understanding of the nature of the convict's conscience. The conscience of
which he speaks is not personal or ethical conscience—that is, in
Webster's definition, "the sense or consciousness of the moral
goodness or blameworthiness of one's own conduct, intentions,
or character together with a feeling of obligation to do right or
be good." The convict opposes the "court of his own milieu" to
the court of law of the authorities and feels "strong in the power

of his conscience," that is, in the power of his tribal or group consciousness. His conscience, in the personal sense, is "at peace." "It is unlikely that a single one of them inwardly acknowledged his lawlessness," remarks Goryanchikov. The convict rationalizes his criminal act. He is guilty only before the authorities' law, the law of the ruling class, not before the law of his own social group—"providing that his sin be not against his peers." But even in the latter case, Goryanchikov notes, the convict does not experience any pangs of conscience. The convict's distinction between two kinds of law—the law of the authorities and the law of his own group—results in a condonation of lawlessness and a de facto evasion of personal moral accountability.

In the years that followed *House of the Dead* the moralist Dostoevsky, as we have noted, tended to retreat from the view that the Russian convict felt no guilt before his crime. Yet clearly the phenomenon of two kinds of law in the popular consciousness continued to disturb him. In *The Brothers Karamazov* Dostoevsky takes up this problem again; the terms of the discussion are different, but the substance of the problem is the same. Ivan Karamazov, troubled by the moral evasiveness of the Russian criminal, comes up with a plan that in his view would overcome all ambivalence in the popular consciousness. "Very, very often today the criminal compromises with his conscience," Ivan explains. " 'I have stolen,' he says, 'but I have not gone against Christ's church.' " Ivan observes that when the Roman Empire desired to become Christian, "it incorporated the church, but itself remained as before a pagan state in very many areas of its life." But "if everything became the church," Ivan reasons, "then the church would cut off the criminal from itself. . . . He would have to separate himself not only from men, but also from Christ. For by his crime he would have risen not only against men but against Christ's church."

Zosima, unlike Ivan, has confidence in the capacity of conscience to act as a deterrent to crime or as chastisement after the crime. "Mechanical punishment," according to Zosima, only "lacerates the heart, while genuine punishment, the only one which inspires fear and at the same time offers some relief, is to be found in the consciousness of one's own conscience." The "law of Christ" expresses itself in the awakening of one's conscience. "Only by recognizing his guilt as a Christian son of society, that is, of the church," insists Zosima, "does [the criminal] recognize also his guilt before society itself, that is, before the church. Thus, the contemporary criminal is capable of recognizing his guilt alone before the church and not before the state."

Ivan and Zosima differ profoundly on how to approach the problem of the compromising conscience, or the existence of two kinds of law in the popular consciousness. But they both recognize that the criminal will not acknowledge any guilt before the state. Ivan is troubled by the manner in which the criminal rationalizes his acts. But instead of viewing the problem in its obvious social context, he hints through his example of the Roman Empire that Christianity has only a superficial impact upon Russia. He suggests that the Russian popular consciousness, though it has formally accepted Christian truth, has not taken the message of Christ to heart. Clearly, what popular consciousness has not taken to heart is the Christian affirmation of the dignity of the individual personality and the freedom, and therefore, the personal moral accountability, of the individual. It is this pessimistic thought that inheres in Ivan's whole approach to the problem of conscience and leads him to seek a bulwark in a stern theological state.

Both Ivan's doubts about conscience in the popular consciousness and Zosima's insistence that the criminal recognize his guilt as a Christian son of society date back to the painful dialectic of Dostoevsky's own thought about crime and the popular consciousness in prison. This was a time when, on the one hand, he was obviously shaken by the absence of any sign of personal conscience in the convict, and on the other, he became deeply convinced that the problem of social relations in general could be resolved only by humanity's embracing the full spirit of Christ's teachings.

3

"Why does what I committed seem so hideous to them?" Raskolnikov asks in his Siberian prison. "Because it was evil-doing? What does that word mean—'evil-doing'? My conscience is at rest." He acknowledges that he violated the criminal code, but he does not regard himself as guilty in any moral sense. In his bitterness he rebels against the "decree of blind fate" that compels him to "resign himself to such 'meaninglessness' and to make the best of such a decree if he wants any peace at all for himself." Raskolnikov's bitterness, of course, is an indication that he is rebellious in his acceptance of defeat.

If the above-quoted lines from the epilogue to *Crime and Punishment* were all that had survived of that novel, the reader might well be inclined to view Raskolnikov as one of the convicts who might have appeared in *House of the Dead*—an unusually articulate one, to be sure, but nonetheless typical in the way he rebuts naive moralists, justifies his crime, and charges his punishment to fate. In fact, Raskolnikov is hardly one of Dostoevsky's typical convicts. First, he is not a man of the common people, a fact that is painfully brought home to him in his Siberian prison; he is a highly educated and sensitive intellectual of gentry origin. Second, as Dostoevsky makes amply clear in *Crime and Punishment*, Raskolnikov's conscience is by no means at rest, either before his crime or after it; it is active even when he is asleep. Though he rejects in argument any moral guilt and haughtily questions the meaning of the word "evil-doing," he is actually a fanatic moralist who is continually preoccupied with moral questions. He has a particularly bad conscience. In both of these respects, then, Raskolnikov is very different from the typical convict from the people, who is uneducated, unconcerned with questions of right and wrong, and who automatically dissolves all questions of personal conscience in a solution of collective social consciousness.

Raskolnikov is a man driven by conscience in spite of himself. The whole message of *Crime and Punishment* is that conscience in man is a transcendent element in his nature. The typical peasant-convict in prison, however, does not exhibit the "slightest sign of repentance" or gnawing conscience. How are we to understand the presence of conscience in one man and the absence of it in another? The answer—at least as far as Dostoevsky approaches the matter in *House of the Dead*—would seem to be that personal conscience is an attribute (though by no means invariably) of a spiritually developed, educated consciousness. Here education must be understood not merely as formal schooling but as involving a total immersion in the moral and spiritual values of Christian culture and civilization. In this sense, an educated man may suffer more intensely than an uneducated man of the people.

Goryanchikov raises this whole question in a discussion of the inequality of punishment for those guilty of the same crime. A person who kills to protect his liberty, for example, should not in Goryanchikov's view receive the same punishment as another person who kills for pleasure. Another inequality, Goryanchikov continues, is the

inequality in the consequences of punishment.... Here is a man who in prison pines away, dwindles away like a candle; but now here is another who before entering prison did not even know that there existed in the world such a gay life, such a friendly group of daring companions. Yes, even such types turn up in prison. Here again, for example, is an educated man with a developed conscience, intelligence, heart. Just the pain of his own heart, prior to any punishments, is enough to kill him with its agonies. He condemns himself for his crime more mercilessly, more pitilessly than the most menacing law. But here alongside of him is another person who does not even once in all his prison term think upon the murder he has committed. He even considers himself innocent. And there are even those who deliberately commit a crime in order to land in prison and in this way avoid a far more penal life of labor in freedom. There this man lived in the deepest degradation, never ate to his fill and worked for his employer from morning till night. But life is easier in prison than at home; there is sufficient bread, and of a kind that he had never seen before; on holidays there is beef,

there are alms, there is the possibility of earning a kopeck.
. . . Is it possible that the punishment these two people experience is felt in an equal way? But really, why busy oneself
with insoluble questions! The drum is beating, it's time to
get back to the barracks. (I, 3)

The narrator, pressing his case for special consideration of the
upper-class convict, paints a particularly unfavorable portrait of
the common convict who does not think upon his crime and
"even considers himself innocent." Indeed, the reader of the
memoirs has a momentary glimpse of the private Goryanchikov
and of that resentment that for the most part remains under control and in the background of the narration.

What is important here, in any case, is Goryanchikov's clear
identification of moral sensibility, of the capacity for moral-spiritual anguish, with a "developed conscience, intelligence, heart."
Goryanchikov himself, of course, emerges in *House of the Dead*
as a prime illustration of a man with such a developed conscience.
In facing the terrible prison world—for him "a completely new
environment"—he characteristically resolves first of all to act "in
a forthright manner" in accordance with the dictates of his "feelings and conscience." This same conscience not only provides him
with a guide for surviving, as he puts it, in the "depths" but
dominates his whole review of his past. "I reviewed all my former
life, went through everything down to the last detail, meditated
on my past, judged myself sternly and implacably, and sometimes
even blessed fate for sending me that solitude without which
there would have been neither judgment of myself nor that stern
reexamination of my earlier life."

Of course, mere formal education or membership in the upper
class is by no means a guarantee of a developed conscience. "Education" Goryanchikov notes, "sometimes exists side by side with
such barbarism and such cynicism that it revolts you." Aristov,
an educated man of noble background, is a "monster" and "moral
Quasimodo," a type especially fearful because of his conscious,
openly cynical renunciation of all standards of morality. Akim
Akimovich, a convict of gentry background, might serve as an
illustration of another kind: "terribly illiterate, a moralist to the

letter, . . . phenomenally honest," and especially sensitive to any injustice, this man, condemned to prison for taking justice into his hands and killing a Caucasian prince, was "somehow completely incapable of understanding of his guilt in any real way." Yet it is clear that Goryanchikov associates the potential for a developed conscience with an educated, cultivated sensibility.

Goryanchikov by no means argues that the uneducated common convict is lacking in fine feeling or that he does not suffer:

> It is difficult to establish any standard with which to measure the soul and its development. Even education itself provides no yardstick here. I would be the first to testify that among these sufferers in the very heart of the most unenlightened and oppressed milieu I encountered instances of a most refined spirituality. It would sometimes happen in prison that you would know a man for several years and you would think of him as an animal, and not as a human being, and you would despise him. But suddenly there would be a moment, a chance one, in which his soul in some involuntary outburst would open itself to you, and you would see in it such richness, feeling, heart, such vivid understanding both of his own suffering and that of others, that your eyes, as it were, would be opened, and for a moment you would not even believe what you yourself had seen and heard. (II, 7)

Certainly Aley, the Old Believer, and Sushilov, among others, are men in whom Goryanchikov discovered feeling and heart. And most certainly the common convicts are people who in their own way suffer deeply the deprivation of freedom.

Nonetheless Goryanchikov insists that the hardships endured by the upper-class, educated man are greater than those endured by the common peasant-convict. This is not necessarily because the nobleman and educated man "feel things in a more refined and sensitive way or because his development is greater," but because he has been plunged into a primitive environment:

> The moral deprivations are more difficult to bear than any physical torments. . . . The educated man, sharing the same

punishments as the common people, frequently loses far more than they do. He must suppress all his needs, all his habits; he enters an environment that is inadequate for him; he must learn to breathe a very different air.... He is like a fish pulled out of the water and put on the sand. And often the punishment, by law identical for all, becomes ten times as painful for him.... (II, 4)

Just as the educated convict typically experiences his crime in an especially acute way, so he experiences certain punishments such as beatings on a moral-psychological as well as physiological plane. The Polish nobleman Miretsky, for example, speaks of his flogging not only with indignation and hatred but with the look of a man suffering from some "internal pain." He flushes and almost tries not to look at Goryanchikov when relating the incident. Miretsky obviously regards physical punishment as a violation of his dignity as a man. To him physical punishment is a moral as well as physical affront. By contrast, Goryanchikov observes, the convicts from the people speak of their beatings "with unusual good nature and lack of malice. . . . Often not even the trace of resentment or hatred could be felt in a story which would sometimes make my heart leap and begin to throb heavily and violently. But they would tell their stories and laugh like children."

The concept of the convict as a child is a recurrent motif in _House of the Dead_ and one that links this work with the legend of the Grand Inquisitor, suggesting the moral distance that separates Goryanchikov from the common convicts. When treated humanely the convicts would "rejoice like children"; their pleasure in dressing up on holidays and parading through the barracks "took on a childlike character"; indeed, "in much the convicts were complete children." In preparing the Christmas theatricals, they "rejoiced like children at the slightest success." Working with animals, "they were as merry as children." The convicts were in general as "credulous as children."

The concept of the convict as a child in these examples suggests his open, naive, and spontaneous nature. Yet this childlike nature in a grown man also suggests an underdeveloped moral and social consciousness. The convict's response to the informer and to the institution of informing, for example, contrasts radically with Goryanchikov's response and is indicative of the former's moral and social immaturity. Goryanchikov looks upon the nobleman Aristov as a man "unrestrained by any inner norm, any sense of law": "I have never in my life met with such utter moral degradation, such total depravity and such brazen vileness." He speaks of Aristov's "vile act of informing" in St. Petersburg, an act that involved the lives of ten men. This same depraved and vile Aristov—with whom Goryanchikov soon severed all relations—regularly informed on the convicts to the prison authorities. Goryanchikov's deep revulsion with Aristov is the measure of his profound moral and social consciousness. But how did the convicts respond to Aristov? Though everybody knew that he informed on them, the "idea of punishing or even reproaching the scoundrel never even occurred to anybody." Informing, Goryanchikov notes, was not looked down upon in any way.[5] Indignation with the informer was unthinkable: "He is not ostracized, people are friendly with him, so that if you tried in prison to point out the whole vileness of informing nobody would understand you in the slightest." This is the voice, of course, of an educated man with a developed conscience.

In contrast to Goryanchikov or Miretsky, then, the common convict does not regard crime as bad, corporal punishment as degrading, robbery in prison as antisocial, or informing as vile. He does not morally suffer over his crime and punishment, nor does he seek to probe his neighbor's conscience. He is not cynical or conscienceless like the educated nobleman Aristov; rather he is without conscience; he is innocent. A concern for moral or social norms strikes him as naive and childish. Goryanchikov, Miretsky, and other gentleman-convicts live together with the common convicts, with these grown-up children, but inhabit an entirely different world. As Goryanchikov observes, the Russian gentleman is separated from the common people by the

profoundest of gulfs, and this fact is *fully* seen only when

the *well-born person* suddenly, by the force of external circumstances, really in fact is deprived of his former rights and
is transformed into a man of the people. Otherwise you may
associate all your life with the people, you may come into
contact with them every day for forty years in a row, in the
civil service for example, in any of the conventional admin-
istrative types of relationships, or even perhaps on a simple
friendly basis, as a benefactor and, in a certain sense,
father,—but you will never know the real essence of them.
It will all only be an optical illusion, and no more. I know,
of course, that everybody, absolutely everybody will say, on
reading my remark, that I am exaggerating. But I am convinced that it is true. I became convinced not through books,
not through ratiocination, but through reality, and I had
quite enough time to verify my convictions. Perhaps in time
everybody will learn to what degree it is correct.... (II, 7)

The shock of reality, a warning, a veiled prophecy is contained
in these last, almost cryptic lines—lines followed, significantly,
by a description of a prison grievance and a discussion of the kind
of limited men who take the lead in this kind of affair. "No, they
don't like the nobles," Akim Akimovich remarks, "especially the
political prisoners, they'd be happy to devour them, and no wonder. First, you're a very different people, not at all like them, and
secondly, they were all formerly landowner's serfs or in the
army. Judge for yourself whether they could be fond of you."
The essence of these people is defined not only by a deep hostility
toward the nobility—the "iron beaks" who peck at them in their
everyday life—but by a complete separation from the moral
codes, the social norms and forms, that were identified with the
nobility and that found embodiment in its best representatives.

Prison convinced Dostoevsky of the full tragedy of the Russian
people and nation. It was a tragedy of alienation and disfiguration
of the masses of people. It was a tragedy of bifurcation of the
Russian nation into two streams of life and history: that of a
ruling upper class and that of an oppressed, disinherited, and dis-
affected lower class. The latter was "subjected to depravity," as

Dostoevsky wrote in "The Peasant Marey," "debauched, tempted, and constantly tortured to such an extent that it is still amazing how it managed to survive and still preserve a human image." In his postexile period, Dostoevsky came to see the bridging—but not by revolutionary means—of the profound gulf between the upper and lower strata of Russian life as the central task of enlightened Russia. It was a task, he believed, that Russian literature had undertaken in seeking out "diamonds in filth," that is, in disclosing the ideals of the people, their "simple-heartedness, purity, gentleness, breadth of mind, and kindliness."

Yet a study of *House of the Dead* suggests that for Dostoevsky bridging the gulf also involved rescuing the Russian people as a whole from "alluvial barbarism," from moral and spiritual disfiguration, from hatred and self-immolation, from imminent catastrophe. It was his critics, Dostoevsky wrote in his notebook in 1875, who were "ignoring facts." The cries of the critics that he was not depicting "real life" in his work, he wrote, have "not dissuaded me":

> There are no *foundations* to our society, no principles of conduct that have been lived through, because there have been none in life even. A colossal eruption and all is crumbling, falling, being negated, as though it had not even existed. And not only externally, as in the West, but internally, morally.[6]

4

More than thirteen years separates Dostoevsky's sketch "Environment" from *House of the Dead.* His memory of the latter work and of the world he depicted in it had not dimmed. But he had begun to see certain aspects of that world in a somewhat different way and to draw certain conclusions that he had not drawn—or in any case, had not expressed openly—in *House of the Dead.* In "Environment" he insists upon the convict's sense of guilt and upon his "long, spiritual suffering . . . the kind that is most purifying and strengthening." He speaks here of the virtues of "self-purification through suffering" and "boldly" declares that "by harsh punishment, by prison and penal servitude, perhaps, you would have saved half of [the convicts]."[7] In another sketch, "Vlas" (1873), Dostoevsky speaks of the Russian people's "craving for suffering"; indeed, he sees in that craving their central attribute:

> I believe that the main and most fundamental spiritual need of the Russian people is the need for suffering,—perpetual and unquenchable suffering—everywhere and in everything. The people, it seems, have been infected by this need for suffering from time immemorial. The suffering stream flows through its entire history, not only because of external misfortunes and calamities; it gushes from the very people's heart. . . . The Russian people seem to enjoy its suffering. What is true of the whole people is also true of its individual types—of course, generally speaking only. Have a look, for example, at the numerous types of Russian debauchee [*bezobraznik*]. Here we do not merely have excessive debauch, sometimes astounding us by the boldness of its scale and the vileness in the fall of the human soul. This debauchee is himself, first of all, a sufferer.[8]

In *House of the Dead* Dostoevsky clearly perceives the centrality of suffering in the historical destiny of the Russian people. But he does not conclude that suffering plays or played a morally or spiritually purifying role in the life of the Russian people. The concept of self-purification through suffering does lie at the basis of Dostoevsky's conception of Goryanchikov's personal drama, however, and it is this conception that Dostoevsky will later superimpose on the drama of the Russian people. Prison for Goryanchikov—and here we are speaking, of course, of Dostoevsky—was a kind of moral and spiritual purgation; he confesses to moments when he revels in his agony of suffering and despair; he sternly judges his past and blesses the fate that sent him to prison and made possible his renewal. Goryanchikov certainly endured long, spiritual suffering of the kind that was "purifying and strengthening." And his journey through the hell of suffering to spiritual salvation serves as a general metaphor for the ultimate journey of the Russian people through their hell. Yet Dostoevsky's central effort in *House of the Dead* is not to idealize the suffering of the Russian people, that is, to extract a compensatory virtue from their miseries. Insofar as he focuses upon the problem of suffering, he seeks to call attention to the terrible social, moral, and spiritual consequences of that suffering.

From the purely psychological point of view the convict's response to his punishment and to his fate in general may be characterized as strongly masochistic. But what Dostoevsky emphasizes in this response is not the enjoyment of suffering (Dostoevsky openly hints at this kind of response in Goryanchikov), but the social and human protest that inheres in it: passive, but unyielding struggle with and hatred for the "Turk"—the authorities, the nobility, the state. It is the revolt of suffering, finally—not suffering as a morally or spiritually productive experience—that primarily concerns Dostoevsky in *House of the Dead*.

In his prison years Dostoevsky more than likely reached the conclusion that in the fate-bound history of the Russian nation suffering had become a permanent feature of the common people's existence and that their revolt had come to express itself in a deliberate choice of suffering (such is the Underground Man's view of the history of man in general). But Dostoevsky does not conclude in *House of the Dead* that the Russian people "crave" suffering or that the need for suffering defines their historical destiny (this reflection of the later Dostoevsky, whatever truth it may contain, undoubtedly reflects a certain element of unconscious bitterness and spite going back to his prison experience). We may note, however, an isolated but important episode in *House of the Dead* that anticipates Dostoevsky's later accent on the importance of suffering in the character and destiny of the Russian people. A convict, noted for his gentle disposition, Goryanchikov recalls, took to reading the Bible day and night. One day he refused to go to work. Confronted by the enraged prison major, he threw a brick at him. He was seized, tried, and beaten. As he lay dying, he said that he bore nobody any ill will but had "simply wished for suffering." This episode—which is echoed in the drama of the painter Mikolka in *Crime and Punishment*—obviously intrigued Dostoevsky. In a return to this episode later on in *House of the Dead*, the narrator suggests that the convict had acted from the loss of all hope. "And since it is impossible to live without hope, he contrived a way out for himself through a voluntary, almost artificial martyrdom. He declared that his attack on the major had been without malice, but solely because he had desired to accept suffering. And who knows what psychological process had taken place in his soul!"

It is noteworthy that Dostoevsky does not interpret this psychological process in moral terms. Yet in a letter to M. N. Katkov in 1865 apropos of *Crime and Punishment*, Dostoevsky observed that the "established legal punishment for a crime is far less frightening for a criminal than legislators think, in part because [*the convict*] *himself morally demands it*. I have observed this even in the most uneducated people, in the most crude circumstances."[9] In the original letter, the word "morally" is penned in above the line. Was Dostoevsky still hesitating between an ethical and a more purely psychological explanation?

"Man does not live his whole life," Dostoevsky wrote in his notebook, "but *composes himself*." The lofty moral and spiritual attitudes in *House of the Dead* take shape against a background of Dostoevsky's own struggle to transcend the often uncontrollable hatred, bitterness, and despair that assailed him in prison. Dostoevsky forges an image of himself in Goryanchikov, who in turn restores the image of the Russian people. So, too, in his later works, Dostoevsky takes the colossal suffering of the Russian people—a suffering full of inexpressible anger, hatred, and despair—and transmutes it into a virtue. He sublimates or diverts the anger into a morality of love, humility, and self-sacrifice. The scene in which the Gospel-reading convict attacks the prison major and then rationalizes his violence with the assertion that he only wished for suffering is thus a kind of model in which we may observe the paradox of violent revolt and passive submission in Russian man that Dostoevsky sought to convert into a moral paradigm.

5

One of the fundamental ideas that Dostoevsky dramatizes in his postexile work is that man is free and that no appeal to environment or fate can justify evasion of responsibility. Goryanchikov is particularly intransigent, as we have seen, with the few careless or dishonest physicians who appeal to environment in defense of their actions. Environment devours much that is in us—but, he insists, not everything. But what of the peasant-convict who feels no guilt over his crime or lawlessness? Is there not some kind of unconscious appeal here to environment or fate? Dostoevsky clearly places the peasant-convicts in a different category from the physicians with their developed conscience. The peasant-convicts are unfortunates, that is, victims of misfortune. Conscience is not a developed faculty in them. And though Dostoevsky certainly disapproves of their acts of violence and crime, at the same time he does not indict or reproach them in any moralistic way.

The peasant-convicts emerge as a people who indeed are devoured by environment. They are not only objectively unfree—their prison servitude is but an extension of their unfreedom as serfs and soldiers—but they are also burdened by an overwhelming sense of helplessness and despair. Lacking in any freedom, they are lacking in any sense of responsibility. Lawlessness and the justification of crime, it would seem, are the inevitable concomitant of existence in a fate-bound world.

Yet as a Christian, Dostoevsky will insist that the very notion of a fate-bound universe is a lie. Man is free, and his first step toward moral and spiritual redemption must be the recognition of his God-given freedom. Dostoevsky holds to these ideas in *House of the Dead*. At the same time, however, he acknowledges in the dead house an absolute denial of that free universe. Dostoevsky, as we shall note again, sees in the convict's violent, irresponsible, and often capricious behavior an essential manifestation of an unquenchable will to freedom. But it is a will that is stimulated not by faith in a God-given meaningful universe, but by despair.

It is in Christian religious and ethical doctrine that Dostoevsky seeks an ultimate answer to the despair and disfiguration he finds in Russian life. Clear evidences of Dostoevsky's own religious faith are apparent both in the overall symbolic design of *House of the Dead* and in many observations made by the narrator. The Russian peasant-convict, on the other hand, responds only to the symbolism and ceremony of the Christian service; with few exceptions, faith as he may experience it does not shape his ethical and social consciousness.

The Russian convict and people, as Goryanchikov finds them in the dead house, are, as it were, doomed. It is Goryanchikov's "Scenes from the House of the Dead"—Dostoevsky's *Notes from the House of the Dead*—that places them back in the circle of redemption. The task of resurrecting the buried humanity of the convict and of bringing his despairing quest for dignity and freedom to the foreground was incompatible with a moralistic or religious-didactic approach that indicted the convict for his failure to comprehend that his acts were blameworthy and evil. In his later writing, however, Dostoevsky sought to combine an idealization of the people's spiritual and religious sensibility with a critical and even moralistic attitude toward crime and irresponsibility.

In his sketch "Environment" Dostoevsky once again discusses the moral-philosophical implications of the folk view of the convicts as unfortunates. He raises the question in connection with his criticism of the contemporary peasant juror, who, he complains, is handing down lenient verdicts in cases involving criminal behavior among the peasants. He speaks of the "mania for acquittal no matter what not only among peasants, yesterday's insulted and injured, but among almost all Russian jurors."[10] Dostoevsky identifies this practice, moreover, with contemporary social-political thought that exculpates the criminal on the basis of environment. The "doctrine of environment," he insists, can only have the effect of undermining any notion of individual personal responsibility.

But what of the fatalistic folk view of the criminal as an unfortunate? Dostoevsky now seeks another meaning in this view; he seeks to challenge the idea of fatalism as an attribute of the psychology of the Russian people. "The people," he writes, "call the condemned criminals 'unfortunates' and extend charity to them. Now what has the people—perhaps for centuries on end—been trying to say by this?" Dostoevsky—clearly with his resolution of this question in *House of the Dead* in mind—then goes on to ask: "Is there expressed here the Christian truth or the truth of 'environment'? Now right here one may find the stumbling block, the concealed lever which the propagandist of 'environment' might seize upon with success."[11] In *House of the Dead* the people resolved this question on the side of the "truth of 'environment'." In "Environment," however, Dostoevsky insists that the people's notion of criminals as unfortunates expresses the Christian truth. "No," he declares, "the people do not deny crime and know that the criminal is guilty." In designating the criminal as an unfortunate, they simply mean to say:

> You have sinned and are suffering, but we too are sinners. If we were in your place, perhaps we might have done worse. If we ourselves were better, perhaps you would not have been sitting in prison. Out of retribution for your crimes and out of a common lawlessness you have accepted a burden. Pray for us and we will pray for you.

In accusing themselves, Dostoevsky continues, the people prove that

> it does not believe in "environment": it believes, on the contrary, that environment depends entirely on it, on its ceaseless repentence and self-perfection. Energy, work, and struggle—here is what overcomes environment. Only by work and struggle is integrity and the feeling of one's own dignity achieved. "By making ourselves better the environment will be better."[12]

Dostoevsky's stance here is didactic, inspiratory, hortatory. He ascribes to the people his own convictions. He finds in them what—in "Environment"—he finds in the criminal: a conscience. He appeals to the citizen in the Russian peasant juror and in Russian man in general. To be a citizen, he explains, means to "raise oneself to the [level of] the opinion of the country at large." It means to exhibit both compassion and awareness of the consequences of environment—"but only up to a point, only as far as is allowed by the healthy opinion of the country and the extent of its enlightenment by Christian morality."[13] Christianity, Dostoevsky insists in one of his most important statements, "while fully recognizing the pressure of environment and declaring forgiveness to the sinner, nonetheless makes man's struggle with environment a moral duty, draws a line where environment ends and duty begins. Making people responsible, Christianity at the same time recognizes their freedom."[14]

But, we may ask, how healthy was Russia and what was the extent of its enlightenment by Christian morality? To what extent did the Russian people really hold to the Christian truth? Dostoevsky himself clearly has real doubts. "And what if our people are especially inclined to the teachings of environment," he remarks in a kind of aside, "even by its very nature, let us say, at least, by its Slavic inclinations?"[15] The psychology of the Russian people as Dostoevsky finds it in the dead house is precisely the psychology of a people inclined by nature toward fatalism, toward justifying crime as misfortune and the criminal as an unfortunate. Clearly the Christian truth that Dostoevsky discovers in the folk designation of the criminal as unfortunate (a "purely Russian idea," he observes, but one existing in the unconscious) is one that in "Environment" he seeks to instill into, or to activate in, the popular Russian consciousness in order to combat the elements of fatalism and irresponsibility. Dostoevsky allows, however, that the people might be led astray by a "false interpretation" of their notion that the criminal is an unfortunate. "The final meaning and last word will no doubt always be their own, but *temporarily* it may be otherwise."[16] Of course, it was the "temporary" truth of environment that Dostoevsky found embodied in the popular consciousness in the dead house.

To the truth of environment, then, Dostoevsky opposes the Christian truth. To the tragic truth of inertia, congealed environment, *fatum*, he opposes the Christian teachings of ethical freedom and redemption, ceaseless repentance, and striving for self-perfection. He stresses the voluntarism of duty and insists upon absolute personal moral responsibility. Dostoevsky's stern, almost Protestant ethic, with its emphasis upon energy, work, duty, and the salutory rigors of punishment, undoubtedly reflects thoughts of his prison period. Here we find not only a version of his own stern self-directed criticism but also echoes of stern thoughts about the conduct and behavior of his fellow convicts. This moralistic, didactic side of Dostoevsky—strengthened no doubt by a deep personal resentment—was muted in *House of the Dead*. It is expressed forcibly in "Environment." It is no accident, of course, that in the same sketch in which Dostoevsky idealizes the Russian people's buried ethical consciousness he creates a fearful, almost vengeful portrait of a merciless peasant who beats his wife, the Beatrice of the Russian village.

Dostoevsky did not accept the truth of environment when he wrote *House of the Dead*, but he recognized that that truth had taken root in the consciousness of the Russian convict. He recognized, too, the grave moral-philosophical implications of the triumph of that truth. "Environment"—in its essential content, a kind of didactic, inspiratory gesture—illustrates his effort to counteract some of the grim truths he discovered in Russian life in his prison period. It illustrates his effort to seek out new and healthy foundations for the development of the Russian people. "I do not want to think and live," Dostoevsky wrote in the conclusion of the January issue of *Diary of a Writer* in 1876, "other than with the faith that all of the ninety millions of us, Russians (or however many there will be) some day will all be educated, humanized, and happy."[17] The truth of environment, then, could only be a temporary truth. It would inevitably give way to the truth of Christianity and its idea of freedom and responsibility.

Dostoevsky's concept that man is his own environment speaks not only of man's imprisonment but of his freedom. Freedom is also part of man's fate—hence his eternal capacity, as Emerson expressed it, to "confront fate with fate."[18] What drew Dostoevsky's attention in prison, and what preoccupied him in *House of the Dead*, was the convict's instinctive unwillingness, in spite of his recognition of the truth of environment, to renounce his freedom. His will to freedom, however, was not expressed in a recognition of his moral freedom, but in a frenzied and often amoral blind confrontation with his fate-ruled prison universe.

Freedom in the Shadow of the Dead House

So absolute is our souls' need of something hidden and
uncertain for the maintenance of that doubt and hope and
effort which are the breath of its life, that if the whole future
were laid bare to us beyond today, the interest of all mankind
would be bent on the hours that lie between; we should pant
after the uncertainties of our one morning and our one afternoon;
we should rush fiercely to the Exchange for our last possibility
of speculation, of success, of disappointment; we should
have a glut of political prophets foretelling a crisis or a
non-crisis within the only twenty-four hours
left open to prophecy.
GEORGE ELIOT, The Lifted Veil

IN *Winter Notes on Summer Impressions* Dostoevsky sets forth his notion on the ideal relation between the individual and society and on the attributes of the authentically free self. Society, he insists, must recognize the individual as possessing the same rights as society. But the "demanding rebellious individual ought first of all to sacrifice to society his whole I, his whole self." Here, in self-sacrifice, Dostoevsky finds the highest expression of man's personality:

> Understand me well: voluntary, fully conscious self-sacrifice, utterly free of outside constraint, sacrifice of one's whole self for the benefit of all, is in my opinion the sign of the highest development of personality, of its supreme power, its absolute self-mastery, and its most complete freedom of its own will. (ch. 6)

The ideal of brotherhood and highest freedom of will that Dostoevsky projects here did not find social embodiment anywhere in the world—certainly not in Russia, and not in the dead house where nobody loved anybody. We need only single out the phrases "supreme power," "absolute self-mastery," and "most complete freedom of its own will" to recognize that these attributes of the highest development of personality were the very attributes the Russian convict craved but could neither comprehend nor experience except in comic or tragic forms of self-assertion, excess, or violence. The convict, in the light of Dostoevsky's highest ethical and spiritual ideals, is profoundly unfree.

Yet in *House of the Dead* Dostoevsky ponders a notion of freedom that is not ethical, but psychological or psychophysiological. Freedom here implies movement, the deployment of man's vital energies. It involves the satisfaction of instincts that in man's evolution have developed in an environment of uncertainty and have been expressed traditionally in an active relation to the surrounding world. This freedom—in the deepest sense, egoistic—is a will to life, a will creatively to affirm oneself and one's right to existence. If suppressed or frustrated, the will to freedom does not disappear, but manifests itself in distorted and even monstrous forms. Yet however distorted, this will to freedom is marked by the pathos of man's instinct for life and survival, an instinct that in its purest form is "beyond good and evil."[1]

"Yes, man is tenacious of life!" Goryanchikov exclaims at the beginning of his memoirs, recalling the seething, boisterous life of the convicts in the midst of the filth and mephitic fumes of the barracks. "Man is a creature who adapts to anything, and, I think, that is the best way of defining him." At the same time, Goryanchikov insists, anyone who approaches a prison feels that "this whole mass of people has not been brought here of their own will, and that regardless of any and all measures taken, a living man cannot be turned into a corpse; he will remain with his feelings, with his thirst for revenge and life, with his passions, and with the need to satisfy them."

Goryanchikov analyzes the convict's will to life and the varied forms it sometimes takes against a background of a radical denial of life: confinement to one location, chains, inhumane conditions, penal labor, senseless and sadistic regulations, brutality of punishment, an obligatory herdlike existence in which man is never alone. The convict outwardly adapts. Yet, as Goryanchikov remarks in connection with one convict's resolute determination to protest violently his unjust treatment, there are "strange outbursts of impatience and rebellion." A convict is "obedient and submissive up to a certain point; but there is a limit which must not be overstepped. . . . Often a man is patient for several years, submits, endures the cruellest punishments, and then suddenly explodes over some little thing, some trifle, almost nothing. From a certain point of view one may regard such a person as mad; and indeed the mad do act this way." Dostoevsky was one of the first writers to explore the psychological content of this kind of madness and its social-cultural roots in the suppression of a man's freedom.

1

"What is more important than money for the convict?" asks Goryanchikov. "Freedom, or at least some dream of freedom." "The whole meaning of the word 'convict' is a person without any will." But when the convict spends money for vodka or other forbidden pleasures, he is "acting *of his own free will.*" He likes to swagger about and "show off before his comrades, and even to convince himself *if only for a moment* that he has incomparably more will and power than he appears to have—in a word, he will go off on a spree, storm about, reduce somebody to dust and prove to him that he *can* do all this, that everything is 'in our hands,' that is, convince himself of what a beggar could not even dream." Such is the underlying motivation, Goryanchikov believes, for the convict's tendency, even when sober, to boast and "puff up his personality in naive and comic ways."

"All this excess has its risks, which means that all this provides a least some illusion of life, at least a distant illusion of freedom. And what will one not give for freedom?" The wild and destructive outbursts or sprees of the convict, sometimes even the exemplary convict, also constitute an

anguished, hysterical manifestation of personality, an instinctive yearning to be oneself, the desire to express oneself, one's humiliated personality; a desire which suddenly takes shape and reaches the pitch of malice, of madness, of the eclipse of reason, of fits and convulsions. Thus, perhaps, a person buried alive in a coffin and awakening in it, would thrust at the cover and try to throw it off, although, of course, reason might convince him that all his efforts were in vain. But the whole point here is that it is not a question of reason: it is a question of convulsions. We must further take into consideration the fact that almost any independent manifestation of personality in the convict is regarded as a crime; and so in this situation it naturally makes no difference to him whether the manifestation is great or small. A spree is a spree; to risk anything is to risk everything, even murder. It is only really the beginning that matters: as he goes on, the man gets intoxicated, nothing will stop him! And thus it would be better in every way not to bring him to this point. It would be more tranquil for everybody. Yes. But how is this to be done? (I, 5)

The wild and irrational revolt of the peasant-convict, humiliated to the last degree, anticipates the tragic underground revolt in *Notes from the Underground*. The same intoxicated rebellion of the convict, in a world where "any independent manifestation of personality in the convict is regarded as a crime," finds a direct counterpart in the sudden and mad rebellion of the embittered serf or soldier. The psychology of irrational prison revolt deeply interested Dostoevsky, but the parameters of his investigation reached beyond the prison environment proper. This kind of transgression began in the oppressive and disordered conditions of Russian life. Goryanchikov describes one type of murderer who was often to be encountered:

This man lives quietly and peaceably. His lot is bitter, but he puts up with it. He may be a peasant, a house serf, a townsman or a soldier. Suddenly something snaps inside him; he can stand it no longer and he sticks a knife into his enemy and oppressor. Now here is where the strangeness sets in: for a time the man suddenly breaks all bounds. The first person he knifed was his oppressor, his enemy; although that was criminal, it was understandable; here there was a motive; but then he goes ahead and cuts up people who are not his enemies, cuts up the very first person who crosses his path, murders for amusement, because of some rudeness, in response to some glance, for a string of beads, or simply—"out of my way, don't cross my path, here I come!" It is precisely as though the man were drunk, precisely as though he were in a feverish delirium. It is as though, once having leaped beyond the boundary that was sacred for him, he now began to revel in the fact that nothing was sacred for him any more; as though he felt an urge at one bound to leap beyond all law and authority and to enjoy the most unbridled and limitless freedom, enjoy the thrill of horror which he could hardly not feel toward himself. He knows, moreover, that a terrible punishment awaits him. All this is perhaps similar to the sensation of a man who gazes down from a high tower into the depths below until finally he would be glad to hurl himself headlong down—as soon as possible, anything to put an end to it all! (I, 8)

With this kind of murderer, the motive for the crime—a bitter lot, privation, exploitation, humiliation—may at first seem incidental to some deeper psychological disorder. Goryanchikov distinguishes between an "understandable" criminal act and running amok. Yet running amok is also understandable from a certain point of view. Whatever the proclivity in the individual toward extreme behavior, both the sudden violent act and, even more, the wild uncontrollable outburst point back to a life of prolonged tension and suppression of feelings. Behind the frenzied overleaping of all restrictions of law and authority and the experience of "the most unbridled and limitless freedom" lies a human calamity. That calamity is poignantly expressed in a phrase that the convicts would repeat: " 'We are a beaten folk,' they used to say, 'our insides have been beaten out of us; that's why we cry out at nights.' " Such was the historical fate of the enserfed Russian people. And what came most frequently to the tongues of the convicts at night—curses, thieves' slang, mention of knives and axes—was the obverse, ominous, active night side of their passive daytime confession, "We are a beaten folk."

FREEDOM IN THE SHADOW OF THE DEAD HOUSE

The convict's experiments with freedom—his varied displays of personality and self-will, his excesses—are the despairing efforts of a defeated individual to reject his defeat. Through excess he affirms his right to possess what in fact has been denied him: self-determination and self-mastery. The sense of freedom he obtains is an illusion. Yet this illusion has psychological reality. If only for one moment, the convict *feels* free. This is one of Dostoevsky's fundamental insights in *House of the Dead*: the consciousness of freedom is at all times a psychological necessity for man; it is the equivalent of life. In this sense, the deprivation of freedom—in the deepest sense, the denial of movement—carries with it the threat of spiritual and physical death. "Our nature is one of movement," Pascal wrote in the *Pensées*. "To be completely still is to be dead."[2] The Underground Man, revolting against the stasis of rational utopia, puts this thought in his own way: "Twice two is four is not life, gentlemen, but the beginning of death."

Dostoevsky maintains that no conditions of material or social economic well-being can obliterate, or substitute for, man's need to be conscious of himself as free. He illustrated his thesis in the pages he prepared but did not insert in *House of the Dead*:

Try an experiment and build a palace. Furnish it with marble, paintings, gold, birds of paradise, hanging gardens, whatever you can think up. And then enter it. You may really never want to leave it. Perhaps, indeed, you never would leave it. Everything is there! As they say, "let well enough alone." But suddenly—a trifle! Your palace is encircled by a fence and you are told: "It's all yours! Enjoy it! But one thing only—do not take a single step out of it!" Well, you may be certain that at this very moment you will want to abandon your paradise and vault right over the fence. But that is not all! All this luxury, all this ease only makes your sufferings more acute. Precisely this luxury will become a torment to you. Yes, only one thing is missing: The trifle of liberty! the trifle of liberty and freedom! One is a man—and yet one is not: one's legs are fettered, a sharp picket fence surrounds you, and behind you is a soldier with a bayonet.[3]

"The deprivation of freedom," Dostoevsky later wrote, "is a most terrible torture which a man almost cannot bear."[4]

Much of the convict's life represents an effort, largely mental, to vault over the wall that surrounds him, to find a means of overcoming the boredom and deadly inertia of prison life. But the need for freedom is a need also for real movement. A man chained to a wall for years looks forward to the time when that part of his sentence will end and he will be permitted to walk about the prison yard, even though he knows that he will never be released from prison. The convict, in fact, is constantly dreaming of changing his lot or changing his fate. What is meant by "changing one's lot," a phrase used constantly by the convicts, is not the attainment of freedom from prison, however, for "the convict knows that this is almost impossible." He seeks rather to land in a different institution, stand trial again for a new crime, go to a new prison, anywhere, but not back to the old prison, which has become boring to him. This need for movement is behind the readiness of the unusually determined convict to risk all ("to risk anything is to risk everything") in an attempt to escape. The experience of others counsels against this attempt: the escapee is usually caught and his punishment made worse. But the hope of movement and change lures the convict. Only "one man in a hundred," of course, will attempt an escape (usually those who are awaiting sentence); but the other ninety-nine "will at least dream of how they might escape and where they might escape to; at least comfort their hearts with the mere desire to escape, the mere notion of its possibility."

Even the escape that is only vicariously experienced by the convict has enormous psychological meaning to him. The news of one escape, for example, was received by the convicts in prison with

> extraordinary hidden joy. The hearts of everybody seemed to leap.... Aside from the fact that this event interrupted the monotonous life of the prison and stirred up the anthill—an

escape, and an escape like this one, appealed to something
that all these souls shared in common, touched in them long
forgotten chords; something like hope, daring, the possibility
of changing one's lot stirred in all these hearts. "People, after
all, have really escaped; why not then...." And with this
thought everyone plucked up heart and looked at others chal-
lengingly. At any rate, everybody suddenly seemed proud,
and began to look condescendingly on the sergeants. (II, 9)

The attempted escape—like the roll of dice or the turn of the
roulette wheel—introduces a long wished-for uncertainty into the
convicts' lives. And for one moment the convicts, like excited
gamblers, speculate on whether the prison break will or will not
succeed. A feeling of life stirs in the prison community. But this
"romantic state of mind" soon dissipates with the news that the
escapees have been captured and will be returned to the prison by
evening. A feeling of vexation and gloom descends upon the convicts. Then an "impulse to jeer manifested itself," and, with
strange cruelty, the convicts "began to laugh, but now not at the
hunters but at the captured quarry; at first only a few laughed,
but then almost everybody, except a few serious and solid people
who thought for themselves and who could not be influenced by
jeers."

The jeers, the mocking laughter, of course, are self-directed. Here
is that bitter, self-lacerating delight in one's own misfortune of
which Goryanchikov, and later the Underground Man, speaks.
"There is so much inner self-mockery in the Russian character,"
Goryanchikov remarks later on in his narrative. Apropos of the
convicts' longing for freedom, their dreaming "about something
almost impossible," their hopes "so utterly without foundation as
almost to border on delirium," Goryanchikov observes that the
most zealous mockers of the convicts who dreamed of freedom
were precisely those convicts who went further in their own
hopes and dreams than the convicts they ridiculed. The mocking
of the convicts who failed to escape, then, is deeply tragic. The
captured convicts have betrayed the secret hopes of the convicts
in the most painful way possible. Most important of all, they

have confirmed them all again as perpetual losers in the game of fate.

Yet however "unrealizable the hopes" of the dreamer (and every convict, Goryanchikov insists, was a dreamer), "he could not renounce them." Despite the hopelessness of his situation, the convict "positively, instinctively, is unable to accept his fate as something definitive, final, as part of real life. Every convict feels that he is *not at home*, but, as it were, on a visit," "stopping over at an inn, or at a bivouac on some march." The convict, of course, is indeed "at home," though not where he would like to be. The pathos and pathology of his situation—and it is one that anticipates the plight of the Underground Man—lies in the contradiction between his knowledge that his situation is fixed and his instinctive refusal to accept that fact. This contradiction constitutes the dynamic of his tragic will to freedom.

Goryanchikov's designation of the prison, therefore, as a "living dead house" perfectly defines the convict's permanent state of psychological limbo: he is neither alive, that is, "living in the real sense," nor dead, that is, immune to all the instincts and passions for life. One convict expresses this condition in a mournful saying: "We are living, but are not even people, we are dead, but are not at rest" (*Zhili—ne liudi, pomerli—ne pokoiniki*). The condition of the convict, then, is precisely that of a man buried alive in a coffin, awakening in it, and pounding on the lid: "Reason might convince him that all his efforts were in vain. But the whole point here is that it is not a question of reason: it is a question of convulsions." The life of the convict, as Dostoevsky defines it, is the unending process of denying death.

The ways in which the convict experiences an illusion of life, or freedom, are varied, but with almost all of them, as Goryanchikov constantly notes, is associated the element of risk: "All this excess has its risks, which means that all this provides at least some illusion of life." The convict's craving for risk and his occasional experiments with freedom link him psychologically with Dostoevsky's gambler Aleksey Ivanovich, the Underground Man, and Raskolnikov. His bravado, squandering of money, card playing, smuggling of vodka, carousing, attempts to escape, and outbursts of violence all constitute an effort to introduce chance into the deadly status quo, an unconscious desire to determine and affirm his ontological status in a seemingly blind universe. The convict, then, is constantly gambling in one form or another, and this more than anything defines his condition of irresponsibility, despair, and desperate desire not to despair.

Risk, danger, and adventure have their positive, creative sides for the convict. The smuggler of vodka, for example, is almost the archetypal gambler. Smuggling is "a passion as strong as cardplaying," Goryanchikov notes. The smuggler sets his wits against the constant vigilance of the authorities. Failure brings severe punishment. Yet, gambler that he is, he is usually back at work after his punishment. "The smuggler works out of passion, out of a feeling of vocation. He is a poet in part. He risks everything, runs terrible dangers, dissembles, invents dodges, wriggles out of difficult situations; sometimes he even seems to act out of some kind of inspiration." The smuggler, in fact, is a kind of Odysseus of the lower depths—*polutropus*—the self-made, versatile man. But his passion conceals as well his Sisyphean fate—the fate of man doomed to move fruitlessly in an endless circle of effort, meaningless achievement, and frustration. The creativity of the smuggler is, like that of his comrades, tragic in nature.

Not without reason did Dostoevsky also refer in 1863 to the gambler-hero of his projected novel, *The Gambler*, as "a poet in his own way" and go on to describe his story of gambling "as a kind of hell."[5] The godless, fate-bound universe of the gambler Aleksey Ivanovich is but a metaphysical incarnation of the finite world of the dead house, which the convict in the depths of his nature refuses to accept. The convict's moment of inflation or intoxication, his challenge to his prison world (he shares the gambler's psychology of excess), is inevitably followed by a fall.

But what is pathological in the compulsive gambler such as Aleksey Ivanovich is normal metabolism in the convict. In the convict, the conventional "sick" or suicidal gesture is a healthy manifestation of life. His penchant for risk and excess emerges from his instinctive striving for self-preservation, his need for life and movement. His momentary states of intoxication with him-

self (in bravado, argument, drink, or violence) or of suspense (as
in the anticipation of the coming of a government inspector who
might improve his state, or in his excited speculation on whether
or not an escape will succeed) are, from one point of view, empty
surrogates for life; but from another, the convict's, point of view,
they are life itself. In these situations his emotional state is tonic
and restorative; it serves to rally his spirits and bolster his feeling
of hope and confidence in himself; it stimulates his entire organ-
ism and pushes it to the peak of activity and resistance—resistance both to his inert and terminal environment and to all those
internal forces (including the deductions of reason and logic) that
might incline him toward psychic fixity, inertia, and spiritual
death. "Our impulses, our spiritual activities," as George Eliot
remarks, "no more adjust themselves to the idea of their future
nullity, than the beating of our heart, or the irritability of our
muscles."[6]

"The teachings of true philosophy," Dostoevsky wrote in his
notebook at the time he was working on Notes from the Underground, "are the annihilation of inertia."[7] The essence of freedom
and life, as Dostoevsky pondered it in prison, is movement and
the constant process of mastering—or resisting the domination
of—environment. Yet these teachings of true philosophy clearly
presented Dostoevsky with a difficult paradox. The dialectic of
freedom that he discloses in House of the Dead is a tragic one.
Starting out in the dead house, with his legitimate "instinctive
yearnings" to be himself and to express his humiliated personality, the convict ends up, in the most extreme instance, in a raging
delirium in which his instincts take on a disfigured and tragic
form. Even the convict's most benign forms of self-expression—
if we exclude his morally liberating experience with the theatricals, that is, with art—draw largely upon primordial egoistic instincts and feelings.

At the conclusion of his study on the anthropological significance of the gambling impulse in human history Clemens J.
France noted that gambling "raises into the consciousness many
egoistic instincts and feelings": the craving for power, the desire
to dominate and humiliate one's fellow man, the love of conflict,

the desire to pit one's courage and power against another's, the satisfaction of being the object of jealousy, the pleasure derived from the exercise of cunning, deceit, and concealment, the interest in the "transcendent, the dark obscure beyond." France concludes with a thought that is strikingly in accord with Dostoevsky's own deep understanding of the drama of the convicts:

> This, together with the general uncertainty of the environment, together with the fluctuations between faith and in self and ever-recurring fear—plus the ever-present seeking for material gain—gives that tension which to many is the very definition of life. Can you find a half dozen deeper things in man than these, which form the very nucleus of this great play? It is, indeed, a simulation of life-feelings. But of life in which all pity and sympathy for man is absent; in which self is the all important center; in which to gain, to fight and to feel God is with you are all in all; in which each of these is intensified and exaggerated.[8]

France's melancholy observations are wholly applicable to Dostoevsky's tragic gamblers in hell, the Russian convicts. In the convicts' ceaseless but chiefly passive struggle with the enemy, Dostoevsky discovers a tragic unity of creative and destructive impulses. These impulses, while constituting the "very definition of life" as man has known it from time immemorial, nonetheless remain—as does everything else in the dead house—untouched by any vision, any higher values or impulse of love and self-sacrifice, honor, pity, or compassion. In prison, Goryanchikov writes, one "almost never observed friendly relations between the convicts; I do not mean general friendliness—there was little of that, to be sure—but the private kind."

2

How do we bridge the gap between man's egoistic instincts—all that Dostoevsky acknowledged to be organic to man's creative life—and the higher ethical ideals of Christianity? In his introduction to "A Series of Articles on Russian Literature" (1861)

Dostoevsky attempted to come to grips with this problem. The man of the people who learns to read and write, Dostoevsky notes, somehow "is involuntarily inclined to consider himself above his surrounding milieu of dark and illiterate people." He behaves in the same way, Dostoevsky observes ironically, as some of our "thinkers, progressives . . . literary generals." And echoing a central thought in *House of the Dead*, while at the same time anticipating some remarks in *Winter Notes*, Dostoevsky continues:

> In a word, we find the same phenomenon in all strata of society, only each stratum expresses itself in its own way. The need to affirm oneself, to distinguish oneself, to stand out, is a law of nature of every individual; it is its right, its essence, the law of its existence, which in the crude unstructured state of society manifests itself in the individual extremely crudely and even savagely, while in the community that has become cultivated it manifests itself in a morally-humane, conscious and completely free subordination of every person to the welfare of the whole community, and, the other way around, in the constant concern of the community itself to put the least constraint possible upon the rights of every individual.[9]

What is not clear is what happens to man's specifically egoistic desire to affirm himself. How does man's need to affirm his individuality accommodate itself to selfless striving? Is there not a permanent contradiction between these two states of being? Dostoevsky's approach to this problem in *Winter Notes* suggests that he was aware of a contradiction. Yet the contradiction does not deter him from outlining an obviously utopian solution. He recognized in the dead house—with its mortal antagonism between man and state, man and his environment, man and fate—a tragic metaphor for the human condition in a meaningless world. It was a metaphor for contemporary man's aggressive recoil from society and society's callous disregard for the dignity and welfare of the individual. It was a metaphor, in the worst case, for anti-utopia (not without reason did he refer to prison as a kind of "compulsory communism" in his letter to Fonvizina in 1854).

The confrontation between the individual and society or the community, Dostoevsky concluded, could never be resolved through any appeal to the egoistic element in man. Western socialism, he wrote in *Winter Notes*, seeks to "make" brotherhood and to seduce man with various promises of material gain or equity. But true brotherhood, Dostoevsky insists, must involve mutual renunciation of demands made on each other by the individual and society. It is absolutely impossible to make brotherhood:

> What is necessary is that it *make itself, that it be organic*, that it lie unconsciously in the nature of the tribe, in a word: in order for there to be a brotherly, loving element one must love. One must be drawn instinctively to brotherhood, to the community, to a state of concord, and drawn there in spite of all the barbarous crudity and ignorance that has taken root in the nation, in spite of centuries-old slavery and foreign invasions—in a word, the need for the brotherly community must be organic in man, he must have been born with it or have acquired such a habit from time immemorial. (ch. 6)[10]

Apropos of the lofty ideal of individual and society freely yielding their rights to one another, Dostoevsky exclaims: "Love one another and all the rest will come to you. There indeed is a real utopia for you, gentlemen! Everything is based on feeling, on that which is organic and not on reason." Indeed, we sense that Dostoevsky means what he says here when he uses the word "utopia" to define his ideal.

In *Winter Notes*, as we noted earlier, Dostoevsky insists that voluntary self-sacrifice is the "sign of the highest development of personality, of its supreme power, its absolute self-mastery, and its most complete freedom of its own will." Only a "highly developed individual," Dostoevsky maintains, could go to the stake or bear the cross for others. Such a person, conscious of his right to be what he is, can do nothing other than "give himself in his entirety so that others too may be equally autonomous and happy individuals. This is a law of nature; the normal man tends in that direction."

Yet where is this normal man to be found in society? Or is Dostoevsky's accent here on the word *tianet* (tends, leans toward), with its suggestion of limited achievement? And again, how do we reconcile the egoistic "I" and its desire to affirm itself with the urge to love and self-sacrifice? In short, how can man on earth pass from one state of being into another without being in contradiction with himself? Clearly such a movement is unrealistic, indeed utopian, as far as the masses of people are concerned. And in the privacy of his notebook in 1864 Dostoevsky bluntly and unambiguously acknowledged this. But at the same time— and this is what is noteworthy—he attempts to resolve the contradiction between the two laws of nature by positing a third.

"To love man *as oneself* according to the commandment of Christ is impossible. The law of personality is binding. *I* stands in the way. Only Christ can, because Christ is eternal, the centuries-old ideal toward which man strives and by a law of nature must strive." With the appearance of Christ, "the ideal of man in flesh," it becomes clear to man that the "highest development of personality" lies in the "annihilation of this *I*," in giving himself totally and selflessly to others. This "union of the *I* and *all* (obviously two extreme opposites)" is the "highest goal of personal development." But the ideal of Christlike love is impossible to achieve on earth. Therefore Dostoevsky envisages not an attainment of the ideal, but a permanent tension toward it on the part of developing, transitional man, a process of "achieving, struggling and—throughout all defeats—a refocusing upon the ideal and eternally struggling for it." "The whole history of mankind and, in part, of everyone separately, is only development, struggle, striving, and achievement of this goal." Christ himself, Dostoevsky notes, prophesied that "to the end of the world there will be struggle and development (the parable of the sword), because this is a law of nature, because on earth life is in development, while there—being."[11]

The third law of nature that Dostoevsky sets forth in his notebook, then, is the law of striving—the only law that can, as it were, set into dialectical motion, not resolve or do away with, the opposing tendencies of man's nature. "And thus, " Dostoevsky concludes:

> man strives on earth for an ideal that is *contrary* to his nature. When man does not fulfill the law of striving for the ideal, i.e. does not *through love* sacrifice his *I* to people or to another being (I and Masha [Dostoevsky's just deceased wife]), he experiences suffering and calls this state sin. And thus man must continually experience suffering, which is balanced by the divine pleasure in fulfillment of the Law, i.e. sacrifice. Precisely here is earthly equilibrium. Otherwise the Earth would be senseless.[12]

The third law of nature, the law of striving for the ideal, is the moving center of Dostoevsky's aesthetic and religious outlook; it is the structuring law of his artistic universe and of the people who inhabit it; it was the law that for him gave meaning to life on earth.

Dostoevsky's experiences in prison led him to look deeply into the nature of man. What he saw of man and the world did not please him. "The countenance of this world," he once remarked, "is not at all to my liking." As he confronted in the late 1850s and early 1860s the rising tide of rationalistic humanism, scientism, and belief in materialism and social utopia, he reached a conclusion that was voiced later by Zosima in *The Brothers Karamazov*: "To transform the world into something new, men must themselves turn onto another path psychologically." The first step on that path for Dostoevsky consisted in the acceptance of the teachings of Christ. But as he also demonstrates amply in the works that follow *House of the Dead*, "*I* stands in the way."

3

House of the Dead constitutes the great divide in Dostoevsky's works. It profoundly influenced every work that followed it, in particular his important writings in the first half of the 1860s— *Winter Notes, Notes from the Underground, Crime and Punish-*

ment, and *The Gambler*. It is the prologue, or *Urtext*, for *Notes from the Underground*, a work whose core endeavor is to explore the implications of the dead house for contemporary man and his rationalistic utopias. *Notes from the Underground* is marked dramatically by the ideological climate and polemics in the early 1860s. Indeed, it was called into being by Dostoevsky's need to respond to the rationalist and ethical utilitarian doctrines of the Russian "enlightenment" of his time.[13] But in its basic psychological and philosophical insights into the problem of beleaguered man, it is deeply rooted in, and indebted to, a master text: *House of the Dead*.

What indissolubly unites *House of the Dead* and *Notes from the Underground*, despite their radical differences in conception and design, is a vision of catastrophe. The essence of the dead house is man's reduction to the status of the living dead. The convict, confronted by the institutionalized suppression of his personality and freedom, sees all his vital energies pass into a desperate, unending, tragic struggle to maintain his sense of life. It is not only his objective loss of freedom that defines his situation, however, but his fatalistic orientation toward the world. The concomitant of that fatalism in the moral realm emerges as the absence of personal moral responsibility. In the face of universal misfortune, there are no guilty ones. The concept of a dead house contains the notion of a universe that is indeed dominated by fate and in which man is a helpless prey to the forces of accident.[14] Yet the convict's entire behavior represents an unconscious protest against the idea of a meaningless universe. It is a protest, however, in which he is not ennobled, but humiliated.

The Underground Man, too, is the convict of a metaphysical underground, or fate-bound universe. *Notes from the Underground* differs from *House of the Dead*, however, and represents a radical shift in Dostoevsky's attitude, in its metamorphosis of the mute, uneducated convict-hero into an embattled, educated, and highly articulate antihero. The ruling paradox of *Notes from the Underground* is that Dostoevsky assigns to his malevolent antihero the essentially heroic task of signaling to his rationalist and utilitarian interlocutors (and to the reader) the basic and irreconcilable conflicts between human nature and all social or philosophical constructs that deny free will. But in Dostoevsky's conception, the Underground Man is not a representative of an oppressed class like the Russian convict or "little man" of his earliest stories (despite his psychological identification with this type), but the representative of an educated class that has lost its religious faith and connections with the national folk element or people. He is a member of a generation (the 1840s) that has yielded to the Western rationalist and skeptical impulse and has been crippled by it. He argues brilliantly with the rationalists and exposes their theories of behavior governed by rational self-interest and utopian societies where free will would be obsolescent (part one). But he also emerges in his own example and history (parts one and two), in the tragedy of his rationalistic intellect and seemingly fate-bound existence, as an embodiment of the very rationalism he rejects. Herein lies the double force of Dostoevsky's polemic against the rationalists in *Notes from the Underground*.

In the "logical tangle" of his own thinking, the Underground Man can conceive only of a meaningless universe, one dominated by fate and the iron laws of nature. Through spite, irrational will, and caprice, he seeks freedom from these laws, laws that have been humiliating him "more than anything else." He seeks to escape from the inwardly experienced and outwardly perceived rule of determinism. He is without moral or spiritual foundation. His life is a treadmill motion—of rebellious will, on the one hand, which hopelessly declares war on reality, and of consciousness, on the other, which, rationalizing will's defeat, sanctions humiliating capitulation to that same reality.

The Underground Man, then, is not only devastated by the rationalistic principle; he is conscious of that devastation and continually in conflict with himself. The rationalists and utilitarians who step forth as the ideologists of the laws of nature and the prophets of a new utopia only exacerbate his sense of outrage and lead him to formulate an irrational will philosophy based upon his own experience. To those who confront him with the seemingly unanswerable certainties of "twice two is four," the laws of nature, the deductions of reason and mathematics, and the "stone wall," he replies:

> Good Lord, what have I got to do with the laws of nature and arithmetic when for some reason these laws and twice two don't please me? It goes without saying I shall not break through such a wall with my forehead, if I am really lacking in the strength to do it, but at the same time I am not going to reconcile myself with it just because it is a stone wall and I am lacking in strength. . . . Is it not much better to understand everything, to be conscious of everything, all impossibilities and stone walls; not to be reconciled to any of those impossibilities or stone walls if it disgusts you to be reconciled to them; and by way of the most inevitable logical combinations to reach the most repulsive conclusions on the eternal theme that even for the stone wall you are yourself somehow to blame, though again it is clear as day that you are by no means guilty, and therefore, silently and impotently grinding your teeth, with a voluptuous feeling to sink into inertia. (I, 3)

The Underground Man's objective compromise before the wall, yet his uncompromising subjective rebellion, which takes the form of a masochistic delight in suffering; his rationalization of his whole situation as one in which he is "guilty but without guilt before the laws of nature"—all this barely conceals, as in a medieval palimpsest, the subjective world of the tortured convict and his unending duel with the authorities. The convict, as we have seen, outwardly accepts what comes to him from the order about him as "ineluctable fact"; he takes into account "fate" and bends his back passively to the terrible beatings and blows of misfortune. But his compromise, like that of. the Underground Man, is part of "an established, passive but stubborn struggle" with the enemy. The convict, however, is unconscious of the tragic dialectic of this struggle, unaware of how the revolt of suffering expresses his profound anger and hatred. It is the Underground Man who brings the whole psychology of the revolt of suffering to the level of a conscious ideology and who identifies it as the last defensive weapon of absolutely abased personality.

The Underground Man recognizes that in "certain circumstances" man may insist on the "right to desire even the very stupid." He may, indeed, deliberately desire something that is harmful and stupid. And this caprice, the Underground Man believes, may be "more advantageous than any advantage, even in a case where it clearly is harmful to us and contradicts the most healthy conclusions of our reason about advantages, because in any case it preserves for us what is most important and dear, that is, our personality and our individuality. Indeed, some people maintain that this is even more precious than anything else for man." Dostoevsky's encounter with tragic circumstances in which man may perversely desire what is harmful took place in the dead house, where "almost any independent manifestation of personality" was regarded as a crime. In the face of the complete negation of his personality the convict often behaved in capricious and irrational ways; he insisted, as it were, upon the right to desire even the harmful and stupid.

For the Underground Man "certain circumstances" are not merely rationalistic utopia or dystopia; they are the whole tragic human condition. The tragedy of the underground, the tragedy of man's humiliation before the laws of nature, is not only a personal tragedy for him but the universal tragedy of man's alienation in a blind, meaningless universe. This universe is his prison, his underground. It is for this reason that he is certain that man will "never renounce real suffering, that is to say, destruction and chaos." Suffering, he insists, is man's defining trait. But in the end the Underground Man declares that he really does not stand "either for suffering or well-being. I stand for my own caprice and for its being guaranteed to me whenever I want it."

The Underground Man cannot escape the endless *perpetuum mobile* of his thought. Starting out with the legitimate idea of defending personality and individuality in certain circumstances by irrational, self-assertive acts, he ends up defending caprice and irrational will "whenever I want it." Indeed, in the whole development of his argument in part one—that is, in the realm of intellectual argument—and in the tragic dynamic of his relations with his school friends and the prostitute Liza in part two, we find an illustration of that very intoxication that Dostoevsky observed in the wild outbursts of convicts and in certain types of murderers: once having transgressed the boundary that had been sacred to them, these men are carried away and nothing will stop them. "And thus it would be better in every way not to bring him to this point," Goryanchikov remarks apropos of the convict's intoxicated rampage. "It would be more tranquil for everybody. Yes. But how is this to be done?" These lines could easily serve as an epigraph for *Notes from the Underground*. Although Dostoevsky's Christian solution is apparent in that work, the question, "Yes. But how?" speaks more directly to the tragic human condition that is exposed there.

The Underground Man finds man where he finds himself: at the "last wall," without hope or goal, yet—figuratively speaking—beating his head against that wall in order to affirm his existence. He posits a meaningless, treadmill existence: "The worker when he finishes his work at least receives his wages and goes to a tavern, ending up in the clink . . . but where can man go?" He suggests that "perhaps the whole aim mankind is striving to achieve on earth merely lies in this incessant process of achievement, in other words, in life itself, and not really in the attainment of any goal, which, it goes without saying, can be nothing more than twice two is four." Man is "instinctively afraid of reaching the goal and finishing the building he is erecting."

Dostoevsky certainly stands behind the Underground Man in his stress upon man's love of process and rejection of the idea of a terminal point to human strivings in life. The Underground Man's rejection of the "crystal palace," with its idea of final achievement and truth, echoes Dostoevsky's own ironical response to the Crystal Palace at the London World's Fair in *Winter Notes*: "Must we then accept all this indeed as the final truth and be rendered silent forever?" Yet the view of man laboring incessantly without any goal or purpose is one that Dostoevsky clearly did not share. Goryanchikov in *House of the Dead* recoils before the idea of Sisyphean, purposeless labor:

> The thought once occurred to me that if one's desire were to crush and destroy a man completely, punish him with the most frightful of punishments, it would be enough to give him work of a totally and utterly useless and nonsensical character. . . . If one compelled a convict, for example, to pour water from one bucket into another, and then back again into the first, to grind sand or to transfer a pile of earth from one spot to another and back again, I think he would hang himself after a few days or would commit a thousand crimes in order at least to die and in that way escape from such degradation, shame and torment. Of course, such punishment would amount to torture, revenge, and would be senseless, because it would not achieve any rational goal. But since some element of this kind of torture, senselessness, degradation and shame inevitably is a part of all compulsory labor, penal labor is incomparably more painful than any free labor just by virtue of the fact that it is compulsory. (I, 2)

The convict, Goryanchikov notes, works efficiently and rapidly when he is given a task that he can bring to a conclusion. In this he is like the free peasant who works better and longer because "he works for himself with a rational goal." Just as a rational, or tangible, goal makes the labor of a free peasant, or even a convict, meaningful and bearable, so in Dostoevsky's view man's strivings on earth are made meaningful by a spiritual goal or ideal. The concrete rational goal that man needs in his day-to-day labor if the labor is not to be torture and humiliation finds a direct counterpart in the spiritual and religious goal and ideal that he needs to make life meaningful. Striving in a world unillumined by lofty spiritual or religious ideals could only take on the tragic character of senseless forced labor in a penal camp. Such is the Sisyphean labor that the Underground Man projects for man in a universe where he has "no place to go." The Underground Man himself emerges in *Notes from the Underground* as a tragic convict of an age that has lost its faith, a prisoner doomed to the torture and humiliation of endless treadmill movement in a fate-bound universe of his own making.

Thus, like the Underground Man, Dostoevsky rejects the idea of a finite goal in human history, but unlike the Underground Man, he posits a transcendent ideal that makes man's striving on earth rational and meaningful. Man, Dostoevsky agrees, prefers movement to inertia. But, he insists, man seeks more than simply movement: he seeks spiritual meaning in his strivings. Dostoevsky thus affirms a kind of Christian existentialist outlook wherein striving for an ideal itself introduces a creative tension and meaning into human existence. In contrast, the Underground Man lays the groundwork in part one of his notes for an atheistic existential outlook. Unlike some existentialists in the twentieth century (philosophers such as Camus), however, the Underground Man is unable to imagine either himself or the orphaned, Sisyphean man as happy.[15]

Dostoevsky's Christian existentialist point of view and the stark, despairing, unidealized, near-atheistic point of view of the Underground Man constitute intimately related polarities in Dostoevsky's philosophical thought. They also reflect the constructive dialectic of his own spiritual struggle in the period of his imprisonment in Omsk. But *Notes from the Underground*, at least in the form that it exists today, does not clearly bring into the foreground this dialectic or play of polarities. The reason lies, in part at least, in the censoring it underwent. In a letter to his brother Mikhail in 1864 Dostoevsky complained of "frightful misprints" in the printed text as well as other damage by the censor:

> It really would have been better not to have printed the penultimate chapter (the main one where the very idea is expressed) [ch. x, part one] than to have printed it as it is, that is, with sentences thrown together and contradicting each other. But what is to be done! The swinish censors let pass those places where I ridiculed everything and blasphemed for show, but where I deduce from all this the need for faith and Christ—this is forbidden. Just who are these censors, are they in a conspiracy against the government or something?[16]

It seems quite likely that Dostoevsky gave oblique expression in the penultimate chapter of the uncensored part one of *Notes from the Underground* to the ideas he had privately set down in his notebook in 1864 on "transitional" man eternally striving on earth for the ideal embodied in Christ. Here, undoubtedly, Dostoevsky in some way disclosed the inner Christian character of the Underground Man's "crown of desires," his hidden "ideals," his yearning for a "crystal palace" at which one would not want to stick out one's tongue. "I myself know, as twice two is four," he remarks at the end of part one, "that it is not at all the underground which is better, but something else, something quite different, for which I thirst but which I can in no way find! To the devil with the underground!"[17] The uncensored chapter, finally, was the counterpart to chapter nine, part two, where the theme of love and self-sacrifice finds symbolic embodiment in Liza and in that epiphanic moment when she and the Underground Man embrace in tears. But Dostoevsky did not restore the original, uncensored pages in subsequent editions of *Notes from the Underground*, and the manuscript of that work is not extant.

In the very first lines of *House of the Dead* Goryanchikov observes that the prison was situated on the "very edge of the fortress next to the fortress wall." Peering through the cracks in the stockade at "God's world," one could see besides the wall "a tiny strip of sky, not the sky above the prison, but another, distant, free sky." Beyond the locked gates of the fortress was

> a bright, free world where people lived like everybody else. But from this side of the stockade that world appeared to one as a kind of impossible fairy tale. Here is a special world unlike anything else; here are special laws, clothes, customs and ways, and a living dead house—life as nowhere else, and a people apart. Now it is this special corner that I have undertaken to describe. (I, i)

Starting out with God's world and the distant, free sky, Dostoevsky steadily narrows his focus until it concentrates on that special corner, the prison, a world he will shortly refer to as

"hell—pitch darkness." The contrast between the outside and inside worlds serves at the very outset not only to accent the central
theme of freedom but to establish in the reader's mind a cosmic
frame for the prison recollections. In the course of his journey
with the narrator, the reader will never lose a sense of the existence of God's world, the macrocosm. The house of the living dead
is a special corner, but it will be presented and evaluated in terms
of the ethical and spiritual values that are associated with God's
world. What is important is not whether historical Russia beyond
the prison walls lives by these values; it does not, and the prison,
with its representatives from all corners of Russia, is clearly a
model for that Russia. What is important, rather, is that in these
opening passages Dostoevsky clearly establishes that vantage
point, those moral-spiritual heights, from which he will survey
his prison, his Russia, his hell, and address the conscience of man.
In this connection it is of signal importance that Dostoevsky has
chosen a narrator who has overcome his bitterness and despair
and *learned how to see.*

The situation is quite different in *Notes from the Underground.* In *House of the Dead* the objective narrator and resentful
convict constitute two separate entities. Here in *Notes* it is as
though the convict has stepped out of his frame to become the
narrator of his own story. His suffering ego (now the ego of the
Underground Man) becomes the center and circumference of
God's world. It eclipses God's world. He perceives the world
through a "crack in the floor," and what he perceives is the same
dark underground that surrounds him. The reader is without a
Virgil in this hell, and his journey is a difficult one. It is up to
him to discern the cosmic frame that encircles the seemingly
boundless underground.

It is not easy to locate Dostoevsky in *Notes from the Underground.* Even in *House of the Dead* Dostoevsky places a fictional
narrator (as well as an editor) between himself and his prison
experiences. He does not want to speak directly about these experiences. Goryanchikov is a distancing device. The Underground
man too is a distancing device, but one that operates in a different
way, affording the author a certain cover or complicity with his

narrator. The Underground Man carries on Dostoevsky's polemic: he discourses with a chilling frankness about human nature and history; he lashes out at the rationalists, the "stone wall," and the laws of nature. The Underground Man's tragedy, we come to recognize, is the central argument in Dostoevsky's polemic against the rationalists; but it is also part of the Underground Man's truth that Dostoevsky shares—up to a point. Again, however, it is for the reader to determine at what point the Underground Man's truth—the truth of a man buried alive— becomes unacceptable (as it indubitably does) to Dostoevsky. The reader, moreover, must decide whether truth in general, always shifting, even yields such a fixed point.

In allowing the Underground Man to dominate the stage, in investing him with the despair of his own darkest moments, and in turning that despair into a paradoxical weapon, Dostoevsky makes it difficult for the reader wholly to view the Underground Man in the didactic design of the work. At issue here is not Dostoevsky's intentional view—the organizing Christian perspective—but whether this view entirely succeeds in refuting those evidences of reality, that outlook on human nature and history that the Underground Man expresses and that, for him at least, validates a posture of despair. The underground paradoxicalist, in the final analysis, *lives*. He is more than a controlled satirical device by means of which Dostoevsky delivers a crushing blow to the rationalists of the 1860s and demonstrates the tragedy of a man divorced from the people and Christian faith. He is, also, quite clearly, a confession of the deep bitterness and despair that assailed Dostoevsky in the dead house. He is not simply a straw man whom Dostoevsky triumphantly exposes in a brilliant polemic. He also provides a certain viewpoint on human nature and history—a disorienting and pessimistic one—that is not easy to refute and that certainly must have been extremely difficult for Dostoevsky himself to transcend.

"You think I am one of those people who save souls, offer spiritual balm, put grief to flight?" Dostoevsky wrote to A. L. Ozhigina in 1878. "Sometimes people write this about me, but I know *for certain* that I am capable of instilling disillusionment and revulsion. I am not skilled in writing lullabies, though I have occasionally had a go at it. And, of course, many people demand nothing more than that they be lulled."[18] *Notes from the Underground* is not a lullaby; it is capable of instilling disillusionment, not because Dostoevsky stands with the Underground Man—he clearly does not—but because he could not stand at a sufficient distance from him.

In retrospect, the manner in which *Notes from the Underground* presented human reality did not wholly satisfy Dostoevsky. "It is really too gloomy," he remarked many years later. "*Es is schon ein überwundener Standpunkt.* Nowadays I *can* write in a more serene, conciliatory way."[19] At the time he was writing part two of *Notes from the Underground* he worried that "in its tone it is too strange, and the tone is harsh and wild."[20] Yet he nonetheless spoke of the work as "strong and frank; it will be the truth."[21] But did he feel in retrospect that its truth was more somber and divided than he had intended? Why did he not restore the pages that had been mangled by the censor? Did he feel, perhaps, that the Underground Man's blasphemy and ridicule had turned out to be more than something for show? Was he dissatisfied with the too tragic content of the work? Did the "external fatalism" of which he complained to his brother at the time he was writing lay too heavy a hand on *Notes from the Underground* itself? The prison recollections of Goryanchikov were broken in places by "some other narrative, some other kind of strange, terrible recollections jotted down in an uneven, convulsive sort of way"; they seemed to have been "written in madness." These recollections, we have suggested, might have dealt with Goryanchikov's domestic life. May we not, however, regard the Underground Man's reminiscences—in the figurative sense— as the other part of Goryanchikov's notebook? *Notes from the Underground*, in any case, lies deep in the shadow of the dead house.

Aristotelian Movement and Design in Part Two of *Notes from the Underground*

Cause and effect is like a wheel.
JAPANESE BUDDHIST PROVERB

"YOU KNOW what a *transition* is in music," Dostoevsky wrote his brother Mikhail on April 13, 1864. "That's exactly what we have here. In the first chapter we have what appears to be chatter," he writes with reference to part two of *Notes from the Underground* in its original tripartite division. "But suddenly this chatter resolves itself in the last two chapters in unexpected catastrophe."[1] Of course, there is an organic, indeed causal connection between the seeming chatter and the unexpected catastrophe. The catastrophe is unexpected only for the reader; for the author it is as inevitable, from the dramatic and ideological points of view, as the catastrophe of Sophocles' Oedipus or Melville's Ahab.

The action of part two in *Notes from the Underground* takes place at least sixteen years before the philosophizing of part one; the Underground Man is writing his "notes" in the early 1860s. The whole romantic and philosophically idealistic atmosphere of the Russian 1840s, moreover, has determined in a literal way the features of the Underground Man as a social type. Such people as the author of the notes, Dostoevsky writes in his footnote-preface to *Notes from the Underground*, "not only can but even must exist in our society, if we take into consideration the circumstances which led to the formation of our society." The Underground Man, he continues, "is one of the representatives of a generation still living. In this extract, entitled 'The Underground,' this person introduces himself, his outlook, and as it were seeks to explain those causes that have led, and were bound to lead to his appearance in our milieu." The writer of the notes has undergone an intellectual crisis since his experiences in the 1840s. Nonetheless, his psychological and philosophical self-exposition in part one reveal to us fundamental patterns of mind and behavior that made inevitable his tragic encounter with the prostitute Liza in the 1840s (the central episode in part two).

1

Dostoevsky's dominant message in *Notes from the Underground* (expressed directly in the penultimate chapter of part one in passages removed by the censor, and dramatically in the denouement of the Liza episode) is that only through Christian love and self-sacrifice—not through self-assertion, caprice, irrational rebellion, "twice two is five"—can man break the chain of an inwardly binding and blinding determinism. Only in this way can he escape from the underground and the deadly dominion of "twice two is four." Only in this way can he attain authentic freedom and the fullest expression of personality. The solution to man's problems is ethical, not numerical.

The self-defeating, destructive nature of irrational will philosophy, of underground "spite," is already evident in part one of *Notes from the Underground*, though the Underground Man's polemics with the rationalist-utilitarians, his tragic stance of revolt, tends to obscure the main figure in Dostoevsky's overall design. It is in part two, however, that the bankruptcy of irrational will philosophy is demonstrated with devastating force. The action here, taking place in the 1840s, forms an ironic commentary on the Underground Man's central notion that capricious behavior may preserve for us "what is most precious and important, namely, our personality and our individuality." The action begins precipitously on that fateful Thursday afternoon (chap. iii) when the Underground Man, unable to bear his solitude, decides to visit his old school friend Simonov; it includes the ill-fated dinner at the Hôtel de Paris, the mad ride to the brothel, the first encounter with Liza, the duel with Apollon at his flat, the second encounter with Liza, and, finally, after a moment of reversal and recognition, the catastrophe.

The movement toward catastrophe is singularly linear and Aristotelian: effect follows cause swiftly and relentlessly. Every attempt by the Underground Man to introduce the irrational into his life only locks him more firmly into an irreversible course that must end in catastrophe. Every attempt to affirm his independence and self-mastery only deepens his sense of psychological dependence and humiliation. In turn, his suffering arouses in him more frenzied attempts to win his freedom, that is, to achieve real self-mastery and self-determination. But his every bit of demonstrative self-expression, every flight of imagination or caprice, only further emphasizes the ineluctable character of the tragic action—his essential impotence in what appears to be, from his point of view, a closed, meaningless, and tyrannical universe.

2

The Underground Man's "bumping duel" with the officer on Nevsky Prospect (part two, chap. 1)—an episode that lies outside the main course of events in part two—is paradigmatic for the whole inner drama of the Underground Man. It exposes vividly to us the mechanism of the psychological experiment, always irrational in character, and the profound *un*freedom of the Underground Man in that experiment.

More than anything the Underground Man craves recognition, respect, a place in the universe. After periods of moral and spiritual stagnation he blindly goes out into the world seeking, as he puts it, "contradictions, contrasts." He is, in a manner of speaking, a gambler playing a game with reality; he is seeking identity or a sense of being in chance encounters with fate. But he himself is the little black ball. He goes into a tavern hoping to pick a quarrel and be thrown out of the window. But he is simply ignored. An officer at a billiard table—the game of billiards itself is symbolic—matter-of-factly moves him out of his way, simply does not notice him, treats him like "a fly." The Underground Man insists, "the quarrel . . . was in my hands": he had only to protest and be thrown out of the window. But he tells us that he "thought the matter over and preferred...rancorously to efface myself." "Even at that time," the Underground Man observes at the beginning of his discussion of this episode, "I carried the underground in my soul." "I preferred," he says; but the exercise

of choice is only apparent; it was for want of "moral courage,"
he observes, that he did not follow through his instinct to protest
and suffer the consequences. What is certain, however, is that the
quarrel was precisely *not* in his hands. Rather, he was caught up
in a hopeless quarrel with reality; he was a victim of compulsive
underground patterns of behavior.

The Underground Man's attempts at a bumping duel with the
offending officer—and the final duel itself on Nevsky Prospect—
form a sequel to the tavern scene. The officer, like all the other
great powers of Nevsky Prospect, is a social embodiment of those
laws of nature that have been humiliating the Underground Man,
moving relentlessly down upon him. Here on Nevsky Prospect
the Underground Man makes a despairing effort to assert his independence before the embodied force of history, to inject the
irrational into the everyday rational order or status quo. Through
caprice he seeks to break the chain of necessity that binds him, to
rise from a humiliated nonentity to a self-respecting, free entity,
to put himself, as he expresses it, on an equal "social footing"
with his enemy.

Dostoevsky underscores the unfree character of the Underground Man's challenge to Nevsky Prospect: "I was simply
drawn there at every possible opportunity," the Underground
Man observes. After the incident with the officer, he says, "I felt
drawn there more than ever." Then, after many failures to engineer a head-on collision with the army officer—" 'Why do you
always have to step aside first,' I would ask myself over and over
again in a state of crazy hysteria . . . 'there's no law about it, is
there?' "—victory finally comes to him, "suddenly," "unexpectedly," accidentally:

> The night before I had definitely determined not to carry out
> my ruinous intentions and to forget all about it, and with
> this goal I went out for the last time onto Nevsky Prospect
> just in order to find out how I would forget all about it.
> Suddenly, three paces from my enemy, I unexpectedly made
> up my mind, shut my eyes and—we knocked solidly against

each other shoulder to shoulder! I did not retreat an inch and passed him by absolutely on an equal footing! He didn't even look around and pretended that he did not notice; but he only pretended, I am certain of this. (II, 1)

Of course, the Underground Man's sense of victory and self-mastery is no more substantial or real than the pawnbroker's sense of victory in his bedside duel in "A Gentle Creature." There is only an illusion of victory, one that in both "duels" is based on a mistaken notion of the adversary's state of mind.

The duel with the army officer on Nevsky Prospect (unlike the bedside duel) has a strong comic, or tragicomic tonality; it does not end in catastrophe. Yet it serves to illustrate the completely abstract, psychological, and essentially amoral character of the Underground Man's experiments. Indeed, it reveals the wholly compulsive and reactive character of his human relations. The army officer—who could be anybody, who indeed is only one of the "generals, officers of the guards, hussars, and ladies" before whom the Underground Man gives way on Nevsky Prospect— only exists to test the lacerated ego of the Underground Man. The latter moves zombielike, as though in the grip of some external force; he is drawn to the field of action as though by a magnet; he goes into action only after he has decided not to take action, and then he does so unexpectedly and almost blindly. In all of these psychological details, the Underground Man's bumping duel anticipates the manner in which Raskolnikov will be drawn into his experiment. The mental atmosphere of fatality and the role of accident after a deceptive moment of freedom from obsession are some of the elements shared by the two experiments.

The irony of the bumping duel episode (like the irony of Raskolnikov's experiment) is clear: there are no manifestations of freedom of will here. Far from being a master of his fate, the Underground Man in his very efforts to declare his independence from the laws of nature demonstrates his enslavement to them.

3

The drama that is played out on the tragicomic plane of Nevsky Prospect—a Gogolian world where everything has the conventional and abstract character of a stage, where "all is deception"—is then replayed as tragedy in the Petersburg underground in the series of interlocking psychological duels that begin with the Underground Man's visit to his friend Simonov. In place of Nevsky Prospect, a relatively harmless testing ground, we have not only the Underground Man's noxious set of friends and the thoroughly obnoxious Apollon but the prostitute Liza. When the Underground Man "bumps into" Liza at the end of his descent into the Petersburg underworld—a descent that is everywhere accompanied by imagery and reminders of death—he will spiritually destroy her, just as decisively as Raskolnikov will physically destroy the old pawnbroker in his quest for self-definition.

The Underground Man's power duels with his old schoolmate Zverkov, deeply rooted in his personal history, result in one catastrophic humiliation after another. He plunges into the adventure at the Hôtel de Paris against his better reasoning, and with a premonition of disaster. "Of course, the best thing would have been not to go altogether," he observes at the threshold of this new encounter with "reality." "But that was now more than ever impossible: once I begin to be drawn into something, then I find myself totally drawn into it, head first." "I could no longer master myself," he recalls, "and I was shaking with fever." Dostoevsky repeatedly emphasizes that the Underground Man is not in control of his own fate. It is with a feeling that "after all everything is lost anyway" that he rushes down the stairs of the Hôtel de Paris in pursuit of his enemies.

As he rides off to the brothel in a sledge, the Underground Man is tremendously active in his imagination: slapping, biting, shoving, and spitting at his enemies. But on closer inspection, we recognize that this is the frenzied action of a man who in his romantic dreams is himself being beaten and dragged about and who is in the complete control of his tormentors. Protest here is as impotent as the groans of a man with a toothache (in the Underground Man's example in part one), who is conscious only that he is "completely enslaved" by his teeth.

In the midst of his romanticizing the Underground Man suddenly feels "terribly ashamed, so ashamed that I stopped the sledge, got out of it, and stood in the snow in the middle of the road." But he leaps back into the sledge again, remarking, "It's predestined, it's fate!" These words fully define his unfreedom. As he rushes on he realizes that there is no force that can stop the course of events: "All is lost." The sense of impending doom manifests itself everywhere. "Solitary street lamps flickered gloomily in the snowy haze like torches at a funeral." Like Euripides's Hippolytus in his carriage, the Underground Man is rushing along out of control—or rather, in the control of the very laws of nature, the implacable logic of humiliation and self-humiliation, of which he is victim. "Twice two is four is not life, gentlemen, but the beginning of death," the Underground Man declares in part one. Not surprisingly, he casts himself early in the sledge scene in the role of a drowning man. When he arrives at the brothel and discovers that his old school friends have departed, he breathes a sigh of relief: "It was as though I had almost been saved from death."

References to death accumulate on this journey into the underground, defining a psychological syndrome in which the impulses to destruction and self-destruction are closely interwoven. The Petersburg underground, the lower depths of Petersburg that the Underground Man inhabits and knows so well, is itself a kingdom of death. The Underground Man repeatedly evokes this funereal atmosphere in his first encounter with Liza in the brothel. With reference to a coffin carried up from a basement brothel, for example, he says, "Some day you too will die, you know, and you'll die just like that one died." He goes on to detail the terrible degradation and death of prostitutes like Liza: "Your name will disappear from the face of the earth just as though you had never been born! Filth and swamp, filth and swamp, and you may knock vainly at your coffin lid at night when the dead arise, crying, 'Let me live a bit in the world, good people! I lived—but I had no life.'" At one point he dilates upon the joys of parenthood, but this sentimental scene is bracketed by the funereal world of Petersburg. The Underground Man's preachment to Liza is outwardly lofty, didactic, detached; inwardly, it is murderous; it is a deep laceration and self-laceration. He emerges from the brothel terribly upset: "It was as though some kind of crime were weighing on my spirit."

The episode in which the Underground Man confronts Apollon the servant is central in defining the true nature of the Underground Man's universe and his place in it. Here the servant is master—and master, servant. Apollon is not a symbol of the god of sunlight, but a kind of plebeian god of death, a rat exterminator who also reads psalms over the dead. He is the precise embodiment of those deadly laws of nature that have been humiliating the Underground Man all his life. "He is my tormentor," the Underground Man says of Apollon. The Underground Man constantly rebels against the suave and contained servant (for example, by withholding his wages), but he always capitulates to him in the end. So, too, in the encounter with Apollon after his visit to the brothel, the Underground Man vainly tries to best Apollon:

> "Listen"—I cried to him—"Here is your money, you see it; there it is . . . but you won't get it, you-will-not-get-it until you come respectfully with bowed head and ask my forgiveness. Do you hear!" "That will never be!" he answered with a kind of unnatural self-confidence. "It shall be!" I screamed. . . . "I can lodge a complaint against you at the police station" [Apollon observes]. "Go and lodge your complaint!" I roared. "Go this very minute, this second! But all the same you are a tormentor, tormentor, tormentor!" But he only looked at me, then turned around and no longer listening to my screams went to his room with measured step. (II, 8)

The Underground Man follows Apollon to his quarters and repeats his demand. Apollon bursts out laughing and remarks, "Really you must be off your head."

This whole scene (part two, chap. viii) echoes in a parodic form the notion of the Underground Man (part one, chap. viii) that

nothing in the world would induce a man to give up his free will.
Even if "chaos and darkness and curses" could be calculated,
"well, man would deliberately go mad in order not to have reason
and to have his own way," in order to prove that he was "a man
not an organ-stop!" The Underground Man is indeed mad in this
scene. But it is a madness that attests more to the tragic bankruptcy of personality than to man's heroic defense of his independence. "The theme of this time is self-preservation," Max
Horkheimer comments in his *Eclipse of Reason*, "while there is
no self to preserve."[2] The words might well be applied to the
Underground Man.

"I'll kill him, I'll kill him," the Underground Man shrieks with
reference to Apollon. Madness and murder, of course, are closely
linked in the tragic drama of Dostoevsky's antihero. The Underground Man threatens to kill Apollon in the presence of Liza who
has just arrived on the scene. Even at this moment he senses the
outcome of his humiliation at the hands of Apollon: "I dimly felt
that she would pay dearly *for all this* . . . I was angry at myself,
but . . . a terrible anger against her suddenly flared up in my
heart; I could almost have killed her, it seemed." For the second
time, the Underground Man takes out his humiliation on Liza.
Indeed, on the moral-spiritual plane, he murders Liza. After his
cruel tirade, in which he savagely exposes the motives of his behavior toward her, the Underground Man remarks: "She turned
white as a handkerchief, wanted to say something, her lips
worked painfully, but she collapsed in a chair as though she had
been felled by an ax." This allusion to murder by ax is closely
linked with the more famous ax murder in *Crime and Punishment*.

The Underground Man's frenzied assault on Liza in this scene
is also a terrible self-laceration in which he exposes and tramples
upon his nature. His violent self-exposure—"I am the most disgusting, most ridiculous, most petty, most stupid, most envious
of all worms on earth"—arouses in Liza a feeling of pity and
compassion: "She suddenly leapt up from her chair in a kind of
irrepressible impulse and all drawn towards me but still feeling
timid and not daring to go further, extended her arms to me...."

It was here that my heart, too, gave way. Then she suddenly rushed to me, threw her arms around me and burst into tears. I too could not restrain myself and burst out sobbing as I never had before...."

This moment, a kind of "recognition scene" following a classic peripety or reversal in the drama of the Underground Man, points the way out of the underground. In the embrace of the Underground Man and Liza, all walls of ego and pride are dissolved. It is a moment of revelation of higher truth, an epiphany, a pietà. The fundamental problem of freedom posed in *Notes from the Underground* is not resolved here; it is dissolved. It is not twice two is four, not twice two is five, but reciprocal love that is the way out of the underground.

4

The Underground Man ironically affixes as an epigraph to chapter ix, part two, of his notes the two final lines from Nikolai Nekrasov's famous poem, "When from the darkness of error" (*Kogda iz mraka zabluzhden'ia*, 1846): "And my house, fearlessly and freely / As mistress you can enter now." (He cites the same lines in chapter viii of part two.) The narrator in this sentimental poem addresses a prostitute whom he would save from her fate. For the epigraph to part two of his notes as a whole, the Underground Man takes the opening fourteen lines from the same poem:

> When, from the darkness of error,
> I saved a fallen soul
> With a fervent word of conviction,
> And, laden with deep anguish,
> Wringing your hands you curses heaped
> Upon the vice that ensnared you;
>
> When you related to me the story
> Of everything that went before me,
> Lashing with memories
> An unheeding conscience;

And suddenly, covering your face with your hands,
Full of shame and horror
You burst into tears,
Aroused, shaken,—
Etc. etc. etc.

In the light of the Underground Man's half-cynical preachment
to Liza on the evils of her way of life and his invitation to her to
visit him, Nekrasov's words are first perceived by the reader in
the sarcastic vein of the Underground Man's "etc. etc. etc."—that
is, as mockery of the romantic and sentimental ethos of the 1840s,
an ironical comment on the tragedy of naive idealism. But the
moment of reversal and recognition in chapter ix reveals Nekrasov's poem in another light. These lines, and in particular the
unquoted stanza that immediately follows the verses cited in the
epigraph, now point to the tragedy of the Underground Man as
perceived by Liza, the one character in *Notes from the Underground* who embodies Dostoevsky's ethical message. The Underground Man's "etc. etc. etc." comes at a crucial point in Nekrasov's poem—just before the lines:

I shared your torments
I loved you passionately
And I swear that not for a moment did I offend
With the wretched thought of turning away.[3]

Dostoevsky's response to Nekrasov's poem was a complex one.
The sentimental pathos of this poem was not alien to Dostoevsky.
The theme of the "restoration of the fallen man," as Dostoevsky
wrote in 1861, is "the basic idea of all art of the nineteenth century. . . . It is a Christian and supremely moral idea." There can
be no question of any contempt on his part for the core ideal of
Nekrasov's poem. Dostoevsky, who later placed Nekrasov as poet
alongside of Pushkin and Lermontov, saw the weak and tragic side
of this naive, noble enthusiasm of the 1840s, an enthusiasm that
he himself had shared with Nekrasov. But he certainly did not
relate to the poem in the sarcastic vein of the Underground Man.
The "etc. etc. etc.," then, comes from the Underground Man, not

from Dostoevsky. The whole epigraph is part of the Underground Man's notes and cannot be regarded as an independent authorial comment.

Indeed, Dostoevsky brilliantly undercuts the Underground Man's sarcasm. In his final encounter with Liza the Underground Man finds himself in the role he had cast for her—a person in need of salvation. The reader perceives Nekrasov's poem in a new, tragic light: it is Liza who expresses the lofty idealistic ethos of Nekrasov's poem; it is Liza who invites the Underground Man—however naively—not into a bookish romantic realm, but into a contract of reciprocal love in the very depths of the Petersburg hell. It is the Underground Man, in contrast, who is full of shame and horror before himself, who, wringing his hands and savagely exposing himself, bursts into tears. At this point, the reader realizes that it is the Underground Man, not Dostoevsky, who has been savagely parodying Nekrasov and that he has now been trapped by his own parody. Dostoevsky did not abandon the idealistic ethos of the 1840s, but reinvested it with a tragic Christian content.

Nekrasov's poem, in the sarcastic interpretation of the Underground Man, thus cannot be viewed as Dostoevsky's epigraph to part two of Notes from the Underground. If there are (or were) any poems that might possibly be viewed as such an epigraph, they would be the poems by Apollon Maikov and Yakov P. Polonsky that Dostoevsky as editor of Epokha (the journal in which parts one and two of Notes from the Underground first appeared) juxtaposed with the opening pages of "The Underground" and "A Story Apropos of Falling Sleet."[4] On page 292 of Epokha (no. 4, 1864), opposite the title page of part two of the Underground Man's notes (with his epigraph), we find the following poem by Polonsky:

All that tormented me—all has been long ago
    Magnanimously forgiven,
    Or indifferently forgotten,
And if my heart were not broken,
Were not aching from weariness and wounds,—

I would think: all is a dream, all an illusion, all a
  deception.
Hopes have perished, tears have dried up—
    Passions that sprang up like storms
    Have vanished like fog.
And you who in bestowing dreams upon me
Were a comfort to my sick soul—
You have been carried away, like a cloud of rising dew
Disappearing behind a mountain.

Polonsky's poem, poignant and elegaic, emerges in the context
of part two of *Notes from the Underground* as a mournful comment on the idealism of the 1840s and the tragic drama of the
Underground Man and Liza. Had Dostoevsky adopted the Underground Man's sarcastic attitude toward Nekrasov's poem and its
romantic ethos, he would hardly have juxtaposed it with Polonsky's poem, a poem that shares the romantic pathos and emotional tone of Nekrasov's verse. Polonsky seems here to converse
with Nekrasov: he speaks of lost hopes, of the illusory, dreamlike,
deceptive character of the past; but he does so in pain, entirely
without mockery. Here in Polonsky's poem, viewed as an epigraph to part two, we begin to approach Dostoevsky's most intimate response to Nekrasov and the idealism of the 1840s—a response that is echoed later in the 1870s in his moving tributes to
Nekrasov and George Sand on the occasion of their deaths.[5]

5

The moment of illumination for the Underground Man is a transitory one. Immediately he is caught up again in a tragic dialectic
of self-will and humiliation. The sexual encounter that follows
his spiritual reconciliation with Liza turns out to be a fresh insult,
a final testimony—openly acknowledged by the Underground
Man—to his conception of love as the "right to tyrannize" and
be "morally superior."
  The last paragraph of *Notes from the Underground*, beginning
with the words, "even now, after all these years, it is with a

particularly *bad feeling* that I recall all this," almost has the character of a detached chorus. Here the disillusioned idealist looks back on his encounter with Liza through sixteen years of remorse and suffering with a crime on his conscience: "never, never shall I recall that moment indifferently." The words of the Underground Man are now devoid of pun or paradox. He distances himself from the events described and places his own tragedy in a general broadly cultural and social light. He defines himself as an antihero. His tone seems to approach the calm objectivity of Dostoevsky's footnote-preface, or prologue, to *Notes from the Underground*. A change in the Underground Man's consciousness has taken place in sixteen or more years. (Indeed, we cannot properly analyze the notes of the Underground Man without taking into account the shift that has occurred in his thinking since the 1840s.) What he failed to achieve in life he has to a considerable extent gained in his notes: perspective on himself and his dilemma, a perception of himself as morally and socially bankrupt.

It was, in part, to seek "relief" from his "oppressive memory," perhaps even to "become good and honorable" through the "labor" of writing, that the Underground Man put down his recollections. And, indeed, something unexpected happened in the process of writing. "I made a mistake, I think, in beginning to write," he remarks at the conclusion of his notes. "At any rate, I have felt ashamed all the while I was writing this story [*povest'*]; consequently this is no longer literature, but a corrective punishment."[6] The Underground Man gives ironical emphasis to the word "story": these are not entertaining or escapist stories; they are unadorned reality; they are shameful tragedy. This is not the reader's kind of literature (the Underground Man's irony is plain). This is not a romantic story: the posturing hero and his play-acting have been brutally exposed. "A novel must have a hero, but here all the features of an antihero have been *deliberately* gathered together, and, chiefly, all this will produce a most unpleasant impression because we are all divorced from life . . . so much so that we sometimes feel a sort of disgust for the real 'living life' . . . and we are all agreed that life in books is better." (The ironical narrative voice of Dostoevsky merges with the voice

of the Underground Man in this final passage.) There is, indeed,
nothing invented in the Underground Man's reminiscences. The
sentimental-romantic "hero" of the 1840s—in fact, the whole
ethos of romanticism—has been presented in the bitter perspective of the disillusioned idealist. What the Underground Man declares at the end of part one, after admitting that he made up the
concluding speech of his imaginary critics, could serve as an epigraph to his reminiscences: "But it is really the only thing I did
invent."

The Underground Man's impulse to play with the material of
his life and his penchant for the phrase may be felt in the notes.
But this impulse to play, or "tell a story," to evade the true sense
of his life, like all of the Underground Man's capricious attempts
to escape his underground fate, does not succeed. He cannot evade
the truth. "I shall not attempt any order or system," the Underground Man remarks on the threshold of part two with characteristic bravado and caprice. "I shall put down whatever I remember." Yet his reminiscences, like his philosophical discourse, are
no more free from order or system than he is free from the laws
of nature.

We must not confuse the Underground Man's subjective rejection of system, order, evolution, or historicism with the objective
conditions of his enslavement to order. His impulse to put down
his notes cannot be separated from his recollection of the episode
with Liza that has been oppressing him for "some time." It cannot be separated from a broader effort to understand himself and
his whole tragedy—or in the words of Dostoevsky, to "explain
those causes which not only led but were bound to lead to his
appearance in our midst." The Underground Man, much like the
pawnbroker in "A Gentle Creature," is caught up in a dialectic of
guilt that relentlessly drives him toward the truth. Beneath the
surface of his seemingly casual notes, as beneath the surface of
the seemingly random adventures of the hero of the 1840s, we
observe a strict "psychological sequence" (a phrase Dostoevsky
uses to describe the undercurrent in the pawnbroker's ruminations), a tragic system and order.

"Within the action," Aristotle remarks in his *Poetics*, "there must be nothing irrational." And again, with respect to plot: "Everything irrational should, if possible, be excluded."[7] The irony of the action in part two of *Notes from the Underground*— and, indeed, in the whole life of the Underground Man—is that the Underground Man himself, contrary to all his intentions, brings about these model Aristotelian conditions in the drama of his life. He puts a fatal order into the episodic plot of his life; he creates his own tragic necessity out of the accidental matter of his everyday life and encounters. The purely literary expression of this fatal ordering of the episodic plot of his life can be found in the notes of the Underground Man—perhaps the most connected, sequential, and tragically coherent "notes" ever written in any language.

By the end of his reminiscences we realize what is already evident from the Underground Man's exposition of his irrational will philosophy in part one: that he has been caught in a master plot that is historical, linear, and Aristotelian, a plot that he seeks, always vainly, to foil. We see him, in short, as he sees Liza—as entangled in a chain that grows tighter the more he seeks to escape from it:

> Though I may be degrading and defiling myself, still I'm not anybody's slave; it's here for a moment, and then off again, and you've seen the last of me. I shake it off and am a different man. But you are a slave from the very start. Yes, a slave! You give up everything, your whole freedom. And even if you should want to break these chains later on you won't be able to; they will only entangle you more and more tightly. That's the kind of cursed chain it is. I know that kind. And I'm not going to speak of anything else, for you wouldn't understand anyway, I dare say. (II, 6)

The Underground Man is the embodiment of irrational behavior. Yet the singularity of his underground is that in it absolute chance is indistinguishable from absolute necessity. His play with chance only masks a surrender to the organized force of a self-conceived fate. In this we find the central message of Dostoevsky. Man, he believed, renouncing faith in God—that is, faith in a coherent Christian universe—must inevitably confront the world as blind fate. Never was a Dostoevsky hero (unless it be Fyodor Karamazov) more railroaded by fate, by the uncontrollable dynamics of his inner being, than the Underground Man. As we see him in part two in his own representation of his life—a drama he understands very well—nothing remains episodic. Every attempt to introduce the irrational into his life and to bring an illusion of authentic freedom, choice, self-determination, every attempt to play with the plot of his life only further underscores his subjection to the power of blind destiny. There is a precipitous movement toward catastrophe, a moment of reversal, and then disaster, followed by a choral response. Borrowing from Aristotle's *Poetics*, we might say that the final reversal, or recognition, arose from the internal structure of the plot, and that this reversal produced "pity and fear," and that "actions producing these effects are those which, by our definition, tragedy represents."[8]

Yet *Notes from the Underground* is not Aristotelian tragedy any more than is *Crime and Punishment*, nor can Raskolnikov and least of all the Underground Man stand in for heroic Promethean types.[9] The Underground Man and Raskolnikov conceive of themselves as victims of fate; but their real tragedy, in Dostoevsky's explicitly Christian outlook, is their despair. W. H. Auden has written that at the end of a Greek tragedy we say, "What a pity it had to be this way"; while at the end of a Christian tragedy we say, "What a pity it had to be this way when it might have been otherwise."[10] Dostoevsky might have directed these final words to the tragedy of the Underground Man. But they would not have prevented him from introducing into his Christian universe the strict laws of ancient tragedy—odious laws, in his view—which become operative whenever man fails to discover in his inner life the governing principles of Christian freedom: love and self-sacrifice.

After his crucial definition of himself as an antihero and his critique of society the Underground Man concludes his notes. "But enough," he writes, "I do not want to write any more 'from the Underground....' " "However, this is still not the end of the 'notes' of this paradoxicalist," Dostoevsky observes in a final passage detached from the body of the notes. "He could not restrain himself and went on writing."[11] There is certainly no doubt that the Underground Man was capable of writing on and on. There is also no doubt that the notes of the Underground Man—what Dostoevsky has entitled *Notes from the Underground*—constitute a unified structure. The drama that unfolds in part two has a beginning, middle, and end. The author of this work, though not its protagonist, is Dostoevsky. His final comment—"But it seems to us, too, that one can also stop here"—suggests that the Underground Man's desire to call a halt to his writing represented an intuitive understanding of the inner dynamics of his own drama. Dostoevsky's comment signals, as a kind of authorial punctuation, that on the dramatic and ideological planes this final chapter of the Underground Man's notes to all intents and purposes is terminal.

Philosophical Pro and Contra in Part One of *Crime and Punishment*

I suffered these deeds more than I acted them.
Sophocles, Oedipus at Colonus

THE BURDEN OF part one of *Crime and Punishment* is the dialectic of consciousness in Raskolnikov. This dialectic propels him to crime and, in so doing, uncovers for the reader the motives that lead him to crime, motives deeply rooted in his character and in his efforts to come to terms with the necessities of his existence. Leo Tolstoy grasped the essence of the matter in "Why Men Stupefy Themselves" (1890), writing that Raskolnikov lived his "true life" not when he murdered the old pawnbroker and her sister and when he was living in a strange flat planning murder, but

> when he was not even thinking about the old woman, but lying on the sofa at home, deliberating not at all about the old woman and not even about whether it was permissible or not permissible at the will of one man to wipe off from the face of the earth an unnecessary and harmful person, but was deliberating about whether or not he ought to live in Petersburg, whether or not he ought to take money from his mother, and about other questions having no bearing at all on the old woman. And precisely at that time, in that region—quite independent of animal activities—the question of whether or not he would kill the old woman was decided.[1]

If the fundamental matters or issues over which Raskolnikov deliberates are immediate and practical ones, his responses to these matters have broad implications that have direct bearing on the crime. Here we may rightly speak of a moral-philosophical pro and contra.

Part one begins with Raskolnikov's test visit to the old pawnbroker and ends with the visit in which he murders the old lady and, incidentally, her sister Lizaveta. The murder itself is also, in a deeper sense, a test or experiment set up to determine whether he has the right to transgress. He starts out in a state of indecision or irresolution and ends with a decisive action—murder—an apparent resolution of his initial indecision. But does the murder really constitute a resolution of Raskolnikov's dialectic? Does he really "decide" to murder the pawnbroker? Or does not chance, rather, serve to mask his failure to decide with his whole being? Is he master or slave here?

The final line of part one alone suggests the answer: "Bits and fragments of some kind of thoughts swarmed about in his head, but he was unable to get hold of a single one of them, he could not concentrate upon a single one of them in spite of all his efforts." Raskolnikov's dialectic of consciousness continues to be dramatized in his thoughts, actions, and relationships after the murder (parts two-six). It is only in the epilogue (chap. 2) that this dialectic is dissolved—not resolved—on a new, developing plane of consciousness. Raskolnikov's inability to focus his thoughts on anything, his inability consciously to resolve anything after his reconciliation with Sonya in the epilogue ("he was simply feeling") constitutes a qualitatively different state of consciousness from the chaos of mind he experienced right after the murder. These two moments of consciousness are in almost symmetrical opposition. The movement or shift from one to the other constitutes the movement in Raskolnikov's consciousness from hate (unfreedom) to love (freedom).

The movement from test to test, from rehearsal to experimental crime, from theory to practice, is marked by a constant struggle and debate on all levels of Raskolnikov's consciousness. Each episode—the meeting with Marmeladov and his family, Raskolnikov's reading of his mother's letter with its account of family affairs, his encounter with the drunken and bedraggled girl and the policeman, and his dream of the beating of the mare—is marked by a double movement: sympathy and disgust, attraction and recoil. Each episode attests to what has been called Raskolnikov's "moral maximalism." Yet each also attests to a deepening skepticism and despair on the part of Raskolnikov, a tragic tension toward crime in both a psychological and a philosophical sense.

The immediate issues of this pro and contra are nothing more or less than injustice and human suffering and the question of how a person shall respond to them. But the deeper evolving question—on which turns Raskolnikov's ultimate response to this injustice and suffering—is a judgment of mankind: is man a morally viable creature or simply and irredeemably bad? Do man and the world make sense? Raskolnikov's murder of the old pawnbroker is the final expression of the movement of his dialectic toward a tragic judgment of man and society. The ideological concomitant of his paralysis of moral will (the scenes following his chance encounter on the street with Lizaveta) is a rationalistic humanism that is unable to come to terms with evil in human existence. Lacking larger spiritual dimensions, this ideology ends by postulating incoherence and chaos in man and his environment and, in turn, in a universe in which man is a victim of fate.

The stark realism and pathos of Marmeladov's and his family's life at first cools the hot and agitated Raskolnikov. The novel rises to its first epiphany in the tavern: out of the troubled posturing and grotesquerie of Marmeladov comes a mighty prose poem of love, compassion, and forgiveness (echoing Luke 7:36-50). It constitutes an antithesis to Raskolnikov's proud and rebellious anger. Raskolnikov visits the Marmeladovs, responds warmly to them, and leaves some money behind. But the scene of misery evokes incredulity and despair in him. If Marmeladov's "confession," which opens chapter two, accents the central redemptive note in *Crime and Punishment*, the final lines of the chapter stress antithetical notes of despair and damnation. The sight of human degradation so overwhelms Raskolnikov that fundamental doubts about man and human nature are called forth in him. Stunned that people can live in this way, that indignity, vulgarity, and discord can become an accepted part of man's life, Raskolnikov explodes: "Man can get used to anything—the scoundrel!" These strange ruminations follow: "But what if man really isn't a *scoundrel*, man in general, I mean, the whole human race; if he is not, that means that all the rest is prejudice, just imaginary fears, and there are no barriers, and that is as it should be!'' These lines are crucial in posing the underlying moral and philosophical issues of *Crime and Punishment*.

The motif of adaptation is heard throughout Dostoevsky's works—from *Poor Folk* through *House of the Dead* to *The Brothers Karamazov*. It attests, from one point of view, to human endurance, the will to survive. Yet from another view, it expresses a deeply tragic idea, implying that man will yield feebly to suffering, oppression, injustice, unfreedom, in short, to triumphant evil. Man in this conception is man as the Grand Inquisitor finds him: weak and vile. Such adaptation arouses only contempt in the rebellious Raskolnikov.

Raskolnikov's rebellion implies a positive standard or norm of human behavior, morality, life. Merely to speak of man as a scoundrel for adapting to evil is to posit another ideal, to affirm by implication that man ought not to yield weakly to degradation and evil. But the thought that occurs to Raskolnikov at this point is one that links him directly with the Grand Inquisitor. We may paraphrase it as follows: what if all this vile adaptation to evil is not a deviation from a norm; that is, what if villainy pure and simple is, *ab ovo*, the human condition? What if, as Raskolnikov later puts it, every one of the people scurrying about on the streets ''is a scoundrel and predator by his very nature''? If such be the case, if man is truly defective by nature, then all our moral systems, standards, injunctions, pejorative epithets (the word ''scoundrel'' itself) are senseless prejudices and imaginary fears. It follows that if human nature is, morally speaking, an empty plain, then ''there are no barriers''; all is permissible, ''and that is as it should be!''

Raskolnikov's intense moral concerns provide evidence that man is not a scoundrel and predator by nature. And it is the idea of adaptation as testimony to man's endurance and will to live that is ultimately accepted by Raskolnikov. Thus, Raskolnikov, after an encounter with prostitutes on the streets, declares that it would be better to live an eternity on a ''square yard of space'' than to die: ''To live and to live and to live! No matter how you live, if only to live! How true that is! God, how true! What a scoundrel man is!" "And he's a scoundrel who calls him a scoundrel for that," he added a minute later.

Svidrigailov, the character who comes closest to an embodiment of the principle that all is permissible, also poses the question that Raskolnikov is deliberating, though more dispassionately and cynically. Defending himself against the charges that he persecuted Dunya in his home, he observes:

> Now let's just assume, now, that I, too, am a man, *et nihil humanum*...in a word, that I am capable of being attracted and falling in love (which, of course, doesn't happen according to our own will), then everything can be explained in the most natural way. The whole question is: am I a monster or am I myself a victim? Well, and what if I am a victim?
> (IV, 1)

Barely concealed in Svidrigailov's jocular question is the issue of human nature. The underlying ethical and philosophical import of his question—"Am I a monster or am I myself a victim?"—is clear: does a consideration of his acts—man's acts ("Just assume, now, that I, too, am a man")—fall under the rubric of ethics or the laws of nature? Are we really responsible for our behavior? Are the morally pejorative epithets "monster" or "scoundrel" really in order? Are we not simply creatures of nature?

Svidrigailov, we note, likes to appeal to natural tendencies. Very much like the Marquis de Sade's alter egos Clement (*Justine*, 1791) or Dolmance (*La philosophie dans le boudoir*, 1795), he appeals to nature as a reason for disposing entirely of moral categories or judgment. "In this debauchery, at least, there is something constant, based even on nature, and not subject to fantasy," Svidrigailov remarks in his last conversation with Raskolnikov. Indeed, Svidrigailov's conception of man would appear to be wholly biological—"Now I pin all my hope on anatomy alone, by God!"—a point of view that certainly undercuts any concept of personal responsibility.

The concept *homo sum, et nihil humanum a me alienum puto* ("I am a man and nothing human is alien to me") was for Dostoevsky a profoundly moral concept, implying the obligation squarely to confront human reality. "Man on the surface of the earth does not have the right to turn away and ignore what is taking place on earth," he wrote in a letter in 1871, "and there are lofty *moral* reasons for this: *homo sum et nihil humanum...etc.*"[2] Svidrigailov, however, takes the concept as an apologia for doing whatever he pleases. To be a man, in his view, is to be open to all that is in nature, that is, to nature in himself; it is to be in the power of nature (if not to *be* nature) and therefore not to be responsible. But his hope for salvation through Dunya and his final suicide are evidence that his confidence in anatomy has its cracks and fissures. In the final analysis, then, even for Svidrigailov (though infinitely more so for Raskolnikov), the question, "monster or victim?"—is he morally responsible or free to commit all vilenesses?—is a fateful question. Posing this question, in Dostoevsky's view, distinguishes man, even the Svidrigailovs, from Sade's natural man.

The problem of human nature raised by Raskolnikov and Svidrigailov, and lived out in their life dramas, is expressed directly by Ivan Karamazov. Apropos of his belief that man is incapable of Christian love, Ivan observes: "The real issue is whether all this comes about because of bad elements in people's character or simply because that is their nature." Raskolnikov's pessimistic conjecture at the conclusion of chapter two (and, even more, the evidence of his dream in chapter five) can be compared with Ivan's bitter judgment of man in his famous rebellion. It can be described as the opening, and dominant motif, in a prelude to murder. The whole of *Crime and Punishment* is an effort to refute this judgment of man, to provide an answer, through Raskolnikov himself, to this tragic conjecture. The action in part one, however, is moved by the almost syllogistic logic of Raskolnikov's pessimistic supposition.

Chapter two of part one contains the extreme moral and philosophical polarities of the novel: affirmation of both the principle of love, compassion, and freedom (which will ultimately embrace Raskolnikov through Sonya) and the principle of hate, the pessimistic view of man as a scoundrel by nature, the projection of the idea that all is permissible. The events of this chapter bring Raskolnikov full circle from compassion to nihilistic rage. Exposed is that realm of underground, ambivalent consciousness where love is compounded of pain and hate, of frustrated love; where extreme compassion for suffering and the good is transmuted into a contempt for man; where that contempt, finally, signals despair with love and the good, and nourishes the urge for violence and the sick craving for power that is born not only from an acute sense of injustice but from a tragic feeling of real helplessness and irreversible humiliation.

Here is our first contact with the matrix of Raskolnikov's "theoretical" crime, with the responses that will find explicit formulation in Raskolnikov's article and arguments. Here is the protean core of those shifting, seemingly contradictory motives: the "idea of Rastignac" (altruistic, utilitarian crime), as Dostoevsky put it, and the idea of Napoleon (triumph over the "anthill," and so forth). Here we see how the raw material of social and psychological experience begins to generalize into a social and philosophical point of view—and ultimately, into those ideas of Raskolnikov's that will tragically act back again upon life and experience.

The same cyclical pattern we have noted in chapter two dominates chapter three. The chapter opens on a subtle note that disputes the depressing and abstract conjectures of Raskolnikov. Nastasya, the servant girl, brings him soup, chattering about food and about Raskolnikov's affairs. She is the epitome of a simplicity, warmth, and goodness that cannot be gainsaid. She is a kind of spiritual harbinger of Raskolnikov's mother, whose letter he receives. This letter, like Raskolnikov's encounter with Marmeladov and his family, evokes a picture of self-sacrificing people who are helpless before the evil in the world, before the Luzhins and Svidrigailovs. Raskolnikov begins reading the letter with a kiss ("he quickly raised it to his lips and kissed it"), but he ends it with "an angry, bilious, malignant smile" curling about his lips. The letter produces the same ugly sensations in him as the scene in the Marmeladov household, the same sympathy and compassion turning into rage and rebellion. Raskolnikov later goes out for a walk as though "drunk," his shapeless body reflecting his inner rage and distress. His initial readiness to protect a helpless girl from the attentions of a pursuing stranger on the street is replaced almost immediately by a sense of revulsion, a raging amoral anger. Starting out with a gesture of goodness, Raskolnikov characteristically ends by abandoning the girl to evil in a classical gesture of underground malice.

Raskolnikov's basic skepticism about man and human nature emerges in his reflections on his mother, his sister Dunya, and their critical situation. He comprehends the sacrifice his mother and sister make for him as an ascent to Golgotha but in bitterness casts them among the innocents, those "Schilleresque 'beautiful souls' " who wave the truth away, who would rather not admit the vile truth about man. Dunya, Raskolnikov realizes, is prepared to suppress her moral feelings for the one she loves, for him. He almost venomously rejects the idea of this sacrifice of her freedom, peace of mind, conscience. It is a rejection, of course, of the Christian spirit of sacrifice that he finds in Sonya as well as in Dunya. "Dear little Sonya, Sonya Marmeladov, eternal Sonya, while the world lasts! But this sacrifice, this sacrifice, have you taken the measure of your sacrifice, both of you? Have you really? Do you have the strength? Will it be of any use? Is it wise and reasonable?" Raskolnikov's choice of words is symptomatic of his ideological illness. To the impulses of the heart he opposes utility, scales, self-interest. And this, of course, is rich soil for the cultivation of ideas of utilitarian crime. The appeal of utilitarian ethics emerges from a despairing sense of the uselessness of all human striving for justice and truth, from a sense of the vileness of human nature and a conviction that "people won't change, and nobody can remake them, and it's not worth wasting the effort over it!"

Raskolnikov rightly understands that what he rejects (the principle of love and self-sacrifice) is eternal. He rejects it in part out of despair with evil. But he also rejects it in the name of a false principle of self-affirmation and "triumph over the whole anthill," a false principle of freedom: "And I know now, Sonya, that whoever is strong and self-confident in mind and spirit is their master!" Raskolnikov's rejection of his family's spirit of self-sacrifice reflects, at least in part, his own distance from Dostoevsky's concept of self-sacrifice and, chiefly, from the ideal of an authentic freedom that such a spirit of self-sacrifice implies.

Raskolnikov's powerful impulses to good and his high potential for self-sacrifice are short-circuited by a sense of overwhelming injustice and evil, of absurd imbalance in the scales of good and evil. In the face of the world's misery, the rapacious Svidrigailovs and Luzhins, the pitiful and loathesome spectacle of man-adapting, Raskolnikov rebels: "I don't want your sacrifice, Dunya, I don't want it, mother dear! It shall not be as long as I live, it shall not, shall not! I won't accept it!"

Dostoevsky uses the word "anguish" to express Raskolnikov's state of mind here. His rebellion, indeed, looks back on the revolt of the Underground Man and forward to Ivan Karamazov's rebellion against divine harmony (if it be based on the innocent suffering of children). Deeply responsive to human suffering, Ivan, in his indignation, returns to God his "ticket" to future harmony. Yet this same humanitarian revolt, with its despair in a meaningful universe, leads him unconsciously to sanction the murder of his father. This same ethical paradox lies at the root of Raskolnikov's crime. Starting out with love and compassion for the "eternal" Sonya and for Dunya and his mother, Raskolnikov ends up with a rejection of love and sacrifice and with a rage at evil—a rage that itself becomes disfigured and evil. This rage, ethically motivated in its origins, deforms Raskolnikov and accentuates in him the elements of sick pride and self-will.

In this state of mind, Raskolnikov's thought is led back to his projected crime. "It shall not come to that," he insists: he would be "robbing" his family; but what can he do? The letter from his mother exposes his helplessness in a realm that is dear to him, drives him onto the path of action. He must either act, he feels, or "obediently" accept his fate, strangle everything in himself, "renounce every right to act, to live and to love!" Suddenly a thought flashes through his mind. It is the "monstrous vision" (*bezobraznaia mechta*) of his crime, and it is now taking on "some new and terrifying, quite unfamiliar form." This new and threatening form is revealed to him in his "terrible dream" or nightmare in chapter five: the beating and killing of the mare.

Raskolnikov's dream, echoing earlier incidents, situations, and emotional experience, is a psychological metaphor in which we can distinguish the conflicting responses of Raskolnikov to his projected crime: his deep psychological complicity in, and yet moral recoil before, the crime. What has received less attention, however, is the way in which the underlying philosophical pro and contra is revealed in the separate elements of the dream (pastoral church and cemetery episode, tumultuous tavern, and mare-beating scene); how the scene of the beating itself, this picture of Russian man and reality, raises the central and grave question of part one: what is the nature of man? In its oppressive realism, and in the pessimism of its commentary on man, this dream yields only to the tale "Akulka's Husband" in *House of the Dead*.

The opening recollection in Raskolnikov's dream, though darkened by an atmosphere of impending evil, embodies Dostoevsky's pure aesthetic-religious ideal. Sacred form, harmony, and reverence define the boy's first memory of the tranquil open landscape, the stone church with its green cupola, the icons, the simple rituals, the cemetery, and, finally, the tombs of his grandmother and younger brother, with their clear promise of resurrection. "He loved this church" and its atmosphere. In Raskolnikov's purified and almost completely submerged memory of sacred form, spirituality, and beauty, there lies the seed of Raskolnikov's own moral and spiritual renewal. But the path to the church and cemetery—to resurrection—goes by the tavern on the edge of town. Here he encounters the crowd of drunken, brawling peasants with their "drunken, fearsome, distorted faces" and their "shapeless and hoarse singing." Here everything is desecration and deformation. The faces of the people in Raskolnikov's nightmare tell the tale: this is a demonized universe. It created an "unpleasant impression" on the boy. On the deepest level of the dream, then, we may speak of the coexistence—passive, we shall see—of two barely contiguous worlds: the ideal world of Christianity, with its aesthetic-religious ideals, and the real world claimed by the devil.

But Raskolnikov dreams again. It is a holiday, a day of religious observance. The peasants, however, are drunk and in riotous spirits. There is an overloaded cart drawn by a poor mare. Suddenly, a crowd of peasants, shouting and singing, emerges from the tavern, "dead drunk, in red and blue blouses." At the invitation of the driver, Mikolka, they pile onto the cart, followed by a "fat, red-faced peasant woman" in a "red calico dress and beaded cap and high shoes; she was cracking nuts and laughing. In the crowd all around they're also laughing." Then the effort to start the cart and the brutal process of beating, and finally killing, the mare commences.

This terrible and terrifying scene is simultaneously a rehearsal for murder and a statement on man. "Don't look," the father tells the boy. But Dostoevsky forces the reader to look—at the beating, at the crowd, at himself ("Man on the surface of the earth does not have the right to turn away"). "My property!" the peasant Mikolka screams repeatedly in his drunken rage, as he violently smashes away at the mare. This is a scene of absolute evil. In it surface in a strange symbiosis what are for Dostoevsky the most predatory instincts in man: those of power, sensuality, and possessiveness. The message of "my property" is clear: the fact that he owns the mare releases him from all moral obligations, because it is *his* good that is involved. The use of the word *dobro* here—with the dual meaning, property-goods, and ethical good—subtly suggests the smashing of all moral norms or "barriers," the triumph of raw egoism over any moral imperative in human relations. "My property! What I want—I go ahead and do!" screams Mikolka. Akulka's husband in *House of the Dead* cries, "Whatever I want to do to all of you now, that's what I'm going to do, because I'm no longer in control of myself." The motif "all is permissible" permeates Raskolnikov's nightmare, as it does "Akulka's Husband" and Ivan's stories of the cruelties inflicted on children. These are grim statements on man.

In Raskolnikov's nightmare, others also participate in the orgy of violence, or watch passively from the sidelines, laugh, and enjoy the spectacle, or just go on cracking nuts. There are some voices of condemnation. But they are drowned out. Even an old man who shouts indignantly, "You've got a cross on you or something, you little devil?" becomes demonized himself. As he watches the mare vainly straining and stumbling about, he too bursts into laughter.

"Thank God, it's only a dream!" exclaims Raskolnikov. But the monstrous dream is drawn from Russian life. Reality, Dostoevsky liked to emphasize, was more fantastic than fiction. The mare-beating scene is the center of world evil. It is not surprising that at this moment, on the threshold of crime, Raskolnikov's soul is "in confusion and darkness."

Are the people who inhabit Raskolnikov's nightmare monsters or victims? Ivan's question—and it is really Raskolnikov's as well—is very much to the point here: "The real issue is whether all this comes about because of bad elements in people's character or simply because that is their nature." The terrible event at the center of Raskolnikov's nightmare provides a tragic answer to this question. And if human nature is a moral wasteland, then "there are no barriers, and that is as it should be!" Raskolnikov's social-philosophical conclusions, here embodied in the action of his own psychodrama, represent a precipitous movement toward murder.

Certainly, the fractured character of Raskolnikov's moral consciousness is revealed in this dream. The boy identifies with the suffering mare, with the victim, as Raskolnikov does initially in his various encounters in part one. He is in anguish to the point of hysteria. He cries and screams and at the end puts his arm around the mare's "dead, bloodstained muzzle, and kisses her, kisses her on the eyes, on the mouth." But, as in Raskolnikov's waking hours, anguish turns into rage, and the boy "suddenly leaps up and in a frenzy rushes at Mikolka with his little fists."

Mikolka is clearly the oppressor, the embodiment of the principle of self-will. He could easily stand in for types like the pawnbroker, Luzhin, or Svidrigailov—all vicious people exploiting and degrading innocent people like Dunya, Lazaveta, or Sonya, quiet timid creatures with gentle eyes like those of the mare. It is against these vicious people that Raskolnikov revolts. But in his revolt, he is himself transformed into a monstrous, shapeless Mikolka. He himself becomes the alien oppressor, exalted by a new morality that crushes the guilty and innocent alike. In the image of the child, Raskolnikov recoils from the horror that Raskolnikov the man contemplates. But in the image of Mikolka, Raskolnikov prefigures his own role as murderer. Raskolnikov's dream has often been described as revealing the last efforts of his moral conscience to resist the crime. And this is true. The dream is a battle; but it is a battle that is lost. On the philosophical plane, as a statement on man, the dream is the tragic finale to the pro and contra of part one, the final smashing of barriers.

The dream also expresses a central paradox. Here is hell, or, in any case, the postfall world plunged into terrible evil. Yet the evil is witnessed and judged in the innocent, prefall mentality of the child. The world of the "fathers"—the adaptors, objectively indifferent to good and evil—is discredited ("Come along, don't look . . . it's not our business"). Their Christianity (witness the old man) is shameful and frightening at best: Christian ethics dissolve into laughter, the enjoyment of suffering, a Sadean realm that Dostoevsky explored in *House of the Dead*. The Christian ethos is not in men's hearts. The church is out of town, literally—but also in a metaphorical sense. It is passive. The real, active tension in the nightmare—dramatic and ideological—is in the almost Quixote-like opposition of absolute innocence to absolute evil, the inflamed demonic violence and brutality of Mikolka to the pure, idyllic sensibility, goodness, and anguish of the child. But the child, though rightfully protesting cruelty and evil, is unable conceptually to integrate evil in his prefall universe. This is the essential problem, as Dostoevsky conceives it, of such types as Raskolnikov and Ivan. Idealists, humanists, they are unable, at root, to disencumber themselves of their utopian dreams, their insistence on the moral absolute. Raskolnikov, very much like his sister, is a chaste soul.

In the final analysis, what Dostoevsky finds missing in Raskolnikov is a calm, reconciling Christian attitude, an attitude that, while never yielding to evil, nonetheless, in ultimate terms, accepts it as part of God's universe, as cloaked in the mystery of God's truth. Such an outlook can be seen in Zosima in *The Brothers Karamazov*. Dostoevsky himself strained to achieve a reconciling Christian attitude, made his final conscious choice in this direction, and indeed gives clear evidence of this choice (Raskolnikov's ultimate choice, we must believe) in the prelude to the nightmare. Yet at the same time, he invested the child's suffering and rage with deep pathos and anguish. The child's pure nature is ill-equipped to cope with reality or even grasp the deeper coherence of life's processes. Yet it seems a cardinal feature of Dostoevsky's own outlook that all genuine moral feeling must arise from an open confrontation of the pure ideal with reality. Such a confrontation, on the plane of everyday life, may be unpleasant, disruptive, unrealistic, and even absurd. But as Ivan Karamazov observes to Alyosha, "absurdities are frightfully necessary on earth. The world rests on absurdities, and without them, perhaps, nothing would ever have taken place in it." In Raskolnikov's nightmare, only the pure vision of a child, only the sacred indignation of an unsullied soul, holds out any hope to the world that is all but damned.

"Freedom, freedom!" is Raskolnikov's predominant sensation after his nightmare. "He was free now from those spells, that sorcery, that enchantment, that delusion." The nightmare is catharsis, purgation, momentary relief. It is only a dream, yet it brings him face to face with himself. "Lord! is it really possible, really possible that I will actually take an ax, will hit her on the head, split open her skull...slip in the sticky warm blood?" he wonders. "Good Lord, is it really possible?" The day before, he recalls, he had recoiled from the idea of crime in sick horror. Now he remarks inwardly, and significantly: "Granted that everything decided upon this month is as clear as day, true as arithmetic. Lord! Yet I really know all the same I shall never come to a decision!" Indeed, Raskolnikov will never decide to commit the crime. He will never consciously, actively, and with his whole moral being choose to kill—or, the reverse, choose not to kill.[3] His "moral resolution of the question" will never go deeper than "casuistry." And yet he will kill! He will lose his freedom (which in any case, after his nightmare, is deceptive) and be pulled into crime and murder—so it will seem to him—by some "unnatural power." Like Ivan Karamazov—but unlike Ivan's brother Dmitry—Raskolnikov will *allow* circumstances to shape his destiny.

Here a contrast with Dmitry is instructive. Dmitry spent the two days before the murder of his father (which he did not, in the end, commit) "literally casting himself in all directions, 'struggling with his fate and saving himself,' as he himself put it later." Dmitry's open, if naive, recognition of his opposing impulses and freedom to kill or not to kill, as well as his awareness of competing "philosophies" within him, is the crucial internal factor that helps to save him in the end from the crime of murder. Raskolnikov's dialectic of consciousness also constitutes a struggle, but his dialectic moves him toward, not away from, the crime. In the end, one philosophy triumphs: he loses his freedom (he blames the crime, significantly, on the devil) and yields to his obsession. Dmitry, on the other hand, triumphs over his obsession. Significantly, he attributes his victory to God.

Raskolnikov's deeply passive relationship to his crime often has been noted. Yet this passivity is not a purely psychological phenomenon. It is, Dostoevsky clearly indicates, closely linked with Raskolnikov's world view, an area of very intense activity for him. As Raskolnikov realizes later on, and as his own thinking and choice of language suggest, he is dominated at the time of the crime by a belief in fate, a general superstitious concern for all sorts of chthonic forces, perhaps even a taste for the occult (elements that, in Svidrigailov, have already surfaced in the form of ghosts). Dostoevsky alludes to Raskolnikov's problem directly in his notes to the novel. "That was an evil spirit: How otherwise could I have overcome all those difficulties?" Raskolnikov observes at one point. And a few lines later these significant lines: "I should have done that. (There is no free will. Fatalism)." And, finally, these crucial thoughts: "Now why has my life ended? Grumble: But God does not exist and so forth."[4] Dostoevsky's own belief emerges even in these few notes: a loss of faith in God, or in the meaningfulness of God's universe, must end with the individual abandoning himself to a notion of fate.

Raskolnikov shares his proclivity toward fatalism with a number of Dostoevsky's heroes—for example, the Underground Man, the hero of "A Gentle Creature," and Aleksey Ivanovich in The Gambler. The similarities between Raskolnikov's and the gambler's problems are striking. Both men are dominated by a sterile,

rationalistic outlook; both place themselves in a position of challenging fate; both lose their moral awareness in the essential act
of challenge (murder, gambling); both seek through their acts to
attain to an absolute freedom from the so-called laws of nature
that are binding on ordinary men; both, in the end, conceive of
themselves as victims of fate. Such types continually are seeking
their cues or directives outside of themselves. Quite symptomatic,
in this connection, is Raskolnikov's prayerful remark after his
dream: "O Lord!" he prayed, "show me my path, and I will
renounce this cursed dream of mine!"

The fateful circumstance that strikes Raskolnikov "almost to
the point of superstition" and that seems a "predestination of his
fate" is his chance meeting with Lizaveta, a meeting that, in Raskolnikov's view, sets into motion the machinery of fate. Raskolnikov returns home after that meeting "like a man condemned to
death. He had not reasoned anything out, he was quite incapable
of reasoning; but suddenly he felt with all his being that he no
longer had any freedom to reason or any will, and that everything
suddenly had been decided once and for all." Similarly, he responds to a conversation he overhears in a restaurant—by "coincidence" two men give expression to "precisely the same
thoughts" that had been cropping up in his own mind—as constituting "some kind of prefiguration, a sign":

> This last day which had begun so unexpectedly and had de-
> cided everything at once, had affected him in an almost com-
> pletely mechanical way, as though somebody had taken him
> by the hand and were drawing him after him, irresistibly,
> blindly, with unnatural force, without objection on his part;
> as though a piece of his clothing had got caught in the wheel
> of a machine and had begun to draw him into it. (I, 6)

Dostoevsky is not projecting an "accident" theory of personal
history; but neither does he deny the role of chance. Chance is
the eternal given. Without it there would be no freedom. Raskolnikov's encounter with Lizaveta was accidental (though not
pure accident), and it was by chance that he overheard the conversation in which he recognized his own thoughts (although, as

Dostoevsky wrote in his letter to M. N. Katkov on the novel, the ideas that infect Raskolnikov "are floating about in the air").[5] But these chance elements only set into motion a course of action that was seeking to be born, albeit without the full sanction of moral self.

What is crucial in Raskolnikov's situation is not so much the factor of chance as *his disposition to be guided by chance*, his readiness, as it were, to gamble, to seek out and acknowledge in chance his so-called fate.[6] What is crucial to his action is the general state of consciousness that he brings to the moment of critical accident; and consciousness here is not only his nervous, overwrought state but the way he conceives of his relationship to the world. Such is the background of Tolstoy's keen perception that Raskolnikov's true existence and true moment of decision occurred not when he met the sister of the old lady, not when he was "acting like a machine," but when he was "only thinking, when his consciousness alone was working and when in that consciousness barely perceptible changes were taking place"—in realms affecting the total scope of his existence.[7]

Raskolnikov seizes upon the various chance incidents that precede the murder as the action of fate, but he does not recognize that fate here has all the iron logic of his own, inner fatality. His passivity—that state of drift in which he evades the necessity of choice and abandons all moral responsibility—is motivated, then, not only by his deep and unresolved moral conflicts but by a muddled rationalistic, fatalistic outlook that itself denies freedom of choice or moral responsibility, an outlook that in the end posits an incoherent universe. This outlook is not something that Raskolnikov merely picked up in reading or table talk. The sense of a blind, meaningless universe, of a loveless world dominated by an evil spirit—and this is conveyed in part one—emerges from Raskolnikov's confrontation with the concrete social reality of Russian life, with the tragedy of its lower depths: its hopeless poverty, its degradation, its desolation. It is this confrontation with the human condition that violates the purity of Raskolnikov's ideal, that ruptures his faith in moral law and human nature, that bends him toward a tragic view of man and toward the view of a universe ruled by blind fate. It is this confrontation, in which compassion and contempt for man form an intimate dialectic, that nourishes the related structures of his ideas or ideology: his altruistic utilitarian ethics and his Napoleonic self-exaltation and contempt for the "herd." It is this confrontation that underlies his murder of the old pawnbroker.

Consciousness, of course, is not passive here. Raskolnikov, half-deranged in the isolation and darkness of his incomprehensible universe (the model of which is his little coffinlike room), actively reaches out into "history," into his loveless universe, to rationalize his own responses to reality and his own psychological needs. He is an intellectual. His ideas, moreover, acquire a dynamic of their own, raise him to new levels of abstraction and fantasy, and provide him, finally, with a theoretical framework and justification for crime. Yet whatever the independence of these ideas, as we find them in his article or circulating freely in taverns and restaurants, they acquire their vitality only insofar as they mediate the confrontation between individual consciousness and social reality, only insofar as they give expression to Raskolnikov's intimate social and psychological experience and his deepest, organic responses to the world about him.

In one of his notebooks, as we have noted earlier, Dostoevsky prided himself as being the first writer to focus on

> the tragedy of the underground, consisting of suffering, self-punishment, the consciousness of something better and the impossibility of achieving that something, and, chiefly, consisting in the clear conviction of these unhappy people that all are alike and hence it is not even worth trying to improve. Consolation, faith? There is consolation from no one, faith in no one. But another step from here and one finds depravity, crime (murder). Mystery.[8]

The profoundly responsive Raskolnikov, we might say, voluntarily takes on himself this tragedy of the underground. He experiences it internally, morally, in all its aspects and agonizing contradictions. His final step should have been love—a step toward humanity. Instead, experiencing the tragedy of life too deeply,

PHILOSOPHICAL PRO AND CONTRA

and drawing from that tragedy the most extreme social and philosophical conclusions, Raskolnikov (a victim of his own solitude,
ratiocination, and casuistry) takes a step away from humanity
into crime, murder, mystery.

Such is the practical denouement of the philosophical pro and
contra—the dialectic of consciousness of Raskolnikov—in part one
of *Crime and Punishment.*

VIII

Polina and Lady Luck in *The Gambler*

Lucky in cards, unlucky in love.
ENGLISH SAYING

IN A LETTER written to N. N. Strakhov from Rome in September 1863 Dostoevsky projected the idea of a story that was to evolve later into the novel *The Gambler (From the Notes of a Young Man)* (1866). The story, he wrote, would reflect the "contemporary moment (as far as possible, of course) of our inner life." The central character would be "a certain type of Russian abroad":

> I take a straightforward nature, a man, however, highly educated, but in all respects immature, who has lost his faith and *does not dare to believe*, who revolts against the authorities and fears them. He sets his mind at rest with the thought that for him there is *nothing to do* in Russia and consequently there is bitter criticism of people in Russia summoning back our Russians living abroad. . . . He's a live character—(he stands before me almost in his entirety). . . . The main thing about him is that his living juices, forces, impetuosity, daring have gone into *roulette*. He is a gambler, and not a mere gambler, just as Pushkin's miserly knight is not a simple miser. . . . He is a poet in his own way, but the point is that he himself is ashamed of this poetry, because he deeply feels its baseness, although the need for *risk* also ennobles him in his own eyes. . . . If *House of the Dead* drew the attention of the public as a depiction of the convicts whom nobody had depicted *vividly* before it, then this story without fail will attract attention as a *vivid* and detailed depiction of the game of roulette.[1]

Dostoevsky's comparison of this story with *House of the Dead* is of particular interest. The link between *The Gambler* and the earlier work goes beyond the fact that both works provide engaging descriptions of novel institutions—the worlds of the prison and the gambling house. In his letter to Strakhov, Dostoevsky indirectly hints at a deeper relationship between these two institutions, or, in any case, between the people who inhabit them. "The piece perhaps is not at all half bad. Why, *House of the Dead* was of real interest. And this is a description of a special kind of hell, a special kind of prison 'bath'."[2]

The allusion to the world of the gambler as a kind of hell points to the basic similarity in the situations of the convict and the gambler: both are prisoners in what appears to be an enclosed fate-bound universe. But whereas the convict lives in a prison world not of his own choice, a world from which, moreover, there is really no way out, the gambler lives in a dead house, or underground, of his own making. In the gambler's world everybody is possessed by the illusion of freedom, but nobody is really free. Through chance, risk, the turn of the wheel, the gambler challenges fate and seeks to escape its tyranny. Alternatives are offered to Dostoevsky's gambler, Aleksey Ivanovich, in his friend Polina and in lady luck. But in the end, he condemns himself to hurling himself eternally against the walls of his universe. He becomes an inveterate gambler, doomed to permanent unfreedom and to an endless process of trying to change his lot.

The tragedy of the gambler in Dostoevsky's view is that of a man who has uprooted himself from his nation and people and who has lost faith in God. "The cause of evil is lack of faith," Dostoevsky insisted in a letter to A. F. Blagonravov in December 1880, "but he who negates the folk element also negates faith."[3] The gambler finds a surrogate father or mother in fate, chance, luck. Yet the abandonment of self to fate is an unmitigated moral and spiritual disaster for man.

The amoral character of gambling is posited by Dostoevsky on three levels. First, gambling is directly equated with the capitalist market. "Why," asks Aleksey, "should gambling be worse than other means of making money—for instance, commerce?" Everything is relative, a "matter of proportion. What is a trifle to Rothschild is really wealth to me, and as for profits and winnings, people everywhere, and not only at roulette, are doing nothing but gaining or taking away something from each other. Whether profits and gain are vile is another question. But I'm not trying to resolve it here."

Gambling is evil, in the second sense, in that it awakens predatory instincts, chiefly greed and the desire for power. The casino strikes Aleksey as "dirty, somehow morally disgusting and dirty." He notes the greedy faces around him. But since he himself was "overcome by the desire for gain, all this covetousness, and all this covetous filth, if you like, were in a sense natural and congenial to me as soon as I entered the hall."

Yet the ultimate evil that preoccupies Dostoevsky in gambling is the evil that is immanent, psychologically speaking, in the gambling itself. The very act of gambling becomes a conscious or unconscious affirmation of the meaninglessness of the universe, the emptiness of all human choice. "All's nonsense on earth!" declares one of the seconds before Pechorin kills Grushnitski in a duel in Lermontov's *The Hero of Our Time* (1840). "Nature is a ninny, fate is a henny and life is a penny."[4] The gambler is a fatalist. Moreover, he challenges the very fate he affirms and seeks to find out if he is favored or unfavored by it. The game, the gamble, the risk itself is by its very nature a dangerous inquiry into the sources of power and an arrogant form of self-assertion; making chance king, the gambler in essence strives to become the king of chance.

The moral correlative of the belief that everything is possible is that all is permissible. Not without reason does the folk language of the market speak of "making a killing." Dostoevsky's gambler speaks of his "hidden moral convictions," but insists that in the gambling halls "there is no place for them": "I notice one thing that of late it has become repugnant for me to test my thoughts and actions by any moral standards whatsoever. I was guided by something else." That something else is fate.

1

The action of *The Gambler* takes place in a kind of no man's land or hell, Roulettenburg.[5] As the fictitious name suggests, the city is nowhere or anywhere in Europe. The mixed French and German components of the name suggest the illegitimate and rootless character of the place. This is the land of Babel, a place without a national language or culture. The gambling salon—the heart of Roulettenburg—is situated, symbolically, in a railway station where people are coming and going, where all is in continuous movement. Everything is in flux in this city: people, languages, currencies, values.

Roulettenburg is the classical city of capitalism: the market is supreme and everyone is engaged in accumulation. Everyone risks money to make money, and what he wins or loses wipes out what he has staked; there are no absolute values, material or moral; everything is relative and changing. Even people, like stakes at the table, move upward or downward in the eyes of other people according to the value judgment of the roulette wheel. Nowhere is the "cash nexus" that Marx discovered in human relations and affairs in bourgeois society more nakedly visible than in Roulettenburg. Aleksey hopes to redeem himself in the eyes of Polina by winning at roulette. "Money is everything," he declares. "It's nothing more than that with money I shall be a different person to you, not a slave." He is convinced that Polina despises him, sees him as a "cipher" and a "zero." To "rise from the dead" to him means to become a millionaire and to reverse the slave-master relationship that he feels exists between Polina and him.

But there are no permanent plateaus in social or psychological status in Roulettenburg. There are no social realities that are not subject to change. Nothing is what it seems. General Zagoryansky, considered by everybody an extremely wealthy magnate, is in fact not a magnate at all; he is a pompous muddled man who dyes his beard and moustache and is heavily in debt. The Marquis de Grieux is not a marquis, but an imposter. Madame Blanche de Cominges is not a respectable woman, but a courtesan masquerading as a de Cominges. Polina's Russian name is Praskovya, but she uses the Latinized form of her name. The inner Praskovya is not quite the same as the outer Polina. She has been in love with the Marquis de Grieux, but has taken his outer refined form for his inner soul. Aleksey sees through de Grieux, but takes Polina for somebody else.

At the outset Aleksey seems to be an objective and trustworthy observer of this strange world. The prestige of the narrative voice is overwhelming, and, initially, we accept his version of Polina as cruel and manipulative and of himself as a jilted lover. But our confidence is misplaced. Midway in his notes he remarks upon the "whirl" that has caught him up and suggests what we have already begun to suspect—that his view of things, people and events, has not been lucid or wholly rational: "Wasn't I really out of my mind last month, and wasn't I sitting all that time in a madhouse somewhere, and am I not still there perhaps—so that it only seems to me to have happened, and still only *seems* so?" The whirl of events, at the center of which both figuratively and literally is the whirling roulette wheel, has jolted him "out of all sense of proportion and feeling for measure" and sent him "spinning, spinning, spinning." Nothing is what it seems in Roulettenburg. All is deception.

Roulettenburg lies in the shadow of Schlangenberg, that is, "Snake Mountain," the highest elevation in the area. The ominous allusions of the mountain's name are not out of place. The city, in the symbolism of the novel, is in the power of the devil; people have lost their moral and spiritual freedom here. Belief in fate has replaced belief in God, and people are continually yielding to temptation in their pursuit of gold. Furthermore, Dostoevsky identifies the act of gambling, or risk, with a suicidal leap, or "plunge." In *House of the Dead* he speaks of the murderer's feverish delirium and enjoyment of the "most unbridled and limitless freedom." He adds, significantly, that all this is "perhaps similar to the sensation of a man who gazes down from a high tower into the depths below until finally he would be glad to hurl himself headlong down, as soon as possible, anything to put an end to it all!" In his delirium, in his craving for risk, the gambler, like the raging murderer or rebellious convict challenging their fate-bound universe, is overcome by the same passion for the abyss. At the gambling tables, Aleksey experiences an "instant of suspense, perhaps, sensation for sensation similar to that experienced by Madame Blanchard in Paris when she plunged to the earth from the balloon." He offers to leap off the Schlangenberg—a one-thousand-foot drop—if Polina but gives the word. "Someday I will pronounce that word," she remarks, "if only to see how you will pay up."

She tests him later when she suggests that he publicly insult the Baron and Baroness Wurmerhelm, an act that for Aleksey is psychologically analogous to leaping off the Schlangenberg: "You swore that you would leap off the Schlangenberg; you swear that you are ready to murder if I order it. Instead of all these murders and tragedies I want only to laugh." Aleksey accepts her "challenge" and agrees to carry out that "crazy fancy." "Madame la baronne," he exclaims in the confrontation scene, "*j'ai l'honneur d'être votre esclave.*" "The devil knows what urged me on?" Aleksey writes of this incident. "It was as though I were flying down from a mountain." "I can't understand what has happened to me," Aleksey writes again in imagery that recalls the convict or murderer who runs amok, "whether I am really in a frenzied state or simply have bolted from the road and am carrying on in a vile way until I am tied up. Sometimes it seems to me that my mind is disturbed."

Aleksey's reference to the devil—he is mentioned a number of times in *The Gambler*—is not without deeper significance in the novel's symbolic religious-philosophical context. The devil, indeed, may be said to have prompted Aleksey to abandon all sense of measure and control and make his leap into the abyss, his irrational underground challenge to fate. Later he suggests, significantly, that he committed his capricious act out of "despair."

The deeper meaning of this episode may be illuminated in part by reference to the second temptation of Jesus in the legend of the Grand Inquisitor. The devil suggests that Jesus cast himself down from the pinnacle of the temple to prove that he is the son of God, "because it is said that the angels would take hold and lift him up and he would not fall and hurt himself." But Jesus refuses to prove his faith in this way and thus buy men's allegiance. "O, Thou didst know then," declares the Grand Inquisitor, "that in taking one step, in making one movement to cast Thyself down,

Thou wouldst be tempting God and have lost all thy faith in Him and wouldst have been dashed to pieces against the earth which Thou didst come to save." But the Grand Inquisitor insists that there are not many like Jesus. "And couldst Thou believe for one moment that men, too, could face such a temptation?" In refusing to leap, in refusing to tempt God and buy men's faith with miracle, Jesus affirms the "free decision of the heart," the principle of freedom that Dostoevsky found at the core of Christian faith.

Aleksey stands in relation to Polina as Jesus to the devil. But Aleksey fails the test that Jesus passes. "The devil knows what urged me on?" he wonders apropos of his irrational underground behavior in the confrontation scene with the baron and baroness. Polina, like the devil in the "legend," certainly plays the role of temptress. Even if we assume (as does the Englishman Astley who may, indeed, reflect Polina's view) that she does not anticipate that Aleksey will "literally carry out her jesting wish," her suggestion nonetheless has the character of a challenge, and Aleksey is put to the test. But while Polina may be the devil's advocate, the ultimate responsibility rests with Aleksey. He *asks* his deity, his devil, to tempt him; and when she gives the command, he leaps—and falls. Aleksey's leap symbolizes his renunciation of free will. It is an act of despair that is comparable in its psychological and philosophical content to the Underground Man's irrational revolt against his "twice two is four" universe. It is an indication of his loss of faith in God and, therefore, in a universe in which man is free to choose between good and evil.

In a conversation with his employer, General Zagoryansky, who is outraged by Aleksey's behavior toward the baron and baroness, Aleksey bridles at the idea that he is answerable in his conduct to the general: "I only wish to clear up the insulting suggestion that I am under the tutelage of a person who supposedly has authority over my free will." The irony of Aleksey's remark—and Dostoevsky's intent is quite clear—is that he is lacking precisely in free will; in all his acts and behavior, he is caught up in an underground syndrome of negation and self-negation. His remark to the general signals indirectly his psychological dilemma: his subservience to Polina and, at the same time, his resentment over that state. "Please observe that I don't speak of my slavery because I wish to be your slave," he remarks to her, "but simply speak of it as a fact that doesn't depend upon me at all." Aleksey relates to Polina in the same rebellious yet rationalizing way that the Underground Man relates to the laws of nature that have been humiliating him.

As D. S. Savage has rightly observed, Aleksey "invests Polina with an authority which he refuses to invest in God. Polina must become God in relation to him or he must become God in relation to Polina—and God is the fatal demiurge of cosmic Necessity."[6] We need only add that this god, in Dostoevsky's view, is not the God of Christianity, but the devil. And, in fact, Polina has become for Aleksey the surrogate for an implacable deterministic fate and as such arouses in him the opposing feelings of love and hate, adoration and revenge. Aleksey is a person who has forfeited his freedom to fate, and his underground relationship with Polina defines that disaster. His symbolic leap from Schlangenberg anticipates his leap at the gambling tables, his transformation into a compulsive gambler and convinced fatalist. At the end of his notes, the penniless gambler, who has renounced "every goal in life excepting winning at roulette," has driven even his memories from his head. He insists, "I shall rise from the dead." But there can be no future without a past. And just as Polina is not the devil—that is Aleksey's illusion—so Aleksey has no hope of salvation. He will never, like Jesus, "rise from the dead." He will never escape the tyranny of his self-created dead universe.

2

"Polina Aleksandrovna, on seeing me, asked why I had been so long, and without waiting for an answer went off somewhere. Of course, she did this deliberately," remarks Aleksey at the end of the first paragraph of the novel. "All the same, we must have an explanation. A lot of things have accumulated." The movement of *The Gambler*, on levels of plot, theme, character, and psychology, takes the reader from accumulated mystery and complication ("a lot of things have accumulated") through tension and expectation to release and disclosure. The center of everyone's concern is the accumulation of money.

At the outset of the novel everyone in General Zagoryansky's "retinue"—Polina, the Marquis de Grieux, Blanche de Cominges, and others—is waiting "in expectation" for news of the death of "Grandmamma" in Moscow and of a windfall legacy. Grandmamma arrives in place of the anticipated telegram, however, and loses huge sums of money at roulette, but she leaves the gambling tables at last and returns to Moscow. Zagoryansky's little retinue then begins to disintegrate. Blanche, who had been preparing to marry into a fortune, abandons the general and attaches herself to Aleksey who has made colossal winnings at the tables. The Marquis de Grieux, who had been anticipating Polina's legacy and had hoped to get back money he loaned to the general, deserts her. Polina, ill, goes off with the family of the Englishman Astley to live in the north of England. And the now confirmed gambler Aleksey, after a period of dissipation in Paris with Blanche and a "number of absurd blows of fate," finds himself back at zero dreaming of rising from the dead "tomorrow": "Let Polina know that I can still be a man."

Grandmamma is the structural and ideological center of *The Gambler*. She appears on the scene in the ninth chapter—the exact center of the novel—and dominates everybody around her. Like the roulette wheel, she is the center of attention of the main characters in the general's retinue, from the beginning to the end of the novel. All are gambling, as it were, on her death, hoping to resurrect their flagging fortunes. *"Il a du chance,"* Blanche remarks apropos of the general toward the end of the novel. "Grandmamma is now really quite ill and will certainly die." Fate and death are joined in everybody's aspirations. The idea of hope in death in the fate-ruled universe of Roulettenburg parodies, of course, the truth of death and resurrection in Dostoevsky's Christian universe. But there is no resurrection for anybody in Roulettenburg; there is only moral and spiritual death, immersion in the river of Lethe where all memories are washed away.

Grandmamma is the only person in the novel who, figuratively speaking, rises from the dead. Her unexpected appearance on the

scene, alive, foreshadows her ultimate escape from Roulettenburg
and its moral and spiritual chaos. A dominating, imperial figure
to all, she is humbled, finally, in her wilful attempt to conquer
fate at the gambling tables. "Truly," she remarks, "God seeks
out and punishes pride even in the old." But in her naive, simple,
and earthy Russian way, she survives the storm of gambling passions, masters her own fate, and returns to Russia, where, significantly, she vows to carry out a promise she had made—to build
a church. Like nature, she is full of excess, but also full of the
powers of restoration. Grandmamma is for Dostoevsky both symbol and embodiment of Russia's wild abundance, its "breadth,"
and, at the same time, its rootedness and residual spiritual health.

The relationship between Aleksey and Polina forms the axis of
the novel. The work begins with the enigma of their relationship
and ends with its clarification. Their lives are complex and portrayed in a moment of crisis and transformation. At the outset of
the novel the two characters are enigmas not only to the reader
but to each other. Aleksey is continually puzzled by Polina's personality and behavior toward him: "Polina has always been an
enigma to me." In turn, Polina's repeated questioning glances at
Aleksey point to her deep puzzlement over his character and mo-
tivations as they pertain to her. In a certain sense Aleksey speaks
for both of them when he confesses that "there was scarcely anything precise and definite" that he could say about his relations
with her. The reader who turns to *The Gambler* for the first time
would certainly share Aleksey's view of the relationship as
"strange" and "incomprehensible." Yet there is no confusion in
Dostoevsky's understanding of his characters.

At the outset of the story Aleksey and Polina face remarkably
similar situations and relate to each other in quite similar ways.
Both are in a state of dependency in the retinue of General Zagoryansky; both are in need of money, though for different reasons; and both place their hopes in roulette. Aleksey is hateful to
Polina, but she needs him and is drawn toward him. Polina is
hateful to Aleksey, but he is irresistibly drawn toward her and
needs her for some deeper psychological reasons.

Polina, robbed of monies rightfully hers by her stepfather General Zagoryansky, in debt and in some kind of psychological or emotional bondage to de Grieux, is in desperate need of money: "I need some money at all costs; it must be got; otherwise I am simply lost." "I place almost all hope on roulette," she remarks pensively at one point. She has evidently borrowed some money and wants to return it. Polina's belief that she will win at roulette is linked with her feeling that she has "no other choice left." She wishes to settle accounts, literally and figuratively, with de Grieux, a man whom she had loved and idealized, but whom "for a long, long time" she has found "detestable." "Oh, he was not the same man before, a thousand times no, but now , but now!" she exclaims to Aleksey when she brings him the letter in which de Grieux as a parting gesture crudely pays her off, as it were, with a fifty thousand franc I.O.U. note. Could she have expected any other outcome, Aleksey asks. "I expected nothing," she replies in a quiet but trembling voice. "I made up my mind long ago; I read his mind and knew what he was thinking. He thought I would seek...that I would insist.... I deliberately redoubled my contempt for him."

Wounded pride, contempt, and disillusionment (still touched by the dying fires of an infatuation) mark Polina's attitude toward de Grieux. Her reliance on roulette derives not only from her objective plight but from the despair of disillusionment. This despair is the origin of her need for Aleksey on the deepest level of their relationship. "Some time back, really a good two months ago," Aleksey notes, "I began to notice that she wanted to make a friend and confidante of me, and to a certain extent really made a try at it. But for some reason things never took off with us at that time; in fact we ended up instead with our present strange relations." In seeking a friend and confidante in Aleksey, Polina made a first step toward self-knowledge and recovery of her inner freedom. Yet it was not a friend that Aleksey sought in Polina. And her cool and at times even cruel behavior toward him was in large part a recognition of this, as it was also in part a reflex of the resentment and frustration she experienced in her relations with another egoist, de Grieux.

Aleksey, like Polina, sees in roulette his "only escape and sal-

vation." For him, as for Polina, winning seems the "only solution." His need for money, too, is linked with a deep feeling of
humiliation and entrapment. Polina's relationship toward de
Grieux finds a parallel in Aleksey's toward Polina. But his sense
of bondage and need for liberation has a particularly disturbing
character; it points to a profound feeling of weakness and inadequacy. He seeks in roulette a "radical and decisive change" in his
fate. Money for him is not an end in itself but a means. What he
seeks in gambling is the restoration of a lost sense of being, self-
determination, and mastery. Through money, through gambling,
he imagines he will become a different man to Polina, will no
longer be a zero and a slave. Yet it is precisely the craving for
power, the need to "challenge fate," that poisons his relationship
with Polina.

Dostoevsky, then, emphasizes the similarities in the psychological states of Aleksey and Polina. Both find themselves deeply
humiliated: Polina before de Grieux and Aleksey before Polina
and fate over which he wishes to triumph. Both are drawn toward
each other, but the relationship is disfigured by psychological
wounds, humiliations, and resentments on both sides. The key to
a positive relationship lies in overcoming wounded pride, self-assertion, and the desire to inflict pain. The denouement of the
story indicates that Polina is capable of taking this step but that
Aleksey is doomed forever to remain in his underground.

3

It is possible to single out in the first pages of The Gambler Aleksey's two unconsummated passions: the first, his feverish passion
for Polina; the second, his obsession with roulette (like Hermann
in Pushkin's "Queen of Spades," Aleksey has never gambled before). But in a schematic way, we might say that Aleksey has an
affair with Polina and an affair with lady luck. Toward the end of
the story both affairs are consummated: Aleksey momentarily
conquers lady luck in what amounts to an orgy at the gambling
tables, and he spends a night with Polina. Both victories are fleeting, however, and they end in reversal and disaster for Aleksey.

These two affairs or passions constitute in their interaction the psychological drama of Aleksey.

The reader easily distinguishes between Aleksey's two passions. What is far less apparent, initially, is their overlapping character in Aleksey's subconscious, that is, the manner in which Polina is drawn into the orbit of Aleksey's gambling obsession and made to serve as a surrogate for the lady luck he seeks to conquer. In a word, the image of Polina that emerges in Aleksey's notes is not merely a biased one; it is, as it were, clouded over by somebody else. "When we are awake we also do what we do in our dreams," remarks Nietzsche, "we invent and make up the person with whom we associate—and immediately forget it."[7] The idea of Polina as a surrogate for an imperious, tantalizing, and, at the same time, cruelly inaccessible lady luck, or fate, is broadly hinted at the end of the first chapter in *The Gambler*. Aleksey ruminates on the nature of his feelings for Polina:

> And now once more I ask myself the question: do I love her? And once more I am not able to answer it, that is, rather, I answered once more for the hundredth time that I hated her. Yes, she had become hateful to me. There were moments (and precisely at the end of every one of our conversations) when I would have given half my life to strangle her! I swear if it had been possible slowly to sink a sharp knife in her breast, I think I would have seized it with pleasure. And yet I swear by all that is holy that if on that fashionable peak of the Schlangenberg she had indeed said to me, "cast yourself down," I should have done so immediately and with pleasure. I know this. One way or another the matter must be settled. She understands all this amazingly well, and the thought that I am clearly and thoroughly conscious of all her inaccessibility to me, of all the impossibility of fulfillment of my dreams—this thought, I am sure, gives her the most extraordinary pleasure; otherwise, could she, cautious and clever as she is, be on such terms of intimacy and frankness with me? I think that up to now she has looked upon me in

the manner of the ancient empress who would disrobe in the
presence of her slave, not considering him a man.... (1)

Aleksey's psychological portrait of Polina here scarcely accords
with the real Polina. Her efforts, two months earlier, to establish
more intimate and frank relations with him were certainly not
based on a desire to humiliate him. She had sought in him a
friend and confidante but had found instead a man who neither
respected himself nor her, who cast himself in the role of an obedient but deeply resentful slave. "I can't endure that 'slave' theory of yours," she remarks. Aleksey is in the grip of an obsession
that only nominally involves the real Polina. He regards her as
inaccessible. She is, of course, not inaccessible to the Aleksey she
imagines, or hopes, him to be. But she is certainly inaccessible to
the Aleksey who cannot relate to her in any other way than that
of a slave or despot. She certainly finds hateful the vindictive
slave who sees in her an almost impersonal object of love and
hate, who sees her as an imperious ancient empress who has been
humiliating him and whom he must vanquish in order to become
a different man. _That_ ancient empress is not some Cleopatra, but
fate—lady luck who flaunts her riches before the rabble. Aleksey's passion for this empress psychologically structures and defines his erotic passion for Polina.

Abjectly and resentfully—characteristically in Joban terms—
Aleksey speaks of his relationship with Polina: "Since I am her
slave and completely insignificant in her eyes, she feels no offense
at my coarse curiosity. But the point is that while she permits me
to ask questions, she does not answer them. At times she doesn't
even take notice of them. That's how things are between us!"
That is how things are between the despairing Job and God. But
while Job ultimately recognizes the true face of God, Aleksey in
his spiritual rebellion and psychological blindness never really
recognizes the real Polina, at least not until the fatal resolution
of his crisis when it is too late.

The psychological character of Aleksey's relationship to Polina
and the ancient empress, fate, may be elucidated against the background of Hermann's relationship to the old countess and her

maid-in-waiting Lizaveta in Pushkin's profound and seminal work, "Queen of Spades." The impact of this work upon *The Gambler* is at least as deep as it is upon *Crime and Punishment*.[8] At the center of Pushkin's story is an affair that Hermann—an ambitious but parsimonious officer who has the "soul of a gambler"—has with a servant girl and with fate. In Pushkin's story fate is incarnated in the figure of an aged countess (the image of a grotesque card queen of spades) who possesses the secret of three winning cards. In order to gain entrance to the bedroom quarters of the old countess, Hermann strikes up an outwardly passionate, though spurious love affair with the countess's maid-in-waiting, Lizaveta. In a midnight encounter with the countess (the result of arranging a rendezvous with Lizaveta) Hermann implores her to give him her secret of the winning cards, importunes her, waves his pistol before her, but to no avail. The countess dies of fright. Later she comes to him in a dream and tells him the secret. The story ends with Hermann's defeat—following two victories—at the gambling tables. "The queen of spades signifies secret ill will," reads Pushkin's epigraph to his story.

The amoral character of Hermann's gambling passion is manifested not only in his encounter with the old countess—a meeting that discloses his disordered psychology and utilitarian outlook—but in his heartless manipulation of the feelings of Lizaveta. "You are a monster!" she cries to him in their arranged tryst immediately after the countess's death. His motives have become apparent to her. "I did not wish her death," he replies, indifferent to the girl who but a little while earlier had been the object of passionate avowals of love. For the egotist Hermann, Lizaveta is but an incidental sacrifice in his quest for power and wealth. This "hardened soul" feels no pangs of conscience either for the old countess or for Lizaveta.

Hermann masks his gambling passion under a simulated passion for Lizaveta. He quite consciously employs this deception to gain entrance to the dwelling of his real lover—lady luck, fate, the old countess. The object of Aleksey's passion is also lady luck, but she is not incarnated in any independent figure or symbol in his drama (there is an allusion to her, of course, in the reference to the ancient empress). Pushkin's play with the fantastic—or play with the real and fantastic—becomes pure theater of the unconscious in Dostoevsky. What Dostoevsky does in *The Gambler* is endow Polina with the function of a fate-figure in Aleksey's unconscious. Lizaveta and the old countess, as it were, merge there into one person.

Aleksey's relation to Polina as a fate-figure is almost identical with Hermann's relation to the mysterious countess. Both Polina and the countes, in the view of their suitors, withhold their favor. Aleksey's comparison of Polina with the imperious ancient empress who expresses her contempt for her slave by calmly undressing in front of him defines what he feels to be Polina's attitude toward him as a lover and—on the plane of his unconscious— as a fate-figure. This is an obvious reminiscence on Dostoevsky's part of the midnight scene in "Queen of Spades" in which Hermann, concealed in the countess's bedroom, is witness to the "repulsive mysteries of her toilet" as she undresses before her mirror.

In a variety of ways Pushkin brings out the unconscious erotic dimension in this episode; indeed, Hermann is compared to a lover of the countess's youth. Hermann now slavishly petitions the countess on his knees, now despotically threatens her with his pistol in his quest for a "favor," the "happiness of his life," the secret of the three cards. He appeals to the countess as "wife, lover, and mother." Though he recognizes that her secret may be linked with a "terrible sin, with the ruination of eternal bliss, with a devil's contract," he announces that he is prepared to take on her sin. As we have noted, the countess does not yield her riches to her impassioned and frustrated suitor. He is not rewarded at this moment by lady luck any more than Aleksey's erotic interests are rewarded immediately by Polina. Hermann is rewarded by the countess when she comes to him in a dream and tells him the secret of the three cards. Aleksey, too, wants his "empress" to come to him. "I was not at all troubled by her fate," he remarks about Polina apropos of the moment Grandmamma was about to gamble away her fortune. "I wanted to fathom her secrets. I wanted her to come to me and say, 'I really love you'." Polina will, indeed, come to Aleksey and provide the psychological motive for him to rush off confidently to the gambling tables and make his colossal winnings. His erotic strivings will be consummated when he returns to his room where Polina is waiting for him.

In outwardly different but psychologically analogous ways, then, Pushkin and Dostoevsky recognize the interaction of the erotic and gambling impulses in their heroes. In *The Gambler*, the psychosexual dimension of Aleksey's gambling passion is openly expressed in his relationship with Polina. Yet in the deepest sense, Aleksey's passion for Polina is no greater than Hermann's interest in Lizaveta. Hermann simulates a passion for Lizaveta; when she no longer serves as an accessory to his gambling passion, he becomes indifferent to her. It seems to Aleksey that he is in love with Polina and that he cannot live without her. But in fact she is only a stand-in for lady luck. When he recognizes lady luck, when he recognizes his gambling passion and succumbs to it at the tables, his passion for Polina vanishes. He no longer needs the real Polina. He has found lady luck.

4

The dramatic denouement of Aleksey's affair with Polina and lady luck is as brilliant in execution as in conception. At a critical moment in Polina's destiny, after Grandmamma's huge losses at the tables and at the time de Grieux abandons Polina, Aleksey pens the following note to her:

> Polina Aleksandrovna, I see clearly that the denouement is at hand which will of course affect you too. For the last time I repeat: do you or do you not need my life? If I can be of use, be it *in any way*—dispose of me as you see fit, and meanwhile I will remain in my room, most of the time at least, and not go out anywhere. If it is necessary, write or send for me. (13)

Shortly after this note is delivered, Polina turns up in Aleksey's room, pale and somber. He cries out, startled, amazed. "What's

the matter? What's the matter?" Polina asks. "You ask what's
the matter?" he replies. "You? here, in my room!" Aleksey's
expression of amazement inaugurates a scene—the climax of their
relationship—which is marked by a dramatic reversal of his whole
notion of her attitude toward him. "If I come, then I come in my
entirety," Polina remarks. "It's a habit with me."

The scene is a significant one. At a critical moment in Polina's
life Aleksey impulsively offers her everything that a lover could
offer, the maximum of devotion: his life. In turn, Polina comes
to him in her entirety and offers him her life. In the language of
the gambling tables both are staking or risking all. But are the
wagers equal in value? The action that follows clearly points to
the radically different values of the wagers. Polina's gamble, at
its deepest level, involves a throwing off of pride, a breaking out
from the underground tangle of her relationship with de Grieux
and Aleksey, an attempt to find salvation not in roulette, but in
a human relationship based upon mutual respect. Her earlier offers to share her winnings at the gambling table were symbolic
of the kind of relationship she sought. In coming to Aleksey she
is making herself vulnerable—the sine qua non in any genuine
human relationship—she is risking annihilation to gain a friend,
that is, to win Aleksey. Her gamble contemplates neither a play
for power nor the annihilation of somebody else's wager.

Aleksey's gamble, on the other hand, on the psychological
plane, turns out to be the same as all his other gambles: an affirmation of ego. He wishes only a signal from Polina and he will
make his suicidal and murderous leap. His offer to help Polina
only masks his desire to win the favor of lady luck and obtain a
momentary illusion of freedom and power. Recalling his triumphant win at the gambling tables, he remarks significantly: "I
staked my whole life." His pledge of his life to Polina, then, involves not only a symbolic self-annihilation but the annihilation
of Polina, her hopes and her high stakes, her last desperate gamble on his love.

In his room Polina shows Aleksey the letter from de Grieux in
which he offers her her stepfather's I.O.U. note to be used
against him. "Oh," Polina cries out, "with what happiness would

I now throw into his vile face those fifty thousand francs and spit at them...and grind the spit in!" Aleksey, groping for ways in which Polina can settle accounts with de Grieux, comes up with, among other things, the proposal that she turn to Astley for fifty thousand francs. "What, dost thou thyself really want me to go from thee to that Englishman?" she cries, looking into Aleksey's face with "a piercing glance" and smiling bitterly. "She called me 'thou' for the first time in my life," he recalls. "It seemed to me that she was dizzy with emotion at that moment, and she sat down suddenly on the sofa, as if worn out." Aleksey remembers thinking at this point, "Why, she loves me! She came *to me* and not to Mr. Astley." The inner content of Polina's gamble for Aleksey is manifested, of course, in her use of the familiar pronoun "thou." But the desperate nature of her gamble is evidenced by her dizziness; literally, "her head was spinning."

Aleksey's notion that Polina is hostile to him is shattered here. The foundations are laid, we might imagine, for a positive denouement to this strange relationship: the slave is loved and there is no longer any need for self-assertion. Yet Aleksey's actions at this crucial point only confirm that his conception of himself as a slave and of Polina as some kind of arrogant ancient empress is rooted in deep, ineradicable psychological necessities. He does not want the love of Polina on the terms of equality that she offers. He does not desire a real human partnership. "She came to me," he recalls. "I still don't understand it." Like the Underground Man, Aleksey can understand love only as a slave or despot. In part, Aleksey had invented Polina. He had mistaken the surface Polina for the real Praskovya, just as Polina had mistaken de Grieux—in the sarcastic words of Aleksey—for an "Apollo of Belvedere."

In order to distinguish "beauty of soul and originality of personality," Aleksey rightly observes, a person needs "independence and freedom." The inexperienced and basically unsophisticated Russian girl Praskovya is attracted to the external elegance and form of the counterfeit Marquis de Grieux even though this beauty is only a part of her imagination. She "takes this form as his own soul," Aleksey remarks, "as the natural form of his heart and soul, and not as dress that he has inherited."[9] But this elegant, "finished, beautiful form," in the deepest spiritual sense, is "no form at all." Aleksey correctly diagnoses the debacle of Polina's affair with de Grieux: she has been carried away by a false notion of beauty and form, but what another hero of Dostoevsky, the ridiculous man, has called the "beauty of the lie." "It is only among Frenchmen," Aleksey remarks sarcastically, "that form has been so well defined that it is possible to appear with extraordinary dignity and yet be quite a scoundrel."

Polina's near loss of identity in the face of the assault of superficial Western culture, her spiritual immaturity, and, to a certain extent, her corruption are signaled in the novel by her use of the Latinized form of her name, Polina. Yet in the case of the Russian heroine, authentic form—all that relates to organic Russian nature and intelligence—lies within. Significantly, it is Grandmamma, the only character in the novel who embodies the element of Muscovite directness and naturalness, who addresses Polina as "Praskovya." "I might get fond of you, Praskovya. . . . You're a fine girl, better than all the others, and you sure have a strong will, I'll say! Well, I have a will, too; now turn around: that's not a switch you're wearing, is it?" Polina answers that it is her own hair, and Grandmamma puts in: "Good, I don't like the silly fashions that are current. You're very pretty. I would fall in love with you if I were a young gentleman. Why don't you get married?"

It is Grandmamma who recognizes the authentic Praskovya beneath the surface Polina. Aleksey, who clearly perceives that Polina was taken in by de Grieux' elegant form, ironically is unable to respond to the authentic Praskovya when she turns to him for help. Polina seeks out in him a friend and confidante at a moment when her relationship with de Grieux is crumbling; later she turns to him in desperation and reveals her deep attraction to him. But in her moment of crucial need he deserts her. Polina is necessary to Aleksey, ultimately, only as ground for a limitless egoism. Thus, when she reaches out to him in need and offers him the possibility of love, he instinctively interprets her gesture as a signal from his deity to make his long-awaited leap for power. A "wild idea" flashed through his mind: "Polina! Give me only one hour! Wait here only an hour and...I will return! It's...it's necessary! You will see!" Aleksey's idea, significantly, is linked with an inner feeling of something "fatal, necessary, predestined."

Polina, of course, has already offered Aleksey his hour by publicly compromising herself and coming to his room. But what Aleksey wants is an hour with lady luck. What he wants is what only gambling can give him: the momentary illusion of power. In essence, Aleksey exchanges happiness with Polina for luck at the tables.[10] "And I rushed out of the room without answering her astonished, questioning glance; she called out something after me, but I did not go back." That questioning glance is one of many that Polina directs at Aleksey, particularly in their last meeting. These glances reveal the extent of Polina's own perplexity over the nature of Aleksey's strange behavior and psychology. More than any words, they reveal to the reader not a domineering ancient empress sadistically bent on tormenting a passionate lover, but a confused and troubled Russian girl who has not yet fully learned to look beneath surface appearances into the moral-psychological underground.

5

Aleksey's state of mind at the gambling tables is frenzied to the point of madness. There is an intoxicated, orgiastic quality about these moments. His winnings are colossal. This kind of storming of the heavens evokes fear in those around him. Two Jews standing by him warn him to leave: "You are bold! You are very bold!" But Aleksey, like the Underground Man rushing off in pursuit of Zverkov, is "driven on by fate"; he speaks of the "arrogance of chance," the "craving for risk." As he sets off for the hotel, finally, in the darkness, staggering under the sheer weight of the gold he is carrying, he has no thoughts in his head: "I experienced only some kind of fearful sense of pleasure—of success, victory, power." He is conscious that he is going back to Polina, but only "to tell her, show her...but I scarcely remembered what she had been saying to me a while ago, and why I had gone, and all those recent feelings of just an hour and a half before seemed to me now something long past, long since taken care of, obsolete—which we would no longer remember because now everything would begin anew."

Aleksey is not thinking as he emerges from the gambling halls. Rather he is feeling the sum total of his experience. The image of Polina, significantly, rises out of the sensations of success, victory, power; he is going to show her the gold, the symbol of his achievement, the evidence that he is no longer a zero. There is an infantile exhibitionism about Aleksey's actions here. There is also a sense of change in his life, as though the experience at the gambling tables had been traumatic and had opened up a new phase in his psychic existence. The words "now everything will begin anew" are ambiguous: seemingly directed toward Polina, they actually point toward an awareness of a radical internal crisis and transformation. Not without reason does Aleksey later remark: "My life has broken into two."

Returning to his hotel room, Aleksey throws the money on the table before Polina. "I remember she looked into my face with frightful intentness." These words, which open chapter fifteen, strike the keynote for the unfolding scene as far as Polina is concerned: her increasing doubt about Aleksey and about the real nature of his feelings and words. Her glance literally pursues Aleksey throughout their last encounter. As he rushes about, almost completely oblivious of her, tidying up his piles of money and gold, Aleksey notes, she is "attentively" watching him, with a strange expression on her face. "I did not like that look! I do not err in saying that there was hatred in it." When Aleksey suggests that Polina take fifty thousand francs and throw it in de Grieux' face, she does not answer but bursts into the kind of mocking laughter that had always greeted his "most passionate declarations." Her laughter, always defensive in character, now points to her growing disillusionment and despair with Aleksey. At last, he writes, she stops and frowns, looking at Aleksey sternly. De Grieux had sought to cancel his sense of obligation to Polina with an I.O.U. note. Aleksey's proposal, in turn, seems to put the cash sign before their relationship. "You think you can buy my respect with money, if not me myself," Polina had remarked to Aleksey in an earlier episode in the novel. Polina refuses the money.

Aleksey seems incapable of understanding Polina's refusal, however. Puzzled by her response, he counters: "I offer it to you as a friend; I offer you my life." But life is not to be measured by the weight of gold or the gambler's bravado at the tables. Again, Aleksey notes, "she looked at me with a long and searching glance, as if she wanted to transfix me with it." Polina is not a commodity to be bought and sold. "You are setting a high price," she says with a bitter smile, "de Grieux's lover is not worth fifty thousand francs." "Polina, how can you talk that way with me?" Aleksey cries reproachfully. "Am I de Grieux?" Of course, that is precisely the question Polina has been trying to resolve: is he any different from de Grieux? "I hate you! Yes...yes!..." she exclaims. But then she equates him with de Grieux in another way: "I don't love you any more than I love de Grieux." Her paradoxical manner of expressing her hate reveals her deeply conflicting feelings over Aleksey, and indeed even over de Grieux, the man toward whom she had "redoubled her contempt."

In this last encounter with Aleksey, however, it is not hatred, contempt, or even wounded pride that emerges as the dominant note, but a desperate appeal for love, for support, for a genuine human partnership. This is not the Polina that the reader first perceived through the eyes of Aleksey at the beginning of his notes. In this last encounter with him she seems delirious, ill. For a brief moment, under the strain of an emotional crisis as profound as that of Aleksey's, she reveals both her inner wounded pride and her deepest, hitherto concealed, hopes. "Buy me! Do you want to? Do you want to? for fifty thousand francs, like de Grieux?" she gasped between convulsive sobs. But, significantly, she continues to use the familiar form "thou." Aleksey embraces her, kisses her hands, feet, falls on his knees before her. Her hysteria passes. "She placed both her hands on my shoulders and examined me intently; it seemed that she wanted to read something in my face. . . . An expression of concern and contemplation appeared on her face." Polina draws him toward her, and then pushes him away, and again "took up examining me with a somber look." Then she suddenly embraces him:

> "But you do love me, you do love me, don't you?" she said; after all, after all you...you wanted to fight with the baron for me!" And suddenly she burst out into laughter, as though something amusing and nice suddenly flickered in her memory. She was crying and laughing all at once. Well, what could I do. I was myself almost delirious. I remember she began to say something to me, but I could understand almost nothing of what she said. It was a kind of delirium, a kind of incoherent babble, as though she wanted to tell me something as quickly as possible, delirium interrupted sometimes by the merriest laughter, which began to frighten me. "No, no, you are sweet, sweet!" she repeated. "You are my faithful one!" And again she put her hands on my shoulders, again began looking at me closely and repeated: "You love me...love me...You will love me?" I did not take my eyes off her; I had never before seen her in these fits of tenderness and love; it is true, of course, that this was delirium, but...on noticing my look of passion she suddenly began to smile slyly. (15)

This extraordinary scene lays bare the pro and contra of Polina's feelings toward Aleksey. Her words express tenderness and love, but her questioning glances express her deep doubts and uncertainties—all that she had previously masked in coldness and contempt. Polina's swan song of love—for that is what it is—is full of a frenzied will to believe something that she knows in her heart to be false; it is a last delirious gamble, a last gambler's illusion that forms a counterpart to Aleksey's delirious gamble at the tables—his passionate wooing of lady luck. For his part, Aleksey can understand almost nothing of what she is saying. But his problem in understanding is not merely due to Polina's incoherence; it is deeply rooted in a neurotic gambling passion that has consumed all his psychic energies.

CHAPTER VIII

Polina's half-believing, half-despairing lovemaking evokes no reciprocal mood of love or tenderness in Aleksey—only a "look of passion." The protestations of love, the impulsive gestures of tenderness, the physical advances come almost entirely from Polina. Except for one moment when he tries to calm her and falls on his knees before her (the gesture is symbolic), his behavior is passive and his mood almost disbelieving. "I wanted her to come to me and say, 'I really love you'," Aleksey confided earlier in his notebook. "And if not, if this madness is unthinkable, well then..., well, what was I to wish for? Do I really know what I wish? I'm like a person without any perspectives; all I want is to be near her, in her aura, in her radiance, eternally, always, all my life. More than this I don't know! And could I possibly go away from her?" Polina does come and say "I love you." But Aleksey goes off to gamble, and when he returns for the last time, he does not understand her words. Aleksey's whole response to Polina in this episode suggests that he has confused her with the aura of radiance of somebody else, that is, with the dazzling ancient empress, lady luck.

At one point in the episode Polina impulsively embraces Aleksey and exclaims, "We'll go away, we really will go away tomorrow, won't we? And we'll catch up with Grandmamma, don't you think?" To catch up with Grandmamma, of course, is to go back to Moscow—back to Russian soil, Russian nationality, Russian identity, and away from the artificial, rootless, spiritually dead world of Roulettenburg. Russia, in Dostoevsky's ideological design, means spiritual salvation. Polina's hope that Aleksey will take her back to Russia is an illusion. He will be heading not to Moscow, but to the Sodom and Gomorrah of Paris—and not with Polina, but with the radiant Blanche. Polina is, indeed, delirious, on the brink of illness. After another fit of laughter, Aleksey writes, "she suddenly was kissing and embracing me again, passionately and tenderly pressing her face to mine. I no longer thought of anything or heard anything. My head was spinning.... I think it was about seven in the morning when I came to my senses."

The night of sex, clearly, does not dissolve the underlying tensions between Aleksey and Polina: conjunctive, physically, it gives expression to a thoroughly disjunctive emotional relationship. For both, it is the denouement of a delusion in which each has mistaken the other for somebody else. In the morning, after three minutes of looking out of the window, Polina turns to Aleksey with loathing and fury, flings the money in his face, and leaves. This action not only points eloquently to the tragedy of loveless sex but climaxes a relationship that on every level must be considered a paradigm of human misunderstanding. Aleksey, characteristically, does not comprehend her behavior. He can only conclude that Polina is "out of her mind." Was it "wounded pride" or "despair," he wonders, that brought her to him. Vanity, he is sure, prompted her "not to trust in me and to insult me." And then, of course, it all happened in a "state of delirium."

Aleksey's ponderings are deeply evasive, egotistical, and lacking in any insight into Polina. What is chiefly noticeable is the absence of any feeling for her. His last act before leaving his room—he hurriedly tucks his whole heap of gold into his bed and covers it—symbolizes the change that has taken place in him since winning at the gambling tables. When he later learns of Polina's illness and of the possibility of her death, he takes account of the change in himself:

> I was sorry for Polina, I swear, but it's strange—from the very moment I touched the gambling table last night and began to rake in packs of money, my love retreated, as it were, into the background. I say this now, but at the time I still didn't see all this clearly. Is it possible that I really am a gambler, is it possible that I really...love Polina so strangely? No, to this day I still love her, as God will witness. (15)

Aleksey's orgy at the gambling tables engulfs him completely. He becomes an obsessive gambler. He discovers his true passion—the pursuit of lady luck—and with that discovery, his driving passion for Polina vanishes.

Aleksey's gamble for lady luck and his emotional crisis are paralleled by Polina's gamble for Aleksey and her ensuing crisis and illness. Yet the outcomes of these crises are different. Aleksey wins his gamble at the tables and "breaks in two"; the conflict between the man with hidden moral convictions and the pathological gambler ends in the victory of the latter. In a certain sense, Aleksey does become a different man. Polina, for her part, loses her gamble for Aleksey but retains her integrity. At the very moment Aleksey ceases to regard her as a fate-figure, the incubus of demonism is lifted from her. The hopeful, though by no means optimally positive resolution of her drama—for Dostoevsky this would mean a return to Russia and to her roots—is suggested by her joining the family of the eminently decent Astley in England and, later, in Switzerland.

In contrast, the psychological and spiritual catastrophe of Aleksey is symbolized by his capitulation to the courtesan Blanche, a carnivalesque embodiment of lady luck, a new fate-figure in his life. He goes with her to Paris, where he spends much of his time lying on a couch. "Is it possible I am such a child?" he wonders at the end of his notes. The slave of Polina becomes the *"vil esclave,"* the *"fils,"* and the *"bon enfant"* of Blanche, the truly infernal woman of the novel. Not without reason does Aleksey refer to Blanche as a "devil" and speak of her face as "diabolical." She is indeed the very incarnation of the beauty of the lie. Aleksey, who so clearly perceives that Polina had been taken in by the superficial elegance and form of de Grieux, is himself taken in by the demon of emptiness and banality, Blanche. She was "beautiful to look at," Aleksey observes. But he remarks further that "she has one of those faces that can be terrifying . . . her eyes are black, with yellowish whites, her glance is bold, her teeth extremely white, and her lips always painted; her perfume is musky. . . . She sometimes laughs aloud, showing all her teeth, but usually sits silent with an insolent stare."

Aleksey's capitulation to Blanche symbolizes on the religious-philosophical plane of the novel his falling away from God. "For as soon as the human soul despairs of God," Vyacheslav Ivanov has written, "it is irresistibly drawn to chaos: it finds joy in all that is ugly and warped, and is greeted, from the deepest ravines of Sodom, by the smile of a beauty that seeks to rival the beauty of Our Lady."[11]

Aleksey, now basically indifferent to anything outside of gambling, does not stay long with Blanche. In a final encounter with the Englishman Astley, Aleksey learns that Polina had loved him. "You are a lost man," Astley tells him. "You've grown numb, you have not only renounced your life, your own interests, and those of society, your duty as a citizen and a man, your friends . . . you have not only renounced every goal except that of winning, but you have even renounced your memories." The special mention of memory here is significant. "Insofar as it is 'forgotten,' the 'past'—historical or primordial—is homologized with death," Mircea Eliade has written in connection with the ancient Greek understanding of memory and forgetting. "The fountain Lethe, 'forgetfulness,' is a necessary part of the realm of Death. The dead are those who have lost their memories."[12] For Dostoevsky loss of memory implies a static view of the universe and, ultimately, moral and spiritual death. In turn, restoration of memory—recollection—is linked with a dynamic understanding of human destiny and ultimately a vision of Christian truth and a perception of eternal renewal.

Aleksey's renunciation of his memories is symptomatic of his spiritual disintegration. He speaks of himself as dead but can conceive of resurrection only in terms that parody Christian theological reality. "Tomorrow," he insists, "I can be resurrected from the dead and once again begin to live." But he is dying in a spiritual sense. "Is it possible that I do not realize that I myself am a lost man?" The terminology of Christian salvation, however, returns to his lips (in the deepest regions of his unconscious, of course, he has not forgotten the vision of truth). He is certain that he can "rise again." "In one hour I can change my whole fate." He has in mind, however, salvation at the gambling tables, a new challenge to fate. His final words and the final words of the novel, "tomorrow, tomorrow all will be over," testify to his determination once again, like the Underground Man, to hurl himself against the wall of fate. But on the deeper plane of the novel's

meaning, these same words signify the despair of unbelief and
the unconscious recognition that in a fate-ruled universe there is
no tomorrow, but only a meaningless finality: death without resurrection. Not without reason did Dostoevsky speak of the gambler's world as "a special kind of hell, a special kind of prison
'bath'."

The Temptation and the Transaction: "A Gentle Creature"

Which way I fly is hell; myself am hell.
MILTON, Paradise Lost

THE STORY can be told in a few words. An officer—the future pawnbroker—unwilling to challenge an offending officer from another regiment to a duel, resigns in disgrace from the army. His self-esteem mortally wounded, he decides to become a pawnbroker: "That was my plan, a personal idea of self-torture and self-exaltation." He meets a young girl of fifteen and incorporates her into his plans. He marries her and takes out on her the humiliation he had endured in the army incident. His wife, the "gentle creature," finally rebels, but, unable to find a way out or to endure the relationship and its violent peripeties, she commits suicide by throwing herself out of a window icon in hand. A few hours later the pawnbroker is trying to collect his thoughts and explain the whole affair to himself. "A series of recollections evoked by him," Dostoevsky writes in the preface to this story, "inevitably leads him at last to the *truth*; the truth inevitably elevates his mind and heart." The whole story of the pawnbroker is told in the framework of his interior monologue.

"A Gentle Creature" posits as the first and cardinal human need the need to communicate, the need for understanding and love. Yet it tells the story of a failure to communicate. It shows how people thrust themselves into isolation, withdraw into their egos, lose themselves in a tangle of ratiocination. Their need for love takes on a self-defeating form: seeking each other, they repel each other. Such is the life story of the pawnbroker. "I needed a friend very much," he acknowledges, "but a friend had to be trained, shaped up, and even mastered." The need for communication and love expresses itself in the pawnbroker in the tragedy of solitude, silence, alienation. "You think I didn't love her? Who can say that I did not love her? Don't you see: there's a piece of irony here; what resulted is some evil irony of fate and nature! We are accursed, the life of people in general is accursed! (mine in particular!)." There is evasiveness and rationalization in this protestation. There is an unwillingness to accept personal responsibility. But there is also an unconscious awareness of a profound self-alienation. The pawnbroker is not an evil demon, but he is in the power of a demon of pride and negation; he is ashamed of his shame; he cannot humble himself and make himself vulnerable.

The very form of the narrative, the interior monologue, expresses its central theme—solitude. Monologue is the medium of a man locked within himself, talking only to himself. Alone in himself, the pawnbroker speaks words that echo endlessly in the chambers of consciousness and conscience. The words are not spoken, but thought in silence. Silence is the man. "I am a master of speaking without words. I have spent my whole life without words. I have lived through whole tragedies without words." Silence is also the "game," the "system," the "plan," the "idea" whereby he hopes to bring his wife to a consciousness of his own suffering and, finally, to communication as he understands it: "I wanted her to stand before me and worship my sufferings . . . 'find out for yourself and come to appreciate me'." Silence, finally, is world solitude: "People are alone, and around them is silence—that is the earth!"

The pawnbroker's interior monologue takes on the form of a dialogue, or dialectic, in which reason seeks "order" and sense in the chaos of self and event but finds itself increasingly isolated in the court of conscience. The final discovery of truth is apocalyptic: "I understand too much." Reason is self-convicting. The pawnbroker's order—the rational principle—is revealed as inner disorder. The whole complex processes of rationalization and repression are revealed for what they are: a gigantic fictive structure designed to limit the individual's relation to the world to the kind he can maintain or understand. In the end this structure collapses under the pressure of the truth that it cannot contain. And the truth that we now perceive as the product of all consciousness (and not just the reasoning faculties) is revealed in its

THE TEMPTATION AND THE TRANSACTION

innermost essence: aesthetically, as movement and reciprocity—
and ethically, as love.

1

The initial recollections of the pawnbroker—how he came to meet
the gentle creature and what thoughts or feelings her helplessness
and innocence aroused in him—are sinister and serpentine. We
are witness to an archetypal seduction scene in which innocence
and evil have a direct confrontation. The place of seduction is not
the garden of Eden, however, but the Sodom of St. Petersburg.
A young girl of fifteen badly needs money to advertise for a position; this throws her into contact with the pawnbroker. Cynically, and in a way that reveals his own innermost impulses and
psychology of entrapment, he points to the kind of advertisement
that she should place: "A young lady, wholly orphaned, looking
for position as governess to young children, preferably with an
elderly widower. Willing to take on some household duties."
   In his first encounters with her in the pawnshop the pawnbroker takes pleasure, as he puts it, in "triumphing" over this "good
and gentle" creature. Humiliating her on one occasion over a
transaction involving two roubles, he wonders whether the
triumph was worth the two roubles involved:

> He! He! He! I remember that I twice put to myself precisely
> this question: "Is it worth it? Is it worth it?" And, laughing,
> I answered in the affirmative sense. And I was really quite
> elated at the time. But this wasn't a wicked feeling: I was
> acting with design, with a motive; I wanted to test her, be-
> cause certain ideas with regard to her had suddenly begun
> stirring in my mind. This was my third *special* thought
> about her. (I, 1)

"I noticed her *specially*," the pawnbroker remarks in connection
with the gentle creature's independent and self-respecting stance
at their first meeting, "and thought something of a special sort
about her." He does not indicate the exact nature of these "special" thoughts, but they clearly have to do with thoughts of hu-

miliating her. His choice of words alone reveals the tempter. "I wanted to test her," he remarks several times. No word more exactly defines the pawnbroker's interest in his victim than *ispytat'*, with its various cognate meanings of "test," "tempt," and "torture."

The more aware the pawnbroker is of the gentle creature's self-esteem (he calls it "pride") and her helplessness, the more his special thoughts occur to him. His plans shape up insidiously out of half-conscious predatory instincts. Evil in him takes the shape of a sensual craving for possession and power over another human being: "And the main thing is that even at that time I already regarded her as *mine* and did not doubt my might for a single moment. This thought is an extraordinarily voluptuous one you know, not to be doubted." The pawnbroker regards the gentle creature with the same proprietary feelings that he regards property and money ("the money is *mine*," he remarks later, rebuking her after their marriage for her generosity with customers). "I knew that a woman, and what's more, a sixteen-year-old one, cannot but submit to her husband entirely," he remarks in another connection. She was to go nowhere without him.

Proprietary feelings telescope here with an attitude toward women as property and with a sensual craving for power over another human being. The thought of his wife as *his* is "a most voluptuous one." Furthermore, the pawnbroker recalls thinking at one point, "I like the proud kind." "Proud ones are especially nice when...well, when you no longer have any doubt of your power over them, eh?" "Oh, base, blundering man! Oh, how satisfied I was!" the pawnbroker adds. But at the time he would enjoy various thoughts. For example, he was entranced by the fact that he was forty-one and she was only sixteen: "This feeling of inequality is a very sweet one, a very sweet one." The acquisitive instinct, sensuality, and the craving for power here form, as they do in other works of Dostoevsky, the diabolical core of evil. Dostoevsky believes that evil and the potential for evil, like good and the potential for good, lie in human nature. His description of the pawnbroker's special thoughts is, in the most organic sense, one of the birth of evil.

The pawnbroker seeks in his relationship with his wife what the Underground Man and the gambler find in the real and psychological "game": a sense of power and self-mastery. His entire relationship with her takes on the character of a psychological duel in which, testing her, he tests himself—and finds proof of his own strength and mastery. At the core of the pawnbroker's duel with his wife, however, lies another duel, an abortive one: the real duel he had failed to fight as an officer in the army. The response of the pawnbroker to this unfought duel reveals the pattern of his whole mentality and is relevant to the story's deepest philosophical statement.

In a theater restaurant an officer declares in a loud voice that Captain Bezumtsev, a member of our hero's regiment, has just created a disturbance, "and, it seems, is drunk." "The talk was not carried further," recalls the pawnbroker. "What's more, the story was a mistake, because Captain Bezumtsev was not drunk and the scandal was, strictly speaking, not a scandal." This is, of course, pure sophistry. Some disturbance involving Captain Bezumtsev had taken place. Moreover, the honor of the regiment was sullied by a false accusation. Some action or recognition of the insult was in order.

Why did the future pawnbroker fail to call the offending officer to account? It was out of pride, he explains at one point. It also had something to do with over-sensitivity, he explains later. He had been afraid, not of a duel, but of appearing ridiculous. Moreover, he insists, "I did not want to submit to their tyrannical verdict and challenge someone to a duel when I myself could find no offense." But the peculiar response of the pawnbroker to his inaction, his quibble that the "story was a mistake," reveals the deepest levels of his pride, the most important aspects of his character and outlook. The sophistical argumentation of the pawnbroker is nothing more nor less than the unconscious effort of a bankrupt, rationalistic mind to evade the real sense of the situation, to stake out an area of complete moral and social independence. At the core of his mentality is the persistent striving of pure thought to rupture or deny the crucial "connections" that distinguish the moral universe of man from an amoral world of disconnected and meaningless happenings, the constant attempt of self to project itself as a victim of some senseless "nature," "tyranny," or fate.

The root of his misfortune, the pawnbroker insists, was "a terrible external circumstance." He stresses that "while the incident in the regiment was, perhaps, the consequence of a feeling of unfriendliness toward me, yet without doubt it had an accidental character. I am saying this because there is nothing more offensive and unbearable than to perish as the result of an accident which might or might not have occurred, as a result of an unfortunate concatenation of circumstances which might have passed by like a cloud." This assertion reveals the salient feature of the pawnbroker's philosophical consciousness: his inability to discover or recognize, in practice, the truth of Heraclitus' observation that "a man's character is his fate." He fails to recognize the necessity of judging his actions in moral and social terms.

The pawnbroker is not ruined by chance incident or by "mistake," of course. He is as much responsible for his fate in the regiment as he is later for the death of his wife. In the latter case, too, we encounter a sterile rationalistic mind feverishly denying—yet, paradoxically, under the pressure of conscience, also seeking—what we have termed "connections." The pawnbroker talks repeatedly and fantastically of mistakes he has made in his relations with his wife. The recurrent words "accident" and "mistake" are master threads in a pattern of evasiveness and rationalization. The bedside duel strikes him as an accidental incident. As his wife lies dead in another room, he ruminates: "It is true, it is undoubtedly true that I made a mistake. And quite possibly many mistakes. As soon as we awoke the next morning (it was Wednesday) I at once suddenly made a mistake: ·I suddenly made her my friend." He imagines that the disaster was due to an error in calculation, in short, the result of another accident like the episode in the theater restaurant:

> The main thing, the offensive, thing, is that all this was an accident—a plain, rotten, blind accident. That's what's so offensive! I was just five minutes too late, just five measly

minutes! Had I come five minutes earlier then the moment would have passed by like a cloud, and the thought would have never entered her head again. . . . I was late!!! (II, 4)

The pawnbroker considers all this "improbable," "wild," "impossible," "fantastic," a "misunderstanding." But there is nothing improbable about the tragedy of his wife. This is not an "unaccountable moment" or accident. The gentle creature's suicide is rooted deeply in the pawnbroker's actions and in his world view, which denies a coherent universe. Those who believe that everything is chance, Dostoevsky insists, who comprehend their world in terms of discrete, floating realia of everyday life, of drifting clouds ever grouping and regrouping into accidental patterns of fate—those who comprehend tragedy as a matter of "five minutes too late"—essentially posit a disaggregated, meaningless universe in which there is no personal accountability and in which the individual is a perpetual and righteous defendant before the bar of injustice. They are innocent and the world is to blame. As he contemplates the death of his wife and the tragedy of his life, the pawnbroker indeed casts himself in the role of such a defendant:

What do I care for your laws? What meaning to me your customs, your morals, your life, your state, your faith? Let your judge judge me, let me be brought before your court, before your public court, and I will say that I do not recognize anything. The judge will cry out: "Silence, officer!" And I will cry out to him: "What power do you possess to exact obedience from me, why did gloomy insensibility smash what was more precious to me than anything else? What do I care for your laws now? I sunder myself from everything." Oh, it is all the same to me! (II, 4)

With the loss of all sense of connections in the moral universe and the denial of all foundations, the threat of the absolute nihilism of personality and the concept that "all is permissible" emerge: "I do not recognize anything," "I sunder myself from everything." What is important to note is that the pawnbroker is here only giving open expression to the nihilism that has been latent in his outlook from the beginning. But in his rebellion, he is discovering, too, the truth of his own anguish and solitude; he is recognizing that his solitude is, perhaps, world tragedy. In a figurative and almost literal sense the pawnbroker is condemned to silence, that is, to death.

2

The concept of the duel is central to the idea and structure of "A Gentle Creature." The story is divided into two chapters, consisting of ten sections in all. At the structural center of the work are two duels: the wife's duel with Efimovich (section 5, chap. 1), a former regimental comrade of the pawnbroker, and the pawnbroker's bedside duel with his wife (section 6, chap. 1). These two duels not only are pivotal in a formal structural sense but they also mark a certain reversal of roles in a relationship that itself has the character of a prolonged psychological duel. In the first half of this relationship, the wife is psychologically dependent upon her husband; in the second half, the husband finds himself psychologically dependent upon his wife. The shift takes place in the pivotal sections five and six of chapter one in which the two duels, dynamically interrelated, are contrasted with each other.

The duel of the pawnbroker's wife with Efimovich is the culmination of a long period of increasing tension between husband and wife. She rebels against his miserliness, laughs in his face, and walks out of the house. She seemed to be looking for trouble, remarks the pawnbroker, but "her gentleness was in her way." Nonetheless, on learning of his expulsion from his regiment, she taunts him with it: "Is it true that they expelled you from the regiment because you were too cowardly to fight a duel?" He insists that it was not cowardice on his part but a refusal to submit to the regiment's tyrannical verdict.

This episode, in which the wounds of the pawnbroker are opened again, precedes the meeting between his wife and Efimovich. She has struck up a relationship, an apparently innocent one from her point of view, with Efimovich, and the pawnbroker arranges to spy upon their first private meeting. But the meeting

turns out differently than the pawnbroker expects. His wife skill-
fully and resolutely rejects Efimovich's advances. Her bold confrontation with Efimovich, moreover, contrasts directly with the
pawnbroker's earlier failure to challenge the offending officer.
The pawnbroker had conducted himself, to all appearances at
least—and appearances are all important to him—in a cowardly
way. In her meeting with Efimovich, however, the pawnbroker's
wife conducts herself with courage and aplomb. Her "duel" with
Efimovich constitutes a direct challenge to the pawnbroker. It provides, indeed, the immediate impetus for the bedside duel.

Efimovich's parting words to the pawnbroker at the scene of
the rendezvous are full of sarcasm: "And, you know, although a
decent man shouldn't be fighting a duel with you, yet out of
respect for your lady, I am at your service." The pawnbroker
chooses to duel not with Efimovich, however, but with his wife.
At home, pale and sarcastic, she takes on the look of "almost a
solemn and stern challenge" as he places his revolver menacingly
on the table. What follows is certainly one of the most fascinating
psychological duels in Dostoevsky's work. The external action is
dramatically simple and stark: he lies on his bed the next morning, eyes closed, feigning sleep; she lifts the revolver to his head,
obviously contemplating murder; he momentarily opens his eyes,
as one does at times when one is really asleep, and then closes
them; she puts down the revolver. That is all.

This episode is rich in moral and psychological content. We can
approach the content by asking the question: who has won this
strange duel—the pawnbroker or the gentle creature? The pawnbroker insists that the victory is his. The theory on which he
bases his claim and his exultant feeling of victory is that his wife
knew that in fact he was awake. She knew, therefore, that he
knew she was pointing a revolver at his head, and she knew,
therefore, that he was holding firm. "If she has guessed the truth
and knows that I was not sleeping," he remembers feeling at the
time, "then I have already crushed her by my readiness to accept
death; and now her hand may falter." The moment of confrontation, as he describes it, was "a struggle, a terrible duel for life
and death, the duel of yesterday's coward expelled by his com-

rades for cowardice. I knew this, and she knew it, if only she guessed the truth that I was not sleeping." But, he adds by way of an afterthought, "perhaps nothing of the sort happened, perhaps I didn't even think this at the time." Yet he holds to his theory. When he finally opened his eyes and found her gone, he tells us, he concluded that he had "conquered and she was conquered forever." He had, in his own memorable words, "passed the test of the gun."

In one sense, the pawnbroker is right in proclaiming victory. The duel, after all, ends with the blunting of a proud will actively to resist, to counterattack, even to contemplate destroying the pawnbroker. The peak of his wife's resistance to his campaign of psychological warfare comes when she raises the revolver to his head. Yet at the crucial moment, her hand falters, she puts down the gun. He, for his part, has "passed the test of the gun" without faltering. The direct consequence of this experience is her illness and, ultimately, suicide.

But, we may ask, does she in fact lower the revolver for the reason that the pawnbroker gives—because she knows that he knows, etc. etc. Does she retreat because she is conscious of his alleged courage? The answer is surely no. Dostoevsky's thought is clear: what is experienced by the pawnbroker as a test of wills is experienced by his wife as a moral conflict. The real reason for her faltering hand is her moral nature, her recoil before crime, her refusal, or inability, to transgress. What the pawnbroker remarks earlier about his wife's violent outbursts against him applies here as well: "Gentleness gets in her way." She therefore accepts practical defeat by refusing, as it were, the shot that is rightfully hers. Figuratively speaking, of course, she is committing suicide. But her de facto defeat, in Dostoevsky's view, is a moral victory of stupendous significance for humanity. This is a victory of gentleness and moral conscience over self-will, of good over evil.

Conversely, the pawnbroker's practical victory is a moral defeat in which pride and self-will triumph over moral conscience and decency; it is in every respect a crime. "Why," he asks himself later, "did I not save her from an evil deed?" Save her from what

THE TEMPTATION AND THE TRANSACTION

deed? Save her from the act alone of contemplating murder, a crime that, for Dostoevsky, is inevitably accompanied by self-disfiguration. In his egoism, in his "gloomy despair," the pawnbroker had psychologically tortured his wife and led her to the brink of crime. She withdrew from this abyss, spiritually shattered and overcome by a guilty conscience, only to throw herself later into another abyss. A few hours before her physical suicide, she tells him that "her crime had been tormenting her all winter, tormenting her now, too." Her guilt expresses itself—as does the guilt of Ivan Karamazov—in physical breakdown. Guilt and illness, along with the final psychological blow of his confession, provides the impetus to suicide.

3

The pawnbroker, in his own estimation, had achieved a victory in his bedside duel: "Having passed the test of the gun, I was avenged on my whole gloomy past." He had won his game. This game, of course, had always been conceived on the conscious level as a finite affair. It had as its avowed goal a happy little future, a self-contained, precious utopia that would serve as a final slap in the face of a world that had rejected him. He would, he explains, "erect a wall," save up thirty thousand roubles, and spend the rest of his life somewhere in the Crimea—on the southern coast, in the mountains and vineyards, on an estate bought for his thirty thousand roubles, "and, mainly, away from you all, but without malice, with the ideal in my heart, with a beloved woman, with a family." But this bourgeois idyll only masks antiutopia, the inherent corruption of the game.

The pawnbroker had won the game. Yet, as he recalls, "I decided to *postpone our future* for as long a time as possible and for the time being to leave things as they were. Yes, just then something strange and peculiar happened to me—I don't know how to put it any other way: I had triumphed, and the consciousness of that alone was quite sufficient for me." The literary reminiscence or allusion here is to the baron in Pushkin's play *The Covetous Knight*: "I am above all desires: I am tranquil; I know my strength; I am satisfied with the consciousness of it." Like the baron, the pawnbroker is a dreamer for whom the concrete pleasures, occupations, and goals of life have been replaced by purely psychological ones. The pawnbroker deliberately puts off the "denouement" of his carefully staged and elaborated marriage to the gentle creature. "What had happened was for the moment more than enough for my peace of mind, and contained too many exciting scenes and a lot of material for my dreams. The rottenness of it all is that I am a dreamer. I had enough material, and as for her, I thought, *she could wait.*"

The pawnbroker had masked his relationship with his wife and indeed his whole life style with conventional bourgeois goals. He had looked forward to a respectable marriage, money, an estate, security. He sought a friend in his wife, "but a friend had to be trained, shaped up, even mastered." The strange and peculiar thing he discovers is what he seems aware of from the beginning of his ruminations: that the means had become the end; that the purpose of the game was the game itself; that the enjoyment of his psychological manipulations and torture constituted the main interest of his relationship.

Dostoevsky's understanding of Pushkin's baron is broadly relevant to his conception of the pawnbroker and similar types in his works. When he was quite a child, remarks the hero of *The Raw Youth*, he learned Pushkin's monologue from *The Covetous Knight* by heart. "Pushkin has written nothing finer in concept than that!" he exclaims. "I have the same ideas now." And he sets forth his ideal:

> I don't need money, or, rather, money is not necessary to me, nor power either; I need only what is obtained by power and what can in no way be obtained without power: the solitary and tranquil consciousness of strength! Here is the most complete definition of freedom for which the whole world is struggling! Freedom! At last I have set down that grand word...Yes, the solitary consciousness of strength is alluring and splendid. I have strength and I am serene. (pt. I, ch. 5, sect. 3)

Yet the solitary consciousness of strength, self-isolation, the hoarding of wealth, and the craving for power, as Dostoevsky illustrates throughout his work, lead to self-destructive impotence. Instead of self-realization, the "secret visitor" remarks in *The Brothers Karamazov*, man "falls into complete solitude." Such is the catastrophe of the pawnbroker. The essence of his self-discovery is that he remains locked in his underground solitude, cut off from humanity and his own intimations of paradise within himself.

4

The denouement of the pawnbroker's drama is unplanned. He continues his game until an unexpected moment of terrible reversal when the "scales fall from his eyes." "Was it chance?" he wonders characteristically. He hears his wife singing at one point and is stunned. His first reaction is that of "sudden bewilderment and a terrible surprise, terrible and strange, painful and almost vindictive: 'She is singing, and with me around! *How can she have forgotten about me?*' " He realizes that if she sings in his presence it means that she has forgotten about him. But "ecstasy," he recalls, glowed in his soul and overcame fear. "Oh, irony of fate!" he exclaims. "Really nothing else had been or could have been in my soul all winter than just this ecstasy, but just where had I been all winter? Had I been with my soul?"

What is the reason for the pawnbroker's strange ecstasy at the moment he has been forgotten? Dostoevsky's understanding of this moment is profound: here is the sick ecstasy of a man who senses a total reversal of roles in his relationship, from that of a despot to that of a slave. Here is the ecstasy of a man who senses the possibility of change—change that for such a person comes not from the heart, however, but from a blow from without, and change that can only take a psychologically destructive form. Like the Underground Man, the pawnbroker can experience love only as a despot or slave. He rushes up to his wife, kisses her feet rapturously. "Let's talk...you know...say something!" But she replies with a look of "stern surprise."

CHAPTER IX

The pawnbroker's relationship with his wife has come full circle: from his system of silence ("stern, stern, stern") to her "stern surprise" and a look that says: "So it's love you want? love?" Yet he ecstatically changes his role. He kisses her feet in rapture and happiness. "Turn me into your plaything, your lapdog." The pawnbroker would reverse everything and recover his dream of happiness. But he remains the same egotist. Overwhelming her with affection, suddenly disclosing to her his ravaged and disfigured soul, he tortures her in a new way. In effect, he tears away the last defense she had erected—withdrawal and indifference—and plunges her into deeper emotional and moral confusion. *"And I thought you would just leave me alone."* This reversal of roles on the pawnbroker's part is, as it were, the last shot of the duel. The suicide of his wife is almost inevitable.

In this whole flurry of affection the pawnbroker remains the egotist and the dreamer. He plans to take his wife to Boulogne: "The main thing here was the trip to Boulogne. For some reason I kept thinking that Boulogne was everything, that there was something definitive about Boulogne. 'To Boulogne, to Boulogne!...' I waited madly for the morning." But like Chekhov's later and more attractive dreamers (in *The Three Sisters*), who see in Moscow the resolution of all their difficulties, the pawnbroker is a victim of illusions. His explanations reveal the sterile rationalism of a mind that has long been divorced from feeling: "I made a mistake . . . I suddenly treated her as my friend. I was in a hurry, far too much of a hurry, far too much." He recognizes his mistake, but he cannot perceive the horror of his relations with his wife.

His final ruminations are nonetheless full of the sense of stark tragedy. Guilt and recriminations against a blind universe (he refuses to accept responsibility) mingle with a vision of lost paradise: "Blind, blind! She is dead, she does not hear! You don't know what kind of a paradise I would have surrounded you with! Heaven was in my soul, I would have planted it around you!" It is spiritual death that lies within his soul now, however. The truth is made manifest to him, finally, but in tragic and ambivalent terms. A blinding flash illuminates the landscape of apocalypse, and he cries out: "Insensibility! Oh, nature! People are alone on earth—that is the misfortune!" This insensibility is the same "gloomy insensibility" that he believes has destroyed his wife; it is the same "blind accident" that he insists has introduced such chaos into his life. Inert, insensible nature: this is the same nature—terrible, senseless, disembodied—that appears to the dying Ippolit Terentiev in *The Idiot*.

A world view, without faith or moral center, Dostoevsky believed, must resolve finally into a vision of a world dominated by senseless accident, inert nature, blind fate. The pawnbroker has only a glimpse of moral-spiritual truth: "They say the sun warms the universe. The sun will rise and—look at it, is it not dead? Everything is dead, and dead men are everywhere. People are alone and around them is silence—that is the earth!" A momentary beam of light intersects this darkness. " 'People, love one another': who said that? whose testament is that?" And again darkness: "No, seriously, when they take her away tomorrow, what will become of me?" The last words of the pawnbroker recall the opening question of his monologue: "But they will take her away tomorrow and—how will I make out alone?"

A "succession of recollections," Dostoevsky remarked in his preface to the story, have brought the pawnbroker to the truth, but only for a moment. He immediately plunges back into spiritual darkness. The ancient words of Sophocles' chorus still seem applicable here:

> Oh. Oedipus, most royal one!
> The great door that expelled you to the light
> Gave at night. . . .
> All understood too late.[1]

5

Like a devil, or a man possessed, the pawnbroker tortures, tests, tempts his wife. Yet if he is the devil—and on the symbolic plane of the narrative, he plays this role—we must say that in his ultimate aim he is, like Goethe's Mephistopheles, ultimately confounded and defeated: he does not win the soul of this good and gentle creature. Yet the dangers besetting her path are real. In the mythopoetic terms of the Faust theme—and Goethe's *Faust* forms a kind of literary subtext to "A Gentle Creature"—her marriage to the pawnbroker could be regarded as a contract with the devil, with a chthonic power that seeks, or is driven to seek, her total spiritual destruction. Viewed in these terms, the story of the gentle creature takes shape as a struggle between good and evil. She comes to him with her innocence and faith, and he takes it in pawn. She seeks to redeem her innocence, but he insists that she sacrifice it completely. She refuses to fulfill the terms of the contract and commits suicide. But like Gretchen in Goethe's *Faust*, she is "saved."

The gentle creature faces three temptations in her relations with the pawnbroker: the first is to resolve her desperate situation by pawning her innocence, that is, by marrying the pawnbroker; the second is to betray him; the third is to kill him. The first temptation, to which she succumbs, is symbolized by her pawning of the family icon of the Virgin and Child. The pawnbroker's guilt and confusion in recalling this episode—an episode that had a central place in his efforts to lure and entrap the gentle creature—are enough alone to suggest the ominous significance of this transaction. The pawnbroker struggles to recall the "little details" of the scene in which he accepts her icon in pawn. *Chertochki* in Russian may mean both "little details" and "little things," but it also means "little devils." The inner content of this first transaction is signaled by the appearance of this word in the pawnbroker's speech: "The point is that I want to remember everything now, every single detail, every little thing." But he gets muddled: "I cannot, it is these little things, little things." The guilt-laden pawnbroker is blocked, significantly, by the *chertochki* that define so perfectly the demonic ideas that had been stirring in his mind, that define his intention to pollute and destroy the moral purity, pride, and idealism of the gentle creature. Finally, however, he brings his thoughts "to a point":[2]

> An icon of the Virgin. The Virgin and Child—one that had
> been in the home, ancient, belonged to the family, embossed

metal of silver gilt—well, worth about six roubles. I see that she treasures the icon, is pawning the whole icon without removing the embossed metal. I tell her that it would be better to remove the metal setting and keep the icon; after all, an icon, really, well, is not something to pawn. "Why, are you forbidden to take it?" "No, it's not that I'm forbidden, but it's simply that you yourself..." "All right, remove it." "But you know, I don't think I'll remove it, I'll just put it over there in the icon case," I said after thinking it over, "along with the other icons under the lamp." (I always had a lamp burning before the icons since I opened the shop.) (I, 1)

How much is the Virgin and Child worth? The pawnbroker magnanimously offers her ten roubles for the icon, though it is worth only six. ("You see," the pawnbroker remarks later on, "youth, as a rule, despises money; therefore I immediately made a special point of money; I laid a great stress on money.") The girl replies that she doesn't need ten roubles: "Give me five and I'll redeem it without fail." "So you don't want ten?" he replies. "The icon is worth it." She remains silent and he hands her five roubles, adding: "Don't scorn anybody, I myself have been in these straits, indeed far worse, and if you now see me engaged in this sort of business...well, it's after everything I have endured...."

The buying and selling of the icon of the Virgin and Child—indeed, of any icon—is, as the pawnbroker himself is aware, a profanation of all that is sacred. Yet his efforts to triumph over the girl's innocence and idealism and his desire to make a kind of god of himself ("I wanted her to stand before me and to worship my sufferings") represent the supreme profanation. Even in her desperation the gentle creature finally refuses to equate the worth of the icon with a specific sum of money. (No detail is without significance in Dostoevsky's art.) Her refusal to accept ten roubles points to her unwillingness to participate wholly in the act of profanation; she will "redeem" the icon. On the moral plane, her action bears comparison to Dmitry Karamazov's insistence on keeping half the money given to him by Katerina Ivanovna, an act testifying to his desire to preserve in his own mind his sense of honor.

We have discussed the second and third temptations: the pawnbroker allows a rendezvous to take place between his wife and Efimovich, thus leaving the door open for adultery; and in the bedside duel he tempts her to murder. Yet she rejects both temptations. Her refusal to commit adultery or murder, like her refusal to rob the poor in the pawnshop, is a refusal to transgress, to fulfill, as it were, her contract, irrevocably to sell her soul. Yet each of the temptations involves an impulse toward transgression on her part. By her final suicide—a symbolic redemption of the icon of the Virgin and Child—she redeems her purity.

Direct allusions to Goethe's *Faust* appear in the first section of the pawnbroker's monologue, where he recollects the pawning of the icon of the Virgin and Child. In response to the gentle creature's taunt at one point that he is seeking revenge upon society for all that he has suffered, the pawnbroker recalls Goethe's Mephistopheles: " 'You see', I said half-jokingly, half-mysteriously, 'I—I am a part of that part of the whole which wants to do evil, but creates good....' "[3]

> She looked quickly at me and with great interest, an interest, I suppose, that was mixed with childish curiosity. "Wait a moment...What kind of a thought is that? Where does it come from? I've heard it somewhere...." "Don't rack your brains, it's in these words that Mephistopheles introduces himself to Faust. Have you read *Faust*?" "Well...not carefully." "That is, you didn't read it at all. You ought to read it. However, I see that sardonic smile on your lips again. Please don't imagine I've so little good taste as to disguise my role as a pawnbroker, to want to present myself to you as a sort of Mephistopheles. Once a pawnbroker, always a pawnbroker." (I, 1)

The pawnbroker's reference at this point to Mephistopheles' words and, in particular, his suggestion that the gentle creature read Goethe's *Faust* may be taken, perhaps, as involuntary warnings of his intentions toward her.[4] He is, to be sure, no Faust. Or,

rather, he is a completely disillusioned and cynical Faust, Faust's
alter ego, that is, "a sort of Mephistopheles." And Mephistopheles, George Santayana writes about Goethe's famous couplet,
"does not admit that his activity, while aiming at evil, contributes
unintentionally to the good. It contributes to the good intention-
ally because the evil it does is, in his opinion, less than the evil
it cures. He is the cruel surgeon to the disease of life."[5]

The pawnbroker knows his *Faust* well. In recalling Mephistopheles' words, he indirectly underscores the "good" he seeks
to work. He would save the naive and innocent from themselves.
Like Mephistopheles he is actively hostile to anything that savors
of romanticism or to any pathos of high feeling. He is constantly
mocking his wife's sincerity, her idealism, her "charming mur-
mur of innocence"—all that he identifies with youth's "striving
for the lofty and noble." "Youth is magnanimous, that is, when
it is good—magnanimous and impulsive"; but youth's impulse to
do good is worth absolutely nothing "because it is only a case of
hot blood and an excess of energies, and there is such a passionate
desire for beauty!"

The pawnbroker is intent on eradicating all the highmindedness
in his wife that he has trampled in himself. He is amazed that
she has maintained any idealism at all. Recalling her desperate
plight at the time she first came to his pawnshop, he is surprised
that she could have laughed as she did that day "or have been so
curious about the words of Mephistopheles." "But—there's
youth for you!" he exclaims, and "magnanimity, too: to be able
to say, 'though I am on the edge of the abyss, yet Goethe's great
words are radiant with light'." The irony of the pawnbroker's
words here is that he too is standing at the edge of an abyss as
he plays with the radiant words of Goethe. Like Faust after Wal-
purgis Night, the pawnbroker is approaching his own *trüber Tag*,
his moment of tragic awakening. This moment will be filled with
angry and impotent rebellion and despair—but it will be without
any hope of redemption.

The pawnbroker's implicit comparison of the gentle creature
with Gretchen—for that is certainly in the subtext of his allusion
to Goethe's *Faust*—points to a certain clear similarity in their

fate. The tragedy of the proud young St. Petersburg girl of the Russian 1870s, conscious of her ideals and rebelling against the feudal proprietary claims of her husband, is a far cry from the tragedy of the provincial Gretchen in eighteenth-century Germany. Yet like Gretchen, the gentle creature is a person of directness, simplicity, and religious conviction. Her only crime, it is true, is the contemplation of crime, but her guilt and despair, compounded by the frenzied confession of her husband, is no less terrible than that of Gretchen and reveals a person both of immense purity of ideal and of tragic stature. What Santayana said of Gretchen may also be said of the gentle creature: she is the only true Christian in the poem.

The gentle creature's suicide, a form of self-sacrifice, takes on a mystical and religious form. Lukerya, the maid, recalls that her mistress had taken down the icon of the Virgin and Child and put it on the table, "as though the mistress almost moments before had been saying her prayers." In the final moment before her suicide, the pawnbroker's wife is depicted by Lukerya as standing framed in the window, icon in hand and ready to jump. In that final moment she herself, like Akulka in *House of the Dead*, becomes an icon—eloquent, albeit mute, testimony to her suffering and her imitation of Christ. In that final moment—one that recalls the conversation about the removal of the icon from its silver embossed setting—she hurls herself out of that "setting," out of the mundane, temporal, profane frame of her life. She jumps from the window, holding the icon in her hand. This extraordinary detail alone amply conveys Dostoevsky's final comment on the crime of the gentle creature. His unspoken comment is the same as Goethe's at the end of *Faust*. Mephistopheles cries out to Faust as they flee from Gretchen's prison: "She is condemned" (*Sie ist gerichtet!*), but his words are followed by a voice "from above": "She is saved!" (*Ist gerettet!*).

6

How could Efimovich or any other upper-class person, wonders the pawnbroker after his wife's duel with Efimovich, imagine that they could entice his wife—"that sinless and pure girl who clung to her ideal"—into sin? Yet the man who blandly asks this question has devoted all his efforts to enticing his wife into sin and destroying her ideal. He drives her, finally, into spiritual solitude. But he does not triumph over her as he imagines. It is she who triumphs over him. This reversal is conveyed with extraordinary force and beauty in the scene where the pawnbroker discovers his wife singing. Her voice, formerly strong, resonant, and healthy, is now

> faint—oh, it was not that it was mournful (it was some kind of love song) but it was as though something in the voice had snapped, broken, as though the song itself was sick. She sang in a low voice and, suddenly, rising on a high note, her voice broke off—such a pathetic little voice, it broke so pitifully; she cleared her throat and again began softly, softly, ever so softly singing.... (II, 2)

The pawnbroker stresses the mournful, faint character of his wife's song. Yet the song also reflects the affirmative voice of the human spirit. It is pitiful and tragic—but it is a song!

The gentle creature journeys from innocence to tragic knowledge, but she preserves her ideal of beauty and her essential humanity. She succumbs to neither cynicism nor self-pity. Hers is the journey of a free person. The pawnbroker casts himself in the role of a victim of external forces—circumstances, nature, ill will and hostility, fate. Yet if anyone could justly complain about being a victim of fate, it would be the gentle creature. An orphan brought up in "poverty and filth," slaving in the house of coarse and conniving relatives, she has to choose, ultimately, between a shopkeeper who would beat her to death and a pawnbroker who would torture her psychologically and drive her to suicide. She is a victim of a hostile family, environment, and circumstances. When she walks out of her husband's house, as the pawnbroker rightly notes, "she had nowhere to go." But in contrast to the pawnbroker, she does not renounce her moral freedom or her sense of personal responsibility. In the conception of Dostoevsky, she is gentle but not weak or meek. Her rebellion is that of a genuinely independent person, conscious of her dignity and rights.

The "blazing eyes" of the gentle creature when she stands up to her husband are a symbol not only of the moral force and idealism of youth but of a new sense of rights among many Russian women in the 1860s and 1870s. Not without reason does the pawnbroker, who is enchanted by the "inequality" of the sexes, wonder at one point whether his wife is "a member of one of the new movements." She is not a member of these new movements, but she embodies the force of independence that was beginning to make itself felt in the world of Anna Karenina. When she walks out of her house, she anticipates by two years Nora's famous declaration of independence at the end of Ibsen's *Doll House*. But unlike Nora, the gentle creature neither lives in a doll's house nor has any place to go.

The pawnbroker speaks sarcastically of his wife's "straightforward character, ignorance of life, cheap convictions of youth, utter blindness of a 'noble soul'." She can indeed be characterized by her idealism, nobility of soul, feeling for justice, moral rectitude, and passionate desire for beauty. These are also, interestingly, the qualities that Dostoevsky admired in the heroine of his youth: George Sand. On the occasion of Sand's death Dostoevsky wrote in the June 1876 issue of *Diary of a Writer*: "I understood what this name had meant in my life, how much delight and veneration this poet evoked in me at one time and how much joy and happiness she gave me!" "Women of the world," he wrote, "should now don mourning garb in her memory because one of their loftiest and most beautiful representatives has passed away and, in addition, an almost unprecedented woman by reason of the power of her mind and talent."

In his moving essay Dostoevsky speaks not only of the great ideals that George Sand "conceived in her soul" but of her heroines. He writes of how as a youth he was impressed by the "chaste, lofty purity of types and ideals" in her work. A heroine of such lofty moral purity, he maintains, would have been unimaginable without "a tremendous moral quest in the soul of the poet herself, without the confession of the most complete duty, without the comprehension and recognition of the most sublime beauty and mercy, patience and justice." But side by side with these qualities was "an extraordinary pride of the quest and of the protest," a pride that "sprang from the most sublime truth without which mankind could never have retained its place on so lofty a moral height," a pride based on "a feeling of the most chaste impossibility of reconciliation with untruth and vice."[6] Without any question, Dostoevsky's story "The Gentle Creature," which appeared in the November 1876 issue of *Diary of a Writer* less than half a year after his articles on George Sand, gives evidence of his veneration of the French writer.

X

The Fourth Window:
"A Boy at Christ's Christmas Party"

> *"He had a dream," they say, "an hallucination, delirium."*
> *Oh! Is that really so clever? And they are so proud! A dream?*
> *What is a dream? And is not our whole life a dream?*
> DOSTOEVSKY, "The Dream of a Ridiculous Man"

IT IS Christmas Eve. A child of five or six, hungry and cold, leaves a dark and deserted slum basement where his mother has just died and makes his way to a fashionable St. Petersburg avenue flooded with light and people. On his journey up the avenue the boy passes three windows, each more fantastic than the last. In the first window he sees a gleaming Christmas tree with children running about laughing and playing. In the second window he sees another Christmas tree and tables loaded with cakes of all kinds. He goes in, but is quickly hustled out by the proprietors. Frightened, he starts to run. But his attention is drawn to a third window full of tiny puppet dolls in little red and green frocks, "so real that they seem alive." Someone grabs him, though, and kicks him violently, and he rushes off to a courtyard where he hides behind a woodpile. There, as he freezes to death, he feels that somebody is clasping him tenderly in his arms; and "suddenly" he finds himself with other happy boys and girls around a splendid Christmas tree. "This is Christ's Christmas party," they tell him. "On this day of the year Christ always has a party for those little children who have no Christmas party of their own."

This story or sketch appears in Dostoevsky's *Diary of a Writer*, January 1876, chapter two. It is bracketed by two other sketches devoted to the plight of poor, homeless street boys. The first extremely brief sketch, "A Boy with his Hand Outstretched for Alms," forms a kind of prologue to "A Boy at Christ's Christmas Party." The third sketch in the trio, "A Settlement for Juvenile Delinquents," is given over to a description of a reform institution and the problem of the "conversion of wanton souls into virtuous ones." "On the third day of the holiday season I saw all these 'fallen' angels, all fifty of them together. Don't think that I am jesting when I refer to them in this manner: that they are 'insulted' children there can be no doubt. Insulted by whom? How and in what way? And who is to blame?"[1]

"A Boy at Christ's Christmas Party" is a moving Christmas story, as ecstatic in its religious idealism as it is brutal in its social realism. At the same time, it constitutes a kind of statement on the nature of reality and the scope of realism. Dostoevsky not only speaks to the reader directly in occasional comments about the writer's art, but also he addresses him, as it were, indirectly, by allowing him to witness the process of artistic creation. He creates a story before the reader's eyes and in this way awakens the reader to the purely conventional nature (at least in his art) of such designations as "fiction" and "reality," "realistic" and "fantastic."

The opening line of "A Boy with his Hand Outstretched for Alms" seems to anticipate an account of a dream or a story: "Children are strange people; they are subjects for dreams and phantasms."[2] But Dostoevsky does not follow these words directly with a dream or a story. Instead, he provides his reader with an account of some recent street encounters he has had with a poor boy:

> Before and during the Christmas season and on the very day of Christmas, I have been meeting on a street, at a certain corner, a little boy no more than seven years of age. At a time of severe frost he was dressed almost as though it were summer. But he had some kind of old piece of cloth around his neck, which would mean that somebody in any case had been attending to him before sending him out. He was going about "with a little hand": this is slang for "begging alms." The phrase was invented by the boys themselves.[3]

Dostoevsky introduces the reader to one particular boy here, but he goes on to generalize about the desperate existence of a multitude of street boys who are exploited by drunken peddlers inhabiting slum basements. He describes the ways in which the children are recruited to beg for money, how they serve their drunken employers, and how they often turn into accomplished little criminals prowling about the town. "Thievery turns into a passion even among eight-year-olds, sometimes even without any awareness of the criminal nature of their acts," Dostoevsky writes in the concluding lines of the first sketch. "Sometimes these wild creatures understand nothing at all, neither where they are living, nor to what nationality they belong, nor whether there is a God or a tsar; such things are even told of them as are incredible to hear and yet they are all facts."[4] Dostoevsky, then, opens "A Boy with his Hand Outstretched for Alms" with a remark that children are subjects for dreams and phantasmas and concludes it with an observation that brings out its central idea: the actual life of these children has a fantastic character. "True events, depicted in all the exclusiveness of their occurrence," Dostoevsky wrote in "Mummer" in *Diary of a Writer*, 1873, "nearly always take on an aura that is fantastic, almost incredible."[5]

The theme of incredible reality or truth is central in "The Golden Age in the Pocket," a brief sketch in *Diary of a Writer* that precedes "A Boy with his Hand Outstretched for Alms." Dostoevsky insists here that the "golden age"—the realization of goodness, purity, and magnanimity in life—lies within people themselves; it is so deeply hidden, however, that "long ago it began to seem incredible." Yet this golden age, he firmly maintains, is "an absolute truth...." The trouble with people is that this truth seems incredible to them, Dostoevsky concludes.[6] The most lofty spiritual truths, like the seemingly fantastic truths of actuality, are not readily perceived or recognized. These truths appear incredible. And yet they are facts, the very essence of reality. With this general notion seeded in his reader's mind, Dostoevsky turns in *Diary of a Writer* to "A Boy at Christ's Christmas Party," a story that indeed appears incredible on all levels of its action—mundane and spiritual:

But I am a novelist and, it seems, I have made up one "story" myself. Why do I write "it seems"? After all, I know for certain that I made it up; yet I keep on fancying that it must have happened somewhere at some time, that it must have happened precisely on Christmas Eve in *some* great city and in a time of terrible frost. I fancy a boy in a basement, but still very little, about five or six. This boy wakes up in the morning in a damp and cold basement. He is wearing a sort of little dressing gown and is shivering with cold. His breathing gives off a cloudy white vapor; sitting on a box in the corner, he puffs the vapor out of his mouth and amuses himself watching it float away. But he is terribly hungry.

The tone of the opening line here seems playful, but Dostoevsky is quite serious. His reluctance to acknowledge that he made up his story casts into question the very notion of the novelist as an inventor of tales. In the preceding sketch, "A Boy with his Hand Outstretched for Alms," he had just given an account of an actual personal encounter with a child-beggar; further, he reported quite factually there on the incredible lives lived by these unfortunate children. The story that he is about to tell clearly involves one such child. Dostoevsky does not insist, to be sure, on exact or literal truth (he acknowledges that he did not meet the particular child in his story). He knows for certain that in a formal sense he has made up the story. But his "it seems" is not empty play. The child in his story—and his fate—is typical among street boys. And as Dostoevsky remarks in "Cultured Little Characters" in the April 1876 issue of *Diary of a Writer*, "the whole depth, the whole content of an artistic work consists . . . only in types and characters."[7]

Dostoevsky's central notion of art as mimesis is involved here. The artist imagines a little child in a basement; he is haunted by phantasmic images from everyday life. Artistic creation here means receiving impressions from reality and forming them into images. This aesthetic forming involves generalization, of course. And for Dostoevsky it involves above all a moral and spiritual reshaping, or transfiguration, of the material of reality. But it does not involve invention or fabrication. Rather, the writer reveals incredible reality or truth in his art; he makes credible to the everyday eye of man all that may seem too extraordinary or improbable to admit of belief. Not art, but reality is fabulous. And reality for Dostoevsky encompasses the full range of human experience, aspirations, visions, and nightmares. "I have my special view of reality (in art)." Dostoevsky wrote in a letter to N. N. Strakhov in 1869, "and what the majority calls almost fantastic and exceptional for me is sometimes the very essence of the real."[8] The story entitled "A Boy at Christ's Christmas Party" is preeminently this kind of fantastic realism.

The theme of incredible reality finds embodiment in Dostoevsky's account of the perceptions of the little boy—first, as he peers into the three great windows, and second, as he participates in Christ's Christmas party at the moment of his death. Fashionable Nevsky Prospect (clearly the great avenue to which Dostoevsky alludes), with its lights, its crowds of excited and festive people, its horses and carriages, is an incredible sight to the little boy. But the three windows hold special wonders. They reveal what he has never seen before and what to him is a fantasy world. He comes to the first:

> Oh, what a large glass window, and behind the glass a room, and in the room a tree that reaches up to the ceiling; it is a fir tree and on it are ever so many lights, gold papers and apples, and right by are dolls and little toy horses; and children, clean and dressed in their finest, are running about the room, laughing and playing and eating and drinking something. Over there a little girl has just begun to dance with a boy; what a pretty little girl! And through the glass one hears the sound of music.

This dazzling and joyous scene, albeit almost unreal, is a child's paradise. And yet, like the adult's lost paradise, this is not one in which he can participate. This is not his reality; it is his fiction. And yet it is a fact!

> The little boy gazes in wonder, even begins to laugh, but his fingers and toes are beginning to hurt, while his hands have

grown quite red and the little fingers won't bend any longer and it is painful to move them. And suddenly the little boy remembers that his fingers are hurting him, bursts into tears and runs on.

Through the second window the boy sees another Christmas tree and another incredible sight: tables heaped with cakes of all sorts, "almond cakes, red cakes, yellow cakes," and—wonder of wonders—"four rich ladies" are handing out cakes to whoever walks in! It appears to the boy that anyone can participate in this wondrous feast of life. But this is an illusion that yields, like the fantasy of the first window, to the actualities of his life and disillusionment. He goes into the store but is ejected. A coin is pressed into his hand, but it rolls onto the ground: he cannot close his fingers upon it, in the same way that he cannot enter into his dream world:

> The little child runs off—running—running as fast as he can, whither he knows not. Once more he wants to cry but is frightened and he just goes on running and blowing at his hands. And despair suddenly overcomes him because suddenly he feels so alone and so badly, but suddenly, oh Lord! What is this again? People are standing in a crowd in wonder.

The third incredible scene that meets the little boy's eye is the third window, behind which can be seen three little puppet dolls— "so real that they seem alive"—little musicians rocking their heads and moving their lips:

> At first the little boy thought they were alive, but when he realized that they were only puppet dolls he suddenly laughed. He had never seen such puppets and did not know that such things existed! And he wanted to cry, and yet the puppets seemed so terribly funny to him.

Few lines convey a more painful sense of exclusion and loss, a sense of lost paradise, than the two phrases that are juxtaposed with one another: he "did not know that such things existed!

And he wanted to cry." Thus, too, the dim memory of a lost paradise evokes anguish in the ridiculous man. But whereas he bears responsibility for the fall, the child is innocent. The crime against the child—his exclusion from the child's paradise—is the most heinous of crimes. The reader of Dostoevsky's story is also implicated in this crime. He perhaps does not know, or does not wish to know, that such terrible things existed; or perhaps he regards them as incredible and therefore exceptional. Or perhaps he has not grasped the terrible truth of everyday reality. Reading Dostoevsky's story, he too wants to cry.

Dostoevsky plays with the theme of incredible reality throughout his story. What is fantasy and what is real? What is illusion and what is reality? Only art with its multiple perspectives provides the answer. The perception of "reality" clearly depends on the viewer and the vantage point from which he sees his surroundings. To the child, the world revealed in the three windows is incredible; and yet it is real. To the ordinary passerby, that same fantastic world holds nothing astonishing.

The three windows and the happy, contented world they reveal are incredible not only to the child, however, but to the reader who recognizes himself and his world on the other side of the glass. By compelling the reader first to look out into the world of the lower depths and then to look back again at his own world through the eyes of the child, Dostoevsky defamiliarizes, indeed almost demonizes, the reader's reality: what had always seemed right and good now seems evil because of its exclusiveness and moral indifference. All that seems the very essence of the Christmas spirit now seems the beauty of the lie. The dazzling windows that amaze the child for the reader bear witness to a world inhabited by soulless people-dolls. This world that fleetingly appears to the reader as he looks out of the window at the child and then back again into the window is the same uncanny, phantasmic world of Gogol's "Nevsky Prospect": the tragic world of St. Petersburg, a world where at night the devil lights up the lanterns and "all is deception."

Yet Dostoevsky appeals in *Diary of a Writer* to the very St. Petersburg society that makes a pariah of the street children. His

sense of the possibility of change in man is apocalyptic. In "A
Golden Age in the Pocket" a fantastic thought comes into his
head as he watches the old folk dance after a children's ball:

> What now—I thought—would happen if all these nice and
> respectable guests became sincere and ingenuous if only for
> one moment? What would suddenly become of this stuffy
> hall? What if each one of them suddenly learned how much
> straightforwardness, honesty, sincerity, heartfelt joyousness,
> purity, magnanimity of feelings, intellect—nay, more than
> intellect—wit of the most refined, communicative kind there
> is in each of them, decidedly in each of them! . . . You do
> not believe that you are so beautiful. . . . But the trouble is
> that you yourselves don't know how beautiful you are! Do
> you know that each and every one of you, if only he wanted
> to, could immediately bring happiness to everybody in this
> hall and captivate everybody? And this power is in each of
> you, but it is so deeply hidden that long ago it began to seem
> incredible. And is it possible, is it possible that the golden
> age exists only on porcelain teacups?[9]

But no dream of the golden age, no vision of happiness or of
a happy humanity is granted to the fashionable inhabitants of
Nevsky Prospect. It is to the freezing and terrified child huddled
behind the woodpile that such a dream comes. As he slips over
the boundary separating life and death, he quite suddenly begins
to feel good, his hands and feet cease to hurt, and he feels warm.
He laughs as he again recalls the puppet dolls. And "suddenly"—
Dostoevsky, as though to intensify the apocalyptic mood, uses
this word twelve times in the last part of the story—suddenly the
boy hears the voice of his mother leaning over him and singing
a song; and he thinks: "Mother, I am sleeping, ah, how good it
is to sleep here." The boy has a sensation of a totally new reality:

> "Come with me, little boy, to the Christmas party," a quiet
> voice above him suddenly whispered. He thought at first that
> this was still his mother, but no, it was not she; just who it
> was who was calling to him he could not see, but somebody

bent over him and embraced him in the darkness; and he stretched out his hand to him and...and suddenly, oh what light! Oh, what a Christmas tree! And yet this was not a Christmas tree, indeed he had never seen such a tree! Where was he now? Everything was bright and shining, and all round him were puppet dolls, but no—these are all boys and girls, only so bright and shining, all of them are circling around him, flying, all of them are kissing him, lifting him up and carrying him along with them, indeed, even he is flying, and he sees his mother looking at him and laughing joyfully. "Mother! Mother! Ah, how good it is here, Mother!" the boy cries out to her and again kisses the children and wants to tell them at once about those puppet dolls behind the glass.

In his early story "White Nights" (1848) Dostoevsky speaks of the way the fantasy of the dreamer unconsciously catches up the passing surroundings in its "playful flight" and "capriciously" weaves "all and everything in its canvas." We are witness to a similar capricious play of fantasy in the last moments of the boy's life, moments when imagination, deprived now of all external stimuli, turns inward. The boy's image of Christ's Christmas party is a last composite image of the magical life he found in the three windows on Nevsky Prospect; the moments of delight and tenderness he associated with his mother; and, probably, the fragments of religious ritual, stories, revelations that made their way into his unconscious.

The child's vision of Christ's Christmas party might be called the fourth window in Dostoevsky's sketch, but it is a window that the child can step through. Here again is a child's paradise. The incredible world of the three windows—a world reserved for the rich and comfortable—has become the paradise for the poor, for the "insulted children," "for those little children who have no Christmas party of their own." "Even he is flying." Here in the imagination of the child illusion becomes reality. The vision of the dying boy in the deepest sense is not a break with reality, but a realization of a dream in a dream. The vision of the fourth window is a moral and social revolution, a vision of paradise on earth.

The little boy's vision of Christ's Christmas party is also Dostoevsky's own moral-religious vision. We cannot doubt for a moment that Dostoevsky's underlying thought at this high point of his sketch is the same as Paul's question to King Agrippa: "Why should it be thought a thing incredible with you, that God should raise the dead?" (Acts 2:8). Yet the accent in the boy's vision is not only upon the idea of the raising of the dead, but also upon the idea of retribution for suffering. In "A Boy at Christ's Christmas Party," as in the chapter entitled "Rebellion" in *The Brothers Karamazov*, Dostoevsky builds up an almost intolerable ethical tension involving the suffering of children. Justice—the demand for some kind of balancing of the scales—becomes not only an ethical but an aesthetic imperative. The little boy's vision is perceived by the reader not only as a psychological phenomenon but as an aesthetic fulfillment of an ethical demand, that is, as poetic justice.

Yet for all his own felt need to balance the sufferings of this world with the joys of another, Dostoevsky does not permit himself, or the reader, to escape the actualities of existence in the here-and-now. Just as incredible actuality is repeatedly interrupted, as it were, by idyllic or paradisiacal scenes (the three windows and the vision of Christ's Christmas party) in the first part of the story, so the pattern is reversed in the last part of the story: the wondrous vision is interrupted by incredible actuality. The reader learns that the angelic little boys and girls were just like the little boy:

> But some had frozen in the baskets in which they had been laid on the doorsteps of well-to-do Petersburg officials; others had been boarded out with Finnish women by the Foundling and had been suffocated; others had died at their starved mother's breasts (in the Samara famine); and still

others suffocated in third class railway carriages from the foul air.

The scenes are brutal and inescapable. But Dostoevsky returns again to the iconographic scene of rejoicing. The little boy's dream has now become almost exclusively his own dream:

> And yet they were all here, they were all like angels about Christ and He was in the midst of them and held out His hands to them and blessed them and their sinful mothers.... And the mothers of these children stood on one side weeping; each one knew her boy or girl, and the children flew up to them and kissed them and wiped away their tears with their little hands, and begged them not to weep because they were so happy.

But the divine moment of rejoicing and reconciliation is interrupted again by a reference to a harsh detail "down below": "In the morning the porter found the little dead body of the frozen child on the woodstack; they sought out his mother, too.... She had died before him." Dostoevsky does not finish the narrative part of his sketch on this harsh note. He insists on a conclusion that is tonic: "They met before the Lord God in heaven." It is noteworthy, however, that this meeting appears only in the second edition of the story (1879). [10] In the original version of *Diary of a Writer* Dostoevsky resisted the obvious urge to soften his stark realism.

The effect of these final rapid alternations between paradise and hell, between the Petersburg palaces and basements, is to bring the reader back to the starting point of the sketch—to incredible everyday reality. Dostoevsky's final lines, recalling the opening words of his sketch, serve to awaken the reader from his trance:

> And why did I make up such a story, one that conforms so little to an ordinary, reasonable diary—especially a writer's diary? And this, after I had promised stories chiefly about real events! But the point is that I keep on fancying and imagining that all this might really have happened—that is, what took place in the basement and behind the wood pile;

but as for Christ's Christmas party, I really don't know what
to say to you, could it have happened or not? Being a novelist I have to invent things.

The last line here, like the entire paragraph that it caps, is intended as gentle irony. Dostoevsky affirms the reality of the incredible vision of Christ's Christmas party as passionately as he
affirms the phantasmic actuality of the Petersburg lower depths.

In "A Boy at Christ's Christmas Party" Dostoevsky brings the
hellish world of the lower depths to the attention of his reader.
Everyday life, all that which may be seen but which in its famil-
iarity is ignored, is realized in the terrible life of a single child.
This actuality, this violation of innocent, childlike happiness and
beauty, is incredible to moral consciousness. It is a phantasma—
and yet it is a fact! In the second part of the sketch Dostoevsky
moves in an opposite direction. What is not seen, that is, all the
incredible potential for goodness, love, and communion that Dostoevsky finds in men's hearts, is realized for a single moment in
the child's vision. This child's paradise, for all its characteristics
of a religious idyll, is neither more nor less than a moment of
authentic love and communion among people on earth.

In the final analysis, Dostoevsky's sketch is a direct response to
Schiller's notion that the idea of a condition of innocent and
happy humanity (die Idylle) "and the belief in the possible reality
of the same is the only thing that can reconcile man to all the
evils to which he is subjected on the path to culture." It was the
task of the man of culture, Schiller believed, to show that this
possible reality is real and can be realized in the sensuous world.
But since "real experience, far from nourishing this belief, much
the contrary continually contradicts it, so here it is the task of
poetry to come to the aid of reason in order to bring this idea to
view and to realize it in a single case."[11]

The Ridiculous Man—Beyond Don Quixote

Time past and time future
What might have been and what has been
Point to one end, which is always present.
T. S. ELIOT, Burnt Norton

" 'HEROES! You gentlemen novelists are always seeking heroes,' a man of vast experience said to me the other day," reads the January 1876 issue of Dostoevsky's *Diary of a Writer.* " 'And not finding heroes in our midst, you feel angry and grumble at all Russia, but I will tell you one anecdote'." The anecdote is about an obscure official who, in the days of serfdom, would set aside money from a negligible salary in order to buy serfs and free them. "Of course," Dostoevsky's interlocutor concludes, "what kind of a hero is he: merely an 'idealist of the 1840s,' perhaps even a ridiculous and incompetent one, since he thought he could cope with the whole calamity through his microscopic personal effort." "These are the people we need!" Dostoevsky notes with enthusiasm. "I am terribly fond of this comic type of little fellow who seriously imagines that through his microscopic effort he will be able to help the general cause."[1]

In "The Dream of a Ridiculous Man" Dostoevsky presents his reader with one of those comic little fellows. Though a vastly more complex figure than the obscure official in the above-mentioned anecdote, the hero of "Dream" ends up as one of those ridiculous idealists of whom Dostoevsky was so fond. After his dream, and at the very end of his account, the ridiculous man informs his reader that he has found the little girl he had rebuffed and is going to help her. The gesture is microscopic in the context of world evil disclosed in the story, but it has enormous importance from the moral-philosophical viewpoint of Dostoevsky. "All is like an ocean, all is flowing and blending," Zosima remarks in *The Brothers Karamazov.* "A touch in one place sets up movement at the other end of the earth." The ridiculous man arrives at a full awareness of this ocean only after his traumatic dream.

1

The central attribute or characteristic of the hero of Dostoevsky's "Dream"—one that defines him in all periods of his life—is his "ridiculousness." From the earliest time he can remember, he has had a sense of being ridiculous. This sense of being ridiculous "in all respects" was deepened not only by his studies in school and university but by his whole life experience. People always laughed at him. They did not guess, he insists, that he more than anybody knew the full extent of his condition. He was just too "proud" to admit it to anyone. He suffered terribly at first, but as he grew up, he became more tranquil about the whole matter. Just why he cannot explain: "Perhaps because a terrible anguish sprang up in my soul over one circumstance which far transcended me in importance: this was a certain conviction that took hold of me—that everywhere throughout the whole world *nothing made any difference.*"

Two things stand out clearly in the ridiculous man's account of his childhood and youth: first, his acute sense of personal identity, of being different, set apart from his peers, even superior to them in some sense (he stresses his pride); second, his profound sensitivity to moral and spiritual values, a sensitivity signaled by his terrible anguish that nothing makes any difference in the world. Because of this sensitivity, he suffers a moral-psychological breakdown of near catastrophic proportions. The point here deserves a certain emphasis. The ridiculous man evolves not from a state of apathy to moral-spiritual conviction, but from a state of elevated moral-spiritual consciousness to apathy and then back again to a new level of heightened sensitivity to man and society. In other words, he remains consistent to his basic moral and spiritual nature.

"What does nihilism mean?" Nietzsche asks in connection with his analysis of "European nihilism." He answers: *"That the highest values devaluate themselves.* The aim is lacking; 'why?' finds no answer."[2] The crisis of values is reflected dramatically in the story of the ridiculous man. But the resolution of his crisis is not in Nietzsche's hoped for "countermovement"—one involving the creation of new values—but in a rediscovery of traditional, essentially Christian values.

Life experience leads the ridiculous man, a "modern Russian progressive" with a "great store of learning in science and philosophy," to a peculiar state of indifference to himself, society, the world. He falls prey to a kind of psychological anomie: seemingly without center or direction, he wills nothing, desires nothing, simply drifts. His condition can be summed up in a phrase that recurs in his speech: *vse ravno*, it's all the same, it makes no difference, nothing matters. He becomes fully convinced a short while before his dream that "it would *make no difference* at all . . . if the world existed or if nothing existed anywhere at all." If he has a world view at this point, it can be summed up in his solipsistic thought that "the world seemed to be created for me alone." In this state of mind, he resolves to kill himself and buys a revolver. But he does not use it. He is just too indifferent. Even suicide requires some impulse to action. One dismal night, however, it suddenly occurs to him that "if the gaslight were to be extinguished everywhere, everything would become much more cheerful, since the gaslight made the heart sadder because it illuminated [the dismal night]." At that very moment he notices a star amidst the "fathomless black patches" of the sky and peers at it intently. The star gives him the idea of killing himself: "Just why the star gave me that idea I don't know."

The significance or role of the star in the ridiculous man's decision to kill himself can only be comprehended, initially, in the context of his gloomy thoughts about the gaslight. The gaslight is oppressive because it illuminates the misery about him; by extinguishing it he would presumably eliminate the misery. The light of the star is analogous to the gaslight, but what it illuminates is more oppressive: "fathomless black patches," ontological emptiness, that is, meaninglessness. "And the light shineth in darkness, and the darkness comprehended it not" (John 1:5). In the deepest sense, Dostoevsky understands suicide as an extinguishing of the light, an objective denial of the Light, a denial of God and immortality. Thus, to kill oneself is—on the symbolic plane—to kill God and to affirm the utter meaninglessness of all life. Yet as the dream of the ridiculous man reveals, the pure light of the star glows in his heart, in the depths of his unconscious; it is associated with an age-old dream of beauty and paradise. "I often told them," he recalls later in connection with his conversations with the "children of the sun"—the inhabitants of his dream-paradise—"that I had had a presentiment of it long before, that all this joy and glory had been revealed to me in the form of a poignant anguish that at times approached insufferable sorrow; that I had had a presentiment of it all and of their glory in the reveries of my heart and the dreams of my mind."

The anguish of the ridiculous man is that of a man who has yearned in his heart for all this beauty and glory but no longer actively believes in it. The majority of Russian suicides, Dostoevsky wrote in "Something about Youth" in the December 1876 issue of *Diary of a Writer* a few months before publishing "Dream," can be traced to one "spiritual disease—the absence of the sublime idea of existence in their souls. In this sense, our indifference—a contemporary Russian disease—is gnawing at our souls." The desire to kill oneself is an impulse of "anguish, unconscious, perhaps, for the sublime significance of life which they have found nowhere."[3] The suicidal act, then, in spite of its conscious denial of life's meaning, paradoxically attests to the soul's longings for the "sublime goals of life." The ridiculous man's impulse to suicide is rooted in spiritual anguish. The star gives him the idea of suicide because it illuminates in the most painful way his own dream and his tormenting despair over it.

"And so, just as I was looking at the sky, this little girl suddenly grasped me at the elbow," relates the ridiculous man. The juxtaposition of the sky and child points to a central truth in Dostoevsky's novelistic universe: the interdependence of the finite and infinite, concrete and abstract, earthly and spiritual. The most lofty spiritual aspirations of man mean nothing if they are not realized, recognized, treasured in their earthly manifestation. The beauty of the child and the beauty of the dream are inseparable. Man—the human image—is the measure of all things.

Goethe's Werther, Dostoevsky wrote in the opening pages of the January issue of *Diary of a Writer* in 1876, before committing suicide expressed "regret that he would never again behold 'the beautiful constellation of the Great Bear'." Why, Dostoevsky asks, were these constellations so dear to the young Werther?

> Because, whenever he contemplated them he was conscious of the fact that he was by no means an atom, by no means a nothing before them, that this whole abyss of mysterious divine miracles was by no means higher than his thought, higher than his consciousness, higher than the ideal of beauty in his soul, and, therefore, was equal to him and made him akin to the infinity of being...and that for the happiness of feeling this great thought which reveals to him who he is, he is indebted exclusively *to his human image.*[4]

The Russian suicide, according to Dostoevsky, had not "even a shadow of suspicion that he is called 'I' and that he is an immortal creature."[5] But in "Dream," Dostoevsky suggests quite the opposite: more than a suspicion of immortality lies behind the mask of indifference of the ridiculous man.

"I gathered that her mother was dying somewhere nearby," the ridiculous man continues with regard to the child who interrupts his contemplation of the sky, "or that something had happened there and that she had run out to call someone, to find someone who would help her mother." At first the ridiculous man tells her to find a policeman, but the child persists. "It was at that point that I stamped my foot at her and shouted," he recalls. The encounter with the child sets into motion a revolution in the consciousness of the ridiculous man. Why did he not help the girl, he wonders. He admits that at the time he had felt pity for her and would have helped her. The thought that his humane impulse contradicted his rational assessment of his situation—his indifference—blocked this human response, however. But surely, he counters, his impending extinction should have had some "slight influence" on his feeling of pity for this girl or his feeling of shame:

> It had seemed clear to me that life and the world in some way or other depended upon me now. It might even be said

that the world had been created, as it were, for me alone: if I were to shoot myself, there would be no more world—for me at any rate. Not to speak of the possibility that, perhaps, nothing really would exist for anyone after me, and that once my consciousness was extinguished the whole world would be extinguished at once like a spectre, as though it were some accessory of my consciousness, and would be abolished, because, perhaps, this whole world and all these people are really nothing more than me alone. (2)

The reflections of the ridiculous man reveal first of all the undisputed authority that pure reason and logic had acquired in his mind. Indeed, it was not so much a specific line of thought—in this case, his solipsistic outlook—that blocked his humane impulse as it was the pure act and habit of ratiocination, that is, consciousness itself. He did not help the child in the first instance "because of an idea" that came to him; he was vexed by a "conclusion" he had drawn from a "reflection"; he was taken up by contradictions between thought and feeling (he had felt "a strange pain" that he found "quite incomprehensible" in his situation).

Consciousness here usurps not only feeling but life itself; it is a veritable disease. "The greater the accumulation of consciousness," Dostoevsky writes in his notebook the same year he published *Notes from the Underground*, "the greater the loss of the capacity to live. Hence, speaking generally, consciousness kills life. . . . Consciousness is a disease. The disease doesn't come from consciousness (this is clear as an axiom) but consciousness itself is a disease."[6] This idea underlies "Dream," as it does *Notes from the Underground*.

The tortured solipsistic formulations of the ridiculous man, though they express his egoism, nonetheless contain the embryo of a different world view in their peculiar dialectic. Thus, as he recalls his reasoning he remembers that he began to examine the "new questions" that swarmed in his head "from quite a different angle and thought of something quite new." What came to his mind, in the form of a question, was the problem of guilt or conscience: if he had committed a terrible crime on another planet and left it forever, he wondered, "would I have felt that it was *all the same* or not? Would I or would I not have felt shame for this act?" The ridiculous man's new viewpoint is concealed in his earlier solipsistic formulation: "It had seemed clear to me that life and the world in some way or other depended upon me now." From one angle these words express the self-centered outlook of the ridiculous man; from a different angle, however, they express the ethical idea that life, people, and the world do indeed depend upon us—not in a way that releases us from moral commitment, but in a way that inexorably commits us through our essential humanity to helping others.

The very posing of the question of shame constitutes an unconscious acknowledgment on the part of the ridiculous man of the existence of conscience and the binding nature of guilt. The answer to the question, "Would I or would I not have felt shame for this act?" lies not in ratiocination, but in direct feeling. A first answer is provided by the strange pain that involuntarily stirs within the ridiculous man in spite of his rational conclusions about his situation. Man, Dostoevsky insists, cannot reason his way to moral and spiritual truth. Truth—the ideal—must be felt. Christ, for Dostoevsky, is the "ideal of humanity." "In what does the law of this ideal consist?" he asks in his notebook in 1864. "A return to a sense of immediacy, to the mass of people, but—a free one, and not even one that is willed, not through reason, not through consciousness, but through a direct, terribly strong, unconquerable feeling that *this* is terribly *good*."[7]

The restoration of moral-spiritual feeling in the ridiculous man is the result of the double action of his dream: first, the overwhelming direct experience of the ideal as good; the second—and equally important—the overwhelmingly felt experience of the loss of the good. Psychologically, the dream is a reflex of his guilt; it explores the macrocosmic implications of his rebuff of the child, the symbol and embodiment of innocence and beauty. The dream of beauty clouds over into the night of the fall, the terrible earthly truth of corruption: "I was the cause of the fall." "The fact is that I...corrupted them all!" In the fall, as the ridiculous man perceives it, the basic unity between man and nature is fractured and consciousness is born. Knowledge is enthroned and the "children of the sun," separated from nature and the cosmos, come to insist that "knowledge is higher than feeling, and the consciousness of life is higher than life." The "joy and glory" of man dissolves into a flood of tears, disorder, egoism, the craving for property, slavery, and war. People come to know suffering and to love it. The scene is one of almost total tragedy and defeat for man and history.

The ridiculous man's question of whether he would feel shame for a crime he committed on another planet is answered by the terrible, unendurable anguish and guilt he experiences over the fall of mankind. Formerly he had "always loved sorrow and affliction"—but for himself alone. Now he weeps and pities men and stretches out his hands to them, "accusing, cursing, and despising" himself. He wishes to pay for the terrible suffering and disaster, to sacrifice himself, and asks to be crucified. But like Jesus, he is mocked and ridiculed; he is threatened with being committed to an insane asylum if he does not hold his peace. "Then grief entered my soul with such force," the ridiculous man continues, "that my heart contracted and I felt that I was dying, and then—well, then I awoke."

The massive shock of the fall that the ridiculous man experiences in his dream overwhelms his consciousness and awakens him to life and feeling: "Oh, now life, life! I raised my hands and appealed to the eternal Truth." The supreme lesson he has learned through suffering is that the demands of life must take precedence over those of reason and consciousness. " 'The consciousness of life is higher than life, the knowledge of the laws of happiness is higher than happiness'—that is what we must struggle against!" the ridiculous man observes in the crucial concluding lines of the story, clearly echoing Dostoevsky's main thought. The worldly missionary Alyosha Karamazov expresses the same thought: "I think that everyone in the world must love life above everything in the world." "Love life more than its meaning?" asks Ivan. "Absolutely so," Alyosha answers, "love it, regardless of logic as you say, it must be regardless of logic."

The ridiculous man, on approaching the "new" earth of his

dream, refuses in advance the conditions of life there: he loves his sinful earth too much. And later he recalls that he loved the earth of the fallen children of the sun "even more than when it had been a paradise, and only because sorrow had appeared in it." Thus, Dostoevsky presents a paradox: the ridiculous man has seen the truth—the truth of absolute moral beauty—yet he does not want to return to it. Dostoevsky's idea is clear. Freedom, the fall, brought man the experience of evil; it plunged him into suffering where he was alone with his agonizing moral conflicts and choice. In contrast to his beatific existence in the womb of paradise, the fall is a disaster. The fruits of freedom and consciousness are often intolerable. But more intolerable would be a world without suffering. Beatitude and innocence on earth after the fall would not be paradise, but hell, for it would deprive man of that which becomes indigenous to him after the fall: his freedom. Man's salvation, Paul Evdokimoff writes apropos of Dostoevsky's idea in "Dream," "lies in the freedom to overcome evil itself." To turn away from life on earth is to renounce the struggle of free man with evil. "Along with the beauty of paradise," Evdokimoff continues, "the ridiculous man has discovered that there is something better than innocence: conscious virtue. The full realization of human potential requires that one go beyond a state of innocence."[8]

Thus, man must accept the burden of his freedom; he must accept a world of tension and struggle; he must accept the essentially tragic conditions of earthly human existence. What, then, of the vision of ideal good and beauty? Dostoevsky confronts the reader with another paradox: the ideal is simultaneously the great imperative and the great impossibility, "a sublime dream," Versilov remarks in *The Raw Youth* of the dream of the golden age, "a sublime aberration of humanity." Dostoevsky affirms the necessity and reality of the ideal (in its ultimate embodiment Christ or the "paradise of Christ") as a point of permanent striving for all mankind. But at the same time, he recognizes, as we have noted before, that it is impossible for developing, transitional man to achieve the ideal on earth.[9] Christlike love is impossible on earth: "Man on earth strives for an ideal that is *contrary* to his nature." And yet, as Dostoevsky insists, it is the law of man's nature to strive.

Man, who is morally and spiritually alive—and Dostoevsky clearly has in mind all mankind and not merely those who explicitly acknowledge Christ—thus consciously or unconsciously is caught up in the paradox of the great imperative and the great impossibility. Moral or spiritual imbalance begins when man rejects one or the other side of the paradox (as in the case of the utopian socialist or of the Grand Inquisitor) and as a result is deprived of that tension toward the ideal that, for Dostoevsky, is the essence of moral and spiritual health.

The ridiculous man, after his dream, grasps the central paradox of man's earthly existence as Dostoevsky perceives it and the law of man's striving. His final observations, which exhibit a clear awareness of both sides of the paradox, constitute in their totality a creative dialectic. He is stirred by his vision of absolute moral and aesthetic truth. He insists that man has the potential to be "beautiful and happy without losing the capacity to live on earth," that is, man has the capacity to achieve a limited ideal. He does not deny evil but simply expresses his belief that it is not the "normal condition" of man on earth. On the other hand, he is perfectly aware that paradise on earth will never come to pass: "Really it's just this that I understand!"

"All the same," the ridiculous man declares, he will go on preaching. Specifically, he wishes to find out "how to preach, that is, with what words and deeds." "It's all very simple," he insists, "even in one day, *even in one hour*—everything could be arranged at once! The main thing is to love one's neighbor as yourself—that is the main thing, and that is everything, for nothing else matters." This is an "old truth, one that has been repeated and read a billion times." "But," adds the ridiculous man in a reflection on the sad actuality of earthly existence, "it has never become part of our lives." Yet this earthly truth does not keep him from affirming that man must struggle against the idea that "consciousness is higher than life, that knowledge of the laws of happiness is higher than happiness," that man must struggle against all that impedes the spontaneous realization of love in men's hearts. "And I will," he vows. In the penultimate line of "Dream," placing the main emphasis upon man's will, he declares: "If only every one wanted it, it could all be arranged immediately."

The ridiculous man expresses Dostoevsky's own belief that the potential for spiritual, or psychological, change lies within man (the "golden age in the pocket"), that "suddenly" the truth could come to man "even in an hour"—*if* man wanted it. Such a moment, of course, would be a moment of revelation. The revelation experienced by the ridiculous man is not an explicitly Christian one, to be sure; he does not acknowledge Christ. Yet his vision of truth, his conception of the ideal in man, is iconographic: "But how can I not believe: I saw the Truth—not something invented by my mind, but I saw, I saw, and its *living image* has filled my soul forever . . . the living image of what I saw will always be with me and always correct and direct me."

The ridiculous man's veneration of the living image of truth is analogous to the Russian people's veneration of the saints and of Christ. The Russian people, Dostoevsky writes, find their ideal embodied in their luminous saints. It is no accident that Dostoevsky emphasizes "living image" here and directly associates that image with the notion of belief. The truth, Dostoevsky insists, is embodied in Christ in the flesh. But the truth that the ridiculous man has seen is likewise embodied in an image of "complete wholeness." The living image here is not that of Christ, but as Dostoevsky noted in "Vlas" in 1873 in his defense of the Christian character of the Russian people, "there is much one may not be conscious of but only feel. One may know a great deal unconsciously." Though the Russian people have a very poor knowledge of the gospels and the "basic rules of. faith," "it knows Christ and carries him eternally in its heart."[10]

The ideal for Dostoevsky was Christ. Yet in his novels, where he expressed his total vision, he did not maintain that virtue, love of man, or the striving for the ideal was only possible or authentic in a person who consciously believed in God or immortality. There are some convictions, he believed, that almost everyone shares secretly, but that they are ashamed to acknowledge. Certainly Dostoevsky included a belief in God among these convictions. It does not follow, he insisted, that even a professed atheist is in fact an atheist or that he accepts in his soul the logical conclusions and consequences of a negation of God. Dostoevsky once expressed this thought in a capricious way. The hero of the *Raw Youth* remarks at one point that he does not believe in God, to which his father significantly replies: "No, you are not an atheist; you are a cheerful person."

It is not faith in God that testifies to virtue or love, Dostoevsky insists in *The Brothers Karamazov*, but love that testifies to God and immortality. "We know that we have passed from death unto life, because we loved the brethren," reads the First Epistle of John. "He that loveth not his brother abideth in death." "God is love." "If a man say, 'I love God,' and hateth his brother, he is a liar." (These lines are marked in Dostoevsky's personal Bible.) Faith is inseparable from love in the preachment of Zosima. "Hell is suffering over the impossibility of loving." "Try to love your neighbors actively and ceaselessly," Zosima counsels Mrs. Khokhlakova. "To the extent that you succeed in love, you will become convinced in the existence of God and in the immortality of your soul. But if you reach the point of total self-renunciation in love for your neighbor, then without question you will believe, and no doubt can possibly enter your soul."[11] *The Brothers Karamazov* is deeply imbued with the ethos of the First Epistle of John.

The ridiculous man stands on the threshold of Christian faith. It is true that he does not *name* God directly. Instead he speaks repeatedly of the radiant vision and of his exaltation with the terms "Truth" and "life." Here, indeed, we have a terminology that is typical of Orthodox Slavic spirituality. In this connection, we may recall the remarks of the Archpriest Avvakum (1621-1681) apropos of the doctrine of Dionysios, the Areopagite. "These are the Divine names: Being, Light, Truth, Life," Avvakum writes, adding that the other names such as Lord, the Almighty, the Unapproachable, the Thrice-radiant, the Omnipresent, the Spirit, God, and so forth are "laudatory" and "contingent." "It were rather better in the Symbol of faith," according to Avvakum, "not to utter the word Lord, a contingent name, than to cut out *True*, for in that name is contained the Divine essence."[12] There is every reason to affirm that the ridiculous man's discovery of the Truth is a discovery of the divine essence. The dream of the ridiculous man—the dream of a Truth that is also beauty and light—indeed expresses the essence of the Orthodox Slavic spirituality.

Zosima, in contrast to Ivan Karamazov, would seem to be closer to Pelagian than to Augustinian doctrine in his trust that the law of Christ will make itself felt in the consciousness of man and in his stress, in general, upon the importance of man's own moral effort in his spiritual salvation. In these convictions, Zosima and the author of *The Brothers Karamazov* echo Goethe in *Faust*: "A good man in his dark striving is conscious of the right way."[13]

It is the ridiculous man who gives expression to Dostoevsky's vision of man eternally striving for the ideal. Those who scoff at him, he notes, say that he is "muddled" and that this muddle of his can be expected to be far worse later on. But he replies:

> It is true, indeed: I am muddled and, perhaps, it will get worse. And, of course, things will get muddled several times before I find out how to preach, that is, with what words and what deeds, because this is a very difficult task. . . . Who doesn't get muddled? And yet everybody is making for one and the same goal, at least all are striving for one and the same thing, from the sage to the lowest robber, only by different paths. It is an old Truth, but this is what is new: I can't get too muddled. Because I have seen the Truth. (5)[14]

The ridiculous man, from one point of view, can be said to stand at the threshold of a discovery of Christ and the Christian faith. In this sense, we can say that there is much that he unconsciously knows or feels. But the fact that he has not yet acknowledged Christ does not place him in some lower category of men for Dostoevsky. Indeed, what gives the ridiculous man his unique character is that he symbolizes man's striving not for a particular faith (however universal that faith), but for an ideal and spiritual goal in general. What is important in "Dream"—and this, perhaps, is one of its cardinal thoughts—is that everybody is striving for one and the same goal *even if by different roads*. This goal is the ideal of love and brotherhood. Man does not move along a straight and easy path in his striving for this ideal. He gets muddled and goes astray. But Dostoevsky's idea would seem to be the same, again, as Goethe's in *Faust*: "Man errs as long as he will strive."[15]

2

"The Dream of a Ridiculous Man," as Dostoevsky's subtitle reads, is "a fantastic story." Fantasy in this story expresses a philosophically idealistic or religious vision of reality. The dream experience of human consciousness—one that "leaps through space and time and through the laws of being and reason"—can be said to express the non-Euclidian geometry of the human spirit. The ridiculous man's overnight conversion from a man to whom nothing mattered (at least on the surface of his consciousness) to a man for whom everything matters may also be viewed as a fantastic leap.

Yet however fantastic a reader might regard the ridiculous man's lightning discovery of the truth, it is not likely that Dostoevsky regarded this aspect of his hero's drama as fantastic. Revelation was a reality to Dostoevsky in every realm of human experience, history, and existence. What is fantastic about the ridiculous man, for Dostoevsky, relates rather to the element of the ridiculous in him as it manifests itself after his dream. "I am a ridiculous man," he remarks at the outset of the story. "They say I am mad now." The peculiarly ethical character of the ridiculous man's madness becomes apparent at the end of his dream when, overcome by pity and remorse, he moves among the people of his fallen paradise and asks to be crucified. But the people laugh at him and speak of him as a *iurodivyi*, that is, a "holy fool," and even a "dangerous one":[16] "They justified me, they said that they had gotten only what they had themselves desired, and that what was now could not have been otherwise."

It is only after his dream that the new ethical dimension in the hero's ridiculousness is perceived as his defining character trait. What is ridiculous about him, what is mad or fantastic, is his insistence on preaching an ideal of love and self-sacrifice in the face of all the opposing proofs of man's nature and desires. He insists on preaching the old truth of loving one's neighbor as oneself in words and deed. The non-Euclidian geometry of the dream experience, then, finds a corollary in the non-Euclidian moral geometry of the ridiculous man.

The Underground Man posits a treadmill life without any goal in which man is constantly and irrationally affirming himself in the face of a meaningless and humiliating universe. "Twice two is five" is his favorite formula. Dostoevsky accepts the idea of an earthly existence in which man is caught up in a continuous struggle, contradiction, paradox, but he posits a luminous ideal in place of a meaningless universe. The ridiculous man has come to discover this ideal and the need to strive for it. He is the underground man turned inside out. In him ridiculousness is a kind of caprice, a deliberate disregarding of the evidences of reason and reality, a kind of "twice two is five"; all of this, however, is done not in the name of self, or out of despair, but in the name of an ideal. What is ridiculous and fantastic about the ridiculous man— what places him beyond Don Quixote—is his striving for the ideal in the full recognition of the impossibility of achieving it on earth. In his own way, the ridiculous man embodies the outlook of Dostoevsky, and of Cervantes.

Thus, the ridiculous man, as the result of his dream, passes from the nihilistic and immobilizing pessimism and skepticism to a new quixotic realistic idealism, an idealism that clearly acknowledges the limits of good on earth but finds the meaning of life in the concrete struggle with evil and the effort to reach those limits. The final lines of "Dream," with their call to struggle with the idea that consciousness is higher than life, signal the reversal that has taken place in the drama of the ridiculous man. With his return to life comes a return to time. Before his dream the ridiculous man in his solipsistic egoism had lost all sense of the past, present, and future. Now, after his dream, a dream in which he discovered the timeless unity of all human existence and the relativity of all concepts of past and future, the ridiculous man is restored to time and to the all-important present. The restoration of memory and the full awakening of conscience inevitably find expression in moral action: "And I sought out that little girl.... And I will go there! And I will go there!"

We cannot overstress the momentous significance for Dostoevsky of the ridiculous man's decision to help the child. Appealing in 1861 to thinking people from the "upper strata" of society, people who have "dreams of grandiose activity," Dostoevsky remarks:

> You are constantly saying that you have no realm for activity. . . . Teach at least one child to read; there's activity for you. But no! You turn away with indignation.... "What kind of activity is this for us! . . . We harbor in our breasts gigantic forces. We have the desire and capability to move mountains; our hearts beat with the purest love for humanity. We should like to embrace all humanity at once. We want work that is commensurate with our strength. . . . True, gentlemen, but if you do nothing you will die without having done anything; while here at least there is a tiny beginning. . . . Stoop down, stoop down to the child. This will be a colossal sacrifice! What is more, you are intelligent and talented, and if you sacrifice yourself, stoop down to the everyday, to that which is small, then, perhaps, here at the very first step you will find some other activity of greater scope, and then still greater and greater. Indeed, the core of the matter is in the beginning, only begin. And now begin! Will you?[17]

Dostoevsky leaves the ridiculous man precisely at this all-important beginning. As Vyacheslav Ivanov has written of Dostoevsky, "the child is the central point of his doctrine concerning the world and concerning man." " 'The child is weeping' is the source of the world's sorrow. The world's unforgivable sin is the sin against children."[18] In returning to help the child, the ridiculous man reestablishes his connection with the universe and with moral order.

XII

Some Considerations on "The Dream of a Ridiculous Man" and "Bobok," from the Aesthetic Point of View

The human race must experience its own history.
ALFRED NORTH WHITEHEAD

TWO SHORT WORKS in Dostoevsky's *oeuvre*—"The Dream of a Ridiculous Man" (1877), subtitled "A Fantastic Story," and "Bobok" (1873), subtitled "The Notes of a Certain Person"—embody in striking ways certain postulates in Dostoevsky's poetics. We can formulate these assumptions as follows: the aesthetic representation of reality is a question of vision; the highest art is revelation (prophecy); this revelation not only explores man's social reality but sees into, or reveals, the ultimate reality of the human spirit and destiny, the invisible world of "ends and beginnings . . . [that] is still a realm of the fantastic for man."[1] "The Dream of a Ridiculous Man" is a programmatic embodiment of this kind of artistic vision. Fantasy here is the aesthetic concomitant of an idealistic or religious world outlook. But the materialistic and atheistic outlook, if perfectly consistent, denies precisely this invisible universe of ends and beginnings. Such an outlook, for Dostoevsky, is likely to see and depict only temporal, surface reality. The aesthetic concomitant of a rigorously materialistic outlook, therefore, might tend toward naturalism and, beyond that— supposing a materialistic imagination—toward a fantasy of the grotesque. "Bobok," on a parodistic plane, gives expression to this second kind of fantasy. It can be defined as a didactic, pseudo-grotesque in which Dostoevsky explores the aesthetic and philosophical implications of a materialistic outlook in order in the end to repudiate it. Fantasy (here the grotesque) gives expression not to a sense of self-renewing, boundless reality, but to the secular imagination of man before a bounded, self-consuming reality.

"DREAM" AND "BOBOK"

The dream of the ridiculous man and the hallucination of the narrator of "Bobok," Ivan Ivanovich, have the same social matrix. Yet one vision represents a transcendence of this society, whereas the other is nothing more than a grotesque projection, or Gogolian representation, of the society itself. Taken together, "Dream" and "Bobok" reveal the extraordinary range of Dostoevsky's realism.

We may take as a starting point for our discussion of these two stories the moment in which the hero of "Dream" finds himself in his grave. There is nothing at all metaphysical about his experience at this point. His fingers and toes are cold: "I lay there and, strangely, expected nothing, unquestioningly accepting the idea that the dead have nothing to expect. But it was damp." The ridiculous man lies there for several days when suddenly a "drop of water" falls from the cover of his coffin, then another and still another. All this evokes a crisis in him: "A profound indignation flamed up suddenly in my heart, and all at once I felt a physical pain in it." At this point, the ridiculous man calls out with his whole being to the "master of everything that was happening" to him. His protest is vitriolic, Voltairian:

> Whoever Thou art, but if Thou exist, and if something more rational exists than that which is now taking place, then let it show itself here, too. But if Thou art revenging Thyself on me for my irrational suicide with the monstrosity and absurdity of future being, then know that no torture, no matter how strong, can ever compare with the scorn which I will silently feel even if it be over the course of millions of years of torment. (3)

If we take this tragicomic scene in isolation, it is evident that it contains the potential for moving in two different directions: up or down. All appearances point to a materialistic reality or truth, that is, to a pessimistic view of man's ultimate fate. The hero himself is at the threshold of physical disintegration. His protest, almost a parody of the rebellion of the Promethean tragic hero, threatens to degenerate into something underground, perhaps even obscene, as the drops of water continue to fall and take effect. That way lies "Bobok," a grotesque, disgusting demi-world of the unresurrected dead, where a few months of "sepulchral animation" and decay precede total extinction.

But to return to the hero of "Dream" in his coffin, his situation may not be hopeless. Appearances to the contrary—and this is the essence of a religious or philosophical idealistic outlook—the drop of water may not be simply a cruel parody of grace. The deity to whom the protest is directed, if He exists, may in fact respond positively to the ridiculous man's outburst, and the truth of reality may be revealed in a more hopeful light. On the mythopoetic dream plane of "Dream," this is what happens. After his protest, the ridiculous man is, in effect, resurrected. Reality is revealed to him in its transcendental, timeless aspect—aesthetically, in the concrete dream experience and in a vision of the highest beauty.

The dream reveals the Truth: "This dream proclaimed to me the Truth" (*Istina*). Does the ridiculous man include the "awful truth" (*uzhasnaia pravda*) of his corruption of paradise, that is, his fall, in his conception of the Truth? Quite clearly he does not. His juxtaposition of the words *pravda* and *istina* suggests an effort to distinguish a lower earthly truth of the flesh from a higher Truth of beauty and spirit. Truth for the narrator is first of all aesthetically and spiritually transfigured reality. His dream reveals to him the Truth that is Beauty. It is a good dream. A bad dream, the ridiculous man seems to suggest, is no dream at all. Significantly, he prefaces the disclosure of his "secret"—his corruption of the "children of the sun" in his dream-paradise—with the observation that "all this, perhaps, was not a dream at all! Because something happened, here, something really of such horror that it could not have been conceived in a dream." What seems to put the final phase of his dream beyond the limits of a good dream of transfiguration, in the view of the ridiculous man, is its ugliness, its untransformed, all-too-human and earthly "awful" truth. "Granted that my heart alone gave birth to my dream, but is it possible that my heart alone is capable of giving birth to that awful truth?" he asks in perplexity. Nonetheless, he resolves to disclose "this truth too." The tendency of the ridiculous man to define the two parts of his dream in ethical terms—to distinguish between a good dream of Beauty and a nightmare of corruption—corresponds in part to a permanent and paradoxical structure in Dostoevsky's philosophical thought: the notion of two kinds of beauty.[2]

Yet it is clear that Dostoevsky regards the phenomenon of dreams as a structure of aesthetic consciousness analogous to art itself, as a phenomenon that gives plastic expression to man's total reality. The ridiculous man dwells in some detail on the phenomenon of dreams. He speaks of the extraordinary clarity, the "jeweller's fine finish of detail" that we find in dreams. Even such artists as Pushkin, Turgenev, or Tolstoy, as Dostoevsky himself insists elsewhere, could not achieve such subtlety of "artistic detail" or invent such a "complex and real reality" as we find in dreams.[3] This reality, of course, can be thoroughly fantastic. In dreams, the ridiculous man notes, "one leaps through space and time and through the laws of being and reason." Yet the dream, like art, imposes an illusion of reality. Apropos of the "tricky things" done by reason in his dreams, the ridiculous man remarks:

> My brother, for example, died five years ago. I sometimes see him in my dreams. He takes part in my affairs, we are very involved with each other, and yet I am fully aware through the dream that my brother is dead and buried. How is it that I am not surprised that, though he be dead, yet there he is beside me busy with my affairs? Why does my reason fully allow this? (2)

This triumph of illusion, or in the words of Coleridge, this "willing suspension of disbelief," also characterizes man's ethical consciousness, that realm where, in Dostoevsky's view, true beauty is always perceived as good. Here, too, man accepts the aesthetic-spiritual illusion in spite of reason or the proofs of earthly truth: "People make fun of me now by saying that this was all nothing but a dream." But the ridiculous man insists on the reality of his dream illusion: "Now isn't it really all the same whether it was a dream or not, if this dream proclaimed to me the Truth?'' And at the end of his tale the ridiculous man is even ready to grant ''that there will never be such a paradise. Really it's just this that I understand!'' But ''all the same,'' he will go on preaching.

What is involved here is nothing other than the triumph of aesthetic illusion. The dream of Truth has nothing to do with reason. As the ridiculous man insists, ''I saw it, I saw it with my own eyes, I saw all its glory! . . . I saw the Truth—not something invented by my mind, but I saw, I saw, and its *living image* has filled my soul forever.'' The promised land is literally a vision, imagic fantasy. Such a vision cannot be translated into language or words without the loss of the deep, affective side of the imagery; it cannot be translated any more than painting can find an exact verbal equivalent. The hero here too complains of his failure to communicate his vision adequately: ''After my dream I lost my words.'' He feels at a loss to ''relate,'' to ''convey in words,'' his dream:

> The real images and forms of my dream, that is, those that I actually saw at the very moment of my dream, were filled with such harmony, were so enchanting and beautiful, and so absolutely true, that on awakening I was, of course, absolutely incapable of embodying them in our feeble words, so that they were bound, as it were, to start fading in my mind; and therefore, perhaps, indeed, I myself unconsciously was constrained later on to make up details and, of course, to distort them, especially in view of my passionate desire to tell about them as quickly as possible and in some manner at least. (4)

Thus, the ridiculous man, under the impact of the powerful aesthetic impression of his dream, begins imaginatively to shape what he saw but could not directly and adequately translate into simple words. Here, as in ''The Peasant Marey,'' memory merges with imagination; indeed, the dream itself here is creative.

''If there is anything that one might criticize in 'Ghosts','' Dostoevsky wrote Turgenev about the latter's story, ''it is that *it is not quite fully* fantastic.''[4] The artist, Dostoevsky is saying, has the right to range as deeply as he wishes into man's unexplored psychic and mythopoetic history. Dostoevsky fully exercised that right in "Dream." Here the fantastic experiences of flight through time belong naturally to the imagic fantasy of the dream; the dream itself is a direct extension, on the psychological and metaphysical plane, not only of the real, problematic existence of the dreamer but of the history of man's collective consciousness. The moral and spiritual void in which the ridiculous man finds himself before his dream leads into the dream voyage "through time and space and the laws of being and reason." The special character of the subconscious that renders possible the timeless, elliptical existence of the dream world finds a certain analogy in Dostoevsky's view of the ridiculous man as flying down time "toward stars in the heavenly distance whose rays take thousands and millions of years to come to earth." The speculations on "repetitions" in the universe and on the possibility of "such a natural law" form an understructure to Christian mythology, which sees in man's past, and in the whole Christian drama, a predication and prefiguration of the future.

The dream of the ridiculous man is the age-old search in darkness for light, for the meaning and purpose of existence. His dream, as a psychic phenomenon—analogous here to poetry and painting—establishes a purely spatial field of man's search. In its moral and spiritual content, this dream involves a repetition of mythopoetic experience in which the recurrent personal drama of guilt and expiation merges with the permanent and collective dream of rebirth and of the Golden Age. Man does not move forward along a temporal line to some point in the future; rather, he is continually discovering himself anew, reiterating primary experience. In this movement toward self-discovery man overcomes and annihilates time. Indeed, the ecstatic dream of higher Beauty, which the ridiculous man experiences visually and which Myshkin in *The Idiot* experiences in a moment of psychic transfiguration, announces that "there shall be no more time."

The dream, then, as a psychic phenomenon, constitutes for Dostoevsky the area in which man's temporal, earthly existence merges with its timeless meaning, where the finite flows into the infinite world of experience and striving. It is at this point that reality is at once most total and most protean, a continuously contracting and expanding universe in which the notions of past and future, time and space acquire a non-Euclidian, relativistic, "fantastic" character. Only art, in particular poetry and painting, which retains the plasticity of the dream, Dostoevsky suggests, can reincarnate anew this imagic fantasy. Art in this sense is by its very nature fantastic, that is, free to explore man's total reality. Such is the underlying aesthetic statement of "Dream."

1

When we turn to "Bobok" after "Dream" our first tendency is to see it as another example of Dostoevsky's fantastic realism. Yet this is not the case; at least the fantasy in "Bobok" is not the kind that is typical of "Dream." We can, of course, place "Bobok," "Dream," and "A Gentle Creature" under the general rubric of "fantastic realism," but the term loses force if we do not take account of the completely different character of fantasy in each of the works. "I have called ['A Gentle Creature'] 'fantastic'," Dostoevsky writes in the preface to that story, "although I regard it as real in the highest degree." In this story fantasy merely consists in the suggestion that a stenographer overhears the thoughts of the pawnbroker and takes them down. The term "fantastic" has a totally different application in "Dream," where the experience, situations, and events described involve man's mythic consciousness and history. It is noteworthy that Dostoevsky did not use either the term "fantastic" or the term "fantastic realism" in connection with "Bobok." If he had, he would unquestionably have defined the terms quite differently, for in "Bobok," fantasy, or the fantasy of the grotesque, involves the aesthetics of naturalism.

We can speak of three descending circles in the grotesque world of "Bobok." The first circle is the social milieu of the narrator, Ivan Ivanovich, a hack writer who spends a great deal of time in his cups and who is beginning to have hallucinations. The second circle is a cemetery—a place of decidedly unholy doings, smells, open graves, and corpses. The third circle is the world beneath the tombstones, where the dead have their last profane communion and from whence Ivan Ivanovich, in the second circle, overhears the last blabberings of unredeemed humanity: "bobok," "bobok." "Here one notices a stench, a moral one, so to speak . . . a kind of stench of the soul." But the strange and ominous sounds, "bobok, bobok," are heard by Ivan Ivanovich as he moves about in the world above, and they relate to society as well.

The opening lines of Ivan Ivanovich's notes provide a kaleidoscopic impression of his world, something like photomontage of shifting images, fragmented scenes, and witty social commentary. The theme of drunkenness in the first line—"The day before yesterday Semyon Ardalyonovich suddenly said: 'Are you ever going to be sober, Ivan Ivanovich, do tell me?' "—merges immediately with the underlying theme of madness: "A strange request. I am not offended, I am a timid man; but all the same they have made me out to be a madman. An artist painted a portrait of me based on physiognomic 'accidentalities'." As Ivan Ivanovich's commentary proceeds it becomes clear that society itself is in the grip of some kind of madness or disintegration. Ivan Ivanovich is one of Dostoevsky's quixotic and ambiguous characters who, though afflicted with the moral and spiritual maladies of their world, nonetheless acutely comprehend its ills. Through the prism of this tipsy and somewhat disturbed mind there emerges a picture of a society that is held together by "rotten ropes," a superficial, empty, banal world where moral and spiritual values have been driven out by materialistic interests and concerns, a world where the spirit is yielding to the flesh, faith to superstition, and the sacred to the profane. The drama of "Bobok" is not a drama of transfiguration, but one of disintegration.

The moral-spiritual calamity of Ivan Ivanovich's world is signaled in aesthetic terms at the outset of the story. The artist who painted Ivan Ivanovich's portrait did not seek out an interior, organizing idea in his subject, but concentrated on chance features, peculiarities, "accidentalities," thus rendering a grotesque impression of a madman. Ivan Ivanovich complains that the artist did his portrait "not for the sake of literature, but for the sake of my two symmetrical warts on my forehead: it's a phenomenon, they say. They have no ideas, so now they go to town on phenomena. Yet how well he succeeded with my two warts in the portrait— they're alive! They call this realism."

Ivan Ivanovich, though in many respects a proverbial "character" and part of the scenery of the absurd in "Bobok," nonetheless represents a masked point of view in the story from which the action may be judged or placed in perspective.[5] His remarks not only provide the aesthetic canon of naturalism but mark off the distance that separates him (and, even more, Dostoevsky) from that canon. Ivan Ivanovich calls into question shallow realism and in the descriptions and commentary that follow obliquely criticizes a world that is lacking any moral or spiritual center. In such a world all of reality quite naturally presents itself in the aspect of chance or accident. Not without reason does the central scene in "Bobok," under the tombstones, open and close with a game of cards.

"Apropos of madness," Ivan Ivanovich remarks, "many people among us were pronounced crazy last year." He himself is not exempt from the breakdown in general mental stability. The word "devil" is on his lips. His own writing, he confesses, is becoming hackneyed, and, in addition, "something strange is happening to me . . . my character is changing and my head is beginning to ache. I am beginning to see and hear some strange things. Not so much voices, rather as though somebody nearby were murmuring 'bobok, bobok, bobok!' What is this 'bobok'? I need some distraction."

Ivan Ivanovich turns up at a funeral. The place is a cemetery, with its church for prayers. The signs and symbols of the sacred and the eternal are everywhere, but the atmosphere is profane. The church and cemetery have the aspect, indeed, of a peculiarly subverted, even demonic reality: "To begin with, the smell. There were about fifteen corpses there already. Palls at various prices; there were even two catafalques: one for a general and one for some fine lady." The mood of the friends and relatives of the deceased is disquieting at the very least: "Many mourners, much pretended mourning and much open gaiety. The clergy can't complain: it's all income. But the smell, the smell. I should not like to be a priest here." The play in this sentence on the word *dukh* (in Russian "spirit," but also "smell" and "breath") underscores the mood of spiritual disintegration: not the spirit of God, but the breath of corruption and a mood of profanation permeate the cemetery.[6]

After the service the narrator goes out into the fresh air. But there is no sense of relief outdoors in the cold, grey October day. Everything bespeaks an earthbound, grim, estranged, singularly Gogolian landscape: the unpleasantly smiling faces of the dead, the graves classified according to price, the open grave pits with their horrible green water, the strange heaviness of the corpses. "Why do these corpses become so heavy in their coffins?" asks Ivan Ivanovich. "They say it's due to some kind of inertia, the body, in a manner of speaking, somehow no longer manages itself...or some nonsense of this sort; it contradicts the laws of mechanics as well as common sense." The obsessive realism, or naturalism, of these speculations is oppressive; it is the realism of a world in which the demands of the spirit have succumbed to the needs of the body. "I noticed plenty of gaiety and genuine liveliness," Ivan Ivanovich remarks of the packed cemetery restaurant. "I had a bite of something and a drink."

Ivan Ivanovich had not been to a cemetery for twenty-five years and therefore does not attend the church services for his deceased relatives on this occasion. He does not appear to be a believer, but neither is he an atheist. His earlier outburst against superficial realism finds a complement in the spiritual realm in his curious ruminations on the theme of astonishment:

To be astonished at everything, of course, is stupid, while to be astonished at nothing is far more elegant and for some reason is regarded as *bon ton*. But this is really hardly the case. In my opinion, to be astonished at nothing is far more stupid than to be astonished at everything. And what is more: to be astonished at nothing is almost the same as respecting nothing. Indeed, a stupid person has no capacity to respect. "But above all, I want to respect something. I *thirst* to respect something," an acquaintance of mine remarked the other day. He thirsts to respect something! And my God, I thought, what would happen to you if you dared to print that nowadays! At this point I became lost in reverie. I don't like to read inscriptions on tombs: eternally the same thing.

These meditations take place in a cemetery where the question of God and immortality is sharply posed. Ivan Ivanovich, though not a believer, unconsciously raises questions of direct relevance to religious belief. A world without astonishment, without anything to respect, is a world without ideals. It is a world without God.

In such a world, without resurrection, the symbols of the eternal must become tedious symbols that signify nothing. The inscriptions on the tombstones, as Ivan Ivanovich notes, are "eternally the same thing." Yet human nature, Dostoevsky believed, unfailingly demands something to worship. In a world without the mystery of resurrection, astonishment must become a parody of true wonderment; it may, for instance, take the debased and covert form of materialistic speculation on the peculiar heaviness of corpses. Furthermore, the sense of mystery of vanished life, overwhelmed by the evidences of death and disfiguration, must surreptitiously come back in half-understood superstitious behavior: "On the tombstone beside me lay a half-eaten sandwich: there was something stupid and inappropriate about it. I shoved it onto the ground, since it is not bread but only a sandwich. Moreover, I don't think it's a sin to crumble bread on the ground; but it's a sin when it's on the floor." The half-eaten sandwich is evocative of the abrupt, uninvited intrusion of death. Yet M. Bakhtin's remark on this "profoundly naturalistic and profanatory detail" is also relevant: "one may crumble bread on the earth—this is sowing, fertilization; but not on the floor—this is sterile ground."[7] For the typical mourner, of course, the cemetery is sterile ground.

The narrator's reflections on astonishment and on the half-eaten sandwich point to ambiguities in his spiritual make-up. *"Le tombeau est-il un abîme sans issue ou le portique d'un autre monde,"* Chateaubriand asks. And he answers, *"La religion a pris naissance aux tombeaux et les tombeaux ne peuvent se passer d'elle."*[8] The scene at the tombs would seem to support Chateaubriand's views on the birth of religion. Yet on a plane of pure superstition or materialistic speculation where religion itself may be parodied, the grave may be the gateway to a real world of the dead. Here shallow realism, or what might be called an aesthetics of the void, finds its own fantasy in the grotesque. The hallucinations of Ivan Ivanovich lead to this kind of fantasy.

2

The reality of a morally and spiritually decadent world is captured in metaphor in the carnival of the dead in the final scene of "Bobok." The profane earthly truth triumphs here. The characters are "contemporary corpses." Hiccuping, grumbling, gossiping generals, army officers, fashionable ladies, engineers, shopkeepers, sycophants and nobodies, young and old, some just arrived and others already familiar with the "new order"—all converse about their worldly affairs and underworld predicament. Only the setting in their lives has changed. "Just what is this new order?" asks one corpse. "Why, we have, so to speak, died, your excellency," another answers. "Why did you lie down here?" a general is asked. "They put me here, it wasn't that I lay down," he replies. "The mystery of death! And I would not have laid down myself beside you for anything, not for gold!" The humor here is that of the grave. It is mordant parody on a world emptied of faith. "Little mother," screams a shopkeeper, "tell me, don't bear me a grudge (*zla ne pomnia*), am I going the way of torments or is something else happening?" The inhabitants of this world, indeed, remember no evil (*zla ne pomnia* is understood to mean "bear me no grudge," but it literally means "remembering no evil") and know no hell.

What is going on beneath the tombstones is explained by the local, "homegrown" philosopher, Platon Nikolaevich. One corpse remarks, "Really, we have died, yet we speak; seemingly move,

and yet we do not speak and do not move." The paradox is resolved, in the view of Platon Nikolaevich, by the simple fact that
"up there" death was mistakenly regarded as death. Platon, or
Plato, advances a materialistic metaphysics of death:

> The body here once again seems to revive, the remains of
> life concentrate, but only in consciousness. It's a matter of—
> how shall I put it to you?—of life continuing by a kind of
> inertia . . . for another two or three months, sometimes even
> half a year.... There is, for example, one such person who
> has almost entirely disintegrated, but once a week at six
> o'clock he will suddenly mutter one little word, to be sure,
> a senseless one, about some sort of "bobok." "Bobok, bo-
> bok." But that only means that even in him an imperceptible
> spark of life is flickering....

But the true philosopher of the "contemporary corpses" is not
Platon. The inspirer and ideologist of sepulchral animation is
Baron Klinevich: "We're some sort of mangy barons, descended
from lackeys. . . . I'm only a scoundrel from the pseudoaristo-
cratic world and consider myself a 'charming *polisson*'." This
thoroughly cynical figure—in all probability, a deliberate allusion
on Dostoevsky's part to the Marquis de Sade—"draws conclusions" on the basis of the "splendid material" he finds around
him. His "active" nature is drawn to debauchery, and he guides
the underworld community toward one final orgiastic revel. Since
only two or three months are left, "and at the very end—'bobok'," Klinevich reasons that the time should be spent agreeably.
"Ladies and gentlemen," he exclaims, "I suggest that we be
ashamed of nothing!" A newly arrived corpse—an engineer—
tries to give a "scientific social" foundation to Klinevich's suggestion of a general debauch: "You propose, then, to organize
our, so to speak, life here on new and tested rational principles."
But the engineer is behind the times. Klinevich doesn't give a
whit for rational principles. What he wants, most of all, is for
people "not to lie":

That's all I want, because that's the main thing. It's impossible to live on earth without lying, because life and lies are synonymous; well, here we'll not lie out of amusement. The devil take it, after all, the grave does mean something! We'll all recite the stories of our lives and won't be ashamed of anything any longer. I'll be the first to tell about myself. I'm the voluptuary kind, you know. Up above there all that was bound by rotten ropes. Away with the ropes, and let's pass these two months in the most shameless truth! Let's strip and bare ourselves!

Klinevich's proposal is greeted enthusiastically by the inhabitants of the grave: "We will bare ourselves, we will bare ourselves!" "The main thing," Klinevich adds, "is that nobody can forbid us."

The theme of nakedness in "Bobok" signals the final assault on all moral culture. It is the theme of "all is permissible," the casting off of all restraint, the breaking of all taboos. The disappearance of shame—and with it memory—marks the complete atrophy of conscience. Klinevich indicts a society based upon hypocritical lies and insists (somewhat anticipating Nietzsche) that "life and lies are synonymous." He emerges as the embodiment of arbitrary self-will and absolute caprice. And the truth he exalts, in the words of the ridiculous man, is the "shameless truth" of unbridled sensuality: "We'll all recite the stories of our lives." This is a strange Decameron of the dead in which death and sex thrive upon each other. And, indeed, necrophilic love is all that is left to the inhabitants of the underworld of "Bobok." "For a long time, now, I...I have nourished the dream of a little blonde...of fifteen...and in just such circumstances...," pants one of the corpses, an old man.

The underworld scene in "Bobok" draws to a close in an atmosphere of moral stench and pandemonium—"a debauch . . . a debauch of last hopes," as the narrator puts it in his concluding remarks, "a debauch of feeble and rotting corpses." The carnival of the dead in "Bobok" parodies Christian revelation: in place of revelation of the spirit, there is a revelation of the flesh, a final moment of sepulchral animation.

"Oh, ho, ho! verily a soul is passing through torments," rings out an ironical voice in the underworld. At this moment, Ivan Ivanovich remarks, he sneezed: "Everything fell silent, as in a cemetery, and disappeared like a dream. A real silence of the tomb settled over everything." And with some concluding observations, and a promise to return to the site, Ivan Ivanovich breaks the spell of the grotesque world of the dead. But the message of "Bobok" is clear: like the *danse macabre* of medieval painting and legend, "Bobok" emerges as a stark and grim admonition, a warning of impending catastrophe for society.

The signal characteristic of the dream of the ridiculous man is that the dream of beauty does not disappear; it continues to exist before the eyes of the ridiculous man like a "living image." The dream is a luminous, transcendental structure, a permanent point of striving for man. This is not the case with the fantasy of the grotesque; this kind of fantasy embodies no ideal, represents no point of striving for man. The fantasy of the grotesque, furthermore, is alien as a genre to Dostoevsky in its fundamental philosophy. In "Bobok," of course, Dostoevsky gives evidence of a brilliant feeling for the grotesque as style, a sense for abstract or naturalistic fantasy. But the style here does not serve an authentic ideology of the grotesque. The grotesque in "Bobok" is a device. The author uses it not to affirm a vision of the grotesque, the authenticity of an estranged universe, but to parody it. The grotesque for Dostoevsky is a caprice, a whimsical fancy, a *reductio ad absurdum* deriving from invalid materialistic and atheistic premises.

It is in his fundamentally transcendental conception of reality that Dostoevsky differs so sharply from the great master of the grotesque, Nikolai Gogol. The disjunctive, absurd, or aberrative elements of reality never acquire in Dostoevsky a dynamic of their own. But the grotesquerie of Gogol's Sobakevich defines Gogol's vision of reality, a reality from which the reader rarely, if ever, escapes. The grotesque aspects of a Marmeladov have real psychological and social content, however, and we never cease to perceive him in that tragic and profoundly human dimension that he, by his grotesquerie, forever seeks to mask.

The Columbus who discovered the grotesque world in himself and in the reality about him and who agonized over it precisely as a quality of experience was Gogol. His art gives expression to his vision of an estranged world and to his own self-estrangement. The same cannot be said of Dostoevsky and his art. If the grotesque, as Wolfgang Kayser maintains, is a subversion of our familiar reality from within, a dehumanization of it by alien, dark, and terrifying forces,[9] the art of Dostoevsky may be defined as a subversion and *humanization* of the estranged spiritual landscape from within, an attempt to regenerate through the discovery and exploitation of man's spiritual resources.[10]

"The Dream of a Ridiculous Man" and "Bobok" can be seen as expressing an identical moral-philosophical point of view: a belief in a moral order and a transcendent reality. But they do so in different ways: the fantastic realism of "Dream" explores the expanding frontiers of an unbounded reality and traces the endless cycle of fall and resurrection; the fantasy of the grotesque in "Bobok" explores the darkening world of a despiritualized reality. The great drama of the fall and resurrection is seen in reverse perspective in "Bobok," and we are witness to a grotesque spectacle of death and disintegration.

The Sentencing of Fyodor Karamazov

In Anna Karenina *is expressed a view of human guilt and
criminality. People are portrayed in abnormal circumstances.
Evil existed before them. Caught in a whirl of deceit, people
commit crimes and inexorably perish: clearly the idea pertains
to one of the most beloved and ancient of European themes.*
DOSTOEVSKY, Diary of a Writer

He got what was due him.
The Brothers Karamazov

TWO SHORT SCENES, "Over the Brandy" and "The Sensualists,"
one following the other, occupy a pivotal place in the tragic destiny of Fyodor Karamazov. In the first scene the theme of desecration (crime), as it relates to Fyodor, attains its sharpest and
most comprehensive expression. In the second scene the theme of
retribution (punishment) surfaces as the inexorable response to
his desecration. Both the crime and punishment of Fyodor, in the
poetics of Dostoevsky, belong to the realm of *bezobrazie* (the
morally and aesthetically "monstrous" or "shapeless") and involve the disfiguration of man made in the image and likeness of
God.

The centrality of the concepts of *obraz* (image, form, icon) and
bezobrazie as antithetical moral and aesthetic categories in Dostoevsky's thought cannot be overstressed. *Obraz,* for Dostoevsky,
is the axis of beauty in the Russian language. It is aesthetic form,
and it is also the iconographic image, or icon, the visible symbol
of the beauty of God.[1] Aesthetically, *bezobrazie* is the deformation of ideal form. The humanization of man is the creation of
form, the restoration of the image. All violence against man is a
dehumanization, which is a deformation, in Dostoevsky's view, of
the divine image. Zosima in *The Brothers Karamazov* recalls how
once, as a young man in a "savage and monstrous" state of mind,
he struck his servant in the face; and he remembers how he then
reproached himself for his act of violence against another being
created, like himself, in the image and likeness of God. On the

symbolic plane, the desecration of the icon (*obraz, ikona*) involves a crime of the most grave nature, an assault upon the very ideal and principle of divine—therefore, also, human—beauty. Fyodor is guilty of precisely this crime of desecration.

Both the crime and punishment of Fyodor, in Dostoevsky's Christian view, are deeply reprehensible and should have yielded to an ethos of love and self-sacrifice. Yet as dramatist, Dostoevsky grasps the character's fate in the somber logic of classical Greek tragedy. "The theme is not the tragic workings of a mind," H.D.F. Kitto wrote in connection with Aeschylus' *Oresteia*, "it is that men of violence do things which outrage Justice, bring retribution, and provoke further deeds of violence."[2] Fyodor is not a victim; he brings his fate down upon himself by his own words and deeds—his criminal neglect of his sons, his persecution of his wife, his debauchery, and his desecration of all things sacred. Fyodor, although the embodiment of a "universal senselessness," is by no means presented to the reader as an unconscionable villain, however. "You are not an evil man, but corrupted," Alyosha once remarks to him. This observation, perhaps more than any other, echoes Dostoevsky's view that the evil that men do rarely serves to define their whole inner nature.

In *The Brothers Karamazov* Dostoevsky discloses Fyodor's complex and many-sided character. As dramatist, however, he is deeply concerned with the ineluctable movement in the novel from crime to punishment and with the tragic rhythm that carries Fyodor to disaster. He captures the elusive dialectical moment in the destiny of a man when quantity turns into quality, when he exceeds all limits, when, like Agamemnon, he steps upon the "purple carpet"—and falls. Such a moment occurs in "Over the Brandy"—a scene of Shakespearean power and conception—when Fyodor loses all moral controls. The full implications of this moment are spelled out in the following scene, "The Sensualists," in which Dostoevsky discloses the real and false denouement of the tragic action in the novel.

The theme of Fyodor is the theme of desecration, or profanation; it is the theme of moral and aesthetic shapelessness and of the loss of all sense of measure and form. The theme is expressed by the very physical appearance of Fyodor, and this is noted by Fyodor's son Dmitry: "I did not like his appearance, there was something about it that was dishonorable, boastful, and trampling on everything sacred, mockery, unbelief—vile, vile!" Dmitry's response to his father is direct: "Why is such a man alive! . . . No, tell me, can one go on permitting him to dishonor the earth?" Fyodor, moreover, is nicknamed "Aesop," an allusion, no doubt, to the legendary ugliness of the ancient Aesop. The theme of desecration is also embodied in the chronic and "boundless drunkenness" of Fyodor. "The word *obrazit'* (re-form)," Dostoevsky wrote in the January 1876 issue of *Diary of a Writer*, "is a folk word meaning to give an image to, to restore in man a human image. One has always said to the drunkard, with reproach: 'Now you ought to go and *re-form* yourself.' I heard the convicts say this."[3] Zosima, in essence, calls upon Fyodor to "re-form" himself. But the moral disfiguration of Fyodor has passed beyond all limits.

The theme of desecration, in its moral-psychological and spiritual content, is developed in the monastery scenes, where Fyodor confronts Dmitry, Zosima, and the monks, and in rising crescendo in "The Scandal," where in his drunken buffoonery he loses all restraint: "he could no longer control himself and plunged as though down from a mountain." Fyodor flies out of control here. Objectively, physically, he is dissolving, sagging, losing his features. Subjectively, he is carried away by evil. "Alyosha, don't be angry that I offended your Superior a little while ago," he remarks in "Over the Brandy." "I can't help feeling vexed. Now if there's a God, if He exists, then, of course, I'm to blame and I shall have to answer for it." In juxtaposing the phrases *menia, brat, zlo beret* ("I can't help feeling vexed," or literally, "I am taken up by evil") and "now if God exists," Dostoevsky awakens a sleeping metaphor and gives the whole sentence symbolic meaning: at this moment Fyodor is in the power of evil (the devil) and not good (God).

What Dostoevsky suggests obliquely through Fyodor here, he defines directly in another context. "But the foolish devil," writes the narrator apropos of Fyodor's behavior in the monastery, "had caught up Karamazov and was carrying him along on his nerves into lower and lower depths of ignominy." "I dare say that there may be an evil spirit in me, too," Fyodor himself remarks at another point in the novel, adding that it must, however, be a "small one." Fyodor's devil triumphs in "Over the Brandy."

The peculiarly repulsive impression created by Fyodor is especially significant in view of Ivan's theory of love of one's neighbor: "One may love one's neighbor in the abstract and even sometimes from a distance, but close-up almost never." Fyodor provides Ivan and Alyosha with a close-up view of himself in the opening scenes of the novel and again in the scene appropriately entitled "Over the Brandy." Fyodor is alone with his two sons here, and he is drunk. This scene is a fatal one as far as Fyodor is concerned; it is the "last act of the performance." He begins to talk, and he cannot stop. He babbles and almost literally bespatters everything. Both dramatically and ideologically the scene escalates in tension toward a stupendous finale, a confrontation between the sacred and the profane. Fyodor begins by expressing his contempt for the Russian peasant: "The Russian peasant, generally speaking, needs thrashing." He moves swiftly on to defile Russia: "Russia's all swinishness. My dear, if you only knew how I hate Russia." He hates Russian vice, but Russia itself, he implies, is vice. The motif of beating leads him to his favorite subject: the beating of women. The shift from Russia to women—from "mother Russia" to the mother of men—represents, ideologically, a new and dangerous escalation of the theme of profanation.

This theme of profanation is closely and fatally interwoven with the novel's moral-philosophical dialectic. The ominous significance of Fyodor's desecration is signaled by a casual remark: "Now if there's a God, if He exists, then, of course, I'm to blame and I shall have to answer for it." As though gambling with his fate, Fyodor puts this question to Ivan: "Is there a God or not?" His fate is linked with Ivan's resolution of this crucial question, a question that in its basic moral content can be rephrased as follows: Is there any moral order or meaning in the universe, or is everything permissible? It is Ivan's tendency to resolve this question negatively that ultimately proves fatal to Fyodor.

The significance of the entire moral-philosophical dialectic in "Over the Brandy" is that Fyodor himself definitively emerges to Ivan, in his personality and outlook, as a hateful embodiment of the human condition, as disgusting proof of the moral disorder of man and universe. Ivan answers his father's question bluntly: "No, there is no God . . . there is no immortality, either." Whether or not this answer truthfully reflects Ivan's views on this question (later he insists to Alyosha that he had been "teasing him on purpose"), it is clear that it expresses his deep skepticism and, on the psychological plane of action at least, leaves the way open for a negative resolution of the moral question that he has linked with immortality.

Fyodor now returns to his favorite topic: women and sensuality. His unbridled sensualism, as it is disclosed here, is the very essence of *bezobrazie*. In behavior and discourse he pollutes the very idea of woman. As Fyodor shifts his attention to a particular woman, the mother of Ivan and Alyosha, and to his dishonorable behavior with her, the confrontation between the sacred and profane intensifies. In Alyosha's memory his mother emerges as a pure, innocent, almost sacrosanct figure. She is linked in his mind with the iconographic Madonna (he remembers her "praying for him to the Mother of God, holding him out in both arms to the icon as though to put him under the Mother's protection"). It is the subject of Alyosha's and Ivan's mother that provides Fyodor with a bridge to a final assault on the sacred. The attack takes the form of a recollection of an act of vileness—the desecration of his late wife's "wonder-working" icon, an object embodying the loftiest spiritual beauty. Fyodor recalls that he had insulted his wife only once, in the first year of their marriage:

> She used to pray a great deal at that time, kept the feasts of
> Our Lady particularly and would turn me out of her room
> at those times. Well now, I thought, I'll up and knock all
> that mysticism out of her! "You see," I say, "you see, here
> is your icon, here it is, and here I take it down. Now just

look, you regard it as a wonder-working icon, but here
now, I'll spit on it in front of you and nothing will happen
to me for it!" (III, 8)

As the narrator observes at this point, the old man "was slobber-
ing all over."

The act of desecration and insult that Fyodor recalls took place
in the past. But on the dramatic and ideological plane of his drunk-
en discourse, this recollection constitutes the high point of a
sweeping assault on fundamental national, social, and spiritual
values: on Russia, the Russian peasant, Russian women, women
in general, the mother of Alyosha and Ivan, and finally, the image
of Our Lady, the incarnation of spiritual beauty. The fatal hubris
of Fyodor is embodied in his astounding, audacious, cruel words:
"Now just look, you regard it as a wonder-working image, but
here now, I'll spit on it in front of you and nothing will happen
to me for it!"

This is one of the most dramatic and psychologically profound
moments in the novel. It is a moment when past and present
merge to determine the future, a moment verifying the indissol-
uble, fatal unity of a man's character and fate. Both Fyodor's vile
act and the utterance that accompanies it, of course, attest to his
deeply superstitious nature. Years later, rising again in his consciousness, the memory of this moment, guilt, secret dread, tracks
him down. The shameless boast that he would not be punished
for his act, now recalled in the presence of his sons, becomes the
instrument of his future punishment. Fyodor is undone by his
own hubris. In the words of Oedipus, the "blinding hand" is his
own. This moment in "Over the Brandy" rivals in depth and
depiction the art of Greek tragedy where, in the words of Kitto,
"the Past is always a menace to the Present, 'the art of Calchas
is unerring'; even the Future throws its shadow behind it."[4]

As Dostoevsky indicates in the novel, and as Fyodor's behavior
suggests, the wonder-working icon of Alyosha's and Ivan's
mother has a certain mystique attached to it. Dostoevsky's use of
the icon at this point adds a touch of the mysterious or fantastic
to the fate of Fyodor. Yet on the deepest level of Fyodor's char-

acterization Dostoevsky, like the ancient Greek philosopher Heraclitus, recognizes that "a man's character is his fate." Dostoevsky is not making a serious attempt to introduce supernatural motivation into Fyodor's drama (in the last analysis, "God," the "Mother of God," or the "devil" are metaphorical embodiments of objective moral and psychological realities). Rather, he is concerned with the manner in which the arrogant act and boast of his hero is fatefully woven into his drama. This boast is uttered in the presence of Ivan, the ideological murderer in the novel. It is Ivan, or his alter ego, the devil, who more than anyone perhaps, is Fyodor's nemesis.

There is nothing mysterious or supernatural here. It is man's worship of aesthetic and spiritual beauty (revealed negatively in the peculiar character of Fyodor's act), not God, that plays the decisive role here. Fyodor's assault on everything sacred in Russian life, passing all limits in his spitting on the image of beauty itself, enters into Ivan's pro and contra and gives a fatal turn to his moral-philosophical dialectic. Fyodor's profane and drunken blabberings not only raise but also tragically answer the fundamental questions that are tormenting Ivan, and indeed, Dostoevsky as well: is man any good? Is there a moral pivot in man? In the microcosmic universe inhabited by Fyodor in "Over the Brandy" evil is rampant, evil is unpunished, evil prevails. There wells up in Ivan a nihilism of outrage, a subconscious readiness to stand aside in the conflict between Dmitry and his father: "One reptile will devour another reptile," Ivan will remark in the next scene, "The Sensualists," "to hell with both of them!"

Alyosha collapses in hysterics as he listens to Fyodor's story about the icon and his mother. "Ivan, Ivan! Give him some water, quickly!" Fyodor exclaims. "It's like her, exactly like her, the way his mother was at that time! . . . He's upset about his mother, his mother," exclaims Fyodor. "But she was also my mother, too, I think, his mother, isn't that so?" Ivan observes acidly. Fyodor's profoundly offensive and degrading attitude toward women now takes the form of a mortal personal insult: He is seemingly oblivious here not only of Ivan's existence as a son, but of his very presence at the moment (one recalls his first ambiguous words in the novel about Dmitry: "Yes, Dmitry is non-existent as yet"). His forgetfulness could even be taken as a hint of Ivan's illegitimacy:

> "What do you mean, your mother," he muttered, not understanding. "What's this all about? Just what mother are you talking about?... Now can it be that she...Oh, the devil! Why, of course, she was yours, too! Oh, the devil! Well, now, my mind has never been so darkened before, excuse me, and I thought, Ivan...He, he, he!" He stopped. A broad, drunken, half-senseless grin spread out across his face.
> (III, 8)

Fyodor's words about a darkening of his mind—more exactly translated, "an unprecedented eclipse" (*zatmenie kak nikogda*)—do more than characterize the drunken muddle of his mind; they ominously portend the disaster that will befall him and the Karamazov family as a whole. In three words he has pronounced his own death sentence, and he has done so in the presence of his ideological executioner, Ivan. Not without reason does the word "devil" twice come to his lips as he stumbles over his shameless thoughts and tries to come to his senses.

At the beginning of his drunken ramblings Fyodor remarks to Alyosha: "I'd put an end to your monastery. I'd like to take all that mysticism and suppress it once and for all, all over the Russian land, so as finally to bring all those fools to reason. And what a lot of gold and silver would flow into the mint!" "But why suppress it?" Ivan asks. "So that the truth would shine forth as soon as possible, that's why," he answers, to which Ivan replies, "But you know, if this truth were to shine forth you would be the first to be robbed and then...suppressed." In the context of Ivan's profound skepticism (to say nothing of the world view of Smerdyakov, the man who will physically rob and suppress Fyodor), the truth that will shine forth is the truth of *eclipse*—the truth of a world without the sun, without the shining image of Jesus, and therefore, without morality. In "Over the Brandy" the drunken Fyodor emerges as the very incarnation of man without God or morality. And it is in this scene and the one that directly follows that Dostoevsky advances Ivan as one of those people who might be capable in a darkened world of suppressing Fyodor.

"Now if there's a God, if He exists, then, of course, I'm to blame and I shall have to answer for it," Fyodor allows. Fyodor's subsequent punishment, his murder, hardly resolves in the novel the question of the existence of God, however. Dostoevsky's own vision of God was not the punitive God of retribution of the Old Testament. Nonetheless, these words of Fyodor's are noteworthy. Fyodor's murder follows from his violation of fundamental moral and spiritual norms. He perishes in part because he represents to Ivan—the ideological murderer—a negation of all that he, Ivan, holds, or at least would like to hold, sacred. On the plane of the novel's moral action, Ivan and his brother Dmitry are bearers of a tragic pre-Christian truth of which Fyodor is quite aware, though he remembers it in a Christian reformulation: "And with what measure you mete, it shall be measured—or however it goes...," Fyodor remarks in "Over the Brandy."

Dostoevsky certainly did not interpret Jesus' words in the spirit of the Old Testament. Indeed, in the Sermon on the Mount, from which these lines come, Jesus specifically says: "Ye have heard that it hath been said, An eye for an eye, and a tooth for a tooth: But I say unto you, That ye resist not evil" (Matthew 5:38-39). The words that Fyodor recalls are prefaced (Matthew 7:1) by the important lines: "Judge not, that ye be not judged. For with what judgment ye judge, ye shall be judged." Dostoevsky, like Tolstoy in *Anna Karenina* essentially affirms that it is for God and not man to judge. He in no way condones the punishment of Fyodor. Like Aeschylus in *The Oresteia*, he rejects the notion of crime as a solution to crime. Yet as novelist-tragedian, he acknowledges in the murder of Fyodor a tragic reenactment of the primitive law of retribution. All is not permissible in the affairs of men. In the words of *The Oresteia*, the "gods do not fail to punish those who trample upon holy things." The meaning of these words is not that good inevitably triumphs over evil but that evil gives birth to evil, and great evil often leads to catastrophe, or in the words of Fyodor, to an unprecedented eclipse.

Fyodor forgets that Alyosha's mother is also Ivan's mother, and then, half coming to his senses, speaks of a darkening of his mind. At this very moment, the narrator observes:

> A fearful thunderous clamor echoed from the hall, frenzied shouts could be heard; the door burst open and Dmitry tore into the room. The old man rushed to Ivan in terror: "He'll kill me, he'll kill me! Don't let him get at me, don't let him!" he screamed, clinging to the skirt of Ivan's coat.
> (III, 8)

These concluding lines of "Over the Brandy" dramatize the dangerous situation Fyodor finds himself in. He is threatened by Dmitry, and he seeks protection from Ivan, whom he has outraged by his behavior: "Don't let him get at me!" Will Ivan let Fyodor be killed? In the immediate situation he will protect his father. But in the subsequent action the internal pro and contra of Ivan will turn on this question. Fyodor's words, then, point to the main area of Ivan's evil: his inaction, his unwillingness to mediate the struggle between Dmitry and Fyodor, his insistence on playing the observer.

In the early scenes of the novel Ivan is characterized almost exclusively through inaction and silence—and silence, for Dostoevsky, epitomizes the moral atrophy of the spirit. Ivan, almost unnoticed by the reader, silently watches the buffoonery of his father in the early monastery scenes but does nothing to stop him. His angry blow directed at Maksimov at the moment he departs from the monastery reflects his suppressed hostility toward his father. The scene "Over the Brandy" brings to the surface the hidden tensions between Ivan and Fyodor. Fyodor rightly suspects that Ivan out of spite will not stop him from telling lies: "You have contempt for me." Ivan deliberately leads him on, baits him. Fyodor, intoxicated, is carried away by his inner demon and seems to embody in this scene the principle that all is permissible.

In the following scene, "The Sensualists," Ivan emerges as the most dangerous threat to Fyodor. What takes place in this scene is a rehearsal for the murder: Dmitry rushes in followed by Grigory and Smerdyakov; as in the real murder scene, he strikes Grigory; then he boots his father in the face, announcing that he deserves to be killed. But in this action Ivan, along with Alyosha, defends his father, whereas in the murder scene that occurs a short while later, he, after reaching a devious understanding with Smerdyakov, lets his father be killed. Even while he defends his father in "The Sensualists," however, the idea of not defending his father enters his mind and becomes part of a complex moral-psychological dialectic. Ivan remarks to Alyosha:

> "The devil take it, if I hadn't pulled Dmitry away, I dare say he would have gone ahead and killed him. It wouldn't take much to do in Aesop, would it?" Ivan whispered to Alyosha. "God forbid!" cried Alyosha. "And why forbid?" Ivan continued in the same whisper malignantly contorting his face. "One reptile will devour another reptile; to hell with both of them!" Alyosha shuddered. "Of course, I won't let him be murdered as I did not let him now. Stay here, Alyosha, I'll go for a walk in the yard, my head has begun to ache." (III, 9)

Noteworthy in this exchange is the way the psychological and mythopoetic planes of action come together. The names of the devil and God emerge in the subtext as central antagonists. Ivan's remark, "and why forbid?" (a zachem sokhranit', or literally, "why preserve or take care of"), echoes Dmitry's question earlier in the novel: "Why is such a man alive! . . . No, tell me, can one go on permitting him to dishonor the earth?" The body of Dmitry hunches up into a deformed shape when he utters these words. Similarly, Ivan's face is contorted by a grimace when he echoes Dmitry's words. He assures Alyosha that he will not let his father be murdered. But the degree to which the idea of letting his father be murdered has taken hold in his subconscious—and at the same time, the degree to which this temptation disturbs him—is suggested immediately by his complaint about a headache. His headache is the first physical symptom of imminent psychological disorder, a disorder that will involve a deep inner split and an encounter with his devil. Ivan's conscious assurances that he will defend his father, then, contradict his deep subconscious disposition to let his father perish.

In the conversation between Alyosha and Fyodor that follows Alyosha's exchange with Ivan, Dostoevsky accents the emergence of Ivan as the main threat to his father. Fyodor's first question on recovering consciousness relates not to the beating he received from Dmitry, as might be expected, but to the conversation with Ivan just before Dmitry burst into the room. "Alyosha, where's Ivan?" Fyodor whispers fearfully. "Outside, he has a headache. He will protect us," Alyosha replies. "What does Ivan say? Alyosha, my dear and only son, I am afraid of Ivan; I am afraid of Ivan more than the other. You're the only one I do not fear...." Fyodor's terrible fear of Ivan, especially at this moment, is an expression in part of his subconscious awareness of the full implications of his behavior in the scene preceding the brawl and of Ivan's dangerous moral-philosophical position. Yet ominously and naively, even after his eclipse, he continues to disown Ivan and refers to Alyosha as "my dear and only son"; he speaks of his first son, Dmitry, not by his name, but simply as "the other." Alyosha assures his father that Ivan will protect them, but the reference to a headache suggests another course of action, or inaction, on Ivan's part.

Ivan in "The Sensualists" is moving toward moral conflict and mental confusion, whereas Fyodor is slowly recovering his senses. As though stepping back from a terrible abyss, he now adopts a wholly different attitude toward the icon he had abused and the monastery he had reviled: "That little icon of the Mother of God, the one I was talking about a moment ago—you take it with you and keep if for yourself. And I give you permission to go back to the monastery.... I was joking a moment ago, don't be angry. My head aches, Alyosha...." Fyodor's head aches from the beating it has received; but on the moral-psychological plane, his headache, like Ivan's, reflects inner conflict and guilt over his words and behavior in "Over the Brandy."

Ivan, as we have noted earlier, insists that he had been "deliberately teasing" in the episode with his father. Fyodor likewise asserts that he was only "joking." Yet the tragedy of words to which "Over the Brandy" bears witness is that the words have a dynamic of their own. The teasing and joking of both Ivan and Fyodor mask a deep and corrosive skepticism. In both father and son, the teasing and joking constitute a cover for their real feelings and for their evasion of responsibility. Both Ivan and his father are constantly playing with ideas. Ivan's play with ideas—he first expounds them before a group of provincial ladies, then allows Miusov to develop them in his own presence, and finally sits by almost silently as his disciple Smerdyakov parodies his thought (in "The Controversy")—is the corollary of his self-deception. In the cases of both Ivan and his father, seemingly innocent or uncontrolled play ends in tragedy. Fyodor's effort to step back from the abyss comes too late, while Ivan lacks the inner moral strength and candor to confront himself directly.

The final episode in "The Sensualists" brings to the foreground the complex moral-psychological game that Ivan is playing with himself and others. When Alyosha returns to Ivan in the courtyard, Ivan is "writing something with a pencil in his notebook." His mood is disturbingly lighthearted in contrast to his ugly state of mind of a few moments before. Alyosha, upset over the "horror" of relations between Dmitry and his father, puts a crucial question to Ivan:

> "Brother, let me ask one thing more: has any man really the right to look at other people and decide which of them is worthy of living and which of them is less worthy?" "Why introduce here a decision about worth? This question most often is decided in the hearts of people not at all on the grounds of worth, but for other reasons much more natural. And as for right, who does not have the right to wish?" "Not for the death of another?" "What even if for another person's death? Why lie to oneself, since all people live so and probably cannot live otherwise? Are you referring to what I said just now—that the two reptiles will devour each other? In that case, let me ask you, do you think me like Dmitry capable of shedding Aesop's blood, say, of murdering

him, eh?" "What are you saying, Ivan? Such an idea never
entered my head! And I don't believe that Dmitry...."
"Thanks if only for that," laughed Ivan. "Be sure I shall
always defend him. But in my wishes I reserve full latitude
for myself in this case. Goodbye, till tomorrow. Don't condemn me, and don't look upon me as a villain," he added
with a smile. (III, 9)

This Russian Hamlet's last words, "don't condemn me," point to
his inner resolution of the question Alyosha poses, a question
that he himself puts more bluntly when he asks Alyosha: "Do
you think me like Dmitry capable of shedding Aesop's blood?"
What is symptomatic of Ivan's evasiveness here is not only his
unwillingness to name his father, but his initial willingness to let
somebody else resolve a question that ought to evoke an immediate and decisive answer from him.

Alyosha poses the problem of the brothers' relation to their
father in an ethical context: does a person have the right to decide
whether another person is worthy or unworthy of living? (Quite
clearly the idea of murder crossed Alyosha's mind as well.) He
places the question squarely in the realm of conscious decision.
Ivan, significantly, removes the question from the realm of ethical
judgment and responsibility and relegates it to the "natural"
realm of feeling and instinct. Man's natural feelings, in Ivan's
view, do not bind him to love his neighbor or to do good. "There
is absolutely nothing on earth that could compel people to love
each other," Miusov reports Ivan as believing. "A law of nature
saying that man must love mankind simply does not exist."
Man's wishes, then, come from the amoral, instinctual, natural
side of his being. And "who does not have the right to wish?"
Ivan will defend his father; such is his rational decision. But as
for his wishes, he reserves for himself full latitude.

Though he has excluded wishes from the realm of ethical judgment, Ivan involuntarily condemns himself ("don't look upon me
as a villain"). He believes nonetheless that he can keep his wishes
separate from his actions. The denouement of the Karamazov
drama demonstrates the naiveté of this belief and the tragedy of

unconscious duplicity. Just as his wishes involuntarily signal to him his guilt, so those same wishes involuntarily will signal to Smerdyakov—the actual physical murderer—his desires. In the end, Ivan adopts his favorite stance of the observer. The moral and psychological content of this stance is well illustrated in the last chapter of the section of the novel entitled "Pro and Contra." After his fatal encounter with Smerdyakov at the garden gate, Ivan goes upstairs and sits up late:

> Remembering that night long afterwards Ivan recalled with especial revulsion how at one point he suddenly got up from the sofa and very quietly, as though he were terribly afraid that he might be watched, opened the door, went out onto the staircase and listened to Fyodor moving and walking about below; he listened, holding his breath and with beating heart; for a long time, for perhaps five minutes, with a sort of strange curiosity; but just why he did all this, or what was the purpose of listening he of course did not know. This "action" all his life afterwards he called "abominable"; for his whole life long, deeply within himself and in the recesses of his soul, he considered it the most vile act of his life.
> (V, 7)

The Wound and the Lamentation:
Ivan Karamazov's Rebellion

I hear the message clear, but am of faith devoid.
GOETHE, Faust

1

AT THE CONCLUSION of the chapter entitled "Rebellion" in part two, book five of *The Brothers Karamazov*, the reader encounters one of the most dramatic perorations in Dostoevsky's work, and indeed in all of world literature: a monologue, or prose-poem, in which Ivan protests the suffering of children and concludes by returning his "entrance ticket" to universal harmony. Ivan's passionate outcry, as far as pure content is concerned, is in large part a reiteration of ideas already advanced in the main body of the chapter "Rebellion" and in the preceding chapter, "The Brothers Get Acquainted." But this final poetic synthesis of his thought has a structure, set of imagery, and dynamic of its own that deserve particular attention.

Ivan's confession in "Rebellion" over the impossibility of loving man at close quarters and his grueling stories about the suffering of children build up an almost intolerable tension of thought and emotion. In these scenes, Dostoevsky reminds us, Ivan speaks "as though in madness," "as though in a delirium." The suffering that Ivan imposes on Alyosha by making him mentally witness scenes of brutalization of children ("I'll stop if you wish," he offers; but Alyosha replies, "No, I too want to bear with the agony") also acts as a terrible self-laceration. In this context, Ivan's final monologue emerges as something of a poetic catharsis, which releases pent-up emotion and at the same time gives his tortured thought the final form of a dialectic of permanent rebellion. Personal anguish escalates into the pathos of universal suffering. In this prose-poem, suffering consciousness—the very rhythms of unassuaged grief—become the essence of Ivan's protest. A kind of Dionysian impulse triumphs in this strange heretical passion—it is precisely the Apollinian structuring principle that is denied—and Ivan and the reader are lifted on a wave of stupendous, almost orgiastic lamentation.

The choice of the word "lamentation" to describe Ivan's prose-poem is not arbitrary. The problem of the lamentation (*prichi-tanie*)—an old Russian chant or song over the dead—is raised as a psychological and philosophical phenomenon early in the novel in the chapter "Women with Faith." This chapter is crucial background to any consideration of the rebellion of Ivan. "There's something from afar off," Zosima observes as a peasant woman approaches him bearing news of the death of her fourth and last child:

> "From afar off, little Father, from afar off, from three hundred versts from here. From afar off, Father, from afar off," the woman pronounced in a singsong voice, swaying her head rhythmically from side to side and resting her cheek in her hand. She spoke as though chanting a dirge. (I, 3)

At this point the narrator pauses to comment on the form and content of the lamentation:

> There is a silent and much-suffering grief among the people; it passes within and is silent. But there is also a heart-rending grief: it bursts out in tears and from that moment passes into lamentations. . . . Such lamentations appease one only insofar as they even further exacerbate and lacerate the heart. Such grief, however, does not desire consolation; it feeds only upon its feeling of despair. Lamentations are only a need perpetually to reopen a wound. (I, 3)

The grief of the lamentation, the narrator stresses, does not desire consolation. Its spiritual or ideological concomitant is doubt in God or even non-belief. It is not surprising, then, that the early Russian Orthodox Church detected dangerous, even rebellious elements in the popular folk lamentation. In the introduction to his collection of folk lamentations in 1872, E. V. Barsov posited a pagan world view at the core of the ancient poetry of lamentation:

> That is why, without doubt the ancient Russian church took action against such folk lamentations. . . . Church preachers spoke out against them. In the old collections of church writings . . . we frequently encounter the injunction—"Oh, do not weep too much over the dead." In explaining the wailings over coffin and grave as coming from a lack of faith in the immortality of the soul, . . . preachers tried to stop them by awakening faith in the resurrection of the dead. "There is much rebellion in your grief for the dead."[1]

Father Zosima, psychologically more astute perhaps than the old church fathers, takes a more conciliatory view toward the wailing of the mothers. "And do not console yourself," he advises, "and there is no need to be consoled, do not console yourself, but weep." Yet he does not let the matter rest there. He is as cognizant as the church fathers of the implications of excessive grief, of the rebellion latent in the lamentation. Like the early church fathers, he seeks to cope with this danger by arousing faith in the resurrection of the dead. Thus, though advising mothers not to console themselves and to weep, he stipulates:

> However, each time that you weep, remember without fail that your little son is united with the angels of God and is looking at you from up there and sees you, and rejoices over your tears, and points them out to God. And this great maternal sorrow will be with you for a long time, but finally it will turn into a quiet joy, and your bitter tears will only be the tears of a quiet emotion and spiritual cleansing, saving you from sins. (I, 3)

Tragic emotion should lead to spiritual catharsis. Yet one thing is clear: for Zosima only the idea of immortality stands between tears and despair, suffering and rebellion.

Such is Zosima's statement on the mystery of suffering. It is an anticipation of his more expressive and detailed treatment of the problem of suffering and death in "The Russian Monk." The lamentation of the mothers, in all its explosive potential, is a forerunner—both in its rhythms and spiritual content—of the wails of despair in Ivan's prose-poem at the end of "Rebellion."

In his prefatory remarks to his legend of the Grand Inquisitor Ivan characteristically identifies the pathos of his legend with that of the Mother of God in the medieval Russian legend, "The Wanderings of Our Lady through Hell." "Shocked and weeping" at the sight of so much suffering in hell, the Madonna prostrates herself before the throne of God and begs mercy for all in hell. "My poem," Ivan remarks, "would have been that kind if it had appeared at that time," that is, in an age of faith. But it belongs to another, later period. Ivan does not implore God the Father to be merciful, but rebels against him, against the stern Pantokrator. Ivan's rebellion takes on the character of an unending lamentation, in the narrator's words, the kind that "does not desire consolation," that "feeds only upon its feeling of despair," that strives again and again to "reopen a wound."

The center of Ivan's lamentation, literally and figuratively, is a wound, an image paralyzing to mind and spirit: it is the mutilation, the physical as well as psychological disfiguration, of children. Zosima envisages the departed child rejoicing in his resurrected state over his mother's tears and pointing them out to God. This representation of mother and child is permeated with Christian symbolism and is, in its own way, a religious painting. In his state of beatific happiness the child finds his mother's tears absurd. The message or moral of this iconographic representation is that immortality renders inconsolable grief meaningless. Ivan, on the other hand, is unable to conjure up visions of angelic children gamboling about the throne of God the Father and rejoicing at the tears of their grief-stricken mothers on earth. Ivan has other visions the contemplation of which lead him neither to quiet emotion, nor to spiritual catharsis, nor to a feeling of absolution for his sins. For Ivan, who essentially takes on the suffering of the mothers, it is the tears of the suffering children that render God's world absurd and meaningless; and in his despairing rebellion, in his lamentation, he points out these tears, as it were, to God.

2

Ivan's so-called long tirade in the second part of "The Brothers Get Acquainted" may be considered a prose rehearsal for the final poetic monologue. In this tirade Ivan attempts to explain to Alyosha "as quickly as possible" his "essence, that is, what I believe in and what I hope for." He is prepared, so he says, to accept God simply and to believe in the meaning of life and eternal harmony. Yet in the final analysis, he does not accept "this world of God." He is convinced, it is true, that

> suffering will be healed and made up for, that all the insulting comedy of human contradictions will disappear . . . that, ultimately, in the world finale, in the moment of eternal harmony, something so precious will come to pass that it will suffice for all hearts, for the assuagement of all indignation, for the expiation of all crimes of people, of all the blood they have shed; that it will make it not only possible to forgive but to justify all that has happened with man. (V, 3)

All this, Ivan concedes, may come to pass, "but I do not accept it and I do not want to accept it! Granted that even parallel lines will meet: I will see them and say that they meet, but I will still not accept it. That is my essence, Alyosha, that is my thesis."

The long tirade presents us with the paradox of Ivan's essence: his willingness to recognize Christian theological reality (at least for the sake of argument), yet his refusal to accept it. But we do not learn why he rejects the evidences of his understanding. The inner dynamic of his paradox is disclosed in the body of the chapter "Rebellion" and, most graphically, in the final dramatic peroration. There is a qualitative leap here from narrative exposition—starkly vivid accounts of cruelty to children—to the tortured rhythms of prose-poetry. It is as though the emotional pressure built up by harrowing anecdote and personal confession now finds release or resolution in the language and rhythm of poetry. Dostoevsky signals the shift to this final phase of Ivan's rebellion by means of a dramatic pause in Ivan's rapid-flowing discourse:

"Ivan fell silent for a moment, his face suddenly became very sad." After this pause he begins:

> Listen to me: I selected only children to make things clearer. Of the other tears of humanity with which the whole earth is soaked from crust to core—I'll not say anything, I have deliberately narrowed my theme. (V, 4)

The abstract, almost academic character of the first and final phrases contrasts sharply with the charged image at the center: the earth bathed in the rain of tears of suffering humanity.

This image of the earth soaked from crust to core with the tears of humanity harks back to the peasant mothers lamenting the deaths of their children. It also looks forward to the moment of Alyosha's mystical union with the earth, when he flings himself down upon the earth, driven by a desire to kiss it. But "he kissed it weeping, sobbing, and watering it with his tears, and madly swore to love it, love it forever. 'Water the earth with the tears of your joy and love those tears of yours'—rang in his soul." The image of the earth watered by tears in this scene is marked by the spirit of reconciliation and universal forgiveness. The earth is watered with tears of joy, and the result of this mystic union with the earth is a sense of renewal. Alyosha "fell to the earth a weak youth, but arose a firm fighter for the rest of his life." Ivan's tears—the tears of humanity—are bitter tears of suffering. They do not augur a harvest of reconciliation and forgiveness. Ivan will have none of the mystical transmutation of tears into the waters of eternal life, of suffering into salvation.

The various images that appear in Ivan's peroration are, like his stories, lacerations. Ivan's conception of himself as a bedbug, for instance, accurately conveys the hostile, underground character of his pose of humility: "I am a bedbug, and I confess with all humility that I cannot understand anything, why everything is arranged as it is." The whole movement of Ivan's monologue—viewed as antitheodicy—is a steady ascent from earth to heaven, from bedbug to God. The ascent is steep and ends in a reversal of roles: the humiliation of God, the representation of Him as a

THE WOUND AND THE LAMENTATION

scurrilous merchandizer of souls, and the transformation of the bedbug, Ivan, into a Christ figure.

What Ivan cannot understand—narrowing his "theme" to its core—is the doctrine of original sin as it applies to children. "People have eaten of the apple and learned to know good and evil, and became 'as gods'," Ivan observes to Alyosha. "But children have eaten nothing and so far are not guilty of anything." Ivan repeats his thought again in his final peroration, but with a significant change. "People themselves, so it goes, are guilty: they were given paradise, they wanted freedom and they stole fire from the heavens, themselves knowing that they would become unhappy, therefore there is no reason to pity them." The allusion to Greek myth at this point is perhaps significant: the figure of the eternally suffering, ever freshly wounded Prometheus reflects Ivan's own choice of permanent suffering in the name of a higher justice.

The tense, spasmodic character of the opening lines of Ivan's monologue prelude a storm of emotion. This emotion breaks out into the barely controlled rhythms of the fourth line. Ivan no longer merely poses the problem here; he responds to it broadly and passionately and in a deeply personal manner. An exclamatory, rhetorical "Oh" opens the floodgates of new movement:

Oh, with my pitiful, earthly Euclidian mind all I know is that there is suffering and that there are none guilty, that one thing follows from another directly and simply, that everything flows and comes into equilibrium—but really that's only Euclidian nonsense, really I know that, but the point is that I can't consent to live by it! What do I care that none are guilty and that one thing follows another directly and simply and that I know this—I must have retribution or I will destroy myself. (V, 4)

This passage in Russian, with its curious rocking, singsong rhythms, its repetitions and alliterations, establishes the sound pattern of Ivan's lamentation. It is remarkable in the way its formal structure expresses its ideas and tensions. The notion that everything flows and comes into equilibrium is expressed in the extraordinary balance of syntactical units or phrases in the passage.

Yet it is one thing to be presented with a formal equilibrium or balance of elements, and it is another thing to accept it. The opposition between "Euclidian mind" and "Euclidian nonsense" perfectly expresses the insupportable contradiction rending Ivan: reason, which he will not relinquish, exposes a cruel mechanism in which people suffer, no one is guilty, and everything balances out. But this abstract balancing of things, or justice, is completely unacceptable to Ivan's moral sense. In spite of all equilibrium, he wants to know "why everything is arranged as it is." In fact, Ivan sees only suffering and finds no justice or equilibrium. He himself seeks the moral satisfaction of real, Old Testament justice, or retribution. But expressing his need for retribution, Ivan reveals his deep sense of guilt and responsibility: if he does not find retribution, he will destroy himself, that is, take upon him the guilt and, through self-annihilation, reestablish the missing equilibrium. The motif of the pseudo-Christ, important throughout the monologue, emerges clearly here. It is paradoxical in character: it not only attests to an extraordinary degree of moral sensibility but to an egotism. "I did not suffer," Ivan declares, "in order with my misdeeds and sufferings to manure some kind of future harmony."

It is apparent, however, that retributive punishment, though instinctively demanded for the satisfaction of a sense of moral outrage, hardly disposes of the problems raised by human suffering. It has no meaning to those who have unjustly suffered. "What can hell correct," Ivan asks toward the end of his lamentation, "when these [children] already have been tormented?" But the notion of retribution, as Ivan develops it, is only partially exhausted by the idea of punishment. The moment of retribution is also a moment of revelation, of fulfillment of divine prophecy. The destruction of the wicked coincides with the exaltation of the good and the final triumph of God's justice. This is the day of judgment when, as Ivan puts it, "all will suddenly learn why everything has been as it is," "when the crown of knowledge will be attained and all will be explained." The notion of retributive justice is for Ivan, then, a bridge or transition to the central problem and phenomenon of divine reconciliation and harmony.

At the outset Ivan insists that he be on earth at the moment of revelation so that he may see it himself:

> I have believed, I want to see it myself, and if I am already dead at that hour, then let them resurrect me, because if it all takes place without me, then it will be too insulting. I did not suffer in order with my misdeeds and sufferings to manure some kind of future harmony. I want to see with my own eyes how the hind lies down alongside the lion, and how the slaughtered creature rises and embraces his slaughterer. (V, 4)

The initial image in Ivan's lamentation—the rain of tears soaking the earth—was a first indication of Ivan's bitter and mocking attitude toward the concept of the universal harvest. His bitterness and cynicism is even more manifest in the second, as it were, agricultural image of his lamentation: the representation of suffering as "manure" for some future harmony. Ivan's notion of the absurd and cruel character of redemption in the divine plan could not, it would seem, be more forcibly presented. The deliberate crudeness of the metaphor perfectly conveys his lacerating and cruel thought.

At the outset of his peroration Ivan deviates from his theme— the suffering of children—and places the emphasis upon his own need for retribution, his desire for resurrection, and his unwillingness to let his sufferings be manure for a future harmony in which he has no part. But he quickly returns to his theme:

> Listen: if everyone must suffer in order with suffering to buy eternal harmony, then what have children got to do with all this, tell me please? It is quite incomprehensible why they have had to suffer, and why they have had to buy harmony with sufferings. Why did they also have to become material and manure for some future harmony? Solidarity in sin among people I understand, I understand solidarity also in retribution, but with children, however, there can be no such

solidarity in sin; and if it is true that they must, indeed, stand in solidarity with their fathers and all the misdeeds of their fathers, then, of course, this truth is not of this world and is incomprehensible to me. (V, 4)

The metaphor of Ivan's suffering as manure for future harmony now develops into something more ugly and ominous: children as "material and manure" for some future harmony. And in a dramatic period marked by the repeated and ironical use of the word "solidarity," Ivan links the repellent notion of suffering as material and manure with the idea of solidarity of men and children in sin.

At the same time, Ivan compares the dynamics of salvation to a commercial transaction. In Dostoevsky's notebook to *The Brothers Karamazov*, we find the lines, "The Inquisitor: '*God as a merchant. I love humanity more than you'*."[2] We do not need any prompting from Dostoevsky's notebooks, however, to realize that the god against whom Ivan rebels is conceived as a supreme merchant or pawnbroker, trafficking in the sufferings of mankind and selling "tickets" to heaven at exorbitant rates of interest. Ivan pursues the metaphor with a vengeance. In his conception, man must "buy" (*kupit'*, *pokupat'*) eternal harmony with suffering, but at an unfavorable exchange rate: harmony is "not worth" even the tiny tears of a tortured child, not worth it because the tears remain "unexpiated" (*neiskuplennye*). "And if the sufferings of children go to make up the sum of suffering which are necessary for the purchase of the truth," then "all this truth is not worth such a price."[3] "We simply cannot afford to pay so much for admission." Ivan will "respectfully" return his ticket.

In the ironic subtext of Ivan's rebellious lamentation, Jesus the Redeemer (the only being, Ivan hints, who might have the "right to forgive") stands opposed to God the merchant. Jesus does not appear in Ivan's lamentation, but his omission is deliberate. Jesus has not yet arrived in the cruel Old Testament world that Ivan posits. He is only an hypothesis in Ivan's legend of the Grand Inquisitor, as he is in the long tirade where Ivan allows that "in the world's finale, at the moment of eternal harmony, something so precious [might] come to pass that it would suffice for all hearts, for the assuaging of all resentments, for the expiation of all the crimes of humanity . . . that it will make it not only possible to forgive but to justify all that has happened with men."

In "Rebellion" and in "Grand Inquisitor" Ivan posits a world that is utterly loveless, freighted down with intolerable suffering and evil. On the one hand, men are utterly undeserving of salvation: "After all, they are vile and not deserving of love and have gotten their reward," Ivan says of the adults who have eaten the apple. On the other hand, a world where such terrible things occur makes a mockery of any concept of a meaningful, God-made world. Ivan's question, "Is there in the whole world a being who could forgive and who would have the right to forgive?" turns not on whether a Redeemer exists, but on whether such a being has the *right* to forgive, can forgive. The real question is whether the idea of Christ, precious and beyond all comprehension, is relevant at all to the fundamental reality of human existence, to man in all his vileness. "Christian love is a kind of impossible miracle on earth," Ivan insists. In Dostoevsky's manuscript of *The Raw Youth* Versilov gives the most extreme formulation to this skepticism: "Without a doubt Christ could not love us, such as we are. He suffered us. He forgave us, but certainly despised us; I at any rate cannot conceive His countenance otherwise."[4] Man, in Ivan's view, is unworthy of the Redeemer. He deserves the Grand Inquisitor.

The full force of Ivan's rebellion is expressed in a final, thrice-repeated image: a general turns an offending eight-year-old boy over to his hunting dogs to be torn to pieces before the eyes of his mother. Ivan visualizes the moment of universal "hosanna," the supreme moment when the crown of knowledge is achieved in the most emotionally charged passage in his lamentation:

> Oh, Alyosha, I am not blaspheming! Now I understand what an upheaval of the universe it will be when everything in heaven and earth blends into one hymn of praise and everything that lives and has lived cries aloud: "Thou art just, O

Lord, for Thy ways are revealed." When the mother embraces the fiend who threw her child to the dogs, and all
three cry aloud with tears, "Thou art just, O Lord!'", then,
of course, the crown of knowledge will be achieved and all
will be made clear. But there's the rub: it is precisely that
which I can't accept. And while I am on earth, I make haste
to take my own measures. You see, Alyosha, perhaps it
really may happen that if I live to that moment, or rise again
to see it, I, too, perhaps, may cry aloud with the rest, looking
at the mother embracing the child's torturer, "Thou art just,
O Lord!'", but I don't want to cry aloud then. While there
is still time, I hasten to put myself on guard, and therefore
I renounce the higher harmony altogether. (V, 4)

Ivan's renunciation of harmony is conveyed not so much verbally
as visually, in his mental image of the mother embracing the
torturer who has torn apart her child with dogs. It is this composite image, or tableau, in which the scenes of murder and reconciliation are juxtaposed, that Ivan forever keeps before his eye
and the eye of the reader. It is this wound or laceration that lies
at the center of his great lamentation.

Thus, in the novel Ivan's anti-utopian tableau, with its triumph
of suffering over harmony, is opposed to Zosima's Christian utopian tableau (the resurrected child rejoicing in the mother's tears
and pointing them out to God), with its triumph of harmony over
suffering. Both pictures are constructed out of contradictory emotional elements. But in Ivan's picture the contradiction is, as it
were, malignant: the jarring elements constitute a permanent laceration; the idea of a reconciliation between the general and the
mother is perceived, literally and figuratively, as both impossible
and repulsive. In Zosima's picture, on the other hand, the jarring
elements (the tears of the mother and the laughter of the child)
are resolved in the triumphant miracle of resurrection. In Ivan's
picture the owner of the dogs, the general, is a satanic figure; the
mother, in effect, embraces the devil. In Zosima's picture, the
satanic figure is replaced by an unseen but ever-present and so-
licitous God.

The images of suffering and harmony in Ivan's picture are organically incompatible with one another. The whole essence of Ivan's rebellion lies in his inability to relate the idea of divine justice and harmony to the reality of injustice, suffering, and death. Ivan's composite picture, or montage, conveys his sense of a meaningless and absurd universe. The "real images and forms" of his dream of paradise, the ridiculous man insisted, were full of harmony and beauty: "I saw, I saw, and the *living image* filled my soul forever." Ivan, too, *sees*, but the images and forms of his vision of harmony are inharmonious and grotesque and constitute a savage blow at the credibility of the dream of harmony. Here, there is no form or beauty—*obraz*; there is only shapelessness—*bezobrazie*.

With Ivan's repellent picture of the mother embracing the general (in the background is the child being torn to pieces by the general's dogs) at the conclusion of "Rebellion," the reader comes full circle to the beginning of that chapter. There Ivan depicts John the Merciful embracing a frozen and hungry beggar and breathing into "a mouth putrid and loathsome from some awful disease." The significance of both these scenes, at the beginning and end of "Rebellion," is clear; as Ivan puts it, "Christian love"—love at close quarters, love for the visible face of man—"is an impossible miracle on earth": "For any one to love a man he must be hidden, for as soon as he shows his face love is gone." John's act of compassion, then, is not a triumph of love, in Ivan's view, but an act of self-laceration. It is of the same moral-psychological order as the mother's embrace of the murderer of her child. Ivan removes the act of John from the realm of ethical inspiration to the subterranean realm of abnormal psychology. The action of Ivan's namesake, John, is possible in Ivan's view only if we wish to enjoy ugliness.[5]

The opening picture of John the Merciful embracing the loathsome beggar thus anticipates the final discordant picture of reconciliation in Ivan's lamentation—the mock scene of universal harmony. Both acts involve a self-renunciation that is instantly perceived by the reader, or viewer, as self-disfiguration. The mother, like John, embraces that which is loathsome and putrid.

In both scenes "parallel lines" meet. But what may be mathematically or theologically possible is disclosed as morally and aesthetically unacceptable. In his two illustrations Ivan reveals that he will have none of the perverse wonders of non-Euclidian Christian moral geometry. His refusal to accept the meeting point, that is, Christian reconciliation and harmony, is presented as an instinctive inability to countenance a marriage of beauty and the beast, in short, to contemplate any violation of the ideal of beauty. The mother and child, of course, are for Ivan the symbol of the inviolable moral-spiritual absolute.

3

Ivan's rebellious lamentation grows more feverish as it approaches its climax. Harmony is not worth even a tear of the tormented child who prays to "sweet little God" with her unexpiated tears. "It is not worth a single little tear because these tears remain unexpiated. They must be expiated, otherwise there can be no harmony. But how, how," asks Ivan, "are you going to expiate them? Is it really possible? Will that indeed happen through the fact that they will be avenged?" The need for expiation again raises the question of retribution. But whereas at the beginning of his lamentation Ivan insists on his subjective need for retribution, here he emphasizes the objectively meaningless character of retribution. Hell for the torturers, he notes, will in no way help those who have already been tortured.

In the sophistic style of his father Ivan rounds off his argument with the rhetorical question: "And what kind of harmony can there be if there is hell? I want to forgive and embrace, I do not want people to suffer any more." The circular character of Ivan's argumentation here is typical of his thought. Like the Underground Man, Ivan is lacking in "foundations." In point of fact, Ivan does not want to forgive and embrace. He does not believe that the mother has the right to forgive the torturer. She may forgive him for her own sufferings perhaps, but not for the suffering of the tortured child—"even if the child were to forgive him for them!"

THE WOUND AND THE LAMENTATION

At this point Ivan asks the central question of his monologue: "Is there in the whole world a being who could forgive and would have the right to forgive?" Earlier in his long tirade he acknowledges that something so precious could appear that might expiate the villainies of men and forgive, even justify, all that had happened to people. But it is precisely this that he does not want to accept. "I do not want harmony, out of love for humanity I do not want it," he exclaims at the end of his monologue:

> I would rather remain with my unavenged sufferings. I would really rather remain with my unavenged suffering and my unsatisfied indignation *even if I were wrong*. Besides, too high a price is put on harmony; we simply cannot afford to pay so much for admission. And therefore I hasten to give back my ticket of admission. And indeed if I am an honest man I am bound to give it back as soon as possible. And that's what I'm doing. It's not God that I don't accept, Alyosha, I'm only most respectfully returning Him the ticket. (V, 4)

Ivan, as Camus has noted, "rejects here the basic interdependence, introduced by Christianity, between suffering and divine truth," an interdependence symbolically witnessed in the Passion of Christ.[6] Even if salvation—reconciliation and eternal harmony—constitutes the divine truth, Ivan rejects it in advance: the price is too high.

In rejecting the interdependence of suffering and Christian truth, however, and in opposing justice to this truth, Ivan in fact establishes an interdependence between hopeless suffering and a new terrible truth: the reality of a tragic universe, an unjust cosmic order, or disorder, in which humanity at large is hopelessly condemned to pain and suffering. Psychologically, Ivan's choice of endless suffering is embodied in his rebellious lamentation. It can be compared to the Underground Man's revolt against the laws of nature or the "stone wall": it is neither victory nor reconciliation, but, figuratively speaking, a permanent, despairing beating of the head against the wall. In Ivan's rebellion the groans of the "man with toothache" in *Notes from the Un-*

derground are raised to the plane of a despairing lamentation over a meaningless and cruel universe.

On the moral plane, however, Ivan's rebellion—taking on the form of an imitation of Christ—paradoxically introduces meaning into the universe and reaffirms the necessity of the Redeemer. "Is there in the whole world a being who could forgive and would have the right to forgive?" asks Ivan. He does not answer this question directly, but he knows that this right is acquired only through suffering and sacrifice. Konstantin Mochulsky has called attention to the element of "imposture" in Ivan's rebellion: "A diabolic deceit is hidden in this imposture. The atheist appeals to the noble human sentiments of compassion, magnanimity, love, but on his lips this is pure rhetoric."[7] Yet it seems there is more than diabolic deceit and conceit here. The very nature of Ivan's imposture is deeply ambivalent. What he sets out to deny, he affirms in spite of himself by his unconscious wish to imitate Christ. The imitation of Christ by its very nature is redemptive.

In his conversation with Alyosha, Ivan in jest recalls the "old sinner in the eighteenth century," Voltaire, "who delivered himself of the statement that if there were no God, it would have been necessary to invent him, '*S'il n'existait pas Dieu il faudrait l'inventer*'." Ivan's usurpation of the role of Christ is, of course, such an invention, but one that attests to a deep, albeit unconscious identity with Christ. Ivan rebels against God's world; he rebels out of despair. But in its inner content, this rebellion bears witness to man's continual need to rediscover his humanity in himself, to sacrifice himself for others, in short, to imitate Christ. The path of Ivan's own moral and spiritual redemption must take him from usurpation to imitation of Christ in deed as well as word. But that path leads him first of all through the fires of negation and denial.

Dmitry Karamazov and the Legend of the Grand Inquisitor

*Man was created in the image of God, that is, free,
for better or for worse.*
RUSSIAN MANUSCRIPT, TWELFTH CENTURY

THE NATURE and implications of man's moral breadth are a central concern of Dostoevsky's in his art. Arkady Dolgoruky in *The Raw Youth* poses the problem: "A thousand times I have been amazed at this faculty of man (and, it seems, chiefly the Russian man) for cherishing in his soul the most lofty ideal side by side with the most extreme vileness, and all this absolutely sincerely. Whether this is a special breadth in Russian man which will take him far, or simply vileness—that is the question!" This is the *karamazov* question. The prosecutor in the trial of Dmitry takes note of the special capacity of the "broad Russian *karamazov* nature"[1] for combining "all possible opposites and contemplating at the same time two abysses, the abyss over us, the abyss of sublime ideals, and the abyss under us, the abyss of the most vile and stinking debasement." But he finds no secret promise in this *karamazov* breadth. "We are broad, broad as our whole Mother Russia," he exclaims in a burst of sarcasm, "we will make room for everything, make our peace with everything!" He suggests that there may be no moral foundations at all to Russian society—a thought that Dostoevsky privately expressed in his notebook[2]—and sees in Dmitry's extraordinary moral breadth only an example of the "mad gallop of our unbridled nature," of the fateful Russian troika rushing headlong perhaps to disaster.

The prosecutor is carried away by his own rhetoric. Yet we would be ignoring the grim reality of the *karamazov* question to Dostoevsky if we did not recognize how much his own doubts and anxieties are embedded in the civic indignation of the prosecutor. Indeed, it is against the background of Dostoevsky's own shadowy doubts that the brilliance of his characterization of Dmitry can best be perceived. Dmitry is Dostoevsky's attempt to find meaning and direction, a moral pivot, in the apparent disorder of man's nature.

Two views of the human condition constitute the dialectic of Ivan's poem, or legend about the Grand Inquisitor. The disputants, Christ and the Grand Inquisitor, are essentially the same as those in the Biblical story of Job or in the Faust legend. Indeed, Ivan's legend functions in *The Brothers Karamazov* much as the prologue does in Job or Goethe's *Faust*: it poses the questions that are debated and lived out in the body of the work. It is in Dmitry, tragically inept at life, that we find an analogue to the generality of mankind. In him the complex dialectic of Ivan's legend is most richly embodied. "Alyosha, my cherubim, various philosophies are tormenting me, the devil take them!" Dmitry exclaims to Alyosha in a conversation that takes place in prison. Dmitry does not rationally choose between philosophies: they are in him; they are the very fabric of his existence; he lives them out. "Precisely because unknown ideas are storming within me did I carouse, fight and rage madly." This is a life and death struggle for Dmitry. He spends the two days before murder of his father "literally casting himself in all directions, 'struggling with his fate and saving himself,' as he himself put it later."

Does Dmitry constitute a refutation of the Grand Inquisitor's view of man? The answer to this question must lead to the roots of Dostoevsky's moral philosophy. The moral incompetence of man is posited by the Grand Inquisitor. Man, though rebellious, is weak and vile, he insists. Nothing is more frightening and insupportable to man "in his simplicity and inborn anarchy" than freedom. He prefers peace, even death, to "freedom of choice in the knowledge of good and evil"; in his misery he is forever seeking somebody to whom he can hand his gift of freedom. Men are as children, the Grand Inquisitor repeatedly emphasizes, "little children," "foolish children," "pitiful children." Rampant in their rebellion, they will in the end grow weary and place their freedom at the feet of the church.

The characterization of Dmitry, from one point of view, is designed to refute this tragic conception of man. Dmitry goes through his ordeal in the full consciousness of his freedom. He affirms that he is "complete master" and can put a stop to his disgrace or carry it through. He is conscious of his freedom to kill or not to kill. He has sunk into the filthy morass "of his own will." Dmitry struggles through with his freedom: he does not kill his father in the crucial encounter ("the devil was conquered"); he does not commit suicide; he does not—in suffering his freedom of choice—reject the image of his God.

Yet the essence of Dostoevsky's characterization of Dmitry— and herein lies its beauty and deeper tragic significance—is that it is always nearly a question, and at times is really a question, whether Dmitry actually escapes the Grand Inquisitor's definition. For example, Dostoevsky endows Dmitry with a distinctly childlike nature (the words "child" and "childlike" are frequently encountered in references to Dmitry's personality and behavior). Like everything else in Dmitry, this fundamental attribute of the childlike has very contradictory implications. The frankness, the sincerity, the gentleness (when he is gentle) of Dmitry as well as the purity of his idealism, are all linked with a curiously artless, naive, childlike quality. This same childlike quality—and with it goes his enthusiasm, his boyish pranks, his ready tears, his volatile moods—constitutes a mitigating element in his favor. We forgive a child; his lack of self-control, his capricious behavior, even his little misdeeds are somehow beyond good and evil. "But we look upon you, Sir, just as a little child, that's how we consider you," remarks the coachman Andrey to Dmitry as he drives him to Mokroe. "And although you are bad-tempered—that is so— yet the Lord will forgive you because of your simplicity."[3] It is not without significance that these words of symbolic absolution for Dmitry are uttered by a man of the people, a peasant.

But, though childlike, Dmitry in fact is not a child, and he does not live in a child's world. Or rather, he is the "child of nature," in Schiller's sense: "The child of nature, when he breaks loose, turns into a madman."[4] The capricious misdeeds of a grown child, a man, are lawless. A moment after the remarks of the coachman Andrey, Dmitry prays that the Lord accept him in all his "lawlessness" and not judge him. The word "lawless" seems to define so much of Dmitry's nature, so many of his actions. "Perhaps I will not kill, but perhaps I will kill," Dmitry remarks to Alyosha in reference to his father. Are these remarks an illustration of Dmitry's moral consciousness, his freedom to choose, or do they simply reflect what the Grand Inquisitor calls the "anarchy of the free mind"?

A short while after this remark to Alyosha, Dmitry almost kills his father; it is only accidental that he does not kill him. "He's getting what he deserves," screams Dmitry after booting his prostrate father three times in the head. "And if I haven't killed him, I'll come again and kill him." A short while later Dmitry confronts the hated face of his father at the window and decides not to kill him, but on his way out he lets fly at the servant Grigory the blow he had reserved for his father.

Dmitry rages across the stage of life, and for the majority of those who come in his way, it is *sauve qui peut*. The communist moralist V. Ermilov reflects a human point of view (though he fails to understand Dostoevsky's characterization of Dmitry) when he is suspicious of a man who "*continuously almost kills people* who get in his way."[5] "There's no order in me," Dmitry confesses, "no higher order." The Grand Inquisitor's view of man as a rampant child is tragically relevant to any really contemplative consideration of the phenomenon of Dmitry and his disorder.

Christ, says the Grand Inquisitor, wanted to replace the "firm ancient law with the free human heart." He came with a freedom that man could not even grasp and that he feared. Has historical man outgrown the need for the firm hand of the ancient law? Ivan answers this question in the negative; his advocacy of a theological state (in his article and later, though ambiguously, in his legend) rests primarily on the conviction that there is nothing on earth that will compel men to love one another, that there are no deterrents in man to crime. The elder Zosima holds to the opposite conviction: the deterrent to crime and the effective punishment for crime lie in man's conscience, in the "law of Christ which reveals itself in the consciousness of one's own conscience."

Dmitry's intense preoccupation with moral questions and,

above all, his profound spiritual upheaval after the death of his father suggest that man may be able to cope with the problem of his disorder through a free heart. At the same time, Dmitry, in the painful consciousness of his ethical dilemma, is at least partially a child of the ancient law. Dmitry is tormented by the terrible and enigmatic character of beauty; he is horrified that man with the ideal of Sodom in his soul does not renounce the ideal of the Madonna, that in his heart this man may continue to nourish the flame of his youthful ideal. "No, man is broad, indeed far too broad," Dmitry remarks in an echo of the Grand Inquisitor. "I would narrow him." Certainly here is one of Dostoevsky's most important insights: it is not the devil, but man himself who gives birth in the suffering of his moral immaturity to the idea of his own narrowing, his own self-limitation. The Grand Inquisitor is not a figment of Ivan's imagination; he is an integral part, an authentic manifestation, of man's moral consciousness in recoil against its own disorder.

The leitmotif of the Grand Inquisitor is heard at the high point of Dmitry's ordeal in the preliminary investigation. At the end of the grilling, and following his dream of the weeping child, Dmitry turns to the investigators and declares:

> Gentlemen, we are all cruel, we are all monsters, we all make people, mothers, infants at the breast weep, but of them all . . . I am the most vile reptile! So be it! Each day of my life, beating my breast, I have promised to reform and each day I go on doing the very same things. I understand now that for such people as I a blow is needed, a blow of destiny, to seize them as in a noose and bind them by an external force. Never, never should I have risen by myself alone! But the thunder has burst forth. I accept the torment of the accusation and public ignominy. I want to suffer and by suffering I will cleanse myself! (IX, 9)

These lines are striking in the way they reveal two entirely different, though intersecting levels of religious consciousness in Dmitry. Certainly relevant to any consideration of Dmitry's consciousness is Alfred North Whitehead's view of the "interweaving of the Platonic ideal in Christian theology and in the pattern of Christian emotion of an older concept of a Divine Despot and a Slavish Universe, each with morals of its kind."⁶ At the very moment when he approaches the Christian ideal of free personality—when he is supremely conscious of the moral ideal, when he is morally transfigured by his dream image of the suffering mother and child—Dmitry casts himself in the role of the weak and vile slave. The blow, the noose, the binding by an external force, all suggest the psychology of a man still dominated by the concept of punitive purification of ancient law; all suggest man as the Grand Inquisitor understands him.

Yet it would be a mistake to regard Dmitry's own view of his catastrophe and his own definition of himself as the dominant truth of his being. He is not a new man, but neither is he inert clay; he is man in transition, full of fears (as the tempter found him), but groping for a new ethic. It is impossible to understand, or accept, Dmitry as anything other than a symbolic figure—a representation of raw, historical man at the fringe of moral evolution, man at the point in which moral self has crystallized in perfect form but still remains embedded in a more ancient, protean consciousness. The shape of that new self, in a combined moral and aesthetic sense, is reflected for Dostoevsky in the image or iconographic representation of Christ and the Madonna.

In the course of his stay in prison Dmitry becomes aware of a "new man" within him: "A new man has risen in me. He was enclosed in me, but never would have appeared if it had not been for that thunder." The ordeal of Dmitry is the birth of a new, embryonic self. "Yes, Dmitry is non-existent as yet," Dmitry's father observes, in the first reference to Dmitry by a character in the novel. The remark is an eccentric way of pointing to an ordinary fact: Dmitry has not yet arrived at the monastery. But the remark points to more than the physical absence of Dmitry (and Fyodor's total and fateful neglect of his children). In its symbolic function it marks Dmitry's point of departure in the tragedy from a state of being that is, aesthetically, inchoate, raw, protean. The novel carried Dmitry to the threshold of moral being and consciousness. "You cannot believe, Aleksey, how much now I want to live, what a thirst [I have] to exist and to be conscious," Dmitry exclaims in prison. "I am! I sit in a pillar, but I exist." The quest of Dmitry's is a quest for moral structure, that is, for form. It is significant that Dmitry's consciousness of a new man within him is accompanied by an aesthetic awareness of himself as an image and likeness of God.

Dostoevsky's conception of the reformation of Dmitry was influenced by Schiller's idea (expressed in both his poetry and critical writings) of the moral regeneration of man through the awakening of his aesthetic sensibility. Man, the child of nature, according to Schiller, emerges from the "long slumber of the senses," recognizes himself as a man, and sets about "transforming the work of blind compulsion into a work of free choice, and of elevating physical necessity into moral necessity." He strives to leave the dominion of blind necessity and forms for himself a conception of "man as Idea," that is, as a moral-aesthetic ideal that becomes his ultimate aim. This aim is not to be found in man's moral character, "which has, *ex hypothesi*, first to be fashioned," but in Art, in Beauty. Schiller posits Beauty as "a necessary condition of Human Being." It restores man to himself and makes him authentically free. For example, it "ennobles . . . the crude character imposed by physical need upon sexual love."[7]

In *The Brothers Karamazov* Dostoevsky attempts to realize in the figure of Dmitry this awakening to consciousness from the slumber of the senses, to depict the transition from naive, and therefore tragic, humanism (as we find it in Dmitry) to a condition of mature self-consciousness. Dmitry, of course, is far from being the new man he senses within. His desire to suffer, his yearning to bear the cross and to sing a "tragic hymn" to God, turns out to be more symbolic than real. At the end of his trial he asks to be spared, and in conversation with Alyosha, declares that he is not able or ready to resign himself to his suffering: "I wanted to sing a 'hymn,' but I am not able to put up with the guard's use of the familiar form 'thou'!" And Alyosha agrees: "You are not ready and not for you is such a cross," adding that "the lawyer in this case spoke the truth. Such heavy burdens are not for all, for some they are impossible." These are the Grand Inquisitor's thoughts about the mass of men.[8] Christ may be justly proud of those several thousand children of freedom who sacrificed in his name, but what of the remaining millions of weak people? "Now is it possible," the Grand Inquisitor asks Christ, "that you come only to the elect and for the elect?"

The Grand Inquisitor's view of the masses as unable to bear the burdens of the elect finds support in the characterization of Dmitry. The same condition of moral frailty of man that moves the Grand Inquisitor to seek to enslave the masses through lying and deception is accepted by Dostoevsky, though with a crucial qualification, as the normal state of average man. In responding to Dmitry's desire but inability to bear the burden of sufferings, Alyosha articulates Dostoevsky's point of view:

> You wanted through suffering to be re-born into another man; in my opinion, remember only and always through your life . . . this other man—and that will be enough for you. The fact that you did not accept the great cross of suffering will serve to make you feel in yourself an even greater duty, and this constant feeling in times to come, in your whole life, will help your rebirth more, perhaps, than if you went *there*. (Epilogue, 2)

The path that Alyosha envisages for Dmitry is one of compromise; but in this compromise there is no indifference, inertia, or defeat. Man yearns for the ideal of beauty, Dostoevsky wrote in 1861 in "Mr. ——bov and the Question of Art." He yearns for perfection, or transfiguration. What he seeks is unattainable, but man "lives most of all at the very moment he is seeking, striving for something."[9]

The creative existence for Dostoevsky is one in which man is in continual tension toward the ideal. What is important in matters of ethical judgment is that man never lose sight of the ideal, the good, the beautiful. Dmitry can look simultaneously into two abysses. But it is crucial, in Dostoevsky's view, that this moral breadth evoke horror in him. The cardinal sin in Dostoevsky's world is inertia. Stavrogin is doomed not because he finds equal pleasure in good and evil, but because he is indifferent to this conjunction of moral-aesthetic experience. Dostoevsky does not condemn an individual because he has evil in him (man must experience evil); he condemns indifference to evil, the absence of the ideal, moral stagnation, inertia.

This outlook is embodied in some very striking formulations. "I repeat," Dostoevsky writes in the February issue of *Diary of a Writer* in 1876, "judge the Russian people not by those abominations which it so often commits, but by those great and sacred things for which even in its abominations it constantly yearns . . . judge our people not by what it is, but by what it would like to become. And its ideals are strong and sacred."[10] Dostoevsky, of course, does not justify abominations committed by people; he simply insists that where there is striving for an ideal man can be judged finally only in reference to his total, evolving being. "If a people preserve the ideal of beauty and its need," Dostoevsky wrote again in his essay on art in 1861, "that means there is a need for health, the norm, and therefore in this way the highest development of a people is guaranteed."[11] This is not, at root, a very demanding ethic, but it is a working ethic for mortals. It is this outlook that underlies Dostoevsky's final attitude of resigned hope with respect to Dmitry.

To conclude with the question raised in the beginning of this chapter, is the Grand Inquisitor's view of man refuted by Dmitry? The answer can only be "yes" and "no," but with the affirmative and negative seen as constituting a constructive dialectic. The key may be found in the letter Dostoevsky wrote to Fonvizina after his release from prison in 1854, where he speaks of his terrible thirst to believe in spite of the accumulation of "opposite proofs" within him: "Even . . . if somebody proved to me that Christ was outside the truth, and it *really* were true that the truth was outside Christ, then I would rather remain with Christ than with the truth."[12] Dostoevsky affirms the existence of opposite proofs, or what we might call a negative truth. He even allows that Christ might be outside the truth. But immediately he makes a leap of faith that in fact places Christ back in the circle of revealed truth, a leap that denies and renders false the opposite proofs.

The positive truth that Christ embodies wins out, but here there is no stasis; it is a truth continually in movement, continually chasing and overtaking its antithesis.

It is difficult to comprehend Ivan's legend of the Grand Inquisitor unless it is recognized that the confrontation here of two views of man is, in the final analysis, a confrontation of two intersecting, relative truths. In this confrontation is the truth of man and his historical existence: man's weakness, his vileness, his childlike groping, his excess, and, above all, his constant temptation to escape and renounce his responsibilities. All this is tragic actuality. But it is a truth that man, through his frenetic searchings and his passionate belief in an ideal, continually negates, and in negating surmounts.

Man cannot stand alone, the Grand Inquisitor insists. He needs somebody before whom he can bow down. Dostoevsky also maintains that man cannot stand alone; but the deity before whom he bows is Christ—aesthetically, transcendent Beauty, the ineffable Ideal. It is the truth (and therefore reality) of this ideal in its various forms and of man's constant yearning for it that renders incomplete the Grand Inquisitor's view of man—and that, in the end, makes viable man's tragic actuality.

The inner dialectic of Ivan's legend finds its counterpart in the drama of Dmitry Karamazov as a whole and, in particular, in his strange approach to the money he received from Katerina. Apropos of sewing half of the money in a little bag or amulet around his neck, he explains:

> While I have that money on me . . . I am a scoundrel, not a thief, for I can always go to my insulted betrothed and, laying down half the sum I have fraudulently appropriated, I can always say to her, "You see, I've squandered half your money, and shown that I am a weak and immoral man and, if you like, a scoundrel . . . but though I am a scoundrel, I am not a thief, or else I shouldn't have brought you back half of the money, but would have appropriated it as I did the first half." (XII, 6)

The prosecutor heaps ridicule upon the explanation of "this wild, but weak man." His final words of rebuttal are particularly noteworthy in the context of the dialectic of Ivan's legend of the Grand Inquisitor. "One cannot imagine anything more in contradiction with reality than this legend of the amulet. One may presuppose everything, but not this." For Dostoevsky, man's striving for, or belief in, the ideal is indeed "in contradiction with reality" and with man's nature, but it is nonetheless a fact. It is the incredible truth of man's striving for the ideal in the face of the earthly truth of his nature that Dostoevsky posits as the moving force in man's historical existence.

The "legend of the amulet," then, refutes the legend of the Grand Inquisitor insofar as we take the latter as a poem in support of the pessimistic philosophy of the Grand Inquisitor. But if we view Ivan's legend, as we do, as a dialectic or argument between two relative truths in which the negative argument is self-defeating ("But...this is absurd!" cries Alyosha. "Your poem is in praise of Jesus, not in disparagement...as you wanted it to be."), then the legend of the amulet—the quintessence of Dmitry's drama—may be seen as giving expression to the same ultimate truth as Ivan's legend of the Grand Inquisitor. From this viewpoint, Dmitry's insistence on preserving half of Katerina's money glows in the novel like the kiss of Jesus in the heart of the Grand Inquisitor.

The concept of dualism in man's nature and between man and his reality as constituting the creative dialectic of human existence is posited by Dostoevsky as early as 1861 in his critique of the radical Russian critic N. Dobrolyubov. But it is only Dmitry Karamazov, of all Dostoevsky's heroes, who embodies this dialectic in a creative sense, who becomes, as it were, the exemplification of the tragic life principle. Dmitry survives the chaos of his breadth. Whether we can speak of an actual conversion in him of the destructive and self-destructive tensions of ambivalent personality into a positive instrumentality is another question. In the final analysis, however, the ethical message of Dmitry's drama, as in Goethe's *Faust*, must be sought in the change that takes place in his attitude toward life. This change would not seem to be without some effect on Dmitry's concrete behavior. "Real swine!" Dmitry, in prison, remarks to Alyosha in reference to Rakitin. "Formerly I used to boot such people out; well, now I listen to them." It would be risky to take Dmitry at his word. But it would also be a mistake not to recognize in this casual remark—if we view Dmitry, as does Dostoevsky, as a symbolic figure—a hope of no small consequence for mankind.

NOTES

Abbreviations for Dostoevsky Sources

I cite the collected works of Dostoevsky in Russian, *Polnoe sobranie khudozhestvennykh proizvedenii*, ed. V. Tomashevskii and K. Khalabaev, 13 vols. (Moscow-Leningrad, 1926-1930), as *PSS*. Volumes XI and XII of this edition contain Dostoevsky's *Diary of a Writer*. Volume XIII contains his miscellaneous critical and journalistic writings covering the period 1845-1878. Where this edition fails, I use *Polnoe sobranie khudozhestvennykh proizvedenii*, ed. V. G. Bazanov, G. M. Fridlender et al., 30 vols. to date (Leningrad, 1972——). I cite this edition as *PSS²*. For Dostoevsky's letters, I cite *Pis'ma*, ed. A. Dolinin, 4 vols. (Moscow, 1928, 1930, 1934, 1959), as *Pis'ma*. For Dostoevsky's notebooks published separately, I cite *Neizdannyi Dostoevskii: zapisnye knizhki i tetradi 1860-1881, Literaturnoe nasledstvo*, ed. V. G. Bazanov, D. D. Blagoi et al. (Moscow, 1971), Vol. 83, as *LN 83*.

All quotations from Dostoevsky's works are from the Russian. I give page references in the notes to all quotations except those from Dostoevsky's fictional works. For passages from novels and stories that are divided into chapters (or parts and chapters) I place roman and arabic numerals (for part and chapter respectively) at the end of major quotations in the text to indicate the approximate location of these passages in translated texts as well as in the original Russian.

NOTES TO THE PREFACE

1. See Robert Louis Jackson, "The Sociological Method of V. F. Pereverzev" (Columbia University, 1949). See also my essay, "The Sociological Method of V. F. Pereverzev: A Rage for Structure and Determinism," in *Literature and Society in Imperial Russia: 1800-1914*, ed. William Mills Todd III (Stanford, Calif., 1978), pp. 29-60.

2. Robert Louis Jackson, *Dostoevsky's Quest for Form—A Study of his Philosophy of Art*, 2nd ed. (Bloomington, Ind., 1978), p. x.

3. The title of Dostoevsky's book is more literally translated *Notes from the Dead House*. Indeed, the first chapter is entitled "The Dead House," and on the first page of that chapter the narrator speaks of a living dead house. The convicts, in Dostoevsky's conception, are people who are buried *alive* in a dead house, a place that the narrator refers to as hell.

4. See Robert Louis Jackson, "The Narrator in Dostoevsky's *Notes from the House of the Dead*," in *Studies in Russian and Polish Literature. In Honor of Wacław Lednicki*, ed. Zbigniew Folejewski (The Hague, 1962), pp. 779-803.

5. *Pis'ma* I, 183-184.

6. Ludwig Wittgenstein, *Remarks on Colour*, ed. G.E.M. Anscombe, trans. Linda L. McAlister et al. (Berkeley and Los Angeles, 1978), p. 4e.

NOTES TO THE INTRODUCTION

1. See *Selected Letters of Friedrich Nietzsche*, ed. and trans. Christopher Middleton (Chicago and London, 1969), pp. 261, 327.

2. See L. N. Tolstoi *v vospominaniiakh sovremennikov v dvukh tomakh*, ed. V. Vatsuro et al. (Moscow, 1978), I, 120, 126.

3. Tolstoi, *Polnoe sobranie sochinenii (Iubileinoe izdanie)*, ed. V. G. Chertkov et al., 90 vols. (Moscow, 1928-1959), XVI (1955), 7.

4. G. Chulkov, *Kak rabotal Dostoevskii* (Moscow, 1939), p. 81.

5. V. Shklovskii, *Za i protiv* (Moscow, 1957), pp. 64-84.

6. I. T. Mishin, "Khudozhestvennye osobennosti *Zapisok iz mertvogo doma*," in *Uchenye zapiski Armavirskogo pedagogicheskogo instituta* IV, no. 2 (1962), 22 (quoted in *PSS*² IV, 290).

7. *Pis'ma* IV, 333-334. Dostoevsky was listing his works in a legal contract.

8. Aleksandr Gertsen, "Novaia faza v russkoi literature," *Polnoe sobranie sochinenii*, ed. V. P. Volgin et al., 30 vols. (Moscow, 1954-1966), XVIII (1959), 219.

9. See, for example, Allan Gilbert, *Dante and his Comedy* (New York, 1963), pp. 1-20, for a recent discussion of the notions of the historical Dante and Dante the traveler, and other questions relating to the narrator.

10. Gertsen, "Pis'ma budushchemu drugu," XVIII, 87.

11. V. Kirpotin, *Dostoevskii v shestidesiatye gody* (Moscow, 1966), pp. 331-332.

12. Tolstoi, *Polnoe sobranie sochinenii*, LXVI (Moscow, 1953), 250.

13. See Shklovskii, *Za i protiv*, pp. 120-121; and Kirpotin, *Dostoevskii*, pp. 367-368.

14. See, for example, Mochul'skii, *Dostoevskii. Zhizn' i tvorchestvo* (Paris, 1947), p. 210.

15. The Russian philosopher Leo Shestov, it should be noted, called attention to the close connection between Dostoevsky's experiences in prison and the philosophy of the Underground Man: "And precisely in those very moments when he felt himself once and for all, indeed, forever, in the position of the last man, there was born in him those new and terrible spiritual elements which were later destined to develop into

a quite different philosophy, into a real philosophy of penal servitude, into the philosophy of the Underground Man" (Shestov, *Dostoevskii i Nitshe. Filosofiia tragedii*, 4th ed. [1903; reprint ed., Paris, 1971], pp. 45-46).

16. Robert Louis Jackson, *Dostoevsky's Underground Man in Russian Literature*, 2nd ed. (1958; reprint ed., Westport, Conn., 1981), p. 14.

17. LN 83: 173.

18. V. G. Belinskii, *Polnoe sobranie sochinenii*, ed. N. F. Bel'chikov et al., 13 vols. (Moscow, 1953-1959), XII (1956), 433.

19. For a discussion of the conflict between individual and state in Pushkin's *Bronze Horseman*, see Wacław Lednicki, *Pushkin's Bronze Horseman. The Story of a Masterpiece*, Slavic Studies, vol. 1 (Berkeley and Los Angeles, 1955).

20. "To Italy, to Italy!" Dostoevsky exclaimed in a letter of July 31, 1861 to the poet Ia. P. Polonskii apropos of his infatuation with Italy from his earliest years. "But instead of Italy I landed . . . in the Dead House" (*Pis'ma* I, 302).

21. The problem and pathos of alienation, freedom, and rebellion is also to be found in Dostoevsky's earliest works, such as "The Double" and *Poor Folk*, but Dostoevsky's experience in prison brought the underlying problems in these and other early works into sharp focus.

22. For a discussion of some of the literary predecessors of Dostoevsky's *The Gambler*, however, see the notes to this novel in *PSS*² V, 401-402; see also Paul Debreczeny, "Dostoevskij's Use of *Manon Lescaut* in *The Gambler*," *Comparative Literature* 28, no. 1 (winter 1976), 1-18.

23. George Eliot, *The Lifted Veil*, in *Miscellaneous Essays* (New York, 1901), p. 456.

24. Peter Fuller, Introduction to *The Psychology of Gambling*, ed. John Halliday and Peter Fuller (New York, 1975), p. 47.

25. Edward Wasiolek rightly refers to *The Gambler* as "a wrenching of biography into fiction and a purification by creation." (See the introduction to Fyodor Dostoevsky, *The Gambler* and *Diary of Polina Suslova*, ed. Edward Wasiolek, trans. Victor Terras [Chicago and London, 1972], pp. xxxviii-xxxix.) The inner content of *The Gambler* transcends the biographical context.

26. D. S. Savage, "Dostoevski: The Idea of *The Gambler*," in *The Sewanee Review* 58 (1950), 283.

27. For a fine analysis of *Diary of a Writer* in the context of Dostoevsky's writings and literature in general, see Gary Saul Morson's *The Boundaries of Genre: The Utopian Traditions of Dostoevsky's "Diary of a Writer"* (University of Texas Press, 1981). See also Morson's essay, "Dostoevskij's *Writer's Diary* as Literature of Process," in *Russian Literature* 4, no. 1 (1976), 1-14; and "Reading Between the Genres: Dostoevsky's *Diary of a Writer*," in *The Yale Review* 68, no. 2 (winter 1979), 224-234.

28. See in particular Edward Wasiolek, *Dostoevsky. The Major Fiction* (Cambridge, Mass., 1964), pp. 144-148; Michael Holquist, *Dostoevsky and the Novel* (Princeton, N.J., 1977), pp. 155-164; N. Rosen, "The Defective Memory of the Ridiculous Man," in *Canadian-American Slavic Studies* 12, no. 3 (Fall 1978), 323-328.

29. *Pis'ma* IV, 91.

30. Aron Steinberg, *Dostoievsky* (London, 1968), p. 104. See Steinberg's earlier discussion of "A Gentle Creature" in his *Sistema svobody F. M. Dostoevskogo* (Berlin, 1923), pp. 130-132.

31. M. Bakhtin, *Problemy poetiki Dostoevskogo*, 2nd ed. (Moscow, 1963), p. 193.

32. In Fyodor's buffoonlike image, we recognize a carnival type, but one who is playing in a real life drama. In "Over the Brandy," we perceive what Bakhtin in another context has called the "main carnival act," "the mock crowning and uncrowning of the carnival king." Bakhtin goes on: "At the basis of the ritual act of crowning and uncrowning of the king one finds the core of the carnival world view—the pathos of change and replacement, death and renewal" (ibid., p. 174). This, of course, is the central mythopoetic theme of *The Brothers Karamazov*.

33. Ivanov speaks of "Dostoevsky's law of epic rhythm, which exactly accords with the essential nature of tragedy: the law of the progressively gathering momentum of events." See Vyacheslav Ivanov, *Freedom and the Tragic Life*, ed. S. Konovalov, trans. Norman Cameron (New York, 1952), p. 11.

34. For a general discussion of this point, see my article "Chateaubriand and Dostoevsky: A Posing of the Problem," in *Scando-Slavica* 12 (1966), 28-37.

NOTES TO CHAPTER I

1. Dostoevsky's brother Andrey observes in his memoirs that the peasant Marey, "probably called Mark," was "not an invented character but one who really existed." He describes him as a handsome, black-bearded peasant around middle age who was known for his expertise with cattle. (See Andrei Dostoevskii, *Vospominaniia A. M. Dostoevskogo* [Leningrad, 1930], pp. 58-59.) There are a number of interesting references to "Marey" in Dostoevsky's notebook at the time he was conceiving his sketch in 1876. In one of them, he writes: "Marey. A little scene from childhood, I had not been thinking about it, i.e. had not forgotten, but once, later, long afterwards—oh, how I dreamed, and often—and suddenly I recalled Marey; really some childhood scenes make it possible to look at things quite differently" (*LN* 83: 411).

2. *PSS* XI, 187.

3. Ibid.

4. For a discussion of the concepts of *obraz* and *bezobrazie* in Dostoevsky's aesthetic thought, see the chapter, "Two Kinds of Beauty," in my *Dostoevsky's Quest for Form—A Study of his Philosophy of Art*, 2nd ed. (Bloomington, Ind., 1978), pp. 40-70 passim.

5. *PSS* XI, 184.

6. *Pis'ma* II, 190.

7. *PSS* XIII, 10-11.

8. *PSS* XI, 185.

9. Dostoevsky does not mention in his notebook being touched on the lips: "And how this peasant Marey patted me on the cheek and head. I had forgotten this, i.e. not forgotten, but had only recalled it in prison. These recollections made it possible for me to survive in prison" (*LN* 83: 401).

10. The Russian sculptor Naum Gabo relates an incident from his childhood that is almost identical in detail and moral with the story Dostoevsky tells in "The Peasant Marey." Wandering off into an "enchanted" woods near his home, the child Gabo encounters a "huge, overwhelming image of a peasant with an ax." He faints but is carried in the arms of the same peasant home to safety. Later in life, Gabo writes, he learned that the fear he had had in general of "Man—of the Stranger" was rather a fear of his unknown image. "And when I found him as my neighbor among the multitude of my contemporaries, I saw that he might be much more afraid of me than I of him, and that it was perhaps up to me to take him into my arms and bring him safely to his home whence he had wandered so frightfully far away." (See *Of Divers Arts*, Bollingen Series XXXV 8 [Princeton, N.J., 1962], pp. 12-13, 15.)

In his *Confessions of an English Opium Eater* in 1821, Thomas De Quincey (whose work Dostoevsky had read much as Gabo unquestionably had read "The Peasant Marey") describes a somewhat analogous childhood incident. A gentleman's butler or person of some lower rank sitting next to him on a mail coach produces an initial impression of a "brutal fellow." But on learning that the wandering child, De Quincey, was ill, this man, while the child was sleeping, put his arm around him to protect him from falling off. De Quincey writes: "And for the rest of my journey he behaved to me with the gentleness of a woman, so that at length, I almost lay in his arms." This incident, along with many others in his life, convinced De Quincey

how easily a man who has never been in any great distress may pass through life without knowing, in his own person at least, anything of the possible goodness of the human heart, or, as I must add, with a sigh, of its possible vileness. So thick a curtain of *manners* is drawn over the features and expression of men's natures that, to the ordinary observer, the two extremities and the infinite field of varieties which lie between them are all confounded, the vast and multitudinous com-

pass of their several harmonies reduced to the meager outline of differences expressed in the gamut or alphabet of elementary sounds.
See Thomas De Quincey, *Confessions of an English Opium Eater* (New York and Toronto, 1966), pp. 50-51.

11. See Andrei Dostoevskii, *Vospominaniia*, pp. 58-59.

12. *PSS* XI, 138.

13. *Pis'ma* I, 147-148.

14. See N. N. Strakhov, "Vospominaniia o F. M. Dostoevskom," in *Biografiia, pis'ma i zametki iz zapisnoi knizhki F. M. Dostoevskogo* (St. Petersburg, 1883), p. 359 (cited hereafter as *Biografiia*).

15. It is difficult to say to what extent Dostoevsky "corrected," or, perhaps even transfigured the original peasant Marey. At one point in his notebook in 1876, however, he recalls Marey in a nonidyllic context:

> Marey. He loves his mare and calls her his benefactress. And if he has moments of impatience and the Tatar bursts forth in him and he begins to lash his benefactress with a whip across the eyes when she gets bogged down in the mud with the wagon, then remember the official courier: here you have upbringing, habits, recollections, vodka, Vorobiev [a name Dostoevsky invented to stand in for a despotic official] (*LN* 83: 416).

Dostoevsky clearly associates "Marey"—is he an individual or type here?—with the peasant Mikolka from Raskolnikov's dream who lashes his mare across her "gentle eyes." In "The Peasant Marey," Marey is in the field "with his mare," but there is no indication of any brutal behavior on his part toward the mare, or, of any hostile feelings on the part of the child toward the peasant, as in Raskolnikov's dream.

Marey appears in the notes in the context of Dostoevsky's remarks about a brutal "official courier." In *Diary of a Writer* in January 1876 Dostoevsky recalls how he once witnessed this official courier strike fierce blows on the neck of his coachman; the latter in turn lashed his horses mercilessly. "This repulsive little scene has remained in my memory all my life" (*PSS* XI, 168-169). This is not just a little scene from his memories, Dostoevsky insists in the pages of his notebook where he discusses Marey, but "a symbol that should be engraved on the seal of the Society for the Protection of Animals" (*LN* 83: 411).

NOTES TO CHAPTER II

1. At the age of thirty-five, Dostoevsky was living in Semipalatinsk in Siberia. He had been released from prison in 1854 and began working on his recollections in 1856.

2. See some of Dostoevsky's own comments about himself during his period of exile in Siberia, e.g. his letter to M. D. Isaeva, June 4, 1855

353

NOTES TO CHAPTER II

(*Pis'ma* I, 152-154), and his letter to A. E. Vrangel, August 23, 1855 (*Pis'ma* I, 160).

3. Leo Shestov, *Dostoevskii i Nitshe. Filosofiia tragedii,* 4th ed. (1903; reprint ed., Paris, 1971), p. 44.

4. Compare this final line with Dostoevsky's words in a letter to his brother Andrey, November 6, 1854, right after his release from prison: "I conceived my departure from prison . . . as a radiant awakening and resurrection to a new life" (*Pis'ma* I, 148).

5. V. Shklovskii, *Za i protiv* (Moscow, 1957), pp. 101-102.

6. The editor of Goryanchikov's reminiscences speaks in the introduction of the latter's notes on a "lost people" (*pogibshii narod*). The same term, *la perduta gente,* appears, of course, at the beginning of the *Inferno* (see *Inf.* III, 3).

7. *PSS* XIII, 525.

8. Ibid.

9. Early Russian critics and readers remarked on certain affinities between *House of the Dead* and Dante's *Inferno.* Alexander Herzen, as we have noted, directly compared the message of Dostoevsky's prison work with Dante's inscription at the entrance to hell in Canto III of the *Inferno.* Turgenev, praising *House of the Dead* in a letter to Dostoevsky, described the bathhouse scene as "simply Dantesque" (see *Pis'ma,* 13 vols. [Moscow-Leningrad, 1961-1968], IV [1962], 320). In a review of *House of the Dead* in 1861, A. Miliukov, a close friend of Dostoevsky's, repeatedly draws parallels between this work and the *Inferno*:

Dostoevsky, like Virgil, leads us into a terrible world of suffering. . . . At the entrance to Dante's hell you encounter the terrible inscription, *lasciate ogni speranza voi ch'entrate;* so here, too, at the first step . . . the author tells you: 'it is probable that there was no kind of crime without its representative here.' . . . There are three divisions in the Dead House as in the circles of Dante's hell.

Miliukov compares the gentle figure of the convict Aley to the sad shadow of Francesca (*Inf.* V). (See *Kriticheskii kommentarii k sochineniiam F. M. Dostoevskogo,* ed. V. Zelinskii [Moscow, 1901], II, 38, 40.)

10. *PSS*[2] IV, 250-251. The word Dostoevsky uses here for "murderer" is, significantly, *dusheguby,* which literally means "destroyers of the soul."

11. P. K. Martyanov, "V perelome veka," in *F. M. Dostoevskii v vospominaniiakh sovremennikov,* ed. A. S. Dolinin (Moscow, 1964), I, 237.

12. Szymon Tokarzewski, *Siedem lat Katorgi. Pamiętniki 1846-1857* (Warsaw, 1918), p. 167. For a discussion in English of Tokarzewski's experiences in prison and his relations with Dostoevsky, see Wacław Lednicki's discussion of Dostoevsky and the Poles in Siberia in his book, *Russia, Poland and the West* (New York, 1954), pp. 262-291.

13. O. F. Miller, "Materialy dlia zhizneopisaniia F. M. Dostoevskogo," in *Biografiia*, p. 128.

14. *PSS* XI, 423.

15. *The Portable Nietzsche*, ed. and trans. Walter Kaufmann (New York, 1974), pp. 517, 511-512.

16. *Pis'ma* I, 135-137.

17. Ibid., I, 138-139.

18. Ibid., I, 143.

19. N. N. Strakhov, "Vospominaniia o F. M. Dostoevskom," in *Biografiia* (St. Petersburg, 1883), pp. 175-176.

20. *Pis'ma* I, 139.

21. Ibid., p. 166.

22. Ibid.

23. Ibid., p. 167.

24. Ibid., p. 164.

25. Ibid., II, 605.

26. Ibid., I, 141.

27. *PSS* XI, 138.

28. To "see," in Dostoevsky's aesthetics, as in the etymological sense of the Slavic word *"videt',"* "to see," is always to "understand"; and to understand is to penetrate to the depths of a phenomenon. Ordinary sight, which rests only on the surface of things, is not sight in the most profound sense. There are types of unimaginable beauty and strength to be found among the people, Dostoevsky wrote in the August issue of *Diary of a Writer* in 1880, shortly before his death. "Do we see them or not?" He replies: "He to whom it is given to see will, of course, see them and understand them, while he who sees only the image of the beast will, of course, see nothing" (*PSS* XII, 395).

29. Joseph Conrad, *Heart of Darkness & Secret Sharer*, introd. by Albert J. Guerard (New York, 1950), p. 123.

30. Strakhov's remarks are cited by Dostoevsky's wife, Anna Grigorievna, in her memoirs. (See *Vospominaniia A. G. Dostoevskoi*, ed. L. P. Grossman [Moscow-Leningrad, 1925], p. 286.) Dostoevsky's wife takes Strakhov to task for his hostile remarks about Dostoevsky.

31. "It was terrible to see how Dostoevsky would go down deeper and deeper into the spiritual abysses, into the frightful abysses of moral and physical corruption (this is his own word)," Strakhov wrote in an early introduction to Dostoevsky's works. "But he comes out of them unharmed, that is, without losing the measure of good and evil, of the beautiful and the monstrous." (Cited in *Istoriko-kriticheskii kommentarii k sochineniiam F. M. Dostoevskogo*, ed. V. Zelinskii [Moscow, 1885], I, 91.) In his reminiscences of Dostoevsky in 1883, Strakhov expresses substantially the same views. Dostoevsky's "tender and lofty humanity," he writes, "may be called his muse, and just this gave him the measure of good and evil with which he descended into the most terrible

spiritual abysses. He firmly believed in himself and in man." (See *Biografiia*, p. 227.) Elsewhere in his reminiscences, Strakhov remarks that Dostoevsky's weaknesses of temperament "had almost no influence on his conduct or the shape of his feelings and actions which were always marked by generosity and the highest standards (*vysota*)." (Ibid., p. 318.)

32. *Pis'ma* I, 178.

33. *On the Genealogy of Morals*, ed. and trans. Walter Kaufmann (New York, 1967), pp. 87-88.

34. *Pis'ma* I, 142.

35. Ibid., pp. 129, 131.

NOTES TO CHAPTER III

1. See *M. Gor'kii: Materialy i issledovaniia*, ed. S. I. Balukhatyi and V. A. Desnitskii (Leningrad, 1931), III, 136.

2. M. Gor'kii, "O karamazovshchine," in *Stat'i, 1905-1916* (St. Petersburg, 1918), p. 151.

3. *PSS* XI, 19.

4. The Russian verb *posiagat'* etymologically combines the meaning of taking a wife and seizing or taking possession of somebody.

5. For a discussion of Dostoevsky's attitude toward the Marquis de Sade, see my article, "Dostoevsky and the Marquis de Sade," in *Russian Literature* IV, no. 1 (January 1976), Special Dostoevsky Issue (I), 27-45.

6. *PSS* XI, 14.

7. Ibid., 19.

8. Ibid.

9. Eugene N. Trubetskoi, *Icons: Theology in Color* (St. Vladimir's Seminary Press, 1973), p. 23.

10. Without doubt artistic considerations were uppermost in Dostoevsky's mind when he decided against including the Marey episode in Goryanchikov's recollection of a recollection of his childhood. Such an extensive digression beyond the confines of prison, although it would have constituted a structural and ideological counterpart to the digression into the convict Shishkov's village, would have opened up the whole realm of Goryanchikov's past life. As we have noted, Dostoevsky sought to play down the strictly personal, subjective element in Goryanchikov's reminiscences and to maintain a strict focus on the convicts, their personalities and lives.

Goryanchikov, of course, like Dostoevsky, also used to dream and recall the past. While lying on his hospital bed, he noted, broad and vivid pictures would come to mind and he would "remember the kind of details that at another time [he] would not remember or feel in the same way [he] did now." These words, however, are not a prelude to a soothing recollection or anecdote about a kindly peasant (as they are in "The

Peasant Marey"), but an introduction to a story of another kind: a tale of peasant violence to which the narrator listens as though in a delirium.

One wonders, in reading *House of the Dead*, if the Marey episode—clearly an amalgam of memory and invention—had been fully shaped or formed in Dostoevsky's artistic imagination at the time he wrote his prison work.

11. *PSS* XI, 34-35.

12. Tolstoy very pointedly juxtaposes the half-deranged "heroism" of Makar Alekseevich with Pierre's unbalanced state of mind and his plan to kill Napoleon. The name and patronymic of Devushkin, hero of Dostoevsky's first novel, *Poor Folk*, was Makar Alekseevich. It seems likely that by his use of this name and patronymic Tolstoy was signaling a friendly exchange with Dostoevsky. In his early story "Mr. Prohartchin," as well as, of course, in *Crime and Punishment*, Dostoevsky was concerned with the psychology and ideology of "Napoleonism."

13. *LN* 83: 388-390. The reference here is to the saying, "Scratch a Russian and find a Tatar."

14. *LN* 83: 449.

15. Ibid., p. 520.

16. V. Shklovskii, *Za i protiv* (Moscow, 1957), pp. 119-120.

17. Isay Fomich belonged to a category of human beings with whom Dostoevsky deeply sympathized: the "insulted and injured." Yet Bumstein was a Jew, and Dostoevsky's anti-Semitism clearly conflicted with his deeper perceptions of this disfigured individual. His portrait of Isay Fomich is brilliantly executed, but within the bounds of both popular prejudice and standard literary convention (Gogol's Jew Yankel). For a more extended discussion of Bumstein and of his impact upon Dostoevsky's literary creation, Foma Fomich Opiskin, see my article, "A Footnote to Selo Stepanchikovo," in *Ricerche Slavistiche* XVII-XIX (1970-1972). For Dostoevsky's attitude toward Jews, see his discussion of the "Jewish Question" and other matters in the March issue of *Diary of a Writer*, 1877. See also David I. Goldstein, *Dostoyevsky and the Jews* (Austin, Tex., 1981). It was not only Jews, but Poles, Frenchmen, Germans and others about whom Dostoevsky often spoke intemperately and with disrespect. The Russian philosopher, Vladimir Solovyov, who warmly responded to Dostoevsky's love for Russia and things Russian, nonetheless spoke bitterly about Dostoevsky's "indubitable duality." "We can agree with Dostoevsky," he wrote in an article entitled "The Russian National Ideal," "that the true essence of the Russian national spirit, its great distinction and advantage, consists in the fact that it can inwardly grasp all foreign elements, love them, reincarnate itself in them. Along with Dostoevsky we can recognize that the Russian people are both capable of, and called upon, to realize the ideal of universality in brotherly union with other peoples. Yet we can in no way sympathize with the attacks of that same Dostoevsky against the 'yids', the Poles, the French, the Ger-

mans, against all Europe, against all foreign faiths." And in his article, "The Historical Sphinx," Solovyov wrote: "In his Pushkin speech, Dostoevsky, more emphatically than all the Slavophiles, calls attention to the all-unifying and all-humanitarian character of the Russian idea, yet whenever the national question is posed in a concrete way he became the spokesman for the most primitive kind of chauvinism." Cited by S. M. Solov'ev in *Zhizn' i tvorcheskaia evoliutsiia Vl. Solov'eva* (Brussels, 1977), pp. 297-298.

18. *PSS* XI, 100-101.

19. V. Kirpotin, *Dostoevskii v shestidesiatye gody* (Moscow, 1966), pp. 353, 366.

20. Paul Evdokimoff, *L'art de l'icône* (Paris, 1970), p. 43.

NOTES TO CHAPTER IV

1. *PSS* XI, 17. The word translated here as "innocent" (*pravyi*) has various meanings: right, correct, righteous, just, and—in a legalistic sense—innocent, not guilty.

2. The convict mentioned here, it has often been noted, served Dostoevsky in part as a prototype for Dmitry Karamazov (also wrongly convicted of the crime of killing his father) in *The Brothers Karamazov*.

3. The Russian word is *neschastnye*, literally, unhappy, unfortunate, unlucky people.

4. *PSS²* XVI, 329.

5. The practice of informing was not only characteristic of prison life; it was also clearly endemic among all classes. Goryanchikov writes of the town in which his prison was located: "I know that in this city *in the not so recent past* there were so many informers, so much intrigue, so many people digging pits for each other, that the authorities naturally were afraid of being informed against."

6. *PSS²* XVI, 329.

7. *PSS* XI, 17.

8. Ibid., p. 35.

9. *Pis'ma* I, 419.

10. *PSS* XI, 11.

11. Ibid., p. 15.

12. Ibid., p. 16.

13. Ibid., p. 12.

14. Ibid., p. 14.

15. Ibid., p. 15.

16. Ibid., pp. 15, 16.

17. Ibid., p. 173.

18. "Fate," in Selections from Ralph Waldo Emerson, ed. Stephen E. Whicher (Boston, 1957), p. 340. "For if Fate is so prevailing, man is also part of it, and can confront fate with fate. . . . If there be omnipotence

NOTES

in the stroke, there is omnipotence in the recoil." But Emerson adds—and his thought here is very close to that of Dostoevsky in *House of the Dead* and *Notes from the Underground*—"Fate against Fate is only parrying and defence: there are also the noble creative forces" (pp. 340-341).

NOTES TO CHAPTER V

1. Nietzsche responded very positively to Dostoevsky's psychological concept of freedom. In *Twilight of the Idols* he introduces the "testimony" of Dostoevsky in *House of the Dead* into his discussion of the criminal as a "strong human being." Here he speaks of Dostoevsky as "the only psychologist . . . from whom I had something to learn. . . . This *profound human being* . . . lived for a long time among the convicts in Siberia—hardened criminals for whom there was no way back to society—and found them very different from what he himself had expected: they were carved out of just about the best, hardest, and most valuable wood that grows anywhere on Russian soil." (See *Twilight of the Idols* in *The Portable Nietzsche*, ed. and trans Walter Kaufmann [New York, 1974], pp. 549-550.) Dostoevsky's observations in *House of the Dead* on the absence of a conventional "conscience" in the Russian convict obviously interested Nietzsche. In some posthumously published notes Nietzsche, discussing the purely "psychological practice" of the church where the criminal is concerned, remarks that "the 'bite' of conscience as such is a hindrance to recovery," only a new sickness from which no "salvation of the soul" can arise. "But a criminal who with a certain sombre seriousness cleaves to his fate and does not slander his deed after it is done has more *health of soul*—The criminals among whom Dostoevsky lived in prison were one and all unbroken natures—are they not worth a hundred times more than a 'broken' Christian?" (See *The Will to Power*, ed. Walter Kaufmann, trans. Walter Kaufmann and R. J. Hollingdale [New York, 1968], pp. 134-135.)

2. Pascal, *The Pensées*, trans. J. M. Cohen (Bristol, England, 1961), p. 82.

3. *PSS*[2] IV, 250-251.

4. *LN* 83: 392.

5. *Pis'ma* I, 333-334.

6. George Eliot, *The Lifted Veil*, in *Miscellaneous Essays* (New York, 1901), p. 456.

7. The whole quotation reads: "The teachings of the materialists—universal stagnation and the mechanics of matter, means death. The teachings of true philosophy—the annihilation of inertia, i.e. thought, i.e. the center and Synthesis of the universe and its external form—matter, i.e. God, i.e. eternal life" (*LN* 83: 175).

8. Clemens J. France, "The Gambling Impulse," in *American Journal*

of Psychology 13, no. 3 (July 1902), 364-376, 382-407; reprinted in *The Psychology of Gambling*, ed. John Halliday and Peter Fuller (New York, 1975), p. 151.

9. *PSS* XIII, 55.

10. Relevant here are some remarks of Dostoevsky's apropos of English people, in his article "Environment" in 1873. Here he speaks of the "humaneness" of the English people and of their

consciousness and lively feeling of Christian duty to their neighbor and, perhaps, carried to a high degree, that of firm and independent conviction; even, perhaps, firmer than among us, bearing in mind their education and centuries' old independence. Over there, after all, that much power did not fall on them "suddenly as though from the sky." Besides, they themselves invented the jury trial without borrowing it from anyone, sanctioning it through the ages, taking it from life itself and not receiving it in the form of a gift (*PSS* XI, 12).

11. *LN* 83: 173-174.

12. Ibid., p. 175.

13. The Soviet Russian scholar A. Skaftymov was the first to examine *Notes from the Underground* carefully in the social context of the 1860s and in the context of Dostoevsky's polemical writings and concerns of that period. See his "Zapiski iz podpol'ia sredi publitsistiki Dostoevskogo," in *Slavia* VIII (1929-1930), 101-117; 312-339. For a more recent examination in English of *Notes from the Underground* along similar lines, see Joseph Frank, "Nihilism and *Notes from the Underground*," in *The Sewanee Review* 69 (winter 1961), 1-33. The approaches of Skaftymov and Frank, while providing an indispensable perspective for understanding *Notes from the Underground*, do not, however, undertake a full presentation of the philosophical complexity and ambiguities of that work.

14. It is interesting to note that in the period when Dostoevsky was working on *House of the Dead* he drew up a list of writing projects that included "A Plan for a tragedy 'Fatum' " (*PSS*² III, 447).

15. "There is no fate that cannot be surmounted by scorn," Albert Camus writes in his "Myth of Sisyphus." Camus leaves his Sisyphus at the foot of the mountain where he finds his burden again. He concludes: "This universe henceforth without a master seems to him neither sterile nor futile. Each atom of that stone, each mineral flake of that night-filled mountain, in itself forms a world. The struggle itself toward the heights is enough to fill a man's heart. One must imagine Sisyphus happy." A. Camus, *The Myth of Sisyphus and other Essays*, trans. Justin O'Brien (New York, 1959), pp. 90-91.

16. *Pis'ma* I, 353.

17. The Underground Man, of course, remains a skeptic and prisoner

of the "underground." But insofar as his skepticism is directed against a rationalism that is devoid of spirituality or life, it serves the higher truth in which he is unable to believe. In all of this he bears a certain resemblance to Turgenev's Hamlet-type. In his important speech on "Hamlet and Don Quixote" in 1861, Turgenev observed: "The skepticism of Hamlet does not represent indifference . . . [Hamlet] who does not believe in the possibility of realizing the truth at the present moment, indefatigably struggles with falsity and in this way becomes one of the main champions of the truth in which he is unable fully to believe. But in negation, as in fire, there is an annihilating force; and how is one to keep this force within limits, how is one to indicate to it where, precisely, it must stop, when that which it must destroy and that which it ought to spare is often joined and indissolubly linked? Here is where one finds that tragic side of human life that has so often been noted: will is necessary for deeds, thought is necessary for deeds; but thought and will are disunited, and grow more and more disunited every day." (See "Hamlet i Don-kikhote," in Turgenev, *Polnoe sobranie sochinenii*, 15 vols. [Moscow-Leningrad, 1960-1968], VIII [1964], 183.) The Underground Man, as we have noted, is unconscious of the higher truth for which he yearns. Skepticism in him, moreover, takes on pathological forms. But in his irony, in the nature of his contradictions and in his uncontrolled instinct for negation, he is linked genetically with Turgenev's Hamlet-type.

    18. *Pis'ma* IV, 4.

    19. V. V. Timofeeva (O. Pochinkovskaia), "God raboty s znamenitym pisatelem," in *F. M. Dostoevskii v vospominaniiakh sovremennikov* (Moscow, 1964), II, 176. Timofeeva recalls saying to Dostoevsky: " 'I read your *Notes from the Underground* all last night. And I can't get over my impressions. What a horror—the soul of man! But also what terrible truth!' Fyodor Mikhailovich responded with a broad and bright smile. 'Kraevsky told me at the time that [*Notes from the Underground*] was my real *chef d'oeuvre* and that I should always write in that manner, but I don't agree with him. It is really too gloomy. *Es ist schon ein überwundener Standpunkt.* Nowadays I *can* write in a more serene, conciliatory way. At the moment I am writing a piece...'." (Ibid.) Dostoevsky was at work at the time on *The Raw Youth*.

    20. *Pis'ma* II, 613.

    21. *Pis'ma* I, 362.

Notes to Chapter VI

    1. *Pis'ma* I, 365.

    2. Max Horkheimer, *The Eclipse of Reason* (New York, 1947), p. 128.

    3. Nekrasov subsequently replaced this quatrain with the lines:

361

NOTES TO CHAPTER VI

> Believe me: I listened with sympathy,
> Greedily I hung on every word ...
> I understood everything, child of misfortune!
> I forgave everything and forgot everything.

4. These poems appear only in the journal *Epokha*. Maikov's poem appears on page 496 of *Epokha*, nos. 1-2 (1864), opposite the opening page of part one of *Notes*, entitled "The Underground":

> Autumn leaves whirl in the wind,
> Autumn leaves murmur in alarm:
> "All is perishing! All is perishing! You are
>   black and naked, O native forest, the end
>   has come for you!"
> The regal forest does not hear the alarms:
> Beneath the cold breath of severe skies
> Mighty dreams are being born
> And the energies of a new spring are gathering.

The somber and autumnal opening lines of Maikov's poem form a fitting prelude to part one of *Notes from the Underground* (and indeed to the work as a whole) where it seems that "all is perishing"—all idealism, all hope. Yet Dostoevsky's faith that the underground would not be the last word in Russian life is expressed in Maikov's notion that "mighty dreams," preparations for a new spring, are stirring in the depths of the Russian forest.

5. Dostoevsky's tributes to Sand and Nekrasov appeared in *Diary of a Writer* in June 1876 and December 1877 issues (see *PSS* XI, 307-317, and *PSS* XII, 346-363).

6. The word *povest'* (story, tale) originally appeared in the title of part two of *Notes from the Underground: Povest' po povodu mokrogo snega*. In subsequent editions of his work, Dostoevsky removed this word from the title of part two and made it the subtitle for *Notes from the Underground* as a whole. The Underground Man's reference to a "story" here refers to part two of his notes. It is significant that the word *povest'* also appears in Nekrasov's poem ("When you related to me the story"). The Underground Man's story of his past in certain respects parallels the prostitute's story in Nekrasov's poem.

7. See *Aristotle's Theory of Poetry and Fine Art*, trans. and with critical notes by S. H. Butcher, 4th ed. (New York, 1951), pp. 54, 97.

8. Ibid., p. 41.

9. "Raskolnikov's story," writes Mochulsky, "is a new embodiment of the myth of Prometheus' revolt and the tragic hero's destruction in a struggle with Fate." See Mochul'skii, *Dostoevskii. Zhizn' i tvorchestvo* (Paris, 1947), p. 255.

10. W. H. Auden, "The Christian Tragic Hero," in *New York Times Book Review*, December 16, 1945.

11. In his preface or footnote to part one in *Epokha*, nos. 1-2 (1864), Dostoevsky noted that "this first extract [from the Underground Man's notes] must be considered the prelude to a whole book, almost a preface." Dostoevsky referred here to "subsequent extracts." But in the 1865 edition of *Notes from the Underground* (in which parts one and two appear together), Dostoevsky removed from his preface all suggestions that there would be any additional extracts from the Underground Man's notes. (See the variants of the text of *Notes from the Underground* and the commentary on these variants in *PSS*[2] V, 342, 375.)

NOTES TO CHAPTER VII

1. Tolstoi, *Polnoe sobranie sochinenii*, 90 vols. (Moscow, 1928-1959), XXVII (1936), 280.

2. *Pis'ma* II, 274.

3. For a discussion of Dostoevsky's use of the word "decide" and the various word formations from the same root, see Vadim V. Kozhinov, "The First Sentence in *Crime and Punishment*, the Word 'Crime,' and Other Matters," in *Twentieth Century Interpretations of Crime and Punishment*, ed. Robert Louis Jackson (Englewood Cliffs, NJ, 1974), pp. 17-19.

4. *PSS*[2] VII, 81.

5. *Pis'ma* I, 418.

6. The same concept is at the basis of Tolstoy's psychologically profound presentation of Anna Karenina's first meeting with Vronsky at the railroad station (see my "Chance and Design in *Anna Karenina*," in *The Disciplines of Criticism*, ed. Peter Demetz et al. [New Haven, CT, 1968], pp. 315-329).

7. Tolstoi, *Polnoe sobranie sochinenii* XXVII, 280.

8. *PSS*[2] XVI, 329.

NOTES TO CHAPTER VIII

1. *Pis'ma* I, 333-334.

2. Ibid., 334.

3. *Pis'ma* IV, 220.

4. *Natura—dura, sud'ba—indeika, a zhizn'—kopeika.* I have availed myself of Vladimir Nabokov's translation of this saying. (See *A Hero of Our Time. A Novel* by Mihail Lermontov, trans. Vladimir Nabokov in collaboration with Dmitri Nabokov [Garden City, 1958], p. 169.)

5. Dostoevsky originally entitled his novel "Roulettenburg" but his publisher insisted on a more Russian title "for the public." Dostoevsky reluctantly changed the title to *The Gambler* (see *Pis'ma* II, 362). In a

legal contract he signed in 1874, however, Dostoevsky still referred to his novel as "Roulettenburg" (see *Pis'ma* IV, 334).

6. D. S. Savage, "Dostoevski: The Idea of *The Gambler*," in *The Sewanee Review* 58 (1950), p. 296.

7. Nietzsche, *Beyond Good and Evil*, ed. and trans. Walter Kaufmann (New York, 1966), p. 88.

8. For a general discussion of the impact of Pushkin's "The Queen of Spades" upon Dostoevsky's work, see A. L. Bem's wide-ranging article, "*Pikovaia dama v tvorchestve Dostoevskogo*," in *O Dostoevskom* (Prague, 1936), III, 37-81. Bem discusses Pushkin's story and *The Gambler* on pages 62-69. He finds the link between the two works in the authors' "moral condemnation" of the hero who violates the love of a girl who has given herself to him. Such a link indubitably exists. But Bem has nothing to say about the deep connections between the two works on the psychological and philosophical planes. Dostoevsky had a profound understanding of Pushkin's story, as is indicated by the new synthesis he gives to Pushkinian materials in his novel.

9. For a discussion of *The Gambler* in the context of Dostoevsky's aesthetic thought, see my *Dostoevsky's Quest for Form—A Study of his Philosophy of Art*, 2nd ed. (Bloomington, Ind., 1978), pp. 129-131.

10. The Russian word *schast'e* signifies both happiness and luck.

11. Vyacheslav Ivanov, *Freedom and the Tragic Life*, ed. S. Konovalov, trans. Norman Cameron (New York, 1952), p. 32.

12. Mircea Eliade, "Mythologies of Memory and Forgetting," *History of Religions* II, no. 2 (winter, 1963), 333.

NOTES TO CHAPTER IX

1. For this translation, see Sophocles, *The Oedipus Cycle*, English version by Dudley Fitts and Robert Fitzgerald (New York, 1949), p. 64.

2. The very language of the pawnbroker betrays his guilt. He wants to remember "every little detail" (*kazhduiu chertochku*) and to "bring his thoughts to a point" (*v tochku mysli sobrat'*). The juxtaposition of *chertochka* and *tochka* is an important one: what the pawnbroker is trying to bring to a point is his demonism. The demonic, of course, is a *tochka*—grammatically, a "period," a full stop; mathematically the "dead center" (*mertvaia tochka*), that is, nothingness. "At the still point of the turning world" (T. S. Eliot).

3. The original in *Faust* (lines 1336-1337) reads: *Ein Teil von jener Kraft, Die stets das Böse will und stets das Gute schafft* ("A part of that force which always wills evil and always creates good"). The pawnbroker actually has replaced the first part of the line ("A part of that force") with a slightly altered version of a later line (1349) spoken by Mephi-

stopheles: "I am a part of that part which in the beginning was every-thing" ("*Ich bin ein Teil des Teils, der Anfangs alles war*").

4. We may recall here Turgenev's story, "Faust," in which the hero introduces the innocent heroine, Vera Nikolaevna, to Goethe's *Faust* and in so doing sets into motion a tragic action. "An amazing creature!" the narrator says of Vera Nikolaevna. "Absolute insight together with the inexperience of a child, a fine common sense and an inborn feeling of beauty, an eternal striving for the truth, for the lofty, and an under-standing of everything, even the depraved, even the ridiculous." "Meph-istopheles frightens her, not as a devil but as 'something that could exist in every person'." Dostoevsky's gentle creature has much in common with Vera Nikolaevna in Turgenev's story.

5. See "Goethe's *Faust*," in *The Works of George Santayana* (New York, 1936), pp. 109-110. A. L. Bem, in his article on Goethe's *Faust* in Dostoevsky's work, misses, I think, the wider implications of Dostoev-sky's use of Mephistopheles' words in "The Gentle Creature." "If Meph-istopheles 'wants to do evil but creates good'," Bem writes, "then the hero of 'A Gentle Creature,' on the contrary 'wants to do good, but does evil'." (See " 'Faust' v tvorchestve Dostoevskogo," in *Zapiski nauch-noissledovatel'skago ob'edineniia* V [old series, vol. X], 116-117.)

6. *PSS* XI, 308, 312-313.

Notes to Chapter X

1. *PSS* XI, 158.
2. Ibid., p. 153.
3. Ibid., pp. 153-154.
4. Ibid., p. 154.
5. Ibid., p. 83.
6. Ibid., p. 153.
7. Ibid., p. 250.
8. *Pis'ma* II, 169.
9. *PSS* XI, 152-153.
10. G. M. Fridlender calls attention to this in his interesting compar-ison of Dostoevsky's sketch with a ballad written on a similar theme by the German writer Friedrich Rückert (1788-1866) (see Fridlender, *Real-izm Dostoevskogo* [Moscow-Leningrad, 1964], p. 307).
11. F. Schiller, *Über naive und sentimentalische Dichtung*, in *Schillers Werke. Nationalausgabe*, ed. Julius Petersen and Hermann Schneider, 42 vols. (Weimar), XX (1962), 467-468.

Notes to Chapter XI

1. *PSS* XI, 166.
2. Nietzsche, *The Will to Power*, ed. and trans. Walter Kaufmann (New York, 1967), p. 9.

3. *PSS* XI, 489-490.
4. Ibid., p. 146.
5. Ibid.
6. *LN* 83: 251.
7. Ibid., p. 248.
8. Paul Evdokimoff, *Dostoievsky et le problème du mal* (Valence, 1942), p. 65. Evdokimoff's analysis of the metaphysical content of the "Dream," which I follow closely at this point in my discussion, seems to me to touch the core of Dostoevsky's idea in this story.
9. It is certainly true that in *Diary of a Writer* in 1876-1877 we encounter a "millenarian" Dostoevsky who seems to insist on the literal possibility of realizing Christ's truth on earth in the very near future. A Russian take-over of Constantinople, the ancient capital of Orthodoxy, should represent, Dostoevsky believed, "a genuine exaltation of Christ's truth . . . a genuine new exaltation of the cross of Christ and the final word of Orthodoxy." He classes himself among the "utopians" who believe that Russia will stand at the head of a united Orthodoxy (*PSS* XI, 329). Later in *Diary of a Writer*, he writes apropos of the possible triumph of the Orthodox idea:

> People will say that this is fantastic . . . that this "Russian resolution of the question" is the "kingdom of heaven" and possible only in the kingdom of heaven. Yes, the Stivas [Oblonskys] would be very angry if the kingdom of heaven came upon us. But one should take into account the fact that in this fantasy of "the Russian resolution of the question" there is incomparably less of the fantastic and incomparably more of the probable than in the European resolution (*PSS* XII, 64).

It is not easy, of course, to separate the purely religious affirmation from the political and nationalistic affirmation. The theme of Russian hegemony is so closely interwoven with the *possibility* of the coming of the kingdom of heaven as to make it difficult to say whether Dostoevsky literally anticipates Christ's heaven on earth, that is, the heaven and the Christlike love of which he speaks in his 1864 notebook.

Indubitably these statements reveal a different emphasis from that which we find in Dostoevsky's notebook (or in the "Dream"). Yet at root, the political-millenarian Dostoevsky is not really contradicting the artist-philosopher Dostoevsky. In his notebook (as in the "Dream"), he maintains that heaven on earth is impossible but insists that man must act as though it were possible, must be inspired by this ideal; man must strive for the ideal even if it is beyond his reach. In *Diary of a Writer*, Dostoevsky—standing before his audience—dramatizes his belief. When he yields (in that same *Diary of a Writer*) to more purely imaginative development of his thought, however (e.g. in the "Dream"), he gives direct expression to the outlook we find in his 1864 notebook.

10. *PSS* XI, 37.

NOTES

11. See, in this connection, the line from Goethe's *Faust*: "The love of man stirs in us, The love of God is stirring now" (*Es reget sich die Menschenliebe, Die Liebe Gottes regt sich nun* [lines 1184-1185]).

12. Archpriest Avvakum, *Zhitie protopopa Avvakuma im samim napisannoe* (Petrograd, 1916), p. 1.

13. *Ein guter Mensch, in seinem dunklen Drange, Ist sich des rechten Weges wohl bewusst* (*Faust*, lines 328-329).

14. The Russian verb *sbit'sia*, which I have translated here consistently in the sense of "get muddled," in fact has several variant meanings: to "go astray," "go wrong," "get off the track," as well as "get muddled" or "get confused."

15. *Es irrt der Mensch, solang er strebt* (*Faust*, line 317).

16. As a type, the ridiculous man certainly belongs in the category of the *iurodivyi* ("holy fool"), or as he is sometimes known, *iurodivyi khrista radi* ("fool for Christ's sake"). For an historical approach to the holy fool in Russia, see F. P. Fedotov's discussion in *The Russian Religious Mind* (Cambridge, 1966), II, 316-343. For a consideration of the holy fool in Russian literature, see Ewa M. Thompson, "Il Folle Sacro e le sue trasformazioni nella letteratura russa," *Strumenti Critici* 27 (June 1975), 157-181. For a brief comment on the religious implications of the scene in which the ridiculous man is called a *iurodivyi*, see K. Onasch's discussion of N. Rosen's "The Defective Memory of the Ridiculous Man," in *Canadian-American Slavic Studies* 12, no. 3 (Fall 1978), 339-340.

17. *PSS* XIII, 59-60.

18. Vyacheslav Ivanov, *Freedom and the Tragic Life*, ed. S. Konovalov, trans. Norman Cameron (New York, 1952), p. 95.

NOTES TO CHAPTER XII

1. *PSS* XI, 423.

2. For a discussion of Dostoevsky's higher aesthetic, see my chapter "Two Kinds of Beauty," in *Dostoevsky's Quest for Form—A Study of his Philosophy of Art*, 2nd ed. (Bloomington, Ind., 1978), pp. 40-70.

3. See Dostoevsky's observations on dreams in *Crime and Punishment*, part one, chap. 5. The devil in Ivan Karamazov's nightmare expresses analogous opinions.

4. *Pis'ma* I, 344. Dostoevsky had a very positive opinion of Turgenev's "Ghosts" in this letter. He stresses here the great importance of "poetic truth" as opposed to what most people look for, "something copied from actual fact" (p. 343).

5. Ivan Ivanovich appears elsewhere in *Diary of a Writer* in 1873. In "A Half Letter of 'A Certain Person'," Dostoevsky presents him ironi-

cally as "one who has already distinguished himself . . . in the matter of 'little graves'," that is, as the "author" of "Bobok" (see *PSS* XI, 61).

6. Bakhtin discusses the "profane and down-to-earth" style of Dostoevsky's description of the cemetery in his study of Dostoevsky (see *Problemy poetiki* [Moscow, 1963], pp. 185-186).

7. Ibid., pp. 186-187.

8. *Oeuvres complètes de M. le Vicompte de Chateaubriand* (Paris, 1826-1828), II, 287; XIII, 197. See also my discussion of Dostoevsky's response to Chateaubriand in my article, "Chateaubriand and Dostoevsky: A Posing of the Problem," in *Scando-Slavica* XII (1966), pp. 28-37.

9. See W. Kayser, *The Grotesque in Art and Literature*, trans. Ulrich Weisstein (Bloomington, IN, 1963), pp. 179-189.

10. Of course, we may also speak of creative tension in Gogol's art. As raisonneur, poet, and romantic thinker, Gogol may be said to call into question his vision of the grotesque. But the impulse toward transfiguration, the element of purification, comes from without. Gogol's characters, like the companions of Odysseus who have been transformed into swine on the island of Circe, humbly—and, it seems, vainly—await the magic wand of their master who will restore their human image.

NOTES TO CHAPTER XIII

1. Dostoevsky speaks of his great respect for the popular cult of the icon in a letter to Apollon Maikov in 1868 (*Pis'ma* II, 154). See also his remarks on this subject to E. P. Opochinin, "Besedy o Dostoevskom," *Zven'ia* 6 (Moscow, 1936), 468.

2. H.D.F. Kitto, *Greek Tragedy: A Literary Study* (New York, 1954), p. 75.

3. *PSS* XI, 167.

4. Kitto, *Greek Tragedy*, p. 76.

NOTES TO CHAPTER XIV

1. *Prichitaniia severnago kraia*, ed. E. V. Barsov (Moscow, 1872), I, vii-viii.

2. *PSS²* XV, 230.

3. Ivan's rebellion in one sense may be said to take the sardonic form, as it were, of "baring the metaphor" in the Nietzschean manner. "Buying and selling," Nietzsche has observed,

> together with their psychological appurtenances, are older than the beginnings of any kind of social forms of organizations and alliances; it was rather out of the most rudimentary form of personal legal rights that the budding sense of exchange, contract, guilt, right, obligation, settlement, first *transferred* itself to the coarsest and most elementary

social complexes . . . together with the custom of comparing, measuring, and calculating power against power. [One arrives finally] at the great generalization, everything has its price; "*all* things can be paid for"—the oldest and naivest moral canon of *justice*, the beginning of all "good-naturedness," all "fairness," all "good will," all "objectivity" on earth (*On the Genealogy of Morals*, ed. and trans. Walter Kaufmann [New York, 1967], p. 70).

Ivan seeks to embarrass Christianity: a child's tears cannot be redeemed; all things *cannot* be paid for. Yet Ivan himself cannot get beyond the primitive psychology of equity or quid pro quo. "There is no virtue," he insists earlier in the novel, "if there is no immortality." In this he resembles the protagonist of Schiller's philosophical poem, "Resignation" (1786), one that Ivan alludes to when he speaks of returning his "ticket" to divine harmony. The protagonist of Schiller's poem, after a life of virtue, holds out his "letter of credit on happiness" to the great "remunerator" who holds the "scales of Justice." A conventionally religious and virtuous person in Schiller's conception, the narrator of the poem has conceived of his virtuous actions in terms of contractual agreement. His language, indeed, is studded with words of a commercial character. He demands his "salary." Schiller's thought in his poem and elsewhere is that sacrifice cannot be made with a view toward payment in an afterlife. "The moral obligation binds us absolutely and not contractually," he wrote apropos of the idea of his poem. "The virtues that one practices only on the legal assurance of future good have no value. Virtue carries in itself a character of inner necessity, even if there is no immortality" (see *Schillers Werke* XXII [1958], p. 178).

In *The Brothers Karamazov*, the artist Dostoevsky accepts this view of the nature of virtue, but he affirms that through love and sacrifice freely given man can attain to a feeling of God and immortality. In affirming that "there is no virtue if there is no immortality," however, Ivan remains, like Schiller's protagonist, a prisoner of the contractual mentality he ascribes to God-the-merchant.

4. *PSS*² XVII, 48.

5. In the view of Leonid Grossman, Ivan's story about "John the Merciful" is based on Flaubert's *St. Julien l'Hôpitalier*, which was translated into Russian by Turgenev in 1877 (see Grossman, *Tvorchestvo Dostoevskogo* [Moscow, 1928], p. 179).

6. Camus, *The Rebel*, trans. Anthony Bower (New York, 1956), p. 56.

7. Mochul'skii, *Dostoevskii. Zhizn' i tvorchestvo* (Paris, 1947), p. 507.

NOTES TO CHAPTER XV

1. The prosecutor creates an adjective with a small "k" out of the name "karamazov," e.g. "we broad karamazov natures" (*my natury shirokie, karamazovskie*).

2. See page 135 of text for Dostoevsky's remarks on this subject.

3. The Russian word translated here as "simplicity" is *prostodushie*, which means the attribute of a naively trusting, good-hearted nature, a simple soul.

4. Friedrich Schiller, *On the Aesthetic Education of Man*, ed. and trans. Elizabeth M. Wilkinson and L. A. Willoughby (Oxford, 1967), p. 27.

5. V. Ermilov, *F. M. Dostoevskii* (Moscow, 1956), p. 243.

6. Alfred North Whitehead, *Adventures in Ideas* (New York, 1956), p. 33. Dostoevsky posits such a union of concepts in man's moral and religious consciousness in the opening part of "Grand Inquisitor." Christ appears quietly before the Seville cathedral. "This might be one of the best places in the poem," Ivan remarks, "that is, precisely why the people recognize Him." The crowd with irresistible force surges toward the radiant and transcendent figure of Christ. But at the appearance of the Grand Inquisitor, attended by his "somber assistants and slaves," the crowd, "trained, cowed, tremblingly obedient," instantly, as one man, prostrates itself.

7. Schiller, *Aesthetic Education*, pp. 11, 15, 19, and 69.

8. Alyosha—and in my opinion, Dostoevsky—on this point is in agreement with the lawyer and the Grand Inquisitor. "Now isn't this just the way the Jesuits talk, this way? Just like you and I do now, eh?" Dmitry remarks. " 'Yes'—Alyosha smiled quietly." Dmitry's remark, though directly referring to the discussion of his escape plans, also alludes to Alyosha's justification of a refusal to bear the cross. Alyosha's quiet, smiling "yes" (as to a child) both acknowledges a point of comparison between his own observation (the cross is not for all) and the views of the "Jesuits," and at the same time clearly suggests that the question is more complex than Dmitry realizes. Dostoevsky's Jesuits, casuists, and philosophers like Fetyukovich and the Grand Inquisitor, do talk realistically about man's weakness, his inability to bear the cross; they are prepared for all sorts of compromises. But unlike Alyosha they have neither a faith in man nor a belief in the central place of striving and aspiration in man's salvation.

9. *PSS* XII, p. 86.

10. *PSS* XI, 184.

11. *PSS* XIII, 95.

12. *Pis'ma* I, 142.

INDEX

truth (cont.)
 image, 292; of man, 344; old, and
 love, 281, 284, 286; and poetry, x,
 43-44; pre-Christian, 312; sublime,
 259
Turgenev, Ivan, 24, 291, 369n;
 "Faust," 364n; "Ghosts," 292-293,
 366n; "Hamlet and Don Quixote,"
 360n

underground, the: convergence of
 chance and necessity in, 186; psychology of, 123; tragedy of, 124-
 125, 163, 206-207

violence, 25, 79, 80, 83, 86, 98, 112,
 113, 138, 139, 146, 195, 199, 201,
 305; and habit, 84; and human nature, 71; and Russian history, 84;

and sensuality, 82, 89-90; as temptation, 85; vicarious enjoyment of,
 85, 91
vision, 292; as aesthetic and religious
 category, 71; aesthetic representation of reality as, 288; artistic, altruism of, 52; Goryanchikov's initial failure of, in House of the
 Dead, 58-59; as revelation, 25, 288;
 and transfiguration, 21
"The Wanderings of Our Lady
 through Hell," 322
Wasiolek, Edward, 249n
Whitehead, Alfred North, 288, 339
Wittgenstein, Ludwig, xii
women: contempt for, 90-91, 104;
 and Fyodor Karamazov, 307, 308-
 311; and George Sand, 258-259; as
 property, 81-82, 89, 240

Library of Congress Cataloging in Publication Data

Jackson, Robert Louis.
    The art of Dostoevsky.

    Includes bibliographical references and
index.
    1. Dostoyevsky, Fyodor, 1821-1881—
Criticism and interpretation.   I.   Title.
PG3328.Z6J3   891.73′3   81-47136
ISBN 0-691-06484-9   AACR2

ROBERT LOUIS JACKSON is a professor of
Russian literature at Yale University.